THE ARABS AT WAR IN AFGHANISTAN

MUSTAFA HAMID
LEAH FARRALL

The Arabs at War in Afghanistan

HURST & COMPANY, LONDON

First published in the United Kingdom in 2015 by
C. Hurst & Co. (Publishers) Ltd.,
41 Great Russell Street, London, WC1B 3PL

Printed in India

Distributed in the United States, Canada and Latin America by Oxford University Press, 198 Madison Avenue, New York, NY 10016, United States of America.

A Cataloguing-in-Publication data record for this book is available from the British Library.

ISBN: 978-1849044202

www.hurstpublishers.com

This book is printed using paper from registered sustainable and managed sources.

To those who passed early, who were the best among us, I dedicate my words.

Mustafa Hamid

To my family for their constant and unwavering support; and to Zainab, for her patient assistance. Without you there would be no book.

Leah Farrall

CONTENTS

People xi
Glossary xix
Camps, Organisations and Publications xiii
Locations xxix

1. Introducing Mustafa Hamid 1
   On how we met 16
   From a rocky introduction, dialogue and, eventually, a book 18
2. The Arab-Afghan Jihad 21
   A low-profile start 27
   The first Arab arrivals 33
   Lack of training for Arabs and Afghans 38
   Pakistan's role 39
3. Early Training and Taliban Origins 45
   Mawlawi Nasrullah Mansur and the real beginnings of the Taliban movement 46
   Arrival of the Pakistani trainer Rashid Ahmad 52
   Mawlawi Mansur and Rashid's establishment of the Qais camp 55
   Rashid and Mawlawi Mansur's contribution to the Afghan and Arab jihad 59
4. Two Memos and an Idea That Spread: The Real Origins of Maktab Al-Khadamat 65
   The two memos: early suggestions for an Arab-led organisation 65
   Azzam, Sayyaf and bin Laden establish Maktab al-Khadamat 75
   Early Arab training and combat efforts 81
   The establishment of Sadda camp by Maktab al-Khadamat 83

5. Jaji and the Establishment of al-Masadah 89
How and why al-Masadah was established 89
Opposition to bin Laden's establishment of al-Masadah 94
The Jaji battle and its aftermath 97
Exclusion of the Afghans 100
On leadership and lessons: the dangers of the Jaji success 102

6. Confused Origins: Al-Qaeda's Post-Jaji Emergence and the Arab Advisory Council 107
The how, when and why of al-Qaeda's formation 108
More than a move: al-Qaeda's relocation to Khost and its turn away from Afghanistan 112
Changing focus: Arab-Afghan efforts to gain bin Laden's support and al-Qaeda's resources 116
Al-Qaeda and the Arab-Afghan Advisory Council 119
The Arab-Afghan yard: disagreements, arguments and power plays 125
Training 133

7. Jalalabad and the Arab-Afghan Training Storm 145
An inglorious defeat 155
Ikhwan Muslimin enters the fray 162
The rise of the current of preparation and the Jalalabad School 164

8. The Afghan Civil War and Arab-Afghan Flight 177
Short on options: bin Laden's journey from house arrest in Saudi Arabia to Pakistan 177
The fall of the Kabul regime, Afghanistan's descent into civil war and Pakistan's crackdown on Arab-Afghans 180
The forgotten men on the mountain: the Arab-Afghans who remained in Khost 196

9. The Arab-Afghan Return and the Rise of the Taliban 207
An unhappy return to Afghanistan 208
From Tora Bora a declaration of jihad 211
The Taliban gain a controversial guest 217

10. Strong Horse, Weak Horse: Arab-Afghan Politics and Al-Qaeda's Realpolitik 247
Bin Laden's invitation to Khattab 248
Bin Laden's outreach to the Pakistanis 249
The politics among the Arab-Afghan groups about giving oaths to Mullah Omar 250

The politics between Abu Musab al-Suri and al-Qaeda 254
Al-Qaeda's support for Abu Musab al-Zarqawi as a counterweight to Abu Musab al-Suri 257
Khaldan closes operations in Jalalabad 259
Al-Qaeda's training efforts in Kandahar and Kabul 261

11. Arab-Afghan Unity Efforts and 9/11 263
The Uzbek–al-Qaeda relationship and Mullah Omar's appointment of Uzbek military leader, Juma Bai, as amir of the foreign brigade in Kabul 273
The al-Qaeda–Tanzim al-Jihad merger 278
Disagreement about al-Qaeda's upcoming (9/11) attacks 280
Al-Qaeda's pre-9/11 preparations for an American retaliation and an absence of warnings 281
The American invasion 284

12. Reflections 293
Concluding reflections 315

Epilogue 327

Notes 329
Index 341

PEOPLE

Abd as-Samia: Shia Afghan commander operating in the al-Masadah base area before being asked to leave by the Arabs at the base.

Abdul Aziz Ali: Egyptian Ikhwan Muslimin member; veteran of the 1948 Palestine War. Influential figure during the first Afghan jihad. Also known as Abu Usama al-Masri.

Abdul Hadi al-Iraqi: Iraqi veteran of first Afghan jihad. Trained in 1993 in Iraqi Ikhwan Muslimin camp in Jalalabad. Joined al-Qaeda after its return to Afghanistan in 1996. Was a commander of the Ansar volunteer force under the leadership of Juma Bai, the military head of the Islamic Movement of Uzbekistan appointed by Mullah Omar to oversee all foreign fighters in Afghanistan.

Abdul Haq: Senior Afghan commander against the Soviets. Executed by the Taliban in late 2001 when attempting to return to Afghanistan from exile. According to Mustafa Hamid, Abdul Haq returned to Afghanistan to stage a coup against the Taliban in Jalalabad, where he was killed during a clash with them.

Abdul Majid al-Jazairi: Algerian who was an early member of al-Qaeda, but left because of dissatisfaction with the organisation. Established a training camp in Jalalabad for Algerians. He later returned to Algeria and became involved in the conflict there.

Abdul Majid al-Zindani: Religious figure and leader of Ikhwan Muslimin in Yemen.

Abdul Qadir: Former governor of Jalalabad. Also known as Hajji Qadir.

Abdul Rahman al-BM: Egyptian who was briefly a member of al-Qaeda during the early period of the first Afghan jihad. Renowned for his proficiency using 'BM' rocket launchers, earning himself the lifelong nickname 'al-BM'.

Abdul Rahman al-Iraqi: Iraqi member of Maktab al-Alami al-Islami.

Abdul Rahman al-Masri: Egyptian member of Maktab al-Alami al-Islami. Worked closely with Mustafa Hamid in Khost battles.

Abdul Rahman al-Surayhi: Saudi who fought at Jaji and Jalalabad and declined to join al-Qaeda.

Abdul Rashid Dostum: Regional chief in Afghanistan's armed forces during the Afghan jihad against the Soviets. Later a commander in the Northern Alliance.

Abdul Rasul Sayyaf: Afghan mujahidin leader during the first Afghan jihad. Amir of the Union of Afghan Parties, the grouping consisting of the various Afghan mujahidin parties fighting the Soviet occupation.

Abdul Wakil: First Taliban member to meet Arab-Afghans and al-Qaeda at Khost encampment as the Taliban began its rise to power.

Abdullah Anas: Algerian. Abdullah Azzam's son-in-law and early member of Maktab al-Khadamat.

Abdullah Assadeq: One of the high-ranking figures in the Libyan Islamic Fighting Group.

Abdullah Azzam: Palestinian. Amir of Maktab al-Khadamat. Senior Arab-Afghan leader in Afghanistan.

Abdullah Nuri: Tajik. Leader of Tajikistan's al-Nahda movement.

Abu Abdullah: Osama bin Laden. Saudi Arab-Afghan financier of Maktab al-Khadamat and amir of al-Qaeda.

Abu Abdullah al-Muhajir: Egyptian who founded Belief Battalions Institute in Khaldan before defecting to al-Qaeda and working in its Institute.

Abu al-Shahid al-Qatari: Name of an al-Qaeda camp in Jalalabad, named in honour of a mujahid who died in Khost.

Abu Ayman al-Yamani: Egyptian who was present at Tora Bora in late 2001 and reportedly met bin Laden and other senior leaders.

Abu Ayoub al-Iraqi: Iraqi Arab-Afghan who ran al-Qaeda training camp in Jalalabad.

Abu Burhan al-Suri: Ex-Syrian army officer. Commander in the camp of Khaldan; trained Arabs. Former Syrian Ikhwan Muslimin who ran Maktab al-Khadamat's Sadda and Khaldan camps before retiring.

Abu Faraj al-Libi: Libyan who rose to become al-Qaeda's head of external operations following the capture and rendition of Khalid Shaykh Muhammad.

Abu Hafs al-Masri: Egyptian. Early arrival to first Afghan war and member of Maktab al-Alami al-Islami. Co-founder of al-Qaeda; military amir of al-Qaeda after the death of Abu Ubaydah al-Banshiri.

Abu Hafs al-Mauritani: Mauritanian who headed up al-Qaeda's religious institute. Disagreed with 9/11; reportedly resigned from al-Qaeda before arriving in Iran.

Abu Hajr al-Iraqi: Iraqi. Senior al-Qaeda member; allegedly involved in 1998 African embassy bombings.

Abu Hamid al-Libi: Libyan who was early member of al-Qaeda before leaving and becoming the head of a small takfiri group.

Abu Hamza al-Qaiti': Saudi who established his own small training group in Kabul.

Abu Harith al-Urduni: Jordanian who commanded his own group during first Afghan war. Worked closely with Afghan mujahidin commander Jalaluddin Haqqani.

Abu Ibrahim al-Iraqi: Iraqi who was a member of the Arab Advisory Council during the first Afghan war.

Abu Islam al-Masri: Egyptian al-Qaeda member who left the group in the early 1990s to go to Chechnya and join Khattab.

Abu Jafar al-Kandahari al-Masri: Egyptian who attempted to join al-Qaeda in its early days but did not pass the entry test. Author of *Memoir of an Arab-Afghan*.

Abu Jandal: Yemeni who was among the first of the Arabs to join al-Qaeda after 1996; Northern Group member.

Abu Jihad al-Makki: Saudi al-Qaeda member. 1998 African embassy suicide bomber; Northern Group member.

Abu Jihad al-Masri: Egyptian Gamaah Islamiyyah figure who led a faction of the group who merged with al-Qaeda in 2006.

Abu Jihad al-Masri: Egyptian Tanzim al-Jihad leader.

Abu Khabab al-Masri: Egyptian. Chemist and explosives engineer. Worked at Khaldan and Derunta. Independent. Subcontracted services to other groups.

Abu Khalid al-Masri: Egyptian senior al-Qaeda figure.

Abu Layth al-Libi: Libyan field commander during American invasion; later joined his faction of the Libyan Islamic Fighting Group with al-Qaeda.

Abu Muhammad al-Masri: Egyptian who allegedly headed al-Qaeda's training programme.

Abu Musab al-Reuters: Egyptian who worked on al-Qaeda's Media Council during its early period before leaving the organisation.

Abu Musab al-Suri: Former Syrian Ikhwan Muslimin who trained in Egypt and Iraq. In Afghanistan provided training to Egyptian groups and others. Viewed by al-Qaeda as competitor to the group.

Abu Musab al-Zarqawi: Jordanian who was supported by Sayf al-Adl and al-Qaeda to establish his own camp and group in Herat to prevent his working with Abu Musab al-Suri.

Abu Omar al-Yamani: Al-Qaeda member who worked in Yemen, handling weapons smuggled in from Somalia in early 1990s.

Abu Qotada: Jordanian imam. Often claimed to be al-Qaeda member. Provided advice and fatawa to a number of militant groups and in the early 1990s contributed to the Armed Group of Algeria's magazine. Involved in takfiri disputes.

Abu Rida al-Suri: Syrian member of Maktab al-Khadamat and mujahidin financier.

Abu Rouda al-Suri: Syrian-American who headed up Hekmatyar's Yarmuk Brigade, before being killed in action in Kabul.

Abu Samha al-Masri: Egyptian Tanzim al-Jihad leader also known as Tharwat Salah Shihatah. Involved in torture and execution of fellow member's son in the 1990s.

Abu Tariq al-Tunisi: Tunisian who along with other Arab-Afghans approached the Taliban in late 1996 to offer assistance in its efforts to protect Kabul.

Abu Ubaydah al-Banshiri: Egyptian. First military commander of al-Qaeda and one of its co-founders. Died in 1996 in Africa. Had resigned from al-Qaeda.

Abu Usama al-Jazairi: Algerian. Listed as the 'Military Supervisor' in documents outlining 'the work of al-Qaeda', which are believed to mark its founding.

Abu Zayd al-Tunisi: Tunisian commander of al-Qaeda's camps in Khost during its time in Sudan. Commander of Jihadwal at time of American retaliatory strikes.

Abu Zubaydah: Palestinian with Saudi citizenship. Along with Ibn Shaykh al-Libi took over Maktab al-Khadamat's infrastructure when the group disintegrated and Abu Burhan retired. Founded Mujahidin Services Centre in 1996.

Ahmad: Friend of Mustafa Hamid, who was among the first three Arabs to join the jihad in Afghanistan.

Ahmad al-Jazairi: Algerian doctor. Among the takfiris of the first Afghan conflict.

Ahmad Gul: Afghan commander, killed in Lija in 1985, who worked with Haqqani.

Ahmad Shah Masud: Afghan. Commander of the Northern Alliance.

Akhtar Abdul Rahman: General in charge of Pakistan's Inter-Services Intelligence (ISI) during most of the first Afghan jihad (1979 to 1987).

Al-Assad: Refers here to the dictatorial regime of Hafiz al-Assad who ruled Syria for close to thirty years until his death in 2000. Also used to refer to the regime of his son and heir, Bashar al-Assad, who at the time of writing was presiding over a civil war in the country.

Ali Abdullah Saleh: Former president of Yemen who served from 1990 until February 2012.

Ali Muhammad: Egyptian-American member of Tanzim al-Jihad who trained group members and al-Qaeda.

Amin al-Haq: Also known as Dr Amin. Afghan mujahidin commander in Tora Bora area; close friends with Abu Abdullah, advised him against basing himself in Tora Bora.

Amir al-Fateh: Al-Qaeda member. Renowned for his tank work during Jalalabad battle.

Anwar Sadat: President of Egypt assassinated by Tanzim al-Jihad.

Arsla Rahmani: Former senior Taliban member.

Ayman al-Zawahiri: Egyptian. Formerly amir of Tanzim al-Jihad. Led faction of five members who merged with al-Qaeda in 2001. Took over as amir of al-Qaeda following death of Osama bin Laden in May 2011.

Basil Muhammad: Journalist and author of *Arab Ansar in Afghanistan.*

Burhanuddin Rabbani: Leader of Afghan mujahidin party and former Afghan prime minister from 1992 to 1996. Assassinated by Taliban.

Enaam Arnaout: Syrian-American. Fought in the first Afghan war. Managed the Benevolence International Foundation.

Engineer Mahmud: Afghan commander. Offered bin Laden and the returning al-Qaeda members and Arab-Afghans and their family protection in Jalalabad upon their return to Afghanistan in 1996.

Engineer Mujahid: Afghan commander. Offered bin Laden and the returning al-Qaeda members and Arab-Afghans and their family protection in Jalalabad upon their return to Afghanistan in 1996.

Gulbuddin Hekmatyar: Founder and leader of Hizb i Islami. Former prime minister of Afghanistan.

Gulzarak: Afghan. General working with Sayyaf; head of al-Ittihad Military Committee.

Hamoud al-Uqla: Saudi scholar; issued first fatwa in support of Taliban.

Ibn Khattab: Former Northern Group member. Left to pursue jihad in Tajikistan and Chechnya. Established his own camp in Jalalabad.

Ibn Shaykh al-Libi: Libyan. Amir of Khaldan following retirement of Abu Burhan al-Suri.

Ibrahim Haqqani: Afghan mujahidin commander and brother of Jalaluddin Haqqani.

Issam al-Libi: Libyan. Senior Arab mujahid.

Jalaluddin Haqqani: Senior Afghan commander and Tribal leader.

Jamal al-Fadl: Sudanese former member of al-Qaeda; became informant after dispute over stolen funds. Early member of al-Qaeda.

Jamil ul-Rahman: Salafi Afghan tribal leader and Mawlawi who ran his own camp in Kunar and received funding from the Gulf. Assassinated in 1991.

Juma Bai: Head of Islamic Movement of Uzbekistan's Military Committee and commander of all foreign fighters in Afghanistan.

Kamal al-Sananiry: Senior individual in Ikhwan Muslimin until he resigned and left.

Khalid Shaykh Muhammad: Planner of 9/11, headed up al-Qaeda external operations for a time.

Khalil Haqqani: Brother of Jalaluddin Haqqani. Commander.

Luay Sakka: Syrian. Senior Mujahidin Services Centre operative who later worked with al-Zarqawi. Ran Mujahidin Services Centre in Turkey as back station for Chechnya and Georgia.

Mawlawi Adam: Afghan. Senior figure sent by Jalaluddin Haqqani to Abu Dhabi in early 1979 to raise funds for jihad in Afghanistan.

Mawlawi Fathallah: Senior Afghan figure. Killed in Lija in 1985.

Mawlawi Ihsanullah: Senior Taliban member. Killed in ambush in Baglan province in 1998.

Mawlawi Nasrullah Mansur: Former deputy leader of Harakat i Inqilab i Islami until he formed and led a splinter group with the same name. Early founder of Taliban movement.

Mohamed Farrah Aidid: Commander of militants in Somalia whose forces downed American Blackhawks in 1993.

Moqbil al-Wadi: Salafi Yemeni cleric who reportedly supported bin Laden's jihad efforts in Yemen before turning to label him an 'agent of sedition'.

Muhammad al-Islambouli: Egyptian. Brother of Khalid al-Islambouli who assassinated Egyptian President Anwar Sadat. A senior member of Gamaah Islamiyyah.

Muhammad Makkawi: Egyptian. Mujahidin fighter formerly in Egyptian military. Famously called Jalalabad battle a 'Goat War'.

Muhammad Nabi Muhammadi: Afghan. First leader of Harakat i Inqilab i Islami.

Muhammad Najibullah: Known as Dr Najibullah. Afghan prime minister from 1986 until 1992, when his government fell and Afghanistan descended into civil war.

Mullah Abdul Razak: Member of Taliban Shurah Council circa 2001.

Mullah Baradar: Member of Taliban Shurah Council circa 2001.

Mullah Jaleel: Influential figure in the Taliban who was close to Mullah Omar, and also Abu Musab al-Suri, whom he favoured over bin Laden.

Mullah Mansur: Member of Taliban Shurah Council circa 2001.

Mullah Omar: Mullah Muhammad Omar. Amir of the Taliban movement.

Mustafa al-Yamani: Yemeni. Involved in fighting around Lija and in Jalalabad during first Afghan war. Author of *Afghanistan ... Memories of an Occupation.*

Mustafa Mashrour: Egyptian. Senior figure in Ikhwan Muslimin.

Mutiullah: Afghan commander active in Paktia during first Afghan war.

Nasir Abbas: Senior figure in Indonesia's Jamaah Islamiyyah.

Omar Abdul Rahman: Egyptian currently jailed in America for conspiracy relating to the 1993 World Trade Center bombings. Senior religious leader in Egypt's Gamaah Islamiyyah.

Osama Azmarai: Saudi. Also known as Wali Khan. Established his own camp in Jalalabad. Pioneer of anti-American focus and involved in early attack plots in the United States and Asia.

Rashid Ahmad: Pakistani Army major instrumental in providing training to the Afghans and Arab-Afghans.

Ramzi Yousef: Pakistani. Carried out the first World Trade Center bombing in 1993.

Saeed al-Masri: Egyptian. Senior al-Qaeda figure.

Salahdin: Former Iranian al-Qaeda member.

Saleh Kamal: Saudi. Financier of Afghan mujahidin during conflict against the Soviets. Financed Badr camp.

Sayed Ahmad: Provided assistance to the mujahidin in Herat.

Sayf al-Adl: Egyptian. Senior al-Qaeda leader.

Sayyid Imam: Egyptian. Former amir of Tanzim al-Jihad before resigning. Wrote *Foundations in Preparing for Jihad*, a book that was highly influential among takfiris.

Saznor: Afghan. Commander who provided protection to Osama bin Laden and those arriving with him upon his 1996 return to Afghanistan.

Shamil Basayev: Leader of the Chechen resistance; travelled to Afghanistan in 1994 to seek assistance for the campaign in Chechnya.

Shammali: Afghan commander during the Jalalabad battle.

Sharif al-Masri: Egyptian. Gamaah Islamiyyah figure and military trainer who led the al-Faruq training camp at the time of its bombing in August 1998.

Sigbatullah Mujaddidi: Leader of the National Front for the Salvation of Afghanistan, a group within the Union of Mujahidin Parties. Was appointed president of Afghanistan after the communist regime fell in 1992.

Tahir Yuldashev: Uzbek. Amir of Islamic Movement of Uzbekistan.

Tamim al-Adnani: Palestinian. Member of the Arab Advisory Council; deputy to Abdullah Azzam.

Turki al-Faisal: Former Saudi intelligence chief.

Wadih al-Hage: Also known as Abdul Sabur. Arab-Afghan who later joined al-Qaeda.

Wael Julaydan: Assisted in the establishment of Maktab al-Khadamat. He was the Saudi head of The Red Crescent in Peshawar and a member of the Peshawar Advisory Council formed by the Arab-Afghans.

Yunis Khalis: Afghan mujahidin commander. Leader of the group Hizb i Islami-Khalis.

Zia ul Haq: Former president of Pakistan.

Ziad Barre: Former president of Somalia.

GLOSSARY

Ablution	Refers here to the cleansing performed prior to prayer.
Amir al-Muminin	Leader of the Faithful. Refers here to Mullah Muhammad Omar, amir of the Taliban.
Andar	Pashtun tribe predominantly present in Afghanistan's Paktia, Ghazni and Paktika provinces.
Arab-Afghan	Initially used in a derogatory manner; the term referred to Arab volunteers who travelled to Afghanistan to fight against the Soviets in the Afghan jihad.
Bayah	Arabic term for an oath. Plural is bayat.
Blood taxes	A term used to refer to the cost in lives.
Dawah	To call or invite. In the context of this book it means the call or invitation back to Islam and Allah.
Fatwa	Religious ruling given by a mufti. Plural fatawa.
Fiqh	Understanding. Refers to the human comprehension of Shariah.
Goat war	A term used by Muhammad Makkawi to refer to the chaotic, ill-thought out and unsuccessful conduct of war.
Guerrilla warfare	A type of warfare when an irregular force fights a stronger 'regular' force of a nation state.
Hajj	The annual pilgrimage to Mecca in Dhu al-Hijjah; obligatory for those who are able.
Hanafi	One of the main schools of Islamic jurisprudence.
Imam	Leader of prayers at a masjid.
Jahiliyyat	Usually translated as 'ignorance' but has a broader

	meaning as a concept referring to how the pre-Islam era in Arabia is understood. The term is subject to differing interpretations, most notably reflected in Sayyid Qutb's work, and the varying interpretations of his meaning when using this term.
Jamaah	Arabic word for group. Plural is Jamaat.
Jihad	Arabic term meaning to strive. Can refer to striving for betterment of the self, or to religiously mandated armed conflict.
Khalifah	Arabic term meaning deputy. Often used to refer to a ruler.
Kuchi	Refers here to Pashtun nomads who move between Afghanistan and Pakistan.
Madhab	Term used to describe a school of thought within Islamic jurisprudence.
Maliki	School of Islamic jurisprudence.
Manhaj	Program and/or method.
Mawlawi	Is a title commonly used in South Asia. Refers to those who are educated in Islamic jurisprudence, but not to the level of a mufti.
Mufti	Religious scholar qualified to issue rulings/judgements (fatawa).
Mujahidin	Arab term for fighters undertaking armed jihad. Singular is mujahid.
Mullah	A religious figure working in a masjid or providing religious lessons.
Mushrikin	Arabic term for polytheists.
Pashtu; Pashtun	Pashtu is a language spoken by Pashtun, an ethnic grouping in Afghanistan and Pakistan.
Persian	Language of Iran. Also spoken in neighbouring countries such as Afghanistan and Tajikistan.
Proxy war	A kind of warfare where major powers use third parties to engage in conflict rather than to fight directly.
Ramadan	The ninth month of the Hijri calendar, and one of the most religiously significant, when Muslims fast.

Rupees	Refers here to Pakistani rupees, the currency of Pakistan.
Sahib	Honorific term used to denote respect.
Salafis	Those who follow an approach to Islam that aims to emulate the way the first generations of Muslims practised Islam.
Shahadah	To bear witness. The first pillar of faith where a person gives witness by stating their belief that there is no God but Allah and that Muhammad is his messenger. Also used in reference to martyrdom, where a person who is martyred has borne witness to their faith by losing their life in the performance of a religious duty, and is called a *shahid*.
Shariah	Islamic law.
Shia	One of the two main branches of Islam comprised of Muslims who believe that the Prophet Muhammad's son-in law Ali was the legitimate successor to the Prophet.
Shirk	Idolatry, or the association of other things, beings or false gods with Allah.
Shurah council	Shurah is an Arabic term meaning consultation. A shurah council refers to a 'consultative council'; although in the context of jihadi groups these councils often lack authority, which usually rests in the hands of the amir, with the council's role being limited to the provision of advice.
Sufi	Adherent of religious practices commonly referred to as Sufism; the beliefs and practices followed by those seeking to purify themselves and reach the truth—that of God. Sufis seek a spiritual path to a direct personal experience of God.
Takfir	Arabic term. The determination that a person is a disbeliever (*kafir*) or their actions and/or beliefs (such as the *kufr* of apostasy) have shown them as such, and the excommunication of them as a Muslim. To make *takfir* is to make the determination that someone is a disbeliever. A takfiri is one who makes *takfir* of others.

Tanzim	Arabic term refers to organisation. Sometimes used to also denote group. For example, al-Qaeda is sometimes called a *tanzim*, other times a *jamaah*.
Tareekh Osama	Arabic label on files found in a computer containing biographical information on bin Laden and al-Qaeda. *Tareekh* means history; as such the file name indicates it contains contents about the history of Osama.
Ulama	Muslim scholars.
Ummah	Muslim nation.
Wahhabi	Form of Islamic faith, in which adherents follow a literal interpretation of the Quran and Sunnah, as first practised by Muhammad ibn Abdul Wahhab. Dominant in Saudi Arabia.

CAMPS, ORGANISATIONS AND PUBLICATIONS

Abu al-Shahid al-Qatari: Name of an al-Qaeda camp in Jalalabad, named in honour of a mujahid who died in Khost.

Afghan Jihad Encyclopaedia: Widely used encyclopaedia compiled by Abu Burhan al-Suri for trainees at Maktab al-Khadamat's camp. It contained most of the training courses offered at Sadda, and later Khaldan.

Al-Qaeda: The organisation founded by Osama bin Laden, Abu Hafs al-Masri and Abu Ubaydah al-Banshiri in late 1987 following the unlikely victory of the Arab-Afghan mujahidin at Jaji against Soviet and Afghan regime forces.

Al-Faruq: A camp established by al-Qaeda in Khost, which operated from 1989 until it was abandoned following American missile strikes in August 1998. Later, a camp with the same name was established in an area outside of Kandahar.

Al-Furqan: Name of project run by Mustafa Hamid, training Tajik and Central Asian volunteers.

Al-Ittihad al-Islamiyyah (Somalia): A Somali militant group reportedly formed in 1984; according to some lore, the group was named in honour of Abdul Rasul Sayyaf, who some members knew from volunteering in the Afghan jihad.

***Al-Jihad* magazine:** Magazine published by Maktab al-Khadamat. Began in 1984; primarily written by Abdullah Azzam. Widely distributed and internationally read. Published from 1984 until Maktab al-Khadamat's disintegration in 1993/4.

Al-Nahda: Tajik resistance group led by Abdullah Nuri. Formed in 1990, banned in 1993 when Tajikistan became independent after the fall of the Soviet Union. The group took up arms and fought with other groups during the Tajik civil war. It later laid down its arms and became a political party.

Al-Saddiq: Refers here to a small camp used by al-Qaeda in Khost.

***Al-Samud* magazine:** Current magazine of Taliban movement. Has been in publication since 2001.

***Al-Surat* magazine:** Magazine founded by Mawlawi Mansur and written primarily by Rashid Ahmad. Several issues were published in 1985 and 1986 until financial shortages forced the magazine's closure.

Al-Wafa: Charity organisation that had an office in Afghanistan and was claimed by the United States to have links to al-Qaeda.

Arab Advisory Council: Also known as the Peshawar Advisory Council, this was formed in the period after the Battle of Jaji to coordinate the efforts of the Arab-Afghans in Afghanistan. Osama bin Laden was nominally the amir of the Council.

Arab Khel: Village named by the Arabs, where they lived in Jalalabad.

Badr: Name of the camp established in 1984 and funded by Saleh Kamal. Also the name of a camp used to train Pakistanis in Khost.

Badr al-Kubra: Reported name of al-Qaeda camp in Jalalabad.

Badr al-Sughra: Reported name of al-Qaeda camp in Jalalabad.

Belief Battalions Institute: Name of the religious institute located at the Khaldan camp and run by Abu Abdullah al-Muhajir.

Benevolence International Foundation: Charity organisation based in Saudi Arabia with offices around the world. Had close links to a number of Arab-Afghans.

East Turkestan Islamic Movement: Name of a Uighur resistance group whose origins trace to the first Afghan jihad. Group's aim is to liberate East Turkestan from Chinese rule. Was first active in the Khaldan camp.

Fatah: Founded by Yasser Arafat, Fatah was the largest faction of the Palestinian Liberation Organisation.

Gamaah Islamiyyah: Egyptian group whose origins trace to the early 1970s. Conducted a violent campaign inside Egypt against the regime. Was also involved in sectarian violence inside Egypt. The group's leaders renounced violence in 2003, and in 2011 the group fielded a political party in Egypt's first democratic elections following the ousting of Hosni Mubarak. One faction of the group did not renounce violence and in 2006 'merged' with al-Qaeda. Its members are predominantly active in Pakistan and Afghanistan.

Gamaah al-Khalifah: Name of a Salafi group operating in Afghanistan from 1992 onwards, after the establishment of the mujahidin government. Was hostile to other groups who did not swear an oath of allegiance to its khalifah. Led by an Arab with British citizenship.

Harakat i Inqilab i Islami: Also known as the Islamic Revolution Movement. Formed in the late 1970s, the Group was part of the Afghanistan's Union of Mujahidin Parties and carried out jihad against the Soviets. Led by Mawlawi Muhammad Nabi Muhammadi, until the group split and its deputy Mawlawi Nasrullah Mansur led a splinter group by the same name.

Hizb i Islam: Formed in the 1970s and led by Gulbuddin Hekmatyar until Mawlawi Yunis Khalis split with the group in 1979 and established a group with the same name. Both groups were part of the Afghanistan's Union of Mujahidin Parties and fought against the Soviets in the Afghan jihad.

Ikhwan Muslimin: Islamist organisation founded in Egypt in 1928 by Hassan al-Banna. Banned by the Egyptian government following the defeat in the 1948 Palestine War. The group initially had a violent agenda, but during its time as a banned movement renounced violence. It remained a banned opposition movement in Egypt for many years. Following the ousting of Egypt's long-term dictator Hosni Mubarak, it fielded a political party and won Egypt's first democratic elections. While Ikhwan had its origins in Egypt, it expanded to have a presence in other countries, in part as a result of the flight of its members following its early banning. See Syrian Ikhwan Muslimin entry for further details on that branch.

ISI (Inter-Services Intelligence): The name of Pakistan's largest and most powerful intelligence agency; comprised of members from Pakistan's armed services.

Islamic Group Algeria: Group that emerged from the civil strife following the election of the FIS in Algeria and the cancellation of election results by the regime. Initially supported by bin Laden until the group splintered and one faction threatened him.

Islamic Movement of Uzbekistan: Group formed around late 1994 by Muhammad Tahir, previously a member of al-Nahda. Announced its existence with 1999 Declaration of Jihad against the Uzbek regime, but in reality had been operating for several years previously. Was among the largest of the foreign groups operating in Afghanistan with a close relationship to the Taliban.

Islamic Relief Agency (ISRA): Sudanese relief agency active in providing support during the Afghan conflict to displaced persons in Afghanistan.

Jamaah Islamiyyah-Indonesia: Formed in Malaysia by Abdullah Sungkar and Abu Bakar Bashir while in exile in the country from Indonesia. Many of its members participated in the jihad in Afghanistan and eventually the group established its own training camp before relocating training to the Philippines. The group has one of the most sophisticated and lengthy preparation periods of any movement.

Jamaat i Islami: Pakistani group formed in 1941 by Abul Ala Maududi. Was initial contact point for a young bin Laden when he first began bringing financial donations for the mujahidin to Pakistan. The group played an important role in facilitating support for the Afghan jihad and Afghan refugees entering into Pakistan.

Jihadwal: Name of al-Qaeda's 'mother' camp in Khost; located in a larger base by the same name owned by Hizb i Islami's Gulbuddin Hekmatyar.

Jundullah: Group formed in Karachi in early 2000s. Rose from university linkages among its founding members. Linked to Jamaat i Islami, Lashkar i Taiba and al-Qaeda. Active in providing support and facilitation to al-Qaeda figures and other Arab-Afghans as they fled Afghanistan in late 2001. Not the same Jundullah group associated with hostilities against Iran.

Khaldan: Camp located in Khost, first associated with Maktab al-Khadamat and then run by Ibn Shaykh al-Libi and Abu Zubaydah following the disintegration of Maktab al-Khadamat.

Khalid bin Walid: Name of al-Qaeda camp in Khost.

Lashkar i Taiba: Pakistani group reportedly formed in 1990. Rose from university linkages from its founding members. Close links with ISI. Predominantly focused on hostilities in Kashmir, but also provided support to al-Qaeda and Afghan-Arabs fleeing Afghanistan in late 2001.

Lashkar Ethar: Name of short-lived combat group formed by Hizb i Islami Gulbuddin Hekmatyar in 1988 during the first Afghan war.

Libyan Islamic Fighting Group: Libyan group founded in early 1990s that aimed to rid Libya of the Gaddafi regime and establish an Islamic state in the country. Many members were veterans of the Afghan jihad against the Soviets. The group was among many active in Afghanistan during the latter period of Taliban rule.

Maktab al-Alami al-Islami: Name of the small working group of Arab-Afghans in the early 1980s. The group, which pre-dated Maktab al-Khadamat, was a loosely formed entity that was attempting to organise better support for the Afghan mujahidin and to organise the Arab effort in support of the Afghan jihad.

Maktab al-Khadamat: Group founded by Abdullah Azzam in 1984 with bin Laden's financial support. Its rationale was to organise Arab efforts to support the Afghan mujahidin and ensure the jihad was adequately supported.

Mujahidin Services Centre: The name of a group formed by Abu Zubaydah in 1996. It was comprised most of explosives experts, document forgers and other facilitators, and provided services to Khaldan camp and others.

Pabbi Military Academy: A military academy established by Abdul Rasul Sayyaf to train Afghans for the jihad. Also trained Indonesians and Arab-Afghans until the relocation to Sadda. Also known as the Mujahidin Military Academy.

Palestinian Liberation Organisation: Organisation established in 1964. Recognised as the official representative of the Palestinian people. Initially an armed guerrilla organisation with many constituent factions. Ousted by Israel from its Lebanon headquarters in June 1982. Had previously been based in Jordan.

Qais camp: Name of a camp established by Mawlawi Mansur in Sadda area in 1984.

Salman al-Farsi: Name of training camp in Khost.

Syrian Ikhwan Muslimin: Syrian branch of the Muslim Brotherhood. Membership of the group was made a capital offence in 1980. The group was distinguishable for its involvement in armed conflict in Hama, Syria in 1982 and Afghanistan. Members were trained in Iraq, Egypt and, after 1990, Afghanistan.

Taliban: A movement of 'students' whose origins trace to Harakat i Inqilab i Islami and that began its rise to power in Afghanistan in 1994.

Tanzim al-Jihad: Egyptian organisation active since the late 1970s, founded in Alexandria. The group was seriously weakened following the crackdown after its assassination of Egyptian President Anwar Sadat. One faction of the organisation merged with al-Qaeda in 2001; another small faction remains.

Union of Mujahidin Parties: Name given to the body representing the Afghan mujahidin parties.

World Islamic Front against Jews and Crusaders: Name of the front formed by bin Laden and al-Qaeda. Other groups who signed on as members included Tanzim al-Jihad, Gamaah Islamiyyah, Jamiat Ulama i Pakistan and Harakat ul Jihad i Islami from Bangladesh.

Yarmuk: Name of a camp and a brigade established by Hekmatyar and Abu Rouda al-Suri in Logar province.

LOCATIONS

Al-Arin	Area behind al-Masadah at Jaji.
Al-Sham	Region of Lebanon, Palestine, Jordan and Syria.
Ali Khel	An area in Jaji.
Amu Daria River	A large river in Central Asia flowing through Afghanistan, Tajikistan and Uzbekistan.
Badakshan Province	Province in north-east Afghanistan.
Dagestan, Republic of	Federal subject of Russia in the North Caucasus.
Faisalabad	City in Pakistan's Punjab region. Location of safe houses used by al-Qaeda and other Arab-Afghans.
Garamwak	Name of the area where al-Qaeda established its new al-Faruq camp outside Kandahar in 2000.
Gardez	City in Afghanistan. Capital of Paktia province.
Herat	City in western Afghanistan; capital of province by the same name.
Islamabad	Capital of Pakistan and location of al-Qaeda safe houses.
Jaji	Location where most Maktab al-Khadamat trainees went to fight and the place of the historic al-Masadah battle. Under the nominal control of Sayyaf. Jaji was located north-east of Paktia on the border with Pakistan.
Jalalabad	Capital city of Afghanistan's Nangarhar province.
Kabul	Current capital city of Afghanistan, and capital of province by the same name.

Kandahar	City in Afghanistan and capital of province by the same name.
Karachi	Largest city in Pakistan where most al-Qaeda congregated in a number of safe houses.
Khost	Province of eastern Afghanistan with capital city by the same name.
Kunar	Province in north-east Afghanistan.
Kunduz	Province in northern Afghanistan with capital city of the same name.
Lahore	Capital city of Pakistan's Punjab; location where al-Qaeda used a number of safe houses.
Lija	An area in Khost, which was the site of battles and also of a training camp run by a Yemeni group.
Logar	Province south of Kabul, where Hekmatyar had a camp called Yarmuk.
Mazar Sharif	City in north Afghanistan's Balkh province.
Mes Aynak	A location in Logar province in Afghanistan where al-Qaeda had a small camp. The area has a large copper mine.
Miranshah	Capital of North Waziristan. Entry point for mujahidin going into north-east Afghanistan during the first Afghan war.
Mount Torghar	Mountain in Khost next to the airport. Also known as Black Mountain. Another mountain of this name also exists in Jalalabad.
Pabbi	Area outside of Peshawar in Pakistan's North West Frontier Province.
Paktia	Province in eastern Afghanistan; capital city is Gardez.
Paktika	Province in south-east Afghanistan; capital is Sharana.
Peshawar	Capital city in Pakistan's North West Frontier Province.
Sadda	Large area in Kurram Agency in Pakistan's Federally Administered Tribal Area; previously part of Peshawar division of the North West Frontier Province.
Samar Khel Mountain	Mountain outside Jalalabad that was important during the 1989 battle.

Shiraz	City in Iran where Sudanese government plane carrying bin Laden back to Afghanistan took a refuelling stop.
Taloqan	Capital of Takhar province in northern Afghanistan.
Tora Bora Mountain	White Mountain, located in Nangarhar province.
Torkham Gate	Crossing from Pakistan into Afghanistan's Nangarhar province.
Urgon	Town in Afghanistan's Paktia province.
Zurmat	Region in Afghanistan's Paktia province. It is south of Gardez, the capital of Paktia.

1

INTRODUCING MUSTAFA HAMID

'Abu Walid, please come with me,' Osama bin Laden said to his old friend Mustafa Hamid, referring to him by the nom de guerre by which he was known during the Afghan jihad. It was November 1996. Hamid had been visiting bin Laden at his house inside Jalalabad's 'Arab village' when a group of armed Taliban arrived to tell the latter that he was wanted in Kandahar by their leader, Mullah Muhammad Omar. A helicopter was waiting at Jalalabad airport to take him, they said, with such stern expressions on their faces that both men immediately feared bin Laden was being summoned for his own execution. The Taliban had only recently seized power, declaring Mullah Omar the 'Amir al-Muminin' (Leader of the Faithful) following their taking of Kabul and establishment of the Islamic Emirate of Afghanistan in September 1996. Almost immediately, they found themselves dealing with a flurry of diplomatic communications about bin Laden, who had followed his August 1996 Declaration of Jihad against the United States with a spate of international media interviews.

Dealing with the bin Laden issue posed a problem because at that time none of the Taliban's senior leadership had met the al-Qaeda leader, despite their repeated efforts to do so. Each time they tried to arrange a meeting, bin Laden avoided attending. He also ignored requests by Taliban figures to cease media activities, which were communicated to him via intermediaries, eventually forcing Mullah Omar to act by dispatching a helicopter to bring bin Laden to Kandahar. After hearing the Taliban men's instructions, and fearing he was to be executed, bin Laden immediately sent for his deputy, Abu Hafs al-Masri, and appointed him leader in the event he did not return. Then, bin Laden turned to Mustafa Hamid and asked that he accompany him to Kandahar. 'What, you want me to be executed with you?' was his incredulous reply.

It was not the deferential answer bin Laden might have received from his own men. But Hamid was not part of al-Qaeda. Nor was it the first time Hamid had spoken so frankly to his younger friend. He had already reprimanded bin Laden for disregarding the Taliban after they came to power and continuing his jihad programme against America despite their repeated requests for him to cease activities. Hamid's efforts fell on deaf ears, but when the Taliban messengers arrived, bin Laden, appreciating the gravity of the situation, wanted his old friend to come with him and mediate on his behalf. He thought Hamid could do so because of his stature among the Afghans.

Mustafa Hamid, or Abu Walid al-Masri as he later became known, was one of only three Arabs to join the Afghan insurgency before the Soviet Union invaded Afghanistan in December 1979 in order to prop up the failing communist regime. By the time Soviet forces rolled in, Hamid had already seen combat in Paktia with Afghan commander Jalaluddin Haqqani. A journalist for *Al-Ittihad* at the time (a newspaper based in Abu Dhabi in the United Arab Emirates), Hamid filed the first front-line reports on the conflict in the Arab media. He and his two friends also arranged for the first fundraising visit to the Gulf by a delegation of senior Afghan commanders from the newly formed Ittihad i Islami Tahrir Afghanistan (The Islamic Union for the Liberation of Afghanistan), a union of Afghan mujahidin parties fighting against the Soviet occupation. Their visit marked the beginning of direct contact between the Afghan mujahidin and the Arabs in the Gulf, after which time financial support for the Afghan jihad began to flow.

Hamid later played an important role in mujahidin activities in Khost, forming the first Arab fighting group in the area, and working closely with Jalaluddin Haqqani. As a result, he was held in high regard by many Afghan commanders as well as within the community of foreign volunteers who joined the fight against the Soviets, and came to be known as Arab-Afghans.

Hamid was also one of only a handful of Arab-Afghans who stayed in Afghanistan following its descent into civil war in 1992, and was eyewitness to the Taliban's rapid rise to power. Most Arab-Afghans and foreign jihadi groups who had joined the Afghan jihad left Afghanistan as it became obvious the country was plunging into civil war. If they could, they returned to their homeland, or in the case of al-Qaeda and others, they travelled to Sudan, which at that time had a government sympathetic to their agendas. In 1994, when Taliban figures visited Khost, the province home to the few Arab-Afghans who remained in Afghanistan, Hamid was the first to actively engage with them. He reconnected with Taliban members he knew from the Afghan jihad and built new friendships with others, some of whom went on to become senior figures in the movement.

It was Hamid's long-standing presence in Afghanistan and friendships with key Afghans, including senior leaders in the Taliban, which led bin Laden to ask him to return to Afghanistan with him in May 1996. Al-Qaeda's return to Afghanistan was not voluntary. Bin Laden wished to stay in Sudan but was forced to leave by the Sudanese government, senior members of which had arranged for a group of Jalalabad area commanders to host bin Laden, as well as the fifty or so men remaining in al-Qaeda and other Arab-Afghans who needed to leave Sudan. At the time, Jalalabad was not yet under Taliban control and the situation in Afghanistan was chaotic.

Hamid was in Sudan when bin Laden's departure was being arranged by the Sudanese government, having stopped there before he was to travel on to Yemen to reunite with his family. He never made it to Yemen. Instead, after an impassioned request from bin Laden to accompany him back to Afghanistan, Hamid, along with bin Laden and fourteen others, boarded an official Sudanese government aircraft and left for Jalalabad.

Bin Laden asked Hamid to travel with him because he thought his friend's experience, stature and relationships with Afghan commanders, including senior Taliban, could be of help as he tried to navigate the uncertain environment in Afghanistan. Before the year was finished, bin Laden was relying upon these same traits when he again asked Hamid for help—this time asking his friend to accompany him to Kandahar, mediate the situation with the Taliban and prevent what he thought could be his possible execution.

Hamid, along with his son in law—al-Qaeda's then head of security, Sayf al-Adl—and a small number of others, did travel to Kandahar with bin Laden and attend a meeting with Mullah Omar. As history attests, it did not result in Mullah Omar ordering bin Laden's execution. Nor did it result in bin Laden ceasing his activities, as Mullah Omar had requested. Tension continued in the relationship between al-Qaeda and the Taliban, and Hamid was often called to mediate.

A staunch defender of the Taliban, whom he believed were key to reforming the corruption and violence that had plagued Afghanistan, Hamid became a loyal friend to Mullah Omar. Some Arabs, annoyed at his loyalty, would refer to him as Taliban, particularly after Hamid's decision to give an oath of allegiance to Mullah Omar in 1998.

Not only did Hamid have a front row view of the Taliban–al-Qaeda relationship, but he was also witness to the emergence of an Arab-Afghan community comprised of individuals and groups who had travelled to the country after the Taliban came to power. Some were returnees who had previously been based in the region during the Afghan jihad against the Soviets. Others were new arrivals. The community was a melting pot of different jihadi groups, some of whom were in competition with one another, not only for recruits, resources and funds, but also for the Taliban's favour. The increasingly competitive and at times tense dynamic among the groups came to destabilise the community and endanger its safety in Afghanistan by creating divisions within the Taliban about the wisdom of hosting such groups.

Al-Qaeda's actions also contributed to the tension. Its 26 May 1998 press conference in Khost to announce the formation of the World Islamic Front not only angered the Taliban but also other Arab-Afghan groups. They believed bin Laden's actions had endangered them by alienating the Taliban and bringing international focus on Khost where many had a training presence. Hamid was furious too—before the press conference he had argued with al-Qaeda's leadership about its disregard for Mullah Omar's instructions.

Later that year, discouraged by al-Qaeda's failure to respect the Taliban's authority and similar behaviour by other groups in Afghanistan, Hamid decided to give an oath of allegiance to Mullah Omar—the first time a foreigner had done so—in the hope that it would encourage others to follow suit. Most groups demurred, preferring to remain independent and outside of Mullah Omar's authority. Some groups refused to recognise the legitimacy of the Taliban—with a few individuals going so far as to make *takfir* against it. Only the leaders of the Islamic Movement of Uzbekistan and the East Turkistan Islamic Movement and, later, Abu Musab al-Suri, followed Hamid's lead.

Bin Laden was among the leaders who demurred before relenting, in part at Hamid's urging, and eventually gave an oath-by-proxy to Mullah Omar. It was Hamid who gave bin Laden's oath to Mullah Omar, believing that an oath-by-proxy was better than nothing—and that it might influence his behaviour. Those leaders who had already given a direct oath to Mullah Omar partly motivated bin Laden's decision. They had good relations with the Taliban leader, and their provision of an oath brought them closer, building a bloc of sorts around him, which was not in al-Qaeda's interest.

The giving of oaths, however, did little to fix the situation. As the number of Arab-Afghans increased in the period from 2000 to 2001, the scene grew more fractured and competitive, causing tensions within the Taliban over their presence on Afghan soil. A significant increase in volunteers from the Gulf arriving in Afghanistan during this period also spurred competition among the Arab jihadi groups.

This increase is commonly attributed to the rising prominence of al-Qaeda. By this time al-Qaeda had already carried out two attacks against the United States: the first near-simultaneous bombings of its embassies in Kenya and Tanzania on 7 August 1998, and the second a 12 October 2000 bomb attack against the naval warship the USS *Cole* while at anchor in Aden harbour in Yemen. Another often-cited reason for the increase in volunteers at this time is the release of rulings (fatawa) by several clerics in the Gulf recognising the legitimacy of the Taliban, and by implication the legitimacy of fighting alongside the group. The fatawa did encourage some youths to travel to Afghanistan to fight with the Taliban against the forces of Ahmad Shah Masud in the north of the country, which was outside the Taliban's control.

What is not commonly noticed is that the increase in youths arriving from the Gulf was also in significant part because they had come with the goal of fighting the Shia in the country's north, rather than specifically assisting the Taliban or wanting to join al-Qaeda. Although fighting the Shia was not new—and Arabs had earlier participated in fighting against Shia tribes in Pakistan's North West Frontier Province during the Afghan jihad—it was not the primary focus of any of the major foreign jihadi groups operating in Afghanistan at that time.

The arrival of these youths did, however, cause competition between some Arab jihadi groups. They sought to attract the new volunteers to their respective training camps and, if possible, to recruit them. Some of these groups had also established their own 'fronts' with either Abu Musab al-Suri, or with the Taliban outside of Kabul, where fighting was taking place against Masud's 'Northern Alliance' force, which they hoped would lure newly arrived volunteers.

As the number of 'fronts' around Kabul multiplied and competition for recruits intensified, al-Qaeda sought to establish one united front in Kabul for all Arab jihadi groups, over which it sought control. The idea was scuttled after a series of meetings. Some of the groups were fearful al-Qaeda would attempt to capitalise on their joining. They were concerned that al-Qaeda might make an international media announcement, bringing unwanted attention, and linking them to the organisation's anti-American agenda, which they did not share.

Meanwhile, tensions developed between some of the Arab jihadi groups and the Uzbeks, whose numerical strength in the spring of 2001 was above that of all the Arab groups combined, and whose leadership had a close relationship with Mullah Omar. At this time, al-Qaeda—as the largest of the Arab groups—had a membership of around 150, and another 100 or so men at its front who had trained at its camp but were not necessarily members of the organisation. The rest ranged in size from around ten persons to several dozen.

By the spring of 2001 the relationship between al-Qaeda and the Uzbeks had reached breaking point, and the situation among the Arab-Afghans had become so fractured that Mullah Omar intervened and summoned the leaders of all groups to Kandahar. After taking an oath from those gathered to obey his order, Mullah Omar appointed a leader (amir) from among them who would have authority over the military actions of all the Arab-Afghans inside Afghanistan. Everyone assumed that bin Laden would be appointed as amir. Instead, against all expectations, Mullah Omar appointed the military chief of the Uzbeks to the position, placing under his control the Arab-Afghans at all the different fronts, who were to be unified into one foreign brigade. Mullah Omar also made each group agree to consult him before undertaking any action outside Afghanistan—a directive that was ultimately ignored by bin Laden, who did not attend the meeting and instead sent his deputy, Abu Hafs al-Masri.

At that time al-Qaeda was making its final preparations for the 9/11 attack against the United States and had granted an interview with its senior leadership to a reporter from the Middle East Broadcasting

Corporation (MBC), which took place in the summer of 2001. Threats were made against the United States in the course of the interview, along with references to a forthcoming attack. Upon hearing of this in late August 2001, Hamid angrily approached al-Qaeda's media officials berating them for the violation of Mullah Omar's orders and for al-Qaeda's comments potentially giving cause for American military action against Afghanistan. Accompanying him was a Taliban official. When bin Laden received word that Hamid had made these comments to al-Qaeda's media people in the presence of a Taliban official, he sought a meeting.

By then, Abu Hafs al-Mauritani, the head of al-Qaeda's purported Shariah Council, had resigned in protest at bin Laden's plans to attack the United States, although this was not made public at the time. Neither he nor anyone else from al-Qaeda's old senior leadership supported the attacks, but they went along with the orders of their amir despite their objections, as they had done many times in the past. The attack project was, however, supported by Ayman al-Zawahiri, who had merged his five-person strong splinter faction of Tanzim al-Jihad with al-Qaeda that summer. The remaining five or so members in the Egyptian group who did not wish to join al-Qaeda continued operating under the name Tanzim al-Jihad, with Abu Samha as their leader. Al-Zawahiri, and the four or five others who joined al-Qaeda with him in mid-2001, all assumed senior leadership positions within the organisation. This caused tension, particularly with some older members of al-Qaeda, who resented their appointments to these positions.

After joining al-Qaeda, al-Zawahiri became bin Laden's deputy. A strong supporter of bin Laden's plan to attack the United States, he was one of those present in the MBC interview that so angered Hamid, and was also present at bin Laden's meeting with Hamid. It was during this meeting that Hamid became aware that the threats made in the MBC interview, which he thought might cause the United States to undertake military action in Afghanistan, were not bluster. Al-Qaeda was, in fact, planning a large attack, the details of which they would not specify—only to say it would cause a huge impact and kill thousands. Shocked, Hamid challenged the wisdom of attacking the United States and questioned their claims that al-Qaeda could withstand a retaliatory onslaught, using the example of Japan's Pearl Harbor attack. Al-Zawahiri interjected, saying 'he who strikes first has the upper hand', seemingly ignoring that the strategy did not work so well for the Japanese who struck the United States first at Pearl Harbor, but ultimately lost the war.[1]

Hamid argued that the United States could absorb a large attack and still retaliate strongly, potentially decimating not only al-Qaeda but also Afghanistan. He was angry al-Qaeda was sacrificing Afghanistan for its own objectives, arguing that Afghans should not pay with their blood for bin Laden's cause. He tried unsuccessfully to remind bin Laden that permission was required from Mullah Omar before undertaking any outside attack, but bin Laden could not be convinced. It would be the last time Hamid saw his old friend; bin Laden left Kandahar shortly afterwards.

By the time bin Laden met with Hamid he was already preparing a location at Tora Bora Mountain where he planned to wait for the arrival of the Americans following al-Qaeda's attack. Bin Laden knew al-Qaeda's attack would cause an armed American reaction, one that he thought would involve paratroopers being sent to capture him. He was planning to lay in wait for them at Tora Bora and thought he could achieve a victory over them on the mountain, as he had done against Soviet paratroopers years earlier at the 1987 Battle of Jaji. Although it made its own defence plans in the event of an American retaliation, al-Qaeda did not advise the Taliban or any of the other Arab-Afghan groups that an attack was coming and preparations were needed.

On 11 September 2001, a little over two weeks after Hamid's last meeting with his old friends, al-Qaeda attacked the United States. There was great anger at al-Qaeda's actions among the Arab-Afghan groups in Afghanistan, who, like Hamid, realised that war was coming and consequently their own safety was in jeopardy. But as the American invasion loomed, infighting among the groups died down as they instead turned to focus on what to do. Most were unprepared for what was coming—many thought it would be like the last Afghan war, where they could keep their families close by, fight at the fronts and be able to move openly behind the front lines.

However, Hamid and some of his friends knew better, and realised this war would be different. Hamid's old friend Haqqani had asked him to travel to Khost and help him coordinate activities there, but Mullah Omar instead requested that Hamid try to arrange a meeting with Iranian officials. He wanted to see if the Iranians would assist the Taliban as it attempted to deal with the invasion. Hamid travelled to Herat and participated in meetings held near the Iranian border, but he was unable to secure any agreement for cooperation.

It was not long after the meeting that Herat suddenly fell, leaving Hamid and other Arab-Afghans in the region cut off. Some in Herat, such as Abu Musab al-Zarqawi, who would go on to lead al-Qaeda in Iraq, risked the journey to Kandahar, which was still under Taliban control. The Arab-Afghan brigade under the command of the Uzbeks had already been decimated in Mazar Sharif. As the rest of the country fell, Arab-Afghans converged on Kandahar where, following the death of Abu Hafs al-Masri in an American air strike, defence activities were being coordinated by al-Qaeda's Sayf al-Adl, along with a number of other senior Arab-Afghans.

Meanwhile, bin Laden was in Jalalabad and would soon head to Tora Bora Mountain, the location where he hoped to lure American forces to their defeat. Al-Qaeda's military leadership along with senior local area Afghan commanders had advised bin Laden against holing up at Tora Bora. They thought the location was ripe for a siege, and supply routes were vulnerable, particularly during winter, but bin Laden was insistent. Perhaps he thought because he had declared war from there, he would finish it there too. Bin Laden went so far as to use radio communications because the Americans would hear it, telling his men who tried to caution him against using the equipment, 'I want them to know where to come.'

Hamid did not return to Kandahar like Abu Musab al-Zarqawi and the others in Herat because the route back to Herat from the border area where he had held his meeting was blocked. Unable to link up with the convoy heading to Kandahar, Hamid instead crossed the border into Iran, where he was subsequently detained and later placed under house arrest. A number of other Arab-Afghans also ended up in Iranian custody. Most were captured as they fled from Afghanistan to Pakistan and then into Iran. They did so after the Taliban leadership issued a withdrawal from combat order for its remaining forces in late November 2001. After several days of debates and discussions, the remaining Arab-Afghans in Kandahar, some of whom were refusing to leave as they wanted to stay and fight, were told by the Taliban they should take their families and leave.

When Kandahar fell on 7 December 2001, the city was largely free of Arab-Afghans who had begun withdrawing several days earlier after accepting the Taliban's order. Bin Laden had also left Tora Bora, having abandoned his dream of defeating the United States on the mountain. He left before the American campaign at Tora Bora began, returning to Jalalabad, despite the city having already fallen. He would stay hidden in the general area until he was smuggled into Pakistan's tribal region and later into urban areas before settling in Abbottabad where he remained until his death in May 2011. Mustafa Hamid, meanwhile, remained under house arrest in Iran until August 2011, when Iranian authorities released him and he returned to his native Egypt.

My name is Leah Farrall and what I have just narrated to you is a very brief summary of some of Mr Mustafa Hamid's and my discussions on the history of the Arab-Afghans in Afghanistan. These discussions took place throughout the course of our ground-breaking and now four-year long dialogue, and form the basis for our book. A conversation on the history and legacy of the Arab-Afghan experience in Afghanistan, the book draws from thousands of hours of in-person discussions, interviews, letters and joint research and analysis. It tells the story of how Arab-Afghans came to volunteer in Afghanistan's war against Soviet occupation, the training and combat experience they shared, the groups they joined and formed, and the schools of jihad they developed and later exported—some of which remain active today.

By now it should be clear that Mr Hamid had an unrivalled front-row seat to history and unique access to key Afghan and Arab-Afghan figures, something Al-Jazeera recognised when it hired him as its bureau chief in Kandahar in 2000. It should also be apparent that Mr Hamid has a strong attachment to Afghanistan, having spent many years in the country. As a result, Mr Hamid is no fan of countries involved in military activities in Afghanistan. However, he is at pains to point out that he is not against the people of these countries, rather the actions of their governing 'regimes'.

Mr Hamid is also the subject of a United States Treasury designation—a Specially Designated Global Terrorist—for his alleged intermediary activities for al-Qaeda in Iran. That designation is for him alone to challenge, however I do note its peculiar irony, given that Hamid has been the most outspoken critic of al-Qaeda within the Arab-Afghan community, many of whom considered him more as Taliban than Arab-Afghan. His sentiments are clearly on display in many of the twelve books and numerous articles he has written over the years.[2] No one else from among the Arab-Afghans has spoken or written at such length and with such frankness about their history and legacy.

Hamid's old friend, Basil Muhammad, perhaps comes closest with his work *The Arab Supporters in Afghanistan*,[3] which is a frank and exceptionally detailed account of early Arab-Afghan history, drawn almost solely from first-hand recollections and material published at the time.

Muhammad's work, however, focuses on the Arab-Afghans during the war against the Soviets and does not cover the Arab-Afghan community in Afghanistan after the Taliban came to power. Abu Musab al-Suri, al-Qaeda's bitter rival and Hamid's one-time neighbour in Khost, gives an account of aspects of the community in his work *The Global Call*.[4] Ultimately, however, his is a book focused on doctrine and methodology for jihad.

Al-Qaeda's current leader, Ayman al-Zawahiri, has also written materials that contain autobiographical reflections and information on the history of the Arab-Afghans, but for the most part they focus on Egypt, or on doctrinal issues.[5] Both al-Suri and al-Zawahiri's books, and indeed much of the autobiographical literature produced by Arab-Afghans, are written for consumption within the jihadist milieu rather than the outside world. A good deal of it also remains available only in Arabic.

More recently, some Arab-Afghans, such as bin Laden's one-time bodyguard, Abu Jandal, have cooperated with an established author to produce their autobiography. Abu Jandal's, based on over a dozen hours of interviews, was released in French.[6] Bin Laden's family members have also written autobiographies with the support of an established author, including one by his son Omar, and former wife Najwa.[7]

This book is different. I am not cooperating with Mr Hamid to help him produce his autobiography. I am not Mr Hamid's biographer and his recollections do not form the basis of a story authored by me. Mr Hamid is an equal co-author of this book; a somewhat unique occurrence given that by rights he and I should be enemies. I am, after all, a former counterterrorism intelligence analyst who has worked on terrorism-related matters for the Australian Federal Police in both Australia and Indonesia. Although I had already left that line of work to finish my PhD and pursue an academic career well before our paths crossed, many of our views remain opposed. This, you could say, makes us among the two people least likely to cooperate on producing a book. Yet we have, although it has not been without its difficulties. To write this book, and even to engage in the now four-year long dialogue that has underpinned it, our communications and, later, meetings, have literally taken place across the lines of our oftentimes opposing viewpoints.

A book like this has never been written before and is what makes our undertaking so unique. However, being unique does not necessarily equate to being important and we have been mindful of this, as we have attempted to contribute a book of substance and value. What makes our book important is the way in which we wrote it, the reasons we wrote it and the contribution it makes to the historical record and to understanding the Afghan history of many groups involved in contemporary events.

With the exception of this introductory section authored by me, our book does away with the standard one-author narrative. We decided against this approach because we wanted to ensure the book was not only accurate on information but also context, and we both wanted to remain true to our viewpoints and keep our own voice; something that would be impossible to do if only one of us wrote the narrative. While we both generally agree on what happened, we have very different opinions on why it happened, and as you will subsequently read, often widely differing interpretations of events and what they mean. This is why we chose to tell the story of the Arab-Afghans and their legacy through our dialogue.

Had we instead chosen to try to write the story together with one unified narrative, chances are we may never have finished, and at the very least, there would have been considerable delays as we navigated through the thorny issues of context and representation. As the book progresses you will see large parts of our discussion indeed focus on establishing and analysing context as well as information. Telling the Arab-Afghan story in dialogue form not only allows us to keep our own voices, but also narrows the scope for misinterpretation and misinformation, and provides, we think, a better, more accurate context. This in itself is an important contribution to the very sparse historical record on the Arab-Afghans and their legacy.

One of the main reasons we wanted to write this book is our belief that it is critically important that history is not solely written by victors. It almost goes without saying that we disagree as to who will be victorious, but it is our sharing of this viewpoint that has allowed us to cooperate, even with this central disagreement unresolved. We believe that future generations must be informed and understand history from both sides. This is particularly important since events, personalities and ongoing legacies of the Arab-Afghans have come to shape so much recent history, not only in Afghanistan but all over the world, and at the cost of great loss of life.

We have not written this book as an academic text because academics tend to write for their peers. We wanted to make our book accessible to the general reader, but we also wanted to offer up new insights, which require accompanying explanatory analysis. This is another reason why we chose to write the book in dialogue format, so our dialogue could be used as a tool for introduction, explanation and analysis.

In our book, we have been able to offer important new insights into the history and legacy of the Arab-Afghans and correct a number of erroneous assumptions—some of which have become enduring myths. This is because of the extensive knowledge we both have on this subject matter. Although I make no claim to know anywhere near as much as Mr Hamid, I have spent over fifteen years conducting academic research in this area, some of which was for my PhD on al-Qaeda and militant Salafist jihad. This involved not only researching the histories of al-Qaeda and other militant Salafist groups operating from Afghanistan in the period from 1979 to 2001, and their evolution following their late 2001 withdrawal from the country, but also their ideological and doctrinal heritage. As a result, I built up a large collection of primary source materials relating to the Arab-Afghans in Afghanistan. This collection has helped me greatly in my research, which has aimed to break down the myths surrounding the emergence and evolution of al-Qaeda and other schools of jihad from the first Afghan conflict onwards.

A contribution I therefore bring to the book is an awareness of what is 'known' in existing research on the Arab-Afghans and their legacy, and what remains 'unknown', untapped or has escaped critical attention in published material to date. I also have the knowledge to participate in a discussion on and analysis of the history of the Arab-Afghans with Mr Hamid, rather than to merely ask him questions. Aside from being one of the reasons he chose to talk me, it is also why our dialogue has continued for such a significant amount of time. Having such a lengthy ongoing discussion has not only resulted in a more interactive experience for both the book's authors (and readers) but it has also allowed us to focus our dialogue and explanatory efforts on gaps in knowledge and, where necessary, on correcting myths about the Arab-Afghan legacy.

In addition to documenting his own experiences as both a combatant and journalist during the Afghan jihad against the Soviets, Mr Hamid has also chronicled, through interviews and the collection of written materials, the experiences of his friends and acquaintances within the Afghan and Arab-Afghan community. Between us, we therefore had a rich baseline of knowledge, primary information and previously 'unknown' insights to work with in support of the book. Since beginning this project we have also jointly undertaken research on issues as they have come to light.

Accepted wisdom on the history and legacy of the Arab-Afghans is very much dictated by an assumption that all that needs to be known is now known. The attention of researchers has instead turned to focus on understanding conflicts that have emerged in recent years across the Middle East, North Africa and Asia. With this book, we hope to change this assumption and show the ongoing relevance and importance of the Arab-Afghan legacy.

By revisiting the history of the Arab-Afghans, particularly what is not known, or what has been misunderstood, we identify and bring into focus the key characteristics of Arab-Afghan history. Doing so not only builds a better understanding of this important period of time, but also of how the Arab-Afghan legacy continues to manifest in contemporary conflicts, most significantly in Syria. To fully explain how would require another study, but in this book wc build an important foundation. We generate new insights into how Arab-Afghan groups formed, splintered and/or consolidated in Afghanistan and into the cooperation, conflict, and competition among them, some of whom remain active today, and we give a fuller picture of their genealogy that has relevance for understanding contemporary conflicts.

In particular we build understanding through our identification and exploration of 'Schools of Jihad' that emerged from the Afghan conflict and the dynamics that drove their development. Of these schools—the Azzam School, the al-Qaeda School, the Khost School of Abu Harith al-Urduni and the Jalalabad School (or the School of the Youth)—two remain active, and continue to have influence over contemporary conflicts in the Middle East, North Africa and Asia. These are the al-Qaeda School and the Jalalabad School—although the latter has come to dominate the former. Understanding them all, however, is crucial not only for better conceptualising Arab-Afghan history, but also for identifying how much of what is taking place in conflicts today traces its ideological and often organisational roots to what took place in Afghanistan. This makes it easier to see historical continuities and where, in some instances, particularly with the Syrian conflict, such strong parallels exist with what took place during the Arab-Afghan jihad that it is tempting to say history is repeating itself.

There are doubtless alternative versions and interpretations of events we describe in our book. We welcome these being shared; our goal here is not only to build a greater level of understanding and break down the myths about this important period, but also to generate discussion. As the dialogue in our book shows, there is much on which we differ and some on which we may never agree, but it is our desire to share knowledge that might help to build understanding and prevent future bloodshed that has kept us going when views have diverged.

Readers may, however, find less debate than they expect in a book written by two 'enemies'. We hope it will become clear through our telling of the Arab-Afghan story and legacy that in many instances we disagree not on what happened, but on why it happened, or what it means. To this end, we have dedicated the final chapter to discussion and debate about the history and legacy of the Arab-Afghans, and after building a foundation of knowledge with this book, we hope to follow it with another publication more dedicated to discussing our areas of disagreement.

For ease of reading and understanding, we chose to write this book by reviewing our conversations, letters and research, placing excerpts of them into a chronological order, and then discussing them again, to form the story we present here. It was necessary to excerpt the dialogue because in many instances a discussion on just one of the many subjects we covered over the years stretched to book length.

At times, explanatory paragraphs accompany dialogue excerpts, setting the scene for the reader and adding historical context. Unless otherwise noted, they should be taken as being written by and agreed to by both of us. Transitions within chapters between dialogue and explanatory paragraphs are denoted by three stars (***).

The bibliographies, glossaries, maps and other points of reference have been prepared by me, for which I assume full responsibility in the event of any mistakes. Moreover, as I have had the final responsibility of editing this English-language version of the book, I too must take responsibility for any mistakes or misrepresentations contained in the text, a responsibility Mr Hamid will likewise hold when he translates and edits the Arabic version of this book.

Since I have opened our book, it is only fair Mr Hamid closes it, and so he writes the last section in the concluding chapter, which reflects on the legacy of the Arab-Afghans. For me to have the final word on a legacy I did not share would undermine the cooperative spirit in which this book was written. My views are clear enough and communicated elsewhere in the book.

Finally, before we begin our journey through the history of the Arab-Afghans, we would like to explain to you in our own words how we first encountered each other and came to decide to cooperate on this book.

* * *

On how we met

LF: I first became aware of Abu Walid al-Masri, as he is known in mujahidin circles, many years ago and read his books with great interest. Mr Mustafa Hamid—the man behind the nom de guerre—I have only more recently come to know; first through our online dialogues and then in person as we met and decided to cooperate on this book. It was some time, however, before Mr Hamid became aware of me. Once he did, he was not initially happy.

Mr Hamid, at that time under house arrest in Iran, came to know of me after I wrote a newspaper article about a book he had released on his blog.[8] In the article, I misrepresented him as an al-Qaeda figure. Understandably, he was not happy at my misrepresentation, which was the subject of our initial contact via intermediaries. It was my first article after leaving the counter-terrorism world for academia. I had rushed it, and failed to push back on reviewers' suggestions to make my explanation of his position in relation to al-Qaeda and the Taliban simpler. The result was that instead of explaining Mr Hamid's independent stance, my article in effect depicted him as al-Qaeda.

This was, however, no excuse. I was embarrassed by my mistake and misrepresentation, and said as much in a letter to him. I think I surprised Mr Hamid when I also publicly acknowledged my mistakes on my blog.[9] I surprised him even more when I asked for a dialogue, telling him how excited I had been to find his books when doing research for my PhD on al-Qaeda and militant Salafist jihad.

For those of us in the academic community, Mr Hamid's twelve books—part personal history, part historical chronicle—provide remarkable glimpses into an important and poorly documented period of history. I remember sitting with colleagues years ago, discussing whom we would most like to talk to from the mujahidin world (a surprisingly common topic of conversation). Mr Hamid topped my list and had done so since I chanced upon two stories he had recounted in his books. In one, he told of forgetting to buy his children sweets while on a trip away and returning to face their wrath; in the other, he recalled encountering the body of a dead Soviet soldier, and the sadness he felt, even for his enemy.

On reading these lines, I sensed a man who although considering the West, and probably me, as an enemy, was not so filled with hate that he had lost all of his humanity. Never did I think I would come to meet him, let alone have a dialogue with him, or co-operate on a book, but it was the humanity in these two stories that made me decide to take a chance and ask if he would talk to me further. I wrote him a rambling letter telling him about how I felt when I read those two stories of his. I also explained my PhD study; how frustrated I was at the gaps, errors and myths in the historical record, and how excited I had been to find his books.

MH: It came as a great surprise when I received word that an Australian lady wanted to have a dialogue with me on the Internet. But my surprise did not last long, because my response was ready; I was going to reject her request, especially when I came to know she had worked with the Australian Federal Police, and was a key terrorism analyst. When I heard this, my reaction turned to anger, and I thought of the picture of the smiling American soldier as she stood near Iraqi prisoners, their bodies torn from torture and piled together in Abu Ghraib. I thought this Australian lady was like that.

After consulting with others, I decided to agree to hold the dialogue, because rejecting it would be seen as a kind of fear and surrendering to defeat. I accepted on certain conditions. The most important of these was that we both had the right to put questions to each other, so it did not look like I was answering questions as if in one of those secret underground interrogation facilities. Ms Farrall accepted that condition, and said I had the right to answer only what I wanted from the questions.

Although her reply was respectful and logical, it offended me, because it reminded me of what we see in the American movies, when someone is arrested and advised of their legal rights, which sounded a lot like what Ms Farrall was saying. I felt challenged by this, and replied that I had nothing to fear and would answer all of her questions. She also committed to answering my questions, and was eager to start the dialogue and for it to continue. Through her letters, it became clear to me that she was a respectful lady, and a serious researcher. From the beginning, she told me she was preparing for a doctorate on armed jihadi groups, and that al-Qaeda was one of them.

Our dialogue was more academic than political; but this did not stop me from making my first message at times sharp and sarcastic, suggesting that she was a researcher working in the police system and was one of those women in Iraq and other places. Now my having done so makes me sorry because this was not her place at all.

From a rocky introduction, dialogue and, eventually, a book

LF: We got off to a bit of a rocky start and Mr Hamid was understandably suspicious of me, but as time went by he came to realise I was genuinely interested in talking to him. So we undertook our public dialogue, which was at times heated, but still civil. After we started talking, it seemed we could not stop. In fact, our public dialogues triggered so many topics of interest that we then proceeded to write a seemingly endless series of letters about the state of the world, meandering from one topic to another. I learned a lot from Mr Hamid, and although we often disagreed, I found myself surprised at how often we shared the same analysis or sentiments. I came to enjoy our correspondence and debates.

I am not so sure Mr Hamid initially did, particularly as my obsession with accuracy meant I was prone to sending emails double- and triple-checking what he or I had said, and by that stage I was also subjecting him to regular updates about the boring minutiae of the life of a PhD student. Why I don't know; perhaps because I wanted him to see that I was not the person he had initially thought, and so I wrote to Mr Hamid the same way I wrote to family and friends. Through these emails—the humdrum of daily life shared with another whose life was so different to one's own—we found common humanity and some space and distance to talk about how important mutual understanding is to respecting difference and achieving peace.

MH: Our dialogue on the Internet continued for three months. It had some supporters as well as critics, who disliked and doubted a dialogue between two opposites who represented the two camps waging 'a war of civilisations', as some have called it. But the dialogue between Ms Farrall and I showed that many of these doubts were baseless. We found many things we could agree on, especially with regard to the common aim of living in safety with security and justice, which is an aim for all humanity—and there is no disputing this. Besides, war is an odious situation that no one desires or seeks, only those owners of illegal ambitions.

In fact, Ms Farrall was the first to propose we engage in dialogue, and then the dialogue was published on both our websites.[10] After this, some Arabs started to email me and put questions to me, all of which I answered, except for a few letters that contained allegations and lies, which I did not answer because I could not match them in this field. But a number of valuable dialogues started from emails that came from people and different Arab organisations. Some Shia in Afghanistan made contact and we had a dialogue that then evolved into a direct conversation with the Taliban. This was an important step in removing mutual doubts between the two sides, and to clarifying truths that were previously unknown, or deliberately hidden by some.

From my side, I do not doubt Ms Farrall was the reason for the start of these other constructive dialogues. She showed a lot of courage, imagination, and firm determination, and these are the qualities that were necessary for the dialogue between us to be successful. I should also point out that Ms Farrall was the first person in a long time to address me as Mustafa Hamid, instead of the name Abu Walid al-Masri, which I once wrote to her was more like a military rank or reference. By doing so, she reminded me of my own humanity.

We are now in the fourth year of our dialogues, and have exchanged many letters on different topics, although much of it remained in essence on Islamic armed groups, which was part of her PhD topic.

LF: By the time Mr Hamid returned home to Egypt in August 2011, after nearly a decade in detention in Iran, we had been corresponding for close on two years, and with his permission I decided to travel to meet him. We'd talked earlier about writing something together, but it wasn't until we met and the conversation flowed that we decided we could debate our way through cooperating on a book.

Thousands of hours of conversations, letters and sometimes-heated debates later, this book has come together. It has not always been easy. Like anyone who has ever talked to someone over the Internet and then met them, the experience is different. It is much harder to have a dialogue in person—you cannot just walk away or leave your response until later.

Perhaps it is a matter of personalities that we could work through our differences to produce a book together. We are both outspoken, share a cynical sense of humour and have a strong stubborn and independent streak. Avid readers, we both have an interest in world politics, and a mutual fascination with the rising power of China. In fact, keeping on track with the book's subject matter was often difficult, as conversations roamed through a myriad of topics, often taking days to return.

Finding a way to put our conversation and our subsequent research into words and a coherent story has not always been easy. Nor has it been easy trying to conduct a dialogue where, on some issues, it seems we may simply never agree. Here, we've had to learn to agree to disagree, to meet in the middle of the road, as it were. It does not mean we have changed our minds or that we have not had heated debates. But there have been moments of humour breaking up heated arguments, like the ruckus surrounding the arrival of a meal, or a distraction on the street. This is not to belittle the importance of what we argued about, but rather to highlight that once people get to know each other and no longer see each other as enemies, they can debate and argue, but they can also step back when need be.

As we come to the end of our journey with the book, which would have seemed utterly impossible a few years ago, we now find ourselves in uncharted territory. With the impossible now becoming a reality, I find inspiration and determination to move further forward into this uncharted territory, and a hope that others, too, will join us in our efforts to build greater understanding and work towards peace.

MH: Although the war is still ongoing between the West and Islamic groups, it is hard for me to consider Ms Farrall an enemy. This is because of her efforts to build mutual understanding between our sides and to work for peace, and this cannot be opposed, but must instead be upheld, because it is a project that brings benefit for all human beings.

In one of my early letters, I wrote that our dialogue is a small step in a journey of 1,000 miles. Ms Farrall too understands that achieving a fair and complete peace between human beings is a long and difficult place to reach; but it is a journey we both seek, no matter how long it takes, or the distance that needs to be covered. In this field, the will of Ms Farrall knows no tiredness, and her ability to work patiently and her true human sense brings these far hopes towards the limit of what is possible. I hope I have the ability to match her in the same goal, and that my determination does not fail me.

2

THE ARAB-AFGHAN JIHAD

In December 1979 the Soviet Union invaded Afghanistan to prop up the communist regime that had seized power a year earlier and was battling an insurrection led by Afghan resistance groups whose leaders were in exile in Peshawar, Pakistan. The insurrection had not, however, taken widespread hold among Afghanistan's population, most of whom remained on the sidelines of the conflict between these groups and the Kabul regime. The Soviet Union's invasion changed this dynamic, turning many Afghans from spectators of a limited insurrection into participants in a fully-fledged armed struggle. Their taking-up of arms to liberate their country from Soviet occupation marked the beginning of what is commonly referred to as the Afghan jihad. Afghan fighters (mujahidin) were soon joined by foreign volunteers, who came to be known as 'Arab-Afghans'. This name came not only to describe foreigners who fought during the jihad, but also those who remained in Afghanistan after the Soviet withdrawal, or who travelled to the country after the Taliban's rise to power in the mid-1990s.

* * *

MH: I first heard the term 'Arab-Afghan' used in 1989. Although it is more commonly used now, back then the term 'Arab-Afghan' was meant derogatorily, as an insult to the Arabs, who were, in fact, in the minority. There were many more non-Arab foreign volunteers than there were Arabs participating in Afghanistan's jihad.

* * *

Much of what is written about the Arab-Afghan role in the jihad against the Soviet Union focuses on the later stages of the conflict, when foreign mujahidin were at their most numerous. But the history of the Arab-Afghans at war in Afghanistan begins much earlier—particularly for the first-generation mujahidin who travelled to the country between 1979 and 1984.

Events taking place in the Arab world in the years leading up to the Soviet Union's December 1979 invasion played a significant role in motivating many early generation Arab-Afghans to join the jihad in Afghanistan. There was a pervasive sense of anger within many Arab states—not only at the corruption and brutal repression taking place at the hands of various regimes, but also at the perceived weakness of these regimes in the face of foreign political interference. As a result, many had come to believe that no real Arab state existed, let alone an Islamic one. Joining the conflict in Afghanistan offered those who felt this way an outlet for their frustrations and a location to take action.

* * *

MH: The Arab world was, quite simply, on the boil. In addition to wanting to liberate Afghanistan, Arabs went to join the jihad because they felt stifled and frustrated at events in the Arab world and in their own countries. They had come to believe that nothing in their countries could be reformed, and that not even the Islamic movements in these countries could offer hope of change. In this way, Afghanistan became an outlet, and the regimes in many countries were happy to see these men leave for jihad, because they thought their leaving would help reduce the political temperature and unrest.

* * *

The political temperature in Arab countries was also affected by the weakness many felt had beset Arabs after their defeat in the Arab–Israeli war of 1967. The capitulation of Arab states to Israel was seen as deeply humiliating and intensified the sense among some Arabs that their own countries had failed. This was exacerbated by the crackdowns on those who had participated in the earlier 1948 Palestine War, particularly Egyptians.

* * *

MH: The defeat of 1967 shocked a generation of Arabs. Israel's siege of an Arab capital (Beirut) in 1982, while other Arab countries looked the other way, in particular Egypt and Syria, had a huge impact. It caused a very big wound in the dignity of the Arab youth, who were left with a sense there were no real states, only oppressive regimes weak in the face of foreign interference. Many of them were angry. It was in this environment the Afghan jihad took people back to Islam, and absorbed the negative feelings in Arab countries; because of this, Islamic ideas and movements began to rise again.

* * *

While Afghanistan offered an outlet, those belonging to Islamic movements already existing in Arab countries, particularly those from Egypt and Syria, were not significantly represented among early Arab-Afghan volunteers. These movements and groups, such as Egypt's Tanzim al-Jihad, Gamaah Islamiyyah and the Syrian Ikhwan Muslimin, grew in the jails of their home countries. Most members of these groups were either jailed, or still seeking to take action in their homelands against regimes they saw as oppressive and illegitimate, rather than travelling to Afghanistan for jihad. It was only when their efforts had failed and they found themselves and their movements hunted and destroyed by the state that they began to seek refuge in Afghanistan in significant numbers, with most arriving in the later period of the jihad between 1986 and 1992.

The first generation of Arabs arriving in Afghanistan between 1979 and 1984 were not generally part of these movements before they travelled to Afghanistan. Some did later join these movements when, after 1986, they began to establish a presence in Afghanistan. Despite lacking formal affiliations to armed groups in their homelands, many early generation Arab-Afghans had military training or experience gained from military service in their home countries or from volunteering for jihad elsewhere. Some had a pedigree tracing back to the 1948 Palestinian War. Others had participated in activities with Palestinian resistance groups in Lebanon and Jordan, or had trained in Iraq or Egypt as part of the activities of the Syrian Ikhwan Muslimin.

As the number of Egyptians grew within the ranks of the Arab-Afghans, a significant number of former military men could be found—many of whom had been involved in the 1967 and 1973 wars.

* * *

MH: Many Egyptians went to Afghanistan because of Israel, because of 1967's complete defeat—from the first seconds of the war to the last; and also from 1973's initial success and then defeat. For example, Muhammad Makkawi, a prominent Afghan mujahid—famous for his criticism of the Battle of Jalalabad—was in the Special Forces in the 1973 war, and among those on the front line. He resigned from the army, and when he got a chance, left for Afghanistan. Abu Hafs al-Masri, one of al-Qaeda's founders, was trained in missile use, and Abu Jihad al-Masri from Tanzim al-Jihad and later al-Qaeda also served in the anti-aircraft missile section. Abu Abdul Rahman al-BM, a one-time al-Qaeda member and mujahid, respected for his proficiency with the BM weapon (from where he got his lifelong nickname), was in the chemical weapons section during the 1973 war. A good number of those who fought in these wars left to join the jihad in Afghanistan.

Of course, there were others who did not have military backgrounds. Abu Ubaydah al-Banshiri, one of the founders of al-Qaeda, was a police officer. Even people not involved in military or police work were still motivated to join the jihad in Afghanistan because of the events of 1967 and 1973, and the relationship between Egypt and Israel.

* * *

In Syria, the failure of the Ikhwan Muslimin-led jihad against the al-Assad regime in the late 1970s and early 1980s led some to look to Afghanistan. The jihad in Afghanistan offered safety from al-Assad's crackdown in Syria, as well as an outlet for those who wished to continue fighting and were angry at the corruption and mistakes of the jihad in their own country.

* * *

MH: Many Syrians from the early generation of Arab-Afghans had been involved in a fight against the al-Assad regime. Depressed by the events in Syria, and feeling betrayed by Ikhwan Muslimin and its corruption, they went to Afghanistan but largely kept to themselves. Some disappeared into the Afghan fronts and just participated in the fighting; nobody really knew where they were.

* * *

A number of Yemenis who travelled to Afghanistan to fight the Soviets were also among the early generations of Arab-Afghans. At that time,

Yemen was split into North and South Yemen, with South Yemen under the control of a communist regime with close ties to the Soviet Union. The two Yemeni states were often in conflict.

* * *

MH: In Yemen there had been tensions between the North and the South, and it was felt the South was under the influence of the Russians. Some men wanted to go to Afghanistan to fight the Russians there, while others wanted to prepare for jihad in Yemen and to liberate the South from communist rule. This was one of the reasons Abu Abdullah (Osama bin Laden) went to Afghanistan: it was because of Yemen. As you know, he was of Yemeni descent.

Yemen was even one of the reasons why Abu Abdullah established al-Qaeda, but he did not announce it. He did not want to cause rivalry within al-Qaeda because at that time, everyone was thinking about his own country. In fact, many Yemenis, especially those who came to fight in Afghanistan after the 1987 Battle of Jaji, were from the south of Yemen. They went to Afghanistan to see Abu Abdullah.

* * *

The occupation of Palestine also factored heavily into the motivations and activities of some from among the early generations who travelled to Afghanistan. The Israeli invasions of Lebanon in 1978 and 1982 also had a significant impact.

* * *

MH: In Egypt, it was the Israeli war of 1973 and Sadat's relations with Israel and the repression of the state. In Syria, it was the al-Assad regime. In Yemen, it was the communists in the South. Then, of course, there was the issue of the occupation of Palestine, and the Israeli Army's invasion of Lebanon in 1978 and later its expulsion of the Palestinian Liberation Organisation, which was a very big insult to all the Arabs.

* * *

Some early generation Arab-Afghans either trained or joined with Palestinian resistance groups in Lebanon or Jordan. Mustafa Hamid was among those who travelled to participate in the Palestinian resistance in Lebanon. He and a friend sought to fight with the Fatah organisation, which was the main Palestinian fighting group, and the only one at that time which had an Islamic faction inside its ranks.

* * *

MH: My friend and I went to Lebanon after Israel's 1978 invasion, which caused a strong reaction among the Arabs. We went by ourselves and sought to find Fatah because we knew that since 1965 it had started to become a religious group. We were welcomed to fight with them because at that time there were only a few Egyptians volunteering for the jihad. I left Lebanon after the ceasefire when it was clear there was no more fighting. Fatah had also put the religious elements in one group and sent them near to the communist elements from another resistance group, and I feared Fatah were playing a bad game and that the outcome would be fighting between the Palestinians.

* * *

Abdullah Azzam, a Palestinian who would go on to be among the most famous of the Arab-Afghans, trained with Fatah in Jordan.

* * *

MH: Abdul Aziz Ali, who was from the Egyptian Ikhwan Muslimin, trained Abdullah Azzam in Jordan. Abdul Aziz Ali was a mujahid in the 1948 war in Palestine and later travelled to Afghanistan and played an important role.

LF: Was Azzam with Fatah at that time, or Ikhwan Muslimin?

MH: Fatah had made a faction inside its organisation for Ikhwan Muslimin people. Abdul Aziz Ali came to train the Ikhwan Muslimin faction.

* * *

When these early generation volunteers went to Afghanistan there was no Arab media campaign in support of the jihad. In fact, until 1984, when Arab-Afghan media efforts began in earnest, the Arab world knew little about the Afghan jihad outside of what Afghan groups were able to communicate via their media efforts and delegations sent to the Middle East. As Wael Julaydan, an early-generation Arab-Afghan reminisced, he first heard about the jihad in Afghanistan through Western media, or 'from the mouths of enemies', as he put it, before he heard it 'from friends ... and supporters'.[1]

A low-profile start

Despite the Afghan jihad initially having a low profile in the Arab world, Afghan groups actively solicited wealthy benefactors in the Middle East, sending delegations to the region to highlight the plight of Afghanistan. In the early days of the jihad, not all Afghan groups were seeking foreign volunteers to join them; rather most sought financial and material support.

* * *

LF: I imagine the Afghans did not want a large influx of volunteers because at that point there was no infrastructure in place to accommodate or train Arabs.

MH: Some Afghans did want Arabs to come and participate in the jihad. In 1980 they asked Abdul Rasul Sayyaf, the leader of the newly formed Ittihad i Islami Tahrir Afghanistan, to campaign for more support for the Afghan jihad during his first trip to Abu Dhabi as head of the Ittihad delegation.

* * *

Ittihad i Islami Tahrir Afghanistan (Islamic Union for the Liberation of Afghanistan) formed in January 1980 and was comprised of the main Afghan groups with Abdul Rasul Sayyaf as its president. The formation of the Union was not the first effort to unite the Afghan parties, but it was the first to take place after the Soviet invasion and to involve Sayyaf, a relative latecomer to Peshawar who had no group of his own at that time. It was in his capacity as president that Sayyaf led the 1980 delegation that travelled to Abu Dhabi to campaign for more support for the Afghan jihad. As with earlier attempts at unification, the formation of the Union was short-lived and resulted in the creation of yet another splinter group. When the Union split, Sayyaf came to lead a group by the same name. Another effort at unifying the Afghan parties was later made and came to be known as Ittihad i Islami Mujahidin Afghanistan, with Sayyaf's group included, and him retaining the presidency of the Union.

* * *

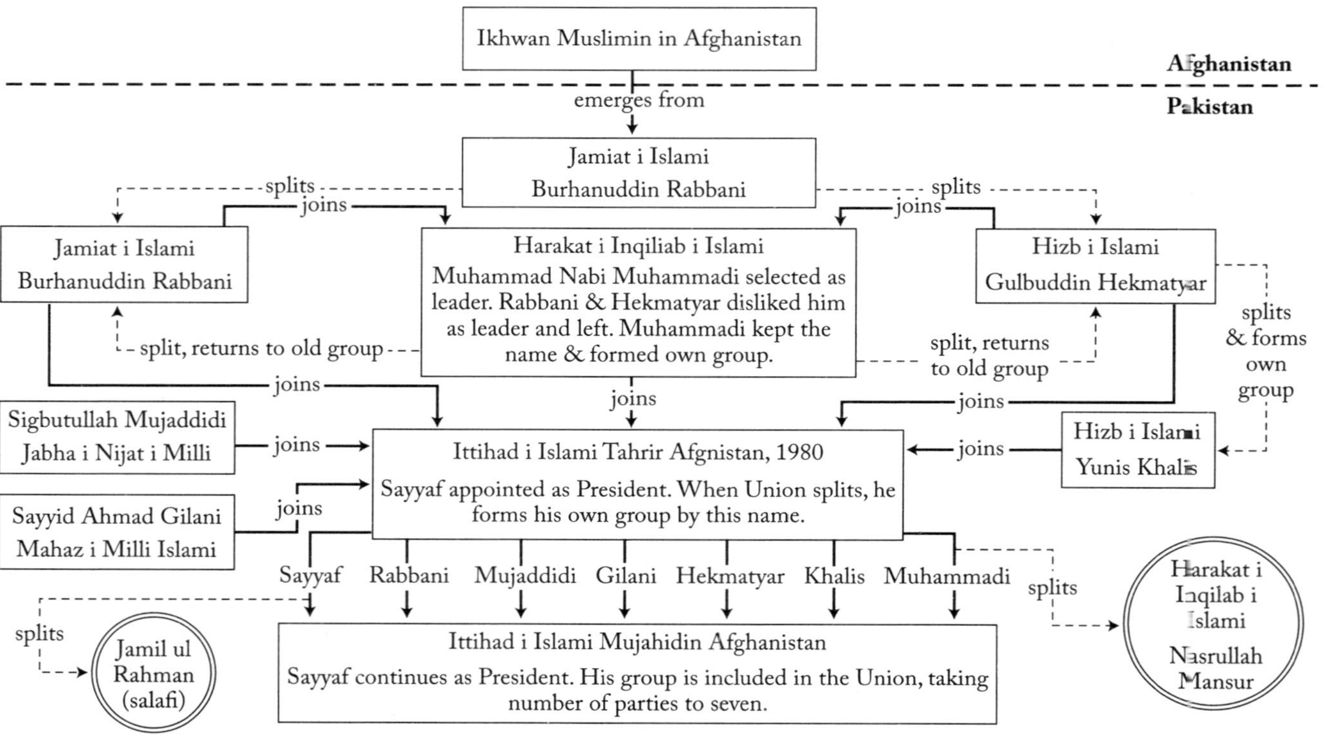

Fig. 1: Links between the Afghan parties

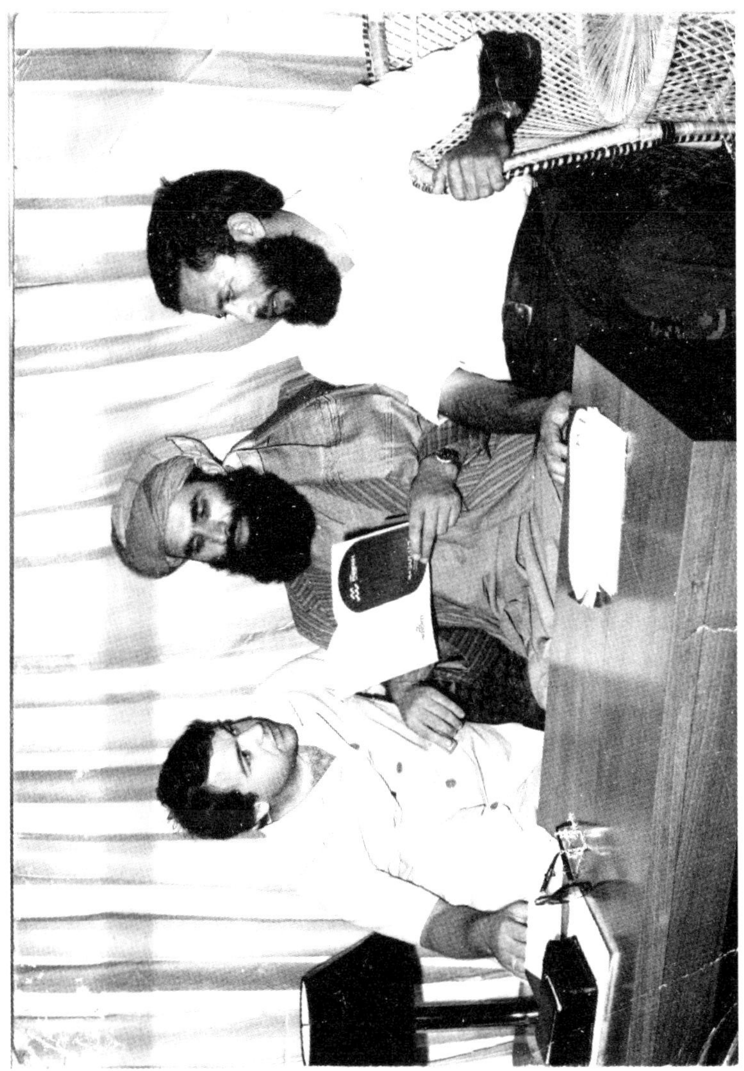

Fig 2: R–L, Mustafa Hamid, Abdul Rasul Sayyaf and another journalist in Abu Dhabi, 1980

MH: Jalaluddin Haqqani, a commander in the group of Yunis Khalis, Hizb i Islami, was among those in the delegation that travelled to Abu Dhabi and who wanted Arabs to come and join the jihad. He asked Sayyaf to call for Arab volunteers to come to Afghanistan, arguing 'the Arabs will not know what we need unless they come here'. Sayyaf agreed to Haqqani's request and said he would call for volunteers at a press conference he was to hold in Abu Dhabi. But other Afghan leaders said, 'we do not need Arab volunteers, we need money'. I attended this press conference and Sayyaf did not call for Arab volunteers as Haqqani had asked. Instead, he only asked for donations and support.

LF: Is this the press conference you and your friends helped organise?

MH: Yes, my friends and I organised this first trip of Union delegates to the Gulf. The delegations from the Afghan parties travelled to a few countries and it was an important move forward for them. During the trip, the delegations made direct contact with Arabs in the Gulf who came to support the Afghan jihad.

* * *

Osama bin Laden, then still a young man, began financing the Afghan jihad almost immediately after the Soviet invasion. He travelled to Pakistan and provided funds for the Afghan jihad to the leaders of Pakistan's Jamaat i Islami who then dispersed them to the Afghan groups. Jamaat i Islami had long-standing links with the leaders of the Afghan mujahidin groups, having supported many of them since the mid-1970s when they sought refuge in Peshawar after the Afghan regime's crackdown on their activities and efforts at insurrection. The Afghanistan conflict was, however, not the only focus of bin Laden's attention in the early 1980s, nor was it the only conflict he was financing.

* * *

MH: At that time Abu Abdullah was still part of Ikhwan Muslimin, and when the conflict began between the Syrian Ikhwan Muslimin and the al-Assad regime, he also provided funding to them to fight the regime.

* * *

While bin Laden delivered funding for the Afghan conflict, he did not stay for long periods. It was not until later that he began spending more time in the region. During the early years of the Afghan jihad, financial

Fig 3: A group photo of Haqqani along with Afghan delegation members and Mustafa Hamid, Abu Dhabi. Haqqani is fourth from left next to Hamid. In front of them are two of the latter's children

donors rarely visited Afghanistan and did not venture to the front lines. They instead limited themselves to Pakistan, where they would assess support options for the jihad, and in some cases for charitable organisations working to assist Pakistan's growing Afghan refugee population.

* * *

LF: Is it true that by the early 1980s Ikhwan Muslimin had sent people to Pakistan to assess options for supporting the jihad and the Afghan refugee population, but that it refused to become directly involved in resistance activities?

MH: Are you talking about the main Ikhwan Muslimin group or the Syrian Ikhwan Muslimin?

LF: The main Ikhwan Muslimin group.

MH: Yes, I think this is probably true, but for the Syrian Ikhwan Muslimin it was different.

LF: Some parts of that group became involved in resistance activities in Afghanistan.

MH: Yes, but it was not an organisational decision on the part of the Syrian Ikhwan Muslimin; the group had essentially collapsed by the early 1980s. After that, the youth came to Afghanistan to share the jihad, and they were angry at the corruption in the Syrian jihad led by Ikhwan Muslimin, and the events that had taken place there.

LF: You discussed the Ikhwan Muslimin position on Afghanistan with some officials from the movement: how would you characterise its position? Did they outline its position to you?

MH: I had two main meetings with them. One meeting was in 1981 with Kamal al-Sananiry, and another was with Mustafa Mashrour in 1984. From the beginning, Ikhwan Muslimin had a position on Afghanistan and military training, and it remained in place for all of the war period against the Soviets, until their 1989 withdrawal. This position was:

1. Use the media to incite Muslims around the world to support the Afghan mujahidin.
2. Collect donations and send them to the mujahidin organisations in Peshawar or distribute them to refugee camps.
3. Send doctors to work in hospitals for treating the mujahidin.
4. Support Abdul Rasul Sayyaf as the leader of the Union. (It was known that Sayyaf represented the international organisation of Ikhwan

Muslimin in Afghanistan, and so most support and media went to him in that capacity.)

Ikhwan Muslimin applied this programme, although they did not clearly disclose the political side of their activities in their data. In my 1984 meeting with Mustafa Mashrour—before he became a guide of Ikhwan Muslimin—I explained to him my point of view about what was happening in Peshawar on both the Arab and Afghan sides. Over a long conversation, I asked for Ikhwan Muslimin to take on the training of Arabs in Afghanistan, and said to him, 'The fact is, this is necessary and is in the interests of jihad and the mujahidin.'

My words made the man angry; he believed the involvement of Ikhwan Muslimin in military action in Afghanistan would turn Arab governments against them, and that this presented significant risks to the group that it could not afford. This position was one Ikhwan Muslimin held throughout the war with the Soviets. Some of its members did participate in the jihad but this was done personally and outside of official guidance. In fact, very few members of Ikhwan Muslimin went to the fronts and they usually only participated for limited periods.

* * *

The first Arab arrivals

The first Arab arrivals to the jihad were not generally affiliated with Afghan groups. Only a small number were directly involved in military work, and because there was no infrastructure in place to support foreign volunteers, they joined whatever Afghan group they could contact. Their numbers were not high, although they were not as low as has been reported by the likes of Abu Musab al-Suri and Abdullah Anas—both Arab-Afghan veterans—who estimate there were only a dozen or so Arabs in Afghanistan prior to 1984.[2] Neither al-Suri nor Anas was present before 1984, and so they were probably unaware that the number of Arabs in Afghanistan before 1984 was higher than they reported. They may have also been basing their estimates on the Arab-Afghans who came to be associated with Maktab al-Khadamat—an organisation founded by Arab-Afghans to support the jihad—and this group was not established until late 1984.

Low estimates of the number of early Arab-Afghans probably also arose because few volunteers remained in Afghanistan for long periods.

Most needed to return to their employment and families. Some found the situation vastly different from their expectations and left, while others struggled to find an Afghan group to house them, and returned home owing to a lack of opportunities to serve on the front. Many were also disgruntled because the scene that greeted them in Peshawar was not what they had imagined.

At that time Peshawar was a town awash with Afghan groups and leaders, many of whom were in competition with one another—despite the existence of the Union of Mujahidin Parties. The Afghan groups lacked resources, and because competition between them often fractured relations, there was no effective coordination mechanism to receive aid and build infrastructure for the jihad. The complicated nature of the relationships between the groups, and the Afghan scene in Peshawar more generally, was not new.

Rivalry among Afghan mujahidin leaders had existed since the mid-1970s—well before the Soviet invasion—when key figures and leaders of Afghan groups sought exile in Peshawar after the Afghan regime cracked down on their resistance activities. This fractured Peshawar scene greeted Mustafa Hamid and his two friends—who were the first Arabs to join the Afghan jihad—when they arrived some six months or so before the December 1979 Soviet invasion.

* * *

MH: My first visit to Afghanistan was in June 1979. My friends and I travelled from Abu Dhabi to Peshawar, and then inside Afghanistan to Urgon in Paktika province to the fronts of Yunis Khalis of Hizb i Islami, and from there, to Paktia province to the front of his commander Mawlawi Jalaluddin Haqqani. Our first trip lasted only around a month and a half, but it left a big impression on us. We participated in two ambushes while we were inside Afghanistan and we could see for ourselves the efforts of the mujahidin. We decided we wanted to return and share in the battle.

LF: How did you come to travel to Afghanistan? Was your experience there different to the one in Peshawar, Pakistan?

MH: I went to Afghanistan after meeting some Afghans in Abu Dhabi where I was working. I heard about the situation from them and the coup that had taken place in the country—putting a communist regime in power. The Afghans I met were part of a delegation that Jalaluddin Haqqani had sent to Abu Dhabi under the command of Mawlawi Adam.

He gave us information about what was happening in Afghanistan—especially in Paktia and Paktika.

I also met Mawlawi Tahir, who was an imam at a mosque in Abu Dhabi, and had previously been a judge in Herat in Afghanistan. He gave us some information about what was happening. At that time, a plane had bombed the area causing a large number of deaths, and the people of Herat revolted and took control. Around 3,000 people were killed in the fighting that followed.

After hearing these stories and meeting Haqqani's delegation, my friend and I asked if we could go to Afghanistan and see for ourselves. They said yes, they could take us. This was in April 1979, and we tried to get donations but we failed because at that time very few people knew or cared about what was happening in Afghanistan. Mawlawi Tahir's eldest son, Sayed Ahmad, told us he was going to Afghanistan the next month and invited us to join him, but we were not ready. He returned after around three weeks and he brought with him photographs showing the success of the mujahidin at Haqqani's front. This made us more determined to go.

We organised the trip with Mawlawi Tahir, who accompanied us in June 1979; he insisted he come with us, even though he was close to eighty years old. We travelled from Peshawar to Miranshah and from there we went into the south-east corner of Afghanistan to see for ourselves the conditions. This was our first trip to Afghanistan. I wrote a ten-page report describing the situation there.

The scene in Peshawar was very different to the one I found inside Afghanistan. In Afghanistan, mujahidin morale was high but they had very limited resources and severe shortages of ammunition. On my first trip—before the Soviets invaded—the problems faced by the jihadis and their weaknesses were not all visible.

By the time of my next visit in 1981, the problems had become clear, in part because the jihad had become international. It was then we discovered many defects in the situation of jihad in Pakistan and Afghanistan; and the relationship between the defects inside Afghanistan and outside became clearer. We concluded we could still lose the war if these defects were not corrected. The problem was these defects were not widely known among the Arabs, because with the exception of Khalis and Haqqani and their people, the Afghan leaders did not like Arabs to join the fighting. When we wanted to join the fight, we went through

Khalis's people. In Paktika, we went via Mutiullah who was one of Khalis's best commanders. After that, we went to Haqqani in Gardez, the capital of Paktia province.

LF: Why did the other leaders not like taking Arabs inside—was it because many were untrained, or they lacked resources to accommodate you? Were there other reasons?

MH: Both of these reasons are true, but the main reason was that if the Arabs went inside they could discover defects in the jihad situation, the most important of which was that the leaders in Peshawar were not the leaders in Afghanistan. In Afghanistan, it was another story, and if the Arabs saw the leaders in Peshawar were not the leaders in Afghanistan, they might directly fund the leaders in Afghanistan. For this reason, some Afghan leaders in Peshawar wanted to keep the Arabs away from Afghanistan and restrict their role to fundraising.

* * *

The influx of aid money following the 1979 Soviet invasion intensified rivalries and competition for resources among the Afghan groups, much to the frustration of overseas donors and the few early Arab-Afghans who attempted to foster unity between the factions. One reason for their frustration was that aid money was often used to strengthen the position of Afghan leaders and their parties, rather than being used to bolster infrastructure for the jihad inside Afghanistan.

Despite this situation, in the early 1980s the number of first-generation Arab-Afghans who were active in Afghanistan slowly began to grow as more became aware of the conflict. Although many Arab-Afghans had prior military experience from armed service or from carrying out jihad elsewhere, an increasing number of volunteers with no military experience but who were eager for battle were also arriving to join the jihad. Their lack of training and often impetuous desire to see combat caused problems for the Afghan commanders who were housing these volunteer guests.

This was the case for the Afghan leader Jalaluddin Haqqani, who in 1981 was hosting a group of Arab volunteers from London. His visiting volunteers were Salafi, and despite lacking training and experience, wanted to participate immediately in combat, believing they were following the example of the Prophet Muhammad and his Companions.

* * *

MH: In 1981 when we were in Lija in Khost some Arabs arrived who were from among the Salafis in London. They were around ten in number. They said to Haqqani, 'Why are you sitting here? You should engage with this garrison in the valley, you should go inside and capture Khost.' He said, 'How?' They said, 'In Islam it is just like this; in the beginning they went and they just captured.' They told Haqqani, 'Islam doesn't ask about the numbers, the weapons or the tactics; just go and capture.' It was a very stupid way of thinking.

LF: What did Haqqani and other senior Afghan leaders think about these volunteers arriving who were so passionate and impetuous about jihad? How did the Afghan leadership look at them?

MH: The Afghans looked to the Arabs as a source of money because every volunteer, when he returned back to his country, was supposed to collect money and send it to the mujahidin, especially to the group on whose front he fought. As a result, they usually, mainly in Afghanistan, treated Arabs as special guests.

That was one thing, but another was that those boys did not care to see and examine what was going on around them. They were eager to fight, to be martyred and to go to paradise quickly. Most of the youth who thought like this were Salafis. These Salafis, especially the Saudis, had a lot of money; they could go to Afghanistan, come home and collect money to donate to the mujahidin, so their influence was very high.

There were many Salafis among the Arab-Afghans and they made big problems inside Afghanistan on the fronts. They also caused problems between the Arabs and the Afghans, and attacked the Afghans over their beliefs, because most of the Afghans were Sufi and Hanafi, and the Salafis hated both of them. That created many troubles; sometimes it came very close to fighting.

* * *

For the Afghan leaders, the behaviour of their volunteer guests could not only be hostile and derogatory to their beliefs, but also dangerous. An impatience to see combat and almost wilful ignorance of the operating environment had the potential to compromise battlefield positions. Organising training for foreign arrivals where attitudes such as these could be addressed before volunteers reached the battlefield was equally problematic.

* * *

Lack of training for Arabs and Afghans

In the early 1980s there existed minimal training resources for Afghans, let alone for a smattering of foreign volunteers, some of whom had no military experience and others who had military backgrounds but no exposure to the type of non-traditional conflict being waged in Afghanistan.

* * *

MH: There were problems securing basic training for the Arabs prior to them going to the front lines. Pakistan was attempting to prohibit the presence of Arabs in the tribal areas, and at that time no special camps had been established. There were also very few Arabs who were qualified to provide training.

The only real group with this capacity was Ikhwan Muslimin in Syria, whose youth had trained in Iraq and Egypt, but as an organisation they refused to participate. At that time, their own organisation was suffering from splits because of accusations of incompetence and corruption.

Many of the Arab volunteers with military experience could not stay for lengthy periods after their participation at the front because they had to return to their homes and work. Most importantly, the majority were not trained for guerrilla warfare, especially in the style needed for the Afghan conflict. They had instead trained in conventional tactics, which were not suitable or effective for the fighting in Afghanistan. Lastly, the Arab presence at that time was still not organised and not supported by any specialised infrastructure.

Volunteers dispersed between the Afghan parties who were willing to accept them and were then sent into Afghanistan according to the conditions of transport and the time the volunteers had available for fighting. While a number of parties accepted the Arabs, it was really only Haqqani and Khalis who said, 'Yes, you can join us as fighters.' The other groups tended to keep the Arabs away from the fighting.

* * *

Training and resources for Afghans were also virtually non-existent, and what training did exist was often haphazard, lacking in resources or carried out by Pakistan's Inter-Services Intelligence (ISI), which was pursuing its own agenda.

* * *

MH: Our Afghan colleagues were using their antique guns and some guns from the spoils of the Soviets. Their lack of basic training on tactics in the field was clear, although the Afghans' religious enthusiasm was overwhelming to the point that only a few had their attention drawn to the severe lack of training.

* * *

Although Pakistani elements were involved in providing some training to the groups, this was often unsuitable for the Afghan conflict. Many Pakistani trainers were members of the ISI, and the training they provided, and Pakistan's support more generally, aimed at gaining strategic control over the conflict and the Afghan groups, rather than assisting the Afghans to liberate their country.

* * *

Pakistan's role

LF: How influential were the Pakistani Army and ISI? *The Bear Trap* by Muhammad Yousaf, which you have read, highlighted how important military aid coming from Pakistan and other countries was to the effort of the mujahidin. *The Bear Trap* outlines extensive involvement of Pakistani military figures at quite high levels helping to coordinate what was happening in Afghanistan.[3] Is that exaggerated?

MH: It is correct from the point of view of Pakistan; they influenced and they pushed things in the ways they wanted, but not for the interests of the Afghans. Pakistan had a big influence inside Afghanistan, but mainly it was harmful. It affected the jihad very badly and made the period of fighting much longer than was necessary. The blood taxes paid were very high.

Pakistan used the Afghans as tools in their hands, and if there was something successful in Afghanistan, they destroyed it. We saw that many times. For example, the Pakistanis destroyed relationships between the Afghan parties, between the tribes and between the ethnic groups. By the way, they were very corrupt.

In fact, the Afghanistan–Soviet war allowed the Pakistani military intelligence apparatus (ISI) an opportunity to turn into one of the most important groups operating in that region of the world, and the most powerful apparatus inside Pakistan. The Pashtun officers working in that apparatus had the most prominent role in penetrating the mujahidin organisations based in Pakistan, and penetrating their armed groups inside Afghanistan. They even dominated many of these mujahidin groups inside Afghanistan, and dealt with them directly, without the supervision of the groups' leadership in Peshawar.

The ISI's greatest concentration was in Pashtun areas, although its activities also reached deep inside the groups of northern Afghanistan, especially since some of the big figures of the jihad were from the north, such as Burhanuddin Rabbani, who was originally from the Tajik of Badakshan province in the far north-east. The fundamentalist leader Gulbuddin Hekmatyar was from the northern state of Kunduz, despite his Pashtun origins. The ISI gave everyone arms and money, but to varying degrees depending on its agenda. Doing so meant it could have a presence everywhere.

The ISI programme throughout the era of Pakistan's President Zia ul-Haq represented a compromise between Zia ul-Haq's aspirations and the requirements of the American strategy, with Zia ul-Haq's aspirations prevailing in most cases. General Zia ul-Haq stood firm against American attempts to have direct relations with the Afghan mujahidin in the fronts. He also placed American communications with the Afghan parties under strict control and trapped it within the narrowest range possible, whether in Islamabad or Peshawar. The ISI was responsible for the distribution of weapons and funds and training, and this was an important factor in its extension of control and its impact and influence.

Another way in which it was able to exert influence, which was no less important, was the presence of a huge number of refugees in Pakistan—most of whom were Pashtun, and whose number sometimes exceeded 4 million people. They relied on the government of Pakistan and its intelligence service for everything. The mujahidin in Afghanistan were not far away from this field of influence either, because many had relatives who were refugees in Pakistan.

The strategy of intervention in the Afghan issue (1979–92) as practised by the ISI was:

1. Setting a strategy for the war against the Soviets in Afghanistan. Brigadier Mohammad Yousaf, who was a former officer in this apparatus, explained this clearly in his important book, *The Bear Trap*.[4]
2. Completely controlling the distribution of weapons and supplies to the mujahidin parties within Afghanistan.

3. Intervening in training and operations to ensure the military action of the mujahidin fitted with the requirements of Pakistan's strategy.
4. Interfering in the relations between the various mujahidin groups, and by doing so, determining the balance of power among these groups, in order to achieve its agenda. Also, exerting control over the work of the 'jihadi' parties within Pakistan, and influencing their relations with each other and the outside world.
5. Prohibiting the 'jihadi' parties from dealing with the political side of the Afghan conflict in order to make Pakistan the sole player in this game. The government of Pakistan, the ISI in fact, even took over acting on the behalf of the Afghans in the outside world. It goes without saying that this was to serve the American strategy and the unique relationship between the two countries of Pakistan and America.

Corruption was also an integral part of the structure of the state's apparatus in Pakistan, and the ISI was no exception to this rule. Hundreds of millions of dollars were streaming into Afghanistan to help its people to break the Soviet Union. Aid came mostly in the form of weapons, ammunition and assistance for the refugees. This stream created a market for corruption in government institutions, as well as in the ISI itself.

In the fronts at which we worked, we saw some of that corruption, although generally it was shrouded in secrecy. Weapons were looted from the aid deliveries and stored in secret caves. They were later transferred to the stores of the arms dealers in the tribal areas and then sold at the weapons bazaars, earning money for the corrupt ISI officers.

We saw the caves being dug and the weapons being stored. They were the hugest caves I have ever seen in Afghanistan, and they were built in solid rock, which means building them was very expensive. These caves could hold trucks, the famous high-sided trucks used in the tribal areas; these trucks could go inside, load and unload. I saw two caves like this, connected from the inside so they formed a unit. In the tribal areas, there were a few like that.

In addition, the ISI 'retained' large quantities of weapons that should have gone to the mujahidin. Outside of those sold on the black market, some were 'retained' for the benefit of the Pakistani Army, while others were used to arm police and government militias in the tribal areas—and such weapons were in fact seen in their hands.

Some weapons were 'retained' because they had the potential to dramatically step up the impact of mujahidin operations. Others were modified, or did not work properly to begin with, and some were very dated. Muhammad Yousaf's book *The Bear Trap* makes this very clear.[5] In my own experience, we saw rocket launchers where the telescopic sights had been removed so they could not be used to target accurately. This occurred with a number of weapons including artillery guns provided to the mujahidin.

LF: Why do you think they did that?

MH: The president of Pakistan, Zia ul-Haq, feared the Soviets' reaction and he also feared America potentially abandoning Pakistan at a dangerous time, and so he gave his advice about this to General Akhtar Abdul Rahman, who was at that time the head of the ISI. It is well known: Zia ul-Haq said to the general, 'the water in Afghanistan must boil at the right temperature'.[6] That meant he did not want the war to be quickly or decisively won. Because of that, the ISI prevented the advanced weapons from reaching the mujahidin and controlled the amount of aid reaching the Afghan groups and their fronts.

In order to subdue the Afghans to their policy, the ISI used methods of enticement with arms and money, and intimidation by threat, siege, isolation and murder. Dozens of Afghan field commanders were assassinated in Peshawar and other areas. Most of these operations were officially announced as 'tribal conflict', but the fact is many were carried out by the ISI to get rid of figures who threatened the programme of Pakistan inside Afghanistan. Hekmatyar's group played an essential role here for the ISI.

In fact, Pakistan enjoyed a tremendous ability to put pressure on the mujahidin parties. A few of the important Afghan leaders realised this and understood the relationship between them and the state of Pakistan was an exchange of interests between two sides.

Some Afghan leaders thought they were the stronger side in the equation, and that Pakistan needed them more than they needed it. Because of this, violent bickering sometimes emerged between the two, which often led to Afghan leaders expelling Pakistani intelligence officers from some areas during raging battles because they were trying to interfere.

* * *

In light of these circumstances, it is unsurprising the Afghans' training had not developed, and that training assistance was essentially designed to keep them dependent on the ISI and under its strategic guidance. It is little wonder that no coherent programme was in place for the Afghans, and why Arab-Afghans with military backgrounds attempted to put in place initiatives for providing assistance.

3

EARLY TRAINING AND TALIBAN ORIGINS

Little progress was made towards developing training for Afghan and Arab volunteers until a confluence of three forces resulted in the establishment of the Qais training camp in 1984, which not only played a crucial role in the history of the Arab-Afghans, but also the Taliban movement. The most important of these forces was Mawlawi Nasrullah Mansur whose efforts after taking control of Harakat-i-Inqilab i Islami in 1981 resulted in the Qais camp's establishment and the beginnings of the Taliban movement.

A number of foreign volunteers helped Mansur in his efforts to establish and expand the Qais camp. Among them were a Pakistani Army major by the name of Rashid Ahmad, who assisted Mansur with hiring Pakistani instructors, and a small group of Arab-Afghans who were working in the field of media and education as well as training. Their coming together with Mansur resulted in the Qais camp's successful training of Arabs and Afghans—including a number of Taliban.

* * *

LF: I have not heard much about the Qais camp. I thought the Badr camp, which was funded by Saleh Kamel, and which began operating in early 1984, was the first significant training camp for the Afghan jihad, and that it too trained Arabs and Afghans?

MH: The Badr camp was the first, and although attended by a number of people who would later become senior figures, like Abu Hafs al-

Masri, it was not the most important. The Qais camp had a great and lasting impact on the war in Afghanistan, and on the future of the country, and so it was more important. Mawlawi Mansur was responsible for establishing and supporting the Qais camp, which provided the first serious education and training for Afghans, including the Taliban, much of whose beginnings came from his reform efforts. The camp also provided training for Arabs.

Mawlawi Nasrullah Mansur and the real beginnings of the Taliban movement

LF: I am quite fascinated to hear about this early history of the Taliban, as conventional wisdom has it that the group emerged a decade later, in 1994.

MH: The Taliban under Mullah Muhammad Omar, which began around 1994, came from three currents from the time of the Afghan war: Hizb i Islami of Yunis Khalis, Harakat i Inqilab i Islami of Mawlawi Muhammad Nabi Muhammadi and Mawlawi Nasrullah Mansur's Harakat i Inqilab i Islami. Of these three, Mawlawi Nasrullah Mansur's group was the most important because it was dedicated to raising a new generation, and focused on education. Of these three currents Mansur's was also the only one that provided military training and management training.

The genuine beginning of the Taliban movement was in the summer of 1981 when Harakat i Inqilab i Islami split, and Mawlawi Mansur—who had previously been a deputy leader under Mawlawi Muhammadi—took leadership of the group. Mawlawi Mansur's objective in assuming control of the group was to initiate a political-jihad movement especially for Afghan Shariat (Islamic law) students. Mawlawi Mansur announced these goals. I heard them directly from him during a lengthy meeting in Peshawar, a gathering that took place at a critical time in the history of the Afghan jihad against the Soviet occupation.

Mawlawi Mansur came to lead Harakat i Inqilab i Islami in what can be described as a revolution within the organisation. It took place because of deviations and corruptions under Mawlawi Muhammadi's leadership, and the harmful influence of his son, Ahmed. These deviations eventually resulted in Mawlawi Mansur separating from the organisation and isolating Mawlawi Muhammadi. Despite being second-in-charge,

Mawlawi Mansur was the most powerful figure in the organisation and the most dynamic and influential, so he kept the name Harakat i Inqilab i Islami for himself.

LF: Can you give some examples of Ahmed's interference, or the corruption more generally within the party?

MH: Mawlawi Mansur had no personal issue with Mawlawi Muhammadi, but he was opposed to the interference of his eldest son Ahmed in the affairs of the organisation because he was not qualified to do so in any form. Mawlawi Mansur said that Ahmed was corrupted and he had corrupt friends around him and was behaving in an un-Islamic manner. He said Ahmed was taking the money of the party and selling weapons and living as a corrupted young man in Pakistan.

Malawi Mansur told me: 'Mawlawi Muhammadi is a good person but he is very weak; he doesn't give enough attention to the party and the mujahidin.' Many mawlawis from inside Afghanistan treated Mawlawi Muhammadi as their spiritual leader; in fact, they had earlier come under his leadership, but day after day, many of them left him because they were not satisfied with the party. It was for these reasons that Mawlawi Mansur undertook this revolution within the party, and separated from Mawlawi Muhammadi.

MH: Mawlawi Mansur was not only worried about activities within his own party. He was also a strong opponent of the corruption and deviations that had gripped all of the jihadist parties and their leadership residing in Peshawar. These deviations were not confined to Peshawar, but they were most prominent there. What happened in Peshawar and the corruption and deviations that took hold there among the parties was a reflection of a battle for control of the jihad in Afghanistan, which turned into a proxy war for America against the Soviet Union.

The corruption and deviations, which stretched from Peshawar in Pakistan to the last remote areas inside Afghanistan, were strongly associated with factors of corruption coming from abroad, particularly from America and its instruments in the region. The most important of them at that time was Pakistan—a country that had embraced 4 million Afghan refugees, as well as the corrupt Afghan jihadist groups operating on its territory.

There was also Saudi Arabia, which had no less important a role than Pakistan, especially in the field of financing the Afghan parties, and supplying armaments of which America decided the type, quantity and source. Saudi Arabia also interfered heavily in the Afghan parties' affairs

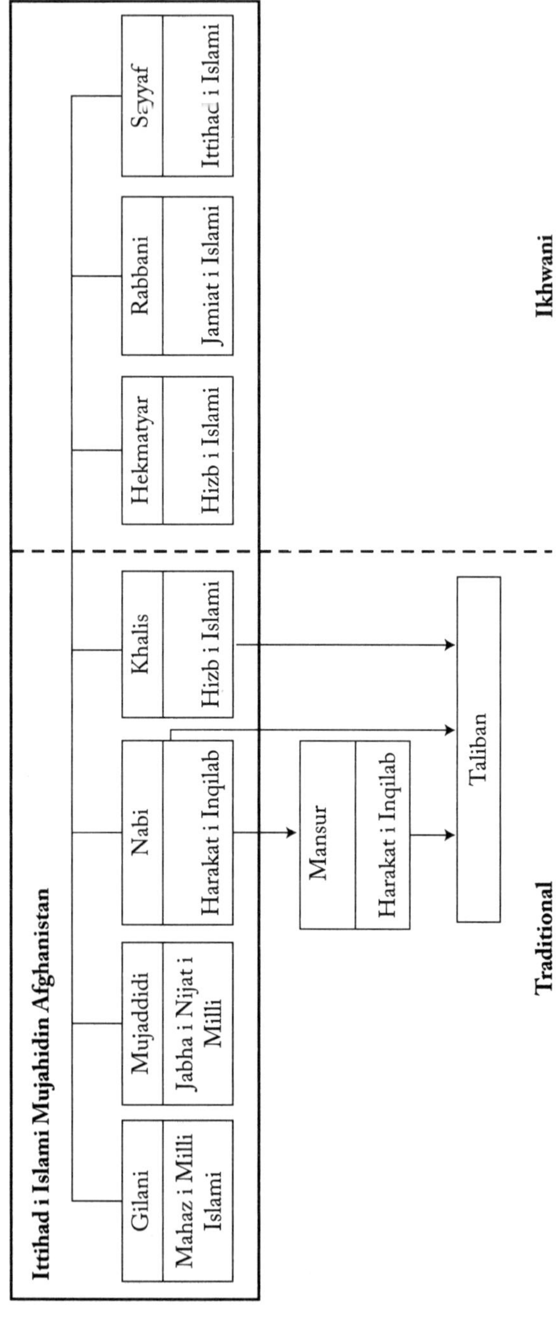

Fig 4: Harakat i Inqilab i Islami and the Taliban

and exerted influence over them in order to benefit Saudi political policy, which was not inconsistent with American strategic interests.

Saudi Arabia's influence also caused disruption and division among the Afghan mujahidin groups, and ideological conflict became a constant part of their disputes in Afghanistan. This is because groups with an affiliation to Salafism could gain access to huge amounts of Saudi money, which caused divisions that even led to fighting among Afghan groups inside Afghanistan. Many Afghan clerics were angry because most of the money was directed to Salafis such as the Jamil ul-Rahman group in Kunar province, and they were unable to access it. The Afghan clerics were also unhappy the Salafi doctrine was propagated so much and other groups were being criticised.

Afghan leaders in Peshawar knew Mawlawi Mansur's views on corruption and external influences, and so when he declared independence from Mawlawi Muhammadi and kept the party name, several leaders moved to stop his attempt. They sent dozens of insurgents to gain control of the headquarters of Harakat i Inqilab i Islami and to prevent Mawlawi Mansur taking it. Mawlawi Mansur did not use force to recover the headquarters and avoided any outbreak of conflict between the armed Afghans in Peshawar. In fact, Mawlawi Mansur absorbed these efforts because he understood the corrupt situation of the Afghan groups.

It was a strange alliance between the Afghan groups against Mawlawi Mansur. Although there usually existed a violent Cold War between these corrupt mujahidin groups in Peshawar, and even between their representatives in other places, they had solidarity against Mawlawi Mansur's party. They united quickly to defend their corrupt interests and to suppress any remedial action introduced to repair the corrupt Peshawar situation, such as Mawlawi Mansur's efforts.

The attempts of the leaders of these Afghan groups to prevent the situation being repaired were more dangerous than financial, political and administrative corruption in Peshawar. This is because they spoiled the jihadist work in Afghanistan in specific and clear ways, which were repeated in almost every area, and led to conflict. The result was the end of cooperation between mujahidin forces inside Afghanistan—on the direct orders of the groups' political leaders in Peshawar.

LF: I didn't realise the competition and conflict expanded to have such an impact inside Afghanistan.

MH: Yes, the groups in Afghanistan were told by their party leaders in Peshawar not to cooperate with others. On the ground in Afghanistan, cooperation was sometimes negotiated without the permission of the leaders in Peshawar. In some cases, they achieved great success. The best example of this was the capturing of Khost in 1991. Haqqani led this with the assistance of other groups who cooperated with him, mostly as a tribal force. If negotiations for cooperation were done on a political basis, they failed because group leaders in Peshawar gave strong instructions against cooperating. Fierce battles also sometimes emerged between the Afghan groups, where dozens of people from both sides were killed.

LF: I remember reading an account from Abu Hafs al-Masri where he said this type of competition and a lack of cooperation was one of the reasons he wanted to get away from Peshawar and go and join the fronts of Haqqani.[1]

MH: Yes, the fighting did cause people to go away from these groups. It also left hostilities that could not be cured, and led not only to a drastic reduction in the combat effectiveness of those groups, but also to a serious imbalance in the security of the population in areas of Afghanistan they controlled. People in these areas often either migrated to Pakistan, or to the cities controlled by the Kabul regime backed by the Soviets.

Despite these difficulties, Mawlawi Mansur's efforts, which began as a rebellion in his group, in fact turned into a rebel political movement focused on the jihad situation and jihadi groups in Peshawar. When Peshawar's corrupted parties suppressed his 'reformist revolution', he realised that confrontation with those parties should be both long and short term. The stage of short-term confrontation he led was not as successful as he had hoped, but his steps of long-term reform had a much deeper impact on the history of Afghanistan.

Mawlawi Mansur outlined the problems and the long-term reforms he sought in a special meeting in his office in Peshawar, Pakistan, in the summer of 1981, which I attended. He said:

- The Peshawar parties are rampant with corruption to a degree that cannot be tolerated or overlooked. The party leaders are working for their own interests and do not care about the fate of Afghanistan, or the life of the mujahidin.
- Each party seeks to obtain the largest amount of money and the largest amount of weapons and aid from Pakistan.
- Every attempt to unify the existing parties has resulted in the appearance of a new party, so the struggles and splits increase, and the last of

these attempts was the process of inaugurating Sayyaf as the head of the Union of Mujahidin Parties—which was sponsored and funded by Saudi Arabia and promoted by the International Ikhwan Muslimin.

- The funds coming from abroad to the Union or to the rest of the parties are spent mostly in Pakistan, and rarely reach the mujahidin inside Afghanistan.
- The parties prevent their followers from collaborating with each other and instead encourage fighting among themselves.
- The parties have distributed arms and money to corrupt elements associated with the [Afghan] regime and the occupation, and seek to increase their followers at home through any means.
- Afghan mawlawis and the senior leaders at home all failed in reforming the political parties, and failed to make a union that brings all parties together in one pragmatic framework.
- Sayyaf has succeeded in attracting most of these mawlawis and leaders. He has given them houses in Peshawar, and paid them salaries and helped them get scholarships for their children in Pakistan and Saudi Arabia. They do not serve the reform movement, but are busy under the auspices of their own interests and the interests of their families in Pakistan.

In the end, Mansur said he doubted the Islam of the Afghan party leaders. He said, 'The people of Afghanistan will not allow such corrupted leaders to govern them.' After Mawlawi Mansur gave a detailed explanation of the situation of the parties and the weakening impact this had on the Afghan jihad, he put forward his idea of long-term reform, saying: 'I see the solution as being to create new generations of students of Shariah science, to take the responsibility for the future leadership. A special section has been established for them within Harakat i Inqilab i Islami to educate and train them, and assign to them work in administrative and military areas and this programme is already being implemented.'

* * *

The students of Mawlawi Mansur, educated and trained under his programme in both military and administrative work, marked the beginnings of the Taliban movement, and it was as part of his efforts to build this new generation that Mawlawi Mansur enlisted the help of foreign volunteers. First among them was former Pakistani Army major, Rashid

Ahmad, who served as chief trainer. Joining him were a small group of Arab-Afghans including Mustafa Hamid, Abdul Rahman al-Iraqi, Abdul Rahman al-Masri, Wadih al-Hage and Abu Hafs al-Masri. They were a small group working together under the name Maktab al-Alami al-Islami, with the aim of providing support to the mujahidin.

The coming together of these individuals resulted in the establishment of the Qais camp, and the provision of the first formal military training for Arabs and Afghans, including guerrilla warfare training, and which produced the first training material on guerrilla warfare and politics. The Qais camp and its training laid the groundwork for the idea of establishing an Arab organisation to support the Afghan jihad.

Arrival of the Pakistani trainer Rashid Ahmad

The training situation for Arabs and Afghans changed with the arrival of Rashid Ahmad. He was one of the most important contributors to the Afghan jihad, but until now his contribution has gone unremarked. Rashid was a Pakistani Army major who volunteered to join the jihad. He worked for a period with Jalaluddin Haqqani, to whom he offered his training services, before moving to join forces with Mawlawi Mansur.

* * *

MH: Few people know about Rashid's contribution to the jihad but it was very important. The story of Rashid is an interesting one that I first heard about in 1981 from my friend Haqqani, and from Rashid himself, as well as others.

Haqqani found Rashid in a market in Miranshah, when he was bargaining to purchase a gun for himself. Rashid was accompanied by his nephew Wahid, who was a very nice young man around eighteen years of age. Rashid did not have enough money to purchase the gun at the price the Kuchi shopkeeper wanted, so he told him, 'Please reduce the price of the gun because it is for jihad'.

One of Haqqani's intelligence people was in the market at this time and overheard the conversation, and returned to tell him. Haqqani sent his men to bring Rashid and then asked him about his story. Haqqani found out Rashid had been in the army but had resigned to join the jihad. The army did not allow its officers to join the jihad, so Rashid told his army bosses, 'If you do not allow us to participate in the forward defence

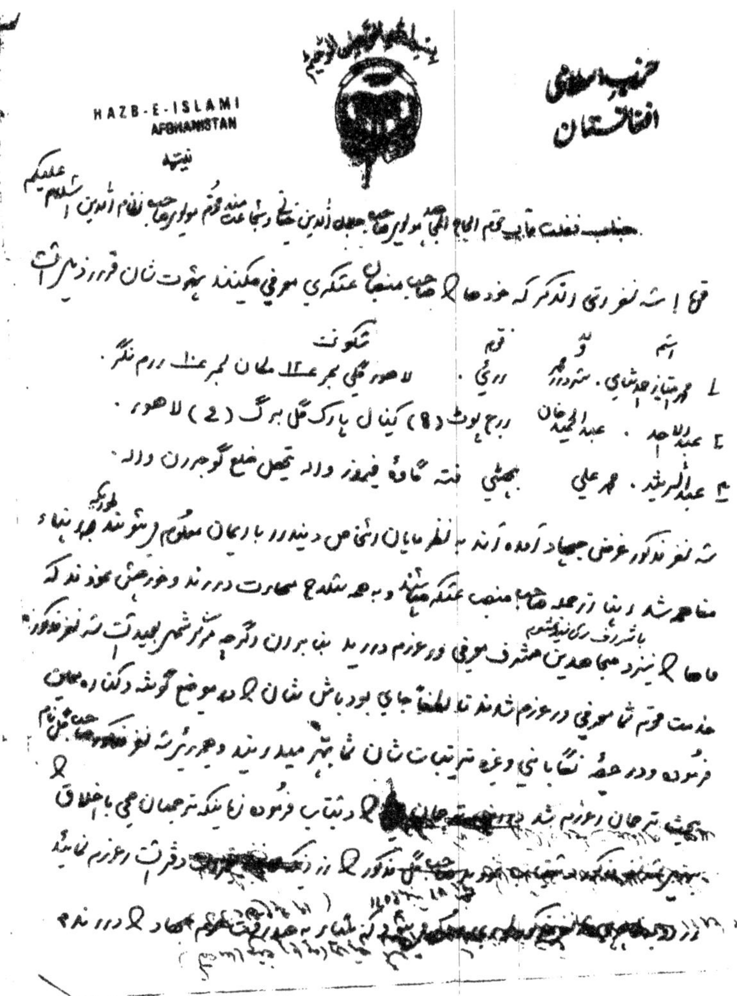
بسم الله الرحمن الرحيم

HAZB-E-ISLAMI
AFGHANISTAN

حزب اسلامی
افغانستان

Fig 5: Haqqani letter appearing to introduce Rashid[2]

of our country in Afghanistan then we cannot defend it inside Pakistan.' He told them, 'We should fight directly in Afghanistan, we should go.' His army bosses said, 'No, our policy is to train the Afghans and give them weapons and courses and help them fight.' Rashid argued, 'We should go inside and organise them and fight with them until they can stand on their own feet.' They did not agree, and so Rashid left. This is what he tried to do in Afghanistan. He was the first to try to do this and he was absolutely right because it needed to be done.

My friend Haqqani was convinced, so Rashid joined Haqqani and went to the front lines, where he did some important and essential work. First, he trained the Afghans on weapons use for the front. This was very good, because before that many of the Afghans had not been properly using their weapons. Rashid trained them on how to use the heavy guns. He trained Haqqani's brothers Khalil and Ibrahim how to use the 122mm howitzer, a Soviet weapon that they used in their attacks against the enemy in Gardez in 1981. Rashid also taught them how to use the 75mm artillery effectively; he taught them how to use it tactically and to absorb the enemy's attack. They put this training to use to hit an enemy barracks in Gardez.

The reaction of the enemy to the new tactics Rashid introduced and the better use of weaponry under his training was very strong. Can you imagine: to hit Gardez with that 122-calibre weapon? It was not a joke. The enemy took this very seriously and used all available artillery to return fire. Although Rashid's men had a limited supply of ammunition, they provoked a strong reaction from the enemy who replied with artillery and helicopters and jets. I was there during this heavy bombardment and fighting. For every one bullet Rashid or his trainees fired, around 100 shells came from the enemy.

You cannot imagine the impact it had. It raised everyone's spirits and the enemy became crazy because of Rashid's clever tactics and his training of Khalil and Ibrahim Haqqani and others. Rashid also used the heavy mortar. I cannot remember the calibre, but it was an Egyptian weapon. They only used it a few times because there were only limited shells available, but it was very effective. We had a big adventure with this gun.

Later, when the SAM7 came, Rashid trained them on this weapon. It was Egyptian-supplied. He trained me too. In fact, I was his assistant for a while, firing these missiles. The missiles themselves were expired and they should have been replaced or disposed of, because the seeking head was no longer effective. The result was that the missiles could not be used to seek a target—they could only be aimed straight at a target.

Rashid also trained the fighters at Haqqani's front to use the Soviet 12.7mm and the 14.5mm heavy machine guns as well as Chinese weapons. He trained them how to fire these weapons but also in the tactics of their use. The tactics were more important to know, because we used these weapons in unusual ways at the front—in ways the mujahidin came to know as guerrilla warfare.

Most of the trainers who gave guidance to the mujahidin, even those volunteers who had previously been in the military, gave training according to the conventional use of weapons. In our environment, this was very dangerous and ineffective, but Rashid was an excellent student and fighter in guerrilla warfare. Because of this, Rashid came to have an excellent reputation with the Afghans in the area, and they all knew his name. I saw children run up to him to say hello. He was also known by the enemy, who released propaganda against him. When I met Rashid in Gardez in 1981, he was only twenty-eight and a major. He said, 'I am the youngest in Pakistan with this rank.' He was a very nice, very good boy.

Rashid also gave Haqqani advice in the battles and Haqqani listened to him and took on his experience as an officer. But in 1983 they had a disagreement during the Lija battle. I was there for this misunderstanding, which turned into a confrontation between them. Haqqani talked with Rashid very roughly, and Rashid became angry and left Haqqani forever. This was the last time I worked with Rashid at the front lines, because after this he left the front and joined with Mawlawi Yunis Khalis and then later Mawlawi Nasrullah Mansur.

Mawlawi Mansur and Rashid's establishment of the Qais camp

MH: When Rashid worked with Mawlawi Mansur, he did many excellent things. One was his work on a magazine called *Al-Surat*, which was issued in Pashtu and Persian, and funded by Mawlawi Mansur. It was a truly unique magazine, with which nothing before or after compared; it was of a very high standard. They made three or four issues. Rashid said to me at the time, 'You should teach the people how to make good analysis.' There was excellent analysis in *Al-Surat*, nearly all of which was comprised of his own political and military analysis, and it was distributed to the Afghans to raise their knowledge.

Unfortunately, Mawlawi Mansur did not have the funding to keep the magazine going. I translated some of Rashid's articles because they were very good. Rashid had fought in Khost before I met him in Gardez, and so his articles about Khost were useful to me. I put two of his articles into my book.

Although his work with Haqqani and on *Al-Surat* was important, I think Rashid's biggest contribution was to training, and the activities he set up when he helped Mawlawi Mansur establish the Qais camp, which operated in 1984. Rashid became the chief trainer and helped Mawlawi Mansur to find other instructors to train the Afghans, Taliban and a group of Arabs. The contribution Rashid made along with Mawlawi Mansur with the Qais camp project came to have a lasting impact. In fact, the Qais camp was the first to receive a large number of Taliban belonging to Mawlawi Mansur, where they were provided with valuable military training. I was an eyewitness to this training and a participant in some of it.

The establishment of Qais was an important step forward, particularly after earlier efforts to develop training activities, including those of my friends and I, had failed to secure support. After our initial efforts to convince others of the need for a project to support the mujahidin came to nothing, we decided we would have to provide some support to the mujahidin ourselves. Although we had no money, we thought we could do some media and research work to make sure that Muslims all over the world knew what was happening in Afghanistan.

We also wanted to create a small training programme to train the Arabs to support the Afghans and to share in the battles on a small scale, because until then, there were few opportunities to share in battle. We needed people to work with us, and we thought to call our project Maktab al-Alami al-Islami. I was responsible for creating this programme, but at the time, Sayyaf and Ikhwan Muslimin had blacklisted me.

LF: Why were you blacklisted? Was this a result of you and your friends' earlier efforts to secure support?

MH: They suspected I was an enemy of jihad, and was working against the mujahidin by trying to exploit them, and that our project was really about making a new party for the mawlawis of Afghanistan.

LF: I am guessing that is not what you were doing, but I am curious as to why that would have been a problem. Was it because of competition and rivalry between the groups and a fear of losing influences and resources?

MH: Yes. The campaign against my friends and I meant that people became afraid to cooperate with our project. At the same time, my friends in Abu Dhabi did not have the money to assist us. I went to Peshawar to try to start the work under these circumstances, and when I arrived, I went to the house of my friend Haqqani. There, do you know who I found?

LF: Who?

MH: I found there a group of Arabs; among them were Abu Hafs al-Masri, Abdul Rahman al-Masri, Abdul Rahman al-Iraqi and Abdul Sabur, who is also known as Wadih al-Hage. As you know Abu Hafs became one of the founders of al-Qaeda and Wadih al-Hage also became close to Abu Abdullah (and played an important role for him in Africa after 1993). This group was waiting for someone to take them to the front, and they had been waiting for a long time because it was winter. I met them all and told them to join our project, Maktab al-Alami al-Islami. I asked them to start first on research about education for the Afghan refugees, because Mawlawi Mansur was trying to focus on this area.

Our group did some excellent research work in this area: Abdul Rahman al-Iraqi and Abdul Sabur in particular made a big effort for several months and produced some very good research and education materials. It was a very good start in our work. In fact, it formed the basis of educational assistance and programmes for most of the Arab relief agencies in the field, but they did not know we started the project.

We also gave this material to others, such as the Sudanese Isra Islamic Relief Agency. It was also the work we built upon at the Qais camp with Rashid and Mawlawi Mansur. As I mentioned earlier, Mawlawi Mansur's programme was not just about military training. He wanted to raise a new generation and realised that this required making sure the youth had a broader education than just learning how to use weapons. This is why his work focused on programs for educating Afghans as well as training in areas of immediate needs like military and administrative work. He was the only one to do so, through his early reform efforts and later with initiatives like the Qais camp, and this is why he was the real founder of the Taliban movement. Of everyone, he was the only one who had a vision for the Taliban into the future and worked towards it.

LF: Where was the Qais camp established?

MH: Mawlawi Mansur set up the Qais camp in the Sadda area of Pakistan, in the border areas, where some training of Afghans had already taken place under the supervision of Pakistani intelligence personnel. This earlier training was low-level, under the direction of conditions set by the then president of Pakistan, General Zia ul-Haq, who as I mentioned earlier told his director of Military Intelligence, Akhtar Abdul Rahman, that he wanted the war in Afghanistan to slowly boil. The Pakistanis had earlier trained Afghans on how to fire weapons, but without training them on combat tactics.

A significant number of Taliban from Mawlawi Mansur's group received their training at Qais. This training was more serious and of a higher quality than other Afghan camps, because it was far away from the politics and the propaganda of the other Afghan parties. In fact, the Qais camp was first in terms of its historical significance in preparing the Taliban for combat missions on the battlefield. The second was a 'front line' camp in the Zurmat area, relatively close to Gardez city. The trainers were Afghan because Pakistani trainers did not work in these areas, although Pakistani military intelligence were roaming everywhere giving instructions, or coordinating certain operations or just monitoring.

The place of training in the Zurmat valley, south of Gardez, the capital of Paktia, was the home area of Mawlawi Mansur and his tribe (Andar), which stretches to the states of Paktia, Ghazni and Paktika. When Mawlawi Mansur was in command of the front in Zurmat, the students of Shariah, 'the Taliban', gathered around him for training and for participation in the field. But it was not until much later that any special grouping or organisation was created for combat, and I think the first to think of this was Jalaluddin Haqqani.

In an interview I had with Mawlawi Mansur, he told me that the Qais camp was independent in its training because he had hired Pakistanis who were no longer part of the military, but had previously served in the armed forces. The person who helped him to locate such trainers was Rashid. Although Rashid worked with Mansur on many projects, the main one was the Qais camp.

By the autumn of 1984, training was underway at the Qais camp, and Arab volunteers attended two sessions. I was present at the first session and with me was my friend Abdul Rahman al-Masri, who was martyred on Mount Torghar in 1988, and Abu Hafs al-Masri, who was one of the three founders of al-Qaeda. In the second session Abu Ubaydah al-Banshiri, who was also a founder of al-Qaeda, attended.

It was this training that made Abu Hafs and Abu Ubaydah excel in guerrilla warfare on the battlefield. That means that the Qais camp played an important role in preparing them to be able to train the others later, at al-Masadah in Jaji where they had an important victory against the Soviets.

LF: How so?

MH: During the first session of the Qais camp, the group of Arabs listened to Rashid's long night lectures on the subject of guerrilla warfare, and his vision for forming a military force of highly trained Afghans. This was the first time that Arab volunteers in Afghanistan listened to lectures in this form and on this subject. In fact, the Qais camp was unique because it was the first time that Arabs or Afghans had been formally trained in such things as guerrilla warfare.

Rashid taught us and gave lectures on guerrilla warfare. He initially did not go too deeply into the subject matter, but instead he gave it as a sort of introduction to the way he thought the project for jihad in Afghanistan should be prepared in order for it to be effective and organised. To explain this, he gave lectures on guerrilla warfare. He was the first one to teach guerrilla warfare to us, and from that point onwards, we started to build a library for ourselves for reading and training. I was already familiar with the term, as I had read about it earlier in Egypt. With Rashid giving the lecture in English, Abdul Sabur and I translated it into Arabic. Abdul Rahman al-Iraqi printed the translations: he was always making jokes with all of us, making trouble. Abdul Sabur was always very nervous, but he worked very hard and was very organised. Actually, the effort we made together was also one of the first steps of training the Arabs in Afghanistan.

Rashid and Mawlawi Mansur's contribution to the Afghan and Arab jihad

LF: It is curious to me that Rashid Ahmad and Mawlawi Mansur clearly made an important contribution to the Afghan jihad, but in all I have read they are barely mentioned. Why is that? Is their history not widely known or did these two fall out of favour and get themselves blacklisted?

MH: They both suffered a lot and their efforts have not been widely recognised. Also, Rashid had left by 1986, and Mawlawi Mansur was killed in 1993, so there was not as much publicity about them as there was with other figures who attracted attention. But yes, they did fall out of favour, largely because of Rashid's involvement in helping Mawlawi Mansur to go to America and meet important people from the Congress and Senate, and to give some speeches and interviews.

By this stage, Rashid had become famous and he introduced Mawlawi Mansur to the Americans. At this stage of the jihad, the mujahidin had the support of the American camp and its allies around the world, so they were travelling in America, Europe and Arab oil countries, holding seminars, meeting people and collecting huge donations. Rashid wanted Mawlawi Mansur to talk to the Americans and to try to get support from them, so he arranged for him to be invited to America. But Mawlawi Mansur disappointed Rashid and everyone by what he said during his visit.

Mawlawi Mansur went to America in 1986, if I remember correctly. He went on the invitation of prominent members of the Congress but he exceeded the limits of diplomatic customs on such invitations. He said in response to a question asked of him that he considered America an enemy as well, and that it was helping the Afghans for its own interests. His trip was not a success because he gave long statements against America while he was there. He was not a diplomatic man and I think he put himself in a certain trap. It was a very big mistake.

After his return from Washington, Mawlawi Mansur experienced the wrath of the Pakistanis and Arabs and all kinds of support and aid to him were stopped, with the exception of small amounts that came from Iran. The anger of America towards Mawlawi Mansur, and the Arab boycott saw him draw closer politically to Iran, and he was alone in doing so. From time to time Mawlawi Mansur visited Iran, and they sent trainers and instructors, and I met some of them in Zurmat in 1988.

Despite this limited aid, Mawlawi Mansur continued to suffer from this experience and the resulting boycott until his life was ended by an assassination organised by Hekmatyar in 1993—according to the belief of those who were close to Mawlawi Mansur. Nonetheless, Mawlawi Mansur made a unique contribution to history because he was responsible for the very early establishment of the Taliban, which changed the history of Afghanistan, and he was the only one to establish relations with Iran at that time.

Rashid suffered too. Pakistan did not tolerate him or Mawlawi Mansur because they had made direct contact with the Americans without passing through the ISI first, which was not allowed. America became angry with Mawlawi Mansur because of his statements, and Pakistan became angry with Rashid because he sidestepped them and made a bridge straight to America.

Rashid started to be chased by the ISI, who told the Afghans not to cooperate with him. They began harassing him. I saw that as an eyewitness. One day I was in Hizb i Islami-Khalis's office in Peshawar. Hajji din Muhammad, the deputy of Khalis, was there and he told me, 'that

Rashid, we don't deal with Rashid. We doubt him, he is an ISI fellow.' At the same time, I knew that the ISI visited this office regularly, and was welcomed. So I came to the conclusion that they were trying to push Rashid out of the arena.

I think Rashid was poorly treated by the Afghans, the Arabs and the Pakistanis, and he deserved better. The Arabs in Lija and Qais did not treat him well because he had no beard and he smoked. For Salafis, anybody who did not have a beard and smoked was not a good man, and they would not cooperate with him. When Rashid asked me to gather the Arabs to form an Arab force for fighting, which he intended to train and to try to collect weapons for, and to help them to launch operations, they would not cooperate fully because they did not trust him. They hardly trusted me, because I was not Salafi, even when they had known me for some time. And so, Rashid's contribution was not fully recognised—despite the ideas and the training he gave us at Qais having such an important impact in Arab and Afghan mujahidin circles long afterwards.

LF: Yes, it seems to me that the ideas taught in Qais are reflected even in the events surrounding al-Qaeda's genesis. When bin Laden went to establish his al-Masadah base in 1986, it was Qais graduates Abu Hafs al-Masri and Abu Ubaydah al-Banshiri who attempted to convince bin Laden not to establish a traditional base, but to instead use it to operate a guerrilla force in the area.

MH: Yes, and Abu Jihad al-Masri was also with them; although he did not attend Qais he became convinced about the benefits of guerrilla warfare. But what was the result? The result was that the three of them ended up joining Abu Abdullah in his work in the conventional war. Why? We will discuss this more later, but it is important here to highlight the effect Abu Abdullah's personality had on others, and in this way on the outcome of particular aspects of the jihad—like the introduction of guerrilla warfare into the conflict.

Abu Abdullah was a courageous, decent man who spent his money for the jihad against the Soviets, so people followed him even if he was doing wrong, because they liked him. The Arabs follow a leader not an idea; they find a person they trust and then they follow him—not the idea. Because of that, Abu Hafs, Abu Jihad and Abu Ubaydah all moved away from the idea of guerrilla warfare, which they were 100 per cent sure was good, and like others, they followed Abu Abdullah because they loved him and trusted him. This is very similar to what happened in 2001, before the 9/11 attacks and in the war in 2001. No one from the older generation of al-Qaeda agreed with Abu Abdullah, but they still followed him.

As for the al-Masadah case at Jaji, the result was that when the Qais graduates tried to convince Abu Abdullah to pursue guerrilla warfare instead of a traditional base and way of conflict, they were unsuccessful. Instead, they ended up joining Abu Abdullah, and a very good chance to carry out some excellent guerrilla warfare in the region was lost. Unfortunately, the victory at Jaji, which we will discuss later, covered over this and other deficits, and meant people did not want to talk about the shortcomings of the Jaji battles. Instead, they argued 'we won'. The impact of this failure to examine the events of Jaji and to learn from them became very clear in the Arab and Afghan folly that was the battle for Jalalabad in 1989.

LF: That is very interesting. Would it be correct then to say that the origins of the Taliban trace to an idea and a movement, while the Arabs, at least in Afghanistan, followed leaders, and this resulted in the establishment of organisations like al-Qaeda that were often personality-based and in competition with one another?

MH: Yes, and if we return to the Qais camp and its results we can see the difference. The Arabs and the Afghans were in the same training, but afterwards the Arab mujahidin followed their leaders, while the Afghan mujahidin followed the ideas they believed in, and the Afghans eventually built a better outcome—the Taliban, and they affected the history of the world.

LF: I think it is safe to say that al-Qaeda too affected the history of the world; don't you?

MH: Yes, but the outcome from al-Qaeda was not better, which we will discuss later. In relation to the Qais camp and its results, there was no Arab organisation at that time, but the ideas that eventually led to one called Maktab al-Khadamat came in large part from the training at Qais. Here we should note that even when an Arab organisation was established in the form of Maktab al-Khadamat, it too became a group that followed a leader, or leaders, and not the ideas, and it became badly affected by mismanagement and corruption, and did not achieve all that it could have in supporting the Afghan jihad.

LF: Competition too also afflicted Maktab al-Khadamat. Now seems to be a good time to talk about the establishment of that organisation, the inspiration for which I believe came from the proposals of you and your friends—proposals that caused Sayyaf to initially brand you all enemies of the jihad.

MH: Yes, it is an interesting story.

4

TWO MEMOS AND AN IDEA THAT SPREAD

THE REAL ORIGINS OF MAKTAB AL-KHADAMAT

The commonly accepted story of Maktab al-Khadamat's creation is that in 1984 Abdul Rasul Sayyaf, Osama bin Laden and Abdullah Azzam held a meeting while they were attending the Hajj in Saudi Arabia, at which they decided to establish an Arab organisation to support the Afghan jihad and facilitate the arrival of foreign volunteers. However, the idea of Maktab al-Khadamat—as an Arab-established and led organisation dedicated to the support of the Afghan jihad—did not originate from any of these three men. Rather, it came from the earlier initiatives of Mustafa Hamid, inspired by Rashid, and with the initial support of two key Afghans, Mawlawi Nasrullah Mansur and Jalaluddin Haqqani.

The two memos: early suggestions for an Arab-led organisation

The ideas and proposals for an Arab-led organisation to support the Afghan jihad were outlined in two of Mustafa Hamid's research papers, which were provided to key Arab and Afghan cadres. These papers drew heavily from early Arab-Afghan experiences on the front lines, as well as from Rashid Ahmad's training at Qais and his recommendations for repairing the Afghan jihad. Together, they outlined the need for an Arab organisation, and laid the groundwork for the creation of Maktab al-Khadamat.

Mustafa Hamid was driven to write the first of the two papers following the 1983 Battle of Urgon, in which ammunition shortages and the poor administration of supplies, logistics and donations had a significant impact on the battle. The paper focused on how to rectify the misdirection and misappropriation of supplies, and was the first to make clear the problem of corruption within the jihad. Parts of the paper were later provided to Jalaluddin Haqqani, who asked Hamid to write something for him to take to the Hajj to secure more assistance and funding.

Prior to the departure of Haqqani and others for the 1984 Hajj, meetings were held in Jaji in an attempt to rectify problems with supplies and mismanagement. At these meetings the idea of an Arab-led organisation was outlined by Hamid, and supported by other early generation Arab-Afghans such as Abdul Aziz Ali, who thought independent Arab oversight could prevent corruption, particularly in the area of ammunition supplies, which was harming success on the battlefield.

* * *

MH: The real origins of the idea for direct Arab support of the jihad inside Afghanistan in areas of logistics, training and ammunition manufacture came because of the Battle of Urgon. During this battle, we found that ammunition for the 12.7mm heavy machine gun was finished and we could not get any more because ammunition and aid were not distributed to the Afghan fronts on the basis of requirements, but politics. This harmed our efforts during the battle, and so afterwards, I began to think about ways in which ammunition could be better supplied.

One idea that I put in my paper was to create a programme for manufacturing or refilling ammunition for light and medium weaponry. Because of the mismanagement of aid and supplies that we witnessed on the fronts and during the Urgon battle, it was also clear we needed to establish a committee to supervise the distribution of aid and ammunition and weapons on the basis of merit and need.

I thought an Arab committee could help ensure that donations, aid and logistics work were guided by the fighting programmes and not by political or tribal factors or corruption. The committee would assist in directing aid to the places it was needed and could best be used. This required people to be inside Afghanistan to know what was happening so they could ensure aid went to the right places.

So I wrote about this in my research paper, highlighting the problems of corruption and misdirected aid, and suggesting this solution: that an

Arab group or committee be formed to oversee supply, logistics and donations. I came under fire for this suggestion, and so too did my friends who supported the initiative.

LF: Why did you and your friends come under fire?

MH: My friends Ahmad, Abdul Aziz Ali and I came under fire because of our committee proposal and the meeting we held about this at Jaji with Sayyaf and other senior leaders on the first night of Ramadan in 1984. We wanted to discuss forming an Arab committee to supervise supplies to the battlefield to ensure they went where they were needed. We based the meeting points on the research paper I had written after the 1983 Battle of Urgon, parts of which I later sent with Haqqani to the 1984 Hajj.

At the meeting, we suggested the Arabs could help to deal with the problem of corruption and supplies not reaching where they were needed, by forming a committee that would ensure supplies were distributed to the battlefronts according to need. To do this, we suggested Arabs should be at the fronts to see for themselves what was needed and they should be in Peshawar too, to control the donations, negotiations and administration of supplies and supply lines. Our main point was that the Arabs needed to be inside, at the fronts, to see what was needed. This was a very essential point, and a new position at that time.

Haqqani and other senior leaders in Paktia like Arsla Rahmani and Mawlawi Mansur agreed to our initiative and suggested we put this in the practical form of a programme to support military operations. According to the military advice of the famous Afghan general, Gulzarak, who was the head of Sayyaf's al-Ittihad Military Committee, and with the agreement of Yunis Khalis, Haqqani, Mansur, Ahmad Gul and others, it was decided the programme be started in Paktia, which would allow a major offensive to be launched in the province.

According to their calculations, the offensive would take three months. Gulzarak made a military programme and calculated the cost would be around 3 million rupees every month. The Arabs would pay, and a committee headed by Azzam would gather and supervise the distribution of donations, while Abdul Aziz Ali would supervise the logistics work and ensure supplies were distributed where they were needed.

Mawlawi Mansur and Haqqani said they would contribute forces and that they were ready to attack the communist strongholds in their area. When this was agreed, it became a practical project, and from this point the Arabs would collect money and come to distribute it and oversee supplies and logistics. Yunis Khalis, who was among those who agreed, asked that the Arabs come to Jalalabad and make a project there once the Paktia offensive was finished.

One of the Arabs present at the meeting said, 'I have 3 million rupees with me to pay for the first month's battle.' Sayyaf initially agreed in front of us, but then he asked for a special meeting of the Afghans without Arabs, and they went to another place to talk. At this meeting I was told Sayyaf said that he did not want to make the Arabs angry but he did not agree with the money being directed by the Arabs for the Afghans without passing through him first, because he was the leader of the Union.

LF: Sayyaf did not like this?

MH: Sayyaf did not like that we had made this proposal, and in doing so had highlighted the problem of corruption within the Afghan parties. Because of this, we became his enemies—although I did not know it at the time of the meeting in Jaji. Later, a Saudi man came to me and asked, 'What is wrong between you and Sayyaf?' I asked, 'Why, we were very good the last time we met in Jaji; all of us, it was a nice meeting.'

The Saudi man said, 'Sayyaf is very angry with you and your friends Ahmad and Abdul Aziz Ali.' I said, 'Why?' The Saudi replied that Sayyaf told him that we were 'going to establish a party for the mawlawis of Afghanistan'. Sayyaf also told the Saudi that all of us were against the jihad in Afghanistan and were agents of the West. I said, 'this is very strange', and he said, 'yes, you should go and settle this'. So, I went to see what the situation was in Peshawar, and discovered that nearly all of the Arabs there knew of Sayyaf's accusations against us.

LF: The meeting, and your proposal and research paper, which caused Sayyaf to react, outlined how to repair the situation and better support the mujahidin?

MH: Yes. This was the main point and Maktab al-Khadamat came from this point. It was a two-part paper; the first part of the paper outlined the problems being faced and the defects within the Afghan jihad. These included corruption as well as inefficiency, which was a problem because the parties were located in Peshawar and at some distance from the Afghan fronts. The second part of the paper presented the solutions. In 1984 Haqqani was going to the Hajj and he said, 'Write something for me to show them what we need.' So this was the paper I gave him.

Haqqani did not take the first part of the paper because I had written about why the jihad was in need of repair. My paper took a strong stand against the parties and their inefficiency. In fact, it was the first paper to outline the problem of corruption and highlight the need for Arabs to supervise the provision of aid to prevent it being misused by corrupt elements. Haqqani thought this might cause further divisions, so he only took the second part, which outlined the solutions.

LF: What were the solutions you suggested?

MH: My solution was that an Arab committee supervise aid and supplies, with members stationed at the fronts inside Afghanistan and also in Peshawar, where they would collect and distribute aid and supplies according to where they were needed. My other solutions involved arranging for the training of Afghans to increase their effectiveness and efficiency. This training was to be in guerrilla warfare, because the tribal way of fighting was wasting too much ammunition and resulting in large casualties.

The mujahidin were also dying from very small wounds because most of the doctors stayed in Peshawar. So, another of my suggestions was for doctors to go inside Afghanistan. The Western doctors went inside Afghanistan, but most of the Arab doctors did not; it was very shameful. My suggestion was to send more doctors with the fighters to save lives.

I also wrote about the need for a big media and education effort. Education programmes were needed for the Afghans because the Soviets were placing a lot of attention on educating Afghan youth. They would take them to Russia to indoctrinate them into communism, so an Afghan education project was needed. An international media effort was also required in Arabic, English and other languages. So, another of my points was to organise this and send people inside Afghanistan to gather the information, photos, films and other materials that could be distributed all over the world to news agencies to give a real and reliable picture of the jihad. This would help Muslims to learn about the conflict, and where and how to assist, and in what way, so money was not wasted. These were the main points I made, which I had discussed with, and were supported by, my friends.

LF: Where did this document you gave Haqqani go?

MH: Haqqani took it to the Hajj and it reached Azzam and Abu Abdullah. They agreed on it, and then they took it to Sayyaf as the leader of the Afghan Union; they went to him and said, 'this is our project' and sought his approval. Because they wanted to support this project Sayyaf had little choice but to agree. Azzam wrote about this and said he was very happy that Sayyaf agreed, and Abu Abdullah was happy too. But neither of them realised that Sayyaf's approval was conditional; that he wanted to make the entire project under the flag of al-Ittihad, and under the flag of Sayyaf as the leader of the Afghan mujahidin.

LF: What about the second paper, the one you wrote for Azzam, what period was this?

MH: I wrote this paper after the Qais training in 1984; it was about building a programme to repair the jihad, especially in the battlefield, by using guerrilla warfare. This paper came mainly from Rashid's training and the programmes he wanted to develop. I built on Rashid's lectures, where he was talking about how to technically repair the Afghan jihad, how to form forces to fight, and in what shape, and what kind of equipment we needed to fight more effectively. In my paper, I gave details about this, and expanded upon Rashid's thinking and vision for an organised and well-trained guerrilla warfare campaign in all of Afghanistan.

When Rashid told us his ideas during the Qais training, he was thinking that we were able to mobilise an Arab campaign to support this project for him. In fact, we were very weak and unsupported, and at that time we had no capacity to bring any youths or money. Still, Rashid planted ideas that grew and he was an important person like that.

So from Rashid's lectures I wrote about how the repair project could be achieved by the Arabs, and what we should do to form well-trained and equipped Afghan strike groups inside Afghanistan and how the Arabs could work alongside the Afghans. I sent it to Azzam for him to read and then it went to a few people in Peshawar, and eventually it reached Sayyaf who did not like it. It was later published in *Al-Jihad* magazine.

LF: How did it reach Sayyaf, and why did he not like it?

MH: Azzam gave it to Sayyaf but it was not intended for Sayyaf. In the beginning, I gave a copy to Azzam because we hoped he would support the project financially. Azzam sent it to his assistant, Abu Akram, a Palestinian who worked with him for a year or two, to be typed and printed. He printed it and I told him, 'Please don't distribute it.'

LF: That is just asking for it to be sent around isn't it?

MH: He did the opposite; he typed it and printed it and it was distributed. He sent it to my enemy, Sayyaf, who read it and said, 'This is a conspiracy to kill jihad.' Sayyaf did not like me, my friends Ahmad and Abdul Aziz Ali, or our projects, and he again accused us of acting against jihad. Really, Sayyaf was trying to protect his own interests. He was also against the idea of guerrilla warfare.

Sayyaf and many others considered the word and idea behind guerrilla warfare insulting, because it basically meant warfare in small groups and running and hiding and not facing the enemy. They believed jihad was not about the small groups and hit-and-run attacks on the enemy, and said other stupid things that showed their limited knowledge about the theory of war. They were against organising anything; anything that was organised was the enemy of jihad. This was what they said.

Because of their reactions I started to specialise in this kind of research, and Rashid helped me a lot, because he opened the door for me. I had previously read about these military topics because material was available in Egypt, but Rashid brought some books from the Pakistani Army library that I had not seen. We studied them all and translated them from English into Arabic, and although he took the books back, we kept the translations and studied them as a group. I later became a teacher of this and bought many military books in Arabic and English until we had a considerable library. Soon I started teaching that subject to the Arabs to help them in their fight against the Soviets, whether in training camps in Afghanistan or in Peshawar.

So, these lectures and the training in Qais, and the Qais camp itself, were a very important step. But nobody has put it in the history of the Arabs or the Afghans—despite these lectures and the camp being so important and showing good results in the battles afterwards. For example, in the winter of 1984/1985, and after the end of the second session of the Arabs in the Qais camp, some of the Arabs who had attended, including Abu Hafs al-Masri and Abdul Rahman al-Masri, participated in the Battle of 'Shahranao' in Paktia province in Afghanistan.

The battle took place in severe winter conditions under the leadership of Mawlawi Fathallah, a senior assistant of Jalaluddin Haqqani. This battle saw Abdul Rahman and Abu Hafs emerge in strong roles, and they fought with great courage, which amazed the Afghans who took to calling them 'those crazy Arabs'. When, at times, the Afghan forces withdrew from enemy fire, Abu Hafs approached using Chinese katyusha rockets, firing them against the enemy from the rocks because there was no launcher available.

In the summer of 1985, Abu Hafs and I used these missiles against Khost city airport, after we introduced some changes in the way they were launched, which was different than what was used by mujahidin, who had been taught by their ISI coaches. We used totally different tac-

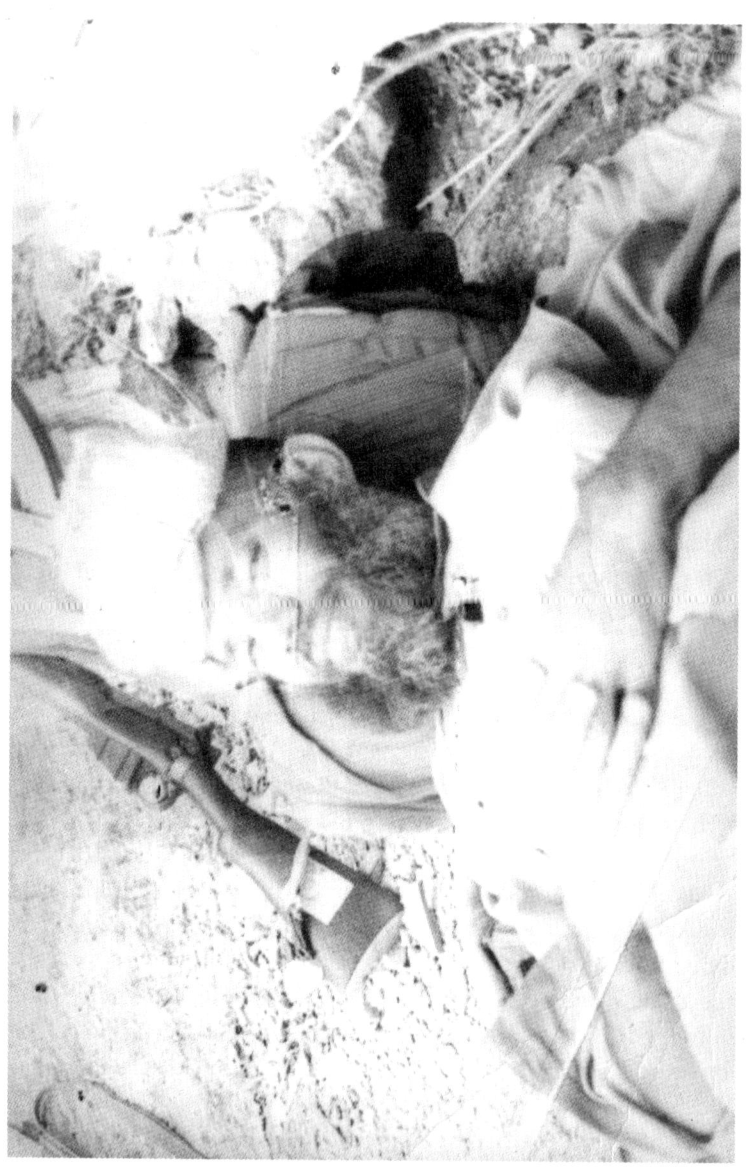

Fig 6: Mustafa Hamid, resting in Khost after scouting activities. Photo by Abu Hafs al-Masri

tics. We made a large disturbance because we engaged in hit-and-run attacks, not attacks to capture territory, and the enemy became angry because it was very new at that time. At that time in Khost, our operation was very small. We were a small group of Arabs, mainly we were three: Abu Hafs, Abdul Rahman al-Masri and me. We made secret and careful movements in the battlefield and even in Miranshah.

* * *

Despite these successes using guerrilla warfare tactics on the battlefield, the Afghans were not always supportive.

* * *

MH: Some of the Afghans who watched our work were not happy about moving in heavy secrecy because we did not launch any battles face to face the way they liked. They thought we were playing some chasing game. During the short time we used these tactics we were able to inflict very heavy losses on the enemy and stop the movement at Khost airport for a day or two at a time. This was a very big achievement for such a small group.

* * *

Another reason some leaders of the Afghan groups did not like the use of such tactics was because it removed their influence. For this reason too, those working for Pakistani intelligence also did not like such methods being used.

* * *

MH: We had to stop our work on the airport in 1985 when we found most of the Afghan groups did not want us to do this work because of Pakistani pressure on them. But our battles in the winter of 1984 through to summer 1985 after Qais training were the most important for the Arabs at that time—both in terms of impact, and where to work independently within the Afghan combat formations.

* * *

The success of the tactics used in these battles did, however, cause Sayyaf to change his view on the project of repair proposals that Mustafa

Hamid had sent to Azzam, including the introduction of guerrilla warfare campaigns.

* * *

MH: Sayyaf changed his mind about the project and then took it as his own, as an al-Ittihad project, and claimed it was for the benefit of 'The Islamic Union of Afghanistan Mujahidin'. This was a complete reversal because at the beginning when he first heard about guerrilla warfare he said it was a conspiracy against jihad. He knew I made that research paper. He did not really change his view about my proposals; he used the ideas in my paper to try to salvage his reputation. He used the paper to claim a project of his own when his activities were being questioned by the Arabs. After Sayyaf failed in Jaji, the Arabs started to suspect his project in Jaji, his fireshow, and a backlash began. So, he took the same paper I had written and which he made accusations against me for writing, and he said: 'This is our project, we are in the third stage of guerrilla warfare, attacking the cities.' He never implemented it, he just wanted to claim it as his own and prevent others from doing something.

There is an irony here, because in my proposals that Sayyaf then claimed as his, were suggestions not only on how to repair the jihad on the battlefield—but also about building unity between the Afghan parties and preventing projects being claimed by one party or another. My proposals were inspired by the teachings and activities at the Qais camp and focused on encouraging broader understanding and cooperation and trying to prevent conflicts between the Arabs and the Afghans, which were increasingly becoming a problem.

I remember when I was putting my paper together, I had sought Haqqani's help, and we were compiling this and another paper on the needs of the mujahidin and how to help them, and as you know Maktab al-Khadamat also came from this other paper. At the time we were working on the paper, Haqqani had a call from Yunis Khalis in Peshawar about a big problem in Kandahar between the Arabs and the Afghans. It came very close to a fight between them because the Arabs had gone to the tombs and taken the flags out. The tomb of every Shahid had a flag on it, and the Arabs had removed all of them because they considered it *shirk*. This angered the Afghans and Yunis Khalis had to travel there himself in order to stop a fight breaking out between the Arabs and the Afghans.

Another example I remember of our trying to build unity and understanding was at the Qais camp when Rashid, Mawlawi Mansur, myself and others tried a new approach. It was a simple idea, and an idealistic one. Our idea was that we call the Salafis of Nuristan to come and join with Mawlawi Mansur (who was Hanafi and Sufi) at the Qais camp. Ten or fifteen of the Salafis from Nuristan came to Qais for training.

In the beginning, it was hard to keep them from clashing, but it stayed peaceful, although at the time of praying it was difficult because of the different ways they prayed. But it succeeded, and it was the first time to mix them together where they sat and trained and lived together in the same place. It has not happened since. It did not happen again because of the corrupt and self-interested nature of the Afghan parties, and the external interference in their activities. They were against reform and repair efforts like this and they pushed many people out. Sayyaf even threatened to kill me. Rashid was pushed out in 1986 and left Pakistan for Canada, and seven years later Mawlawi Mansur was assassinated.

* * *

Despite self-interest often dominating the landscape and preventing many projects from coming to fruition, the idea Mustafa Hamid and his friends outlined—for an Arab-led organisation to be established—was eventually put into place by Abdullah Azzam, bin Laden and Sayyaf, in what would become Maktab al-Khadamat.

Azzam, Sayyaf and bin Laden establish Maktab al-Khadamat

The creation of an Arab-led organisation did come to be supported by Azzam, Sayyaf and bin Laden, but the organisation they established and subsequently called Maktab al-Khadamat differed significantly from what Mustafa Hamid and his friends had proposed.

* * *

MH: The bottom line is both my papers made it to the same people, and together helped influence the decision to create an Arab organisation. But it turned out very differently to the one initially suggested, both in its scope and application in the field.

LF: How did Maktab al-Khadamat differ in relation to what you and your friends had proposed?

MH: Military training was poorly done—until the arrival of Abu Burhan al-Suri, who lifted the quality of training, which we will talk some more about later. The ammunition project was never adopted as part of Maktab al-Khadamat; no manufacturing was every carried out.

Aid dispersal, one of Maktab al-Khadamat's main jobs, was not done well. Maktab al-Khadamat gave money to the Afghans who were transferring weapons and ammunition inside. But the Afghans tricked them. Because most of Maktab al-Khadamat's people were based in Peshawar, there were few to supervise the aid going over the border. Some Afghans took advantage of this and used to take the same shipment back and forth several times and claim money for its transport each time. One shipment went back and forth four times before the fraud was discovered.

LF: How about the media work—it seems they did that well? *Al-Jihad* magazine, for example, was very successful.

MH: The media work was for Ikhwan Muslimin, and for Sayyaf and then after for Jamil ul-Rahman. It was for the cause of Afghanistan from the point of view of Ikhwan Muslimin and for their interest. The media work was done well for their view, but it was a limited view that did not fully represent the Afghan cause.

LF: Would it be correct then to say that Maktab al-Khadamat's alternative path and function came because of the differing and perhaps competing agendas of its three sponsors? It seems to me that bin Laden's decision to support the establishment of Maktab al-Khadamat was influenced by his visits to the front lines where he became aware of the poor conditions in which the mujahidin were living and fighting. I read that at Azzam's urging, bin Laden went inside Afghanistan to one of Sayyaf's fronts to see the conditions for himself.[1] I think it was in the Jaji-Ali Khel area.

MH: It was Jaji, but it was after Maktab al-Khadamat had already been formed. Abu Abdullah went secretly to the front because he was afraid of the reaction of the Saudi government. As Azzam said, 'At first Abu Abdullah was afraid even to go to Peshawar.' When Abu Abdullah first started travelling, he only went to Lahore to Jamaat i Islami; he paid the money and then it was transferred to the mujahidin. This continued until the formation of Maktab al-Khadamat.

After the formation of Maktab al-Khadamat, Azzam convinced Abu Abdullah to come to Peshawar and visit with Sayyaf, and then later he told Abu Abdullah to go and see Sayyaf in Jaji. Azzam supported Sayyaf and he wanted Abu Abdullah to go so he could see that Sayyaf was the most competent leader. Abu Abdullah visited, secretly of course, but he visited in winter, and Sayyaf was not there. So, Abu Abdullah found himself alone with a few mujahidin in miserable conditions. They started to complain to him, and so he came to know that Peshawar was very different to the front.

In Jaji, the mujahidin were living in tents on the mountains. There were no caves, the planes came and bombed them; there were no medical facilities, and all the groups were organising themselves separately. Abu Abdullah became angry at Maktab al-Khadamat and the others and asked them: 'What are you doing there? Where are you spending the money and the millions that come to you?' He had also heard there were corruption problems inside Maktab al-Khadamat.

LF: I am curious as to why Azzam hadn't seen the same thing?

MH: Usually when Arabs travelled to the front their trips were prepared, and they were treated and housed as guests, and travelled with a big leader. They did not see the real picture. Azzam did not get the chance Abu Abdullah had, because he never travelled to the front and sat alone with the mujahidin when there was no big leader there. So Abu Abdullah, unlike Azzam, got to see the real situation.

When he saw the conditions Abu Abdullah said he felt guilty for taking so long to visit, and he felt it was a big sin that he had not come earlier; he found himself wanting to be martyred there. He started diverting money from Maktab al-Khadamat and started to spend it himself inside Afghanistan. From that point onwards, Abu Abdullah began to insist on working inside Afghanistan and on the battlefield. That meant the Arabs had a leader, money and a direction of work.

LF: If bin Laden's first real visit to the front came after Maktab al-Khadamat was established, why then do you think he initially supported its establishment? Did Azzam influence him?

MH: Abu Abdullah did briefly visit in 1984, and he went because Sayyaf was making a big circus with a battle in the Ali Khel area, which he put in a two-part video called Chawni One and Two. In that battle, they were firing the anti-aircraft gun, and they told me every day they were spending 2 million rupees on ammunition using this gun against the aircraft. This made me very angry because it was too much and it was very wasteful.

LF: Two million rupees a day, when the campaign in Paktia that Sayyaf vetoed was to cost 3 million rupees a month, correct?

MH: Yes. He spent too much. All they were doing was making a show for the video and for the Arab guests! This was because there was no supervision or accountability for how supplies were used or divided up and shared. Abu Abdullah soon realised the problem when he later visited the front without Sayyaf there and saw the real conditions.

Before then, Abu Abdullah just gave the money to Azzam to spend for the mujahidin. In fact, this was the idea Abu Abdullah initially liked and the reason he supported Maktab al-Khadamat because he thought the money would go directly to the mujahidin on the fronts. It did not, which he saw when he visited the front in 1986 and saw the extremely poor conditions of the mujahidin. He wondered where his money was going and thought it was a crime they were operating in such poor conditions.

LF: How about Azzam's motivations? I thought his support for establishing Maktab al-Khadamat centred on his desire to build unity between the various Afghan groups, and he believed the Arabs could do this if they could build the infrastructure and support necessary for the jihad. Is this correct? I also read Azzam thought the lack of Afghan ulama to support the jihad and educate the people and the mujahidin was a problem because so many had been martyred, and he wanted to help in this area. At least that was according to the account of his widow.[2]

MH: The thing is the ulama of Afghanistan had their own way of teaching and learning; they had their own schools. This was the special teaching of Islam, away from the governments and institutions. The purpose of Maktab al-Khadamat in the education area was to inject the teachings of Ikhwan Muslimin into a new generation of Afghans, and to inject the teachings of the Salafis. This caused a large divide in Afghanistan, and they are continuing to suffer the consequences of this.

LF: Was the Ikhwan Muslimin element really so influential?

MH: Yes, Azzam was Ikhwan, Sayyaf was the leader of Ikhwan in Afghanistan and Maktab al-Khadamat was essentially an Ikhwan project. Abu Abdullah too was initially Ikhwan.

LF: What of Sayyaf's motivations then? I thought he was seeking more religious support from Saudi Arabia and elsewhere, as well as higher levels of aid? But from what you've told me about the events leading up to Maktab al-Khadamat's creation it seems Sayyaf's support was at least in part to ensure he could capture a significant amount of funding and exercise influence over the direction of the organisation?

MH: Sayyaf realised that since two of the most powerful Arabs wanted to start this organisation it would be coming anyway, and so he wanted it to be near him. He agreed to support it under his name, his party and his leadership, in part because he was hoping most of the money would come to him. He was not happy about it, but having it near was the best option for him.

LF: I would like to divert a little here and ask you a question about your view of Sayyaf. You have made quite a lot of negative comments about Sayyaf and I want to ask you frankly whether your views on Sayyaf are influenced by the fact that he is now part of the Afghan government, while you favour the Taliban? Some readers will be wondering whether this has some influence on your accounts.

MH: When we talk about Jaji, I will tell you what Abu Hafs said to me about his experiences with Sayyaf. You will see that it is the same as Basil Muhammad's account of what Abu Hafs told him, and that was written before the Taliban came to power. So there were these problems with Sayyaf, and with others. In fact, as I have said, most of the Afghan yard was corrupt and this is why Mawlawi Mansur put into place his programme of long-term reform, which was the beginning of the Taliban.

LF: Okay that should make for an interesting discussion.

MH: Yes.

* * *

Maktab al-Khadamat was founded in October 1984 by Azzam with support from Sayyaf and funding from bin Laden. Azzam was the amir of Maktab al-Khadamat but he did not reside in Peshawar permanently because at that time he was still teaching in Islamabad. A deputy amir had day-to-day control of the organisation. Bin Laden too was not yet permanently based in the region, and although as founding financier he had a place on Maktab al-Khadamat's Shurah Council and Finance Committee, he held, at least formally, no special authority.

Maktab al-Khadamat was initially a small organisation, beginning with around a dozen or so members. It was also an organisation of leaders; at one time during its early period, when membership numbers reached thirty, half were designated as committee heads. With a small membership, most early activities focused on media, fundraising and religious education in support of the jihad and for the Afghan population. As it grew, Maktab al-Khadamat later also supported health and education initiatives, in partnership with charities, to assist Pakistan's Afghan refugee population.

By 1985 Maktab al-Khadamat had begun to expand and swelled rapidly after the 1987 Jaji battles, as it sought to facilitate an influx of foreign volunteers who arrived seeking to join the jihad. Even after Maktab al-Khadamat reached its peak, very few Arab-Afghans associated with the organisation had a military role or operated inside Afghanistan, with most working on logistics and support in Peshawar. By then, Maktab al-Khadamat had serious administrative problems and was fraught with allegations of corruption within its ranks.

* * *

LF: How widespread was the corruption problem within Maktab al-Khadamat, or was it more a case of mismanagement?

MH: There was some misbehaviour with the money. I think some of the people working there misused money. It was not common for all of them; it was a small group who came from the same country and the same area. Abu Abdullah was very angry.

* * *

In bin Laden's eyes, Maktab al-Khadamat's mismanagement prevented the jihad being better supported inside Afghanistan, an issue on which he had become more focused after his earlier visit to the Jaji front. He believed narrowing the organisation's focus and trying to improve the way it was managed would help to ensure military support and activities were prioritised and corruption eliminated. Azzam supported broadening Maktab al-Khadamat's activities because he believed this would help foster unity among Afghan groups, the lack of which was harming the jihad. Maktab al-Khadamat's activities outside the military realm continued despite bin Laden's disapproval, largely because by then Azzam had alternative sources of funding. This would prove important when in 1986 the two men's differences over the administration of Maktab al-Khadamat and how to support the Afghan war resulted in bin Laden's withdrawal of funding.

These differences came to a head when bin Laden moved to base himself in Peshawar to more closely supervise activities around the same time Azzam relocated from Islamabad for the same purpose. While their conflict was ostensibly over administrative issues within Maktab al-Khadamat, it was based on their deeply divergent beliefs about the purpose and function of the organisation, and the Arab-Afghan jihad in general.

This became apparent in their different opinions on where military aid and funding should be directed, how Arab training should be coordinated and how the Military Council of Maktab al-Khadamat should be administered. Their difference of opinion eventually resulted in bin Laden focusing on establishing his own independent group. Much of his desire to do so came because of earlier failed efforts at training the Arabs, and the conditions he witnessed on a visit to the front lines at Jaji.

Early Arab training and combat efforts

Early efforts to organisc training for the Arab-Afghans were unsuccessful. The most prominent of these efforts was the 1984 Badr 'camp', established with financing from a wealthy Saudi by the name of Saleh Kamel and with Abdullah Azzam as its nominal head, responsible for religious education.

* * *

MH: The first effort of the Arabs associated with Azzam to train publicly was in 1984, when the Badr camp was held in the Pabbi area on the southern outskirts of Peshawar, which was controlled by Sayyaf. Abdullah Azzam supervised the camp in aspects of religious guidance. He hoped that Afghans and Arabs would gather under the leadership of Sayyaf as the formal leader of jihad in Afghanistan, after he was named president of the Union of Mujahidin Parties (Ittihad i Islami Mujahidin Afghanistan).

The Badr camp was made especially for the Afghan mujahidin and was financed by a rich and famous Arab, Saleh Kamel, who had chosen Azzam as the spiritual guide for Arab and Afghan camp trainees. The immediate objective of the Badr camp was to bring together Afghans from rival fronts within a single programme and highly spiritual atmosphere offered by Azzam's lessons in the hope that hostilities between them would disappear. Abdullah Azzam was a traditional Islamic leader: he wanted the Afghans to sit together in one place and be friends, and to recite the Quran and pray at night and fast two days every week. He was seeking to encourage them to follow such religious practices and to sit together; not to train them how to fight.

It was also hoped the training would lead to the formation of a battalion of mujahidin, whose number would be 313—the same number as the Muslim army in the Battle of Badr. It is from here the name for the camp came. The camp did not concentrate on fighting and training. This is because those running the camp were themselves not fighters. Abdullah Azzam trained with Fatah, but he was not a good military man and did not have much in the way of real combat experience. That was Badr; the Arabs just went there to assist in that programme, which was to help build unity between the Afghan mujahidin. It was not helpful in any way inside Afghanistan, because after that 'training' the Afghans returned to their groups inside Afghanistan and kept working independently, the same way as before.

A number of Arabs did train in that camp and some of them had important roles in the phases of the conflict that followed. Generally speaking, the training was less than was required, and the focus was on the spiritual and moral side, rather than the military side. The camp did not achieve any of its objectives. The Afghans did not unite at all. While the Arabs did for a time gather around Sayyaf—as Azzam had hoped—they began to scatter away from him after the Battle of Jaji in 1987, which revealed his weak leadership and the corruption of Sayyaf's groups at the front. In fact, Abu Abdullah was the biggest reason they left Sayyaf. Abu Abdullah had made his own large contribution in that battle and had unintentionally exposed these flaws in Sayyaf's leadership and his groups.

Azzam was right on many things, but at the same time he did not do the job properly. Azzam was a very good speaker; and he gave excellent speeches because he could talk very well about the Quran, Sunnah and Islamic history. But this was not sufficient at that time, and in fact may have been misused in some places.

LF: How so?

MH: Because these speeches put the youth in the mood of loving to die; to go to paradise and not to care about anything else. Although training was given on how to use the weapons alongside this religious training, there was no training on tactics, or more importantly on the political side of the military work and the implications of this regionally and internationally.

Despite this, the experience of the Badr camp did show that the idea of training had taken hold among the Arab-Afghans of Peshawar. Still, there were those who rejected the need for training and considered it a 'secular' tendency, which contradicted the principle of 'putting our trust in God'. I remember in a meeting I had in 1986, one of the youths against training angrily said: 'The liberation of Afghanistan will come from ablution hands, not trained hands.'

LF: I presume this changed somewhat with Maktab al-Khadamat's formal establishment of the Sadda camp in 1986?

MH: Yes, although it was not really until after the 1987 Battle of Jaji that support for training really increased.

* * *

The establishment of Sadda camp by Maktab al-Khadamat

In mid-1986, Maktab al-Khadamat began looking to create its own separate camp for training Arab-Afghans, as efforts at other camps had not proven particularly successful. The Sadda camp was established after negotiations with Sayyaf to host it in the area of Sadda controlled by Sayyaf. What is not known about Maktab al-Khadamat's moving of resources to Sadda was that it had as much to do with Azzam's need for protection as it did with setting up training.

* * *

MH: The first training for Arabs alone was in the Sadda camp in the tribal area of Pakistan under Sayyaf's control. Azzam sought protection and refuge in Sayyaf's territory after Hekmatyar made strong threats against him. Hekmatyar was angry with Azzam because he thought Azzam was making propaganda in favour of Sayyaf and financial support of his activities. Burhanuddin Rabbani too was angry with Azzam, but unlike Hekmatyar, he did not resort to threats. Both Hekmatyar and Rabbani were angry that Azzam was giving too much money to Sayyaf and not supporting their organisations with anything. Hekmatyar said, 'I am going to kill him [Azzam]; he damaged our work, he took our money; Maktab al-Khadamat came to the mujahidin, and they took our money and behaved freely without asking or consulting us.'

Sayyaf was angry at Maktab al-Khadamat for similar reasons: for not getting enough money and supplies. Although when Sayyaf found out that his competitors did not like what had happened, and that leaders like Hekmatyar had threatened Azzam, Sayyaf told Azzam: 'Take refuge, go to Sadda, to my camp, you will be under my protection.'

During his security asylum in the Sadda camp Azzam thought of summoning a group of young Arabs in Peshawar to hold a religious/military session under his supervision. That session and others that followed were characterised by religious training, and the military training was weak.

In fact, in the early days of Sadda, before the arrival of Abu Burhan al-Suri, what Azzam created was a mosque, not a training camp.

The weakness of this training was evident when Azzam took those who had trained at Sadda to Khost after the end of the Battle of Zhawar in April 1986.

LF: This is the Brigade of the Humorous.

MH: Yes.

* * *

The 'Brigade of the Humorous', as the lore goes, was formed from those who had been through early training at Sadda. Azzam put out a mobilisation call for them to join him in the Battle of Zhawar. The brigade's poor levels of organisation as well as their unfamiliarity with the terrain saw the Afghans decline their participation—with some reports claiming the 'brigade' was in fact asked to leave the area.[3] The utter failure of the mission led Abu Hajr al-Iraqi to coin the name 'Brigade of the Humorous'.[4]

* * *

LF: I thought the brigade did see action.

MH: No. They were unable to even march in the mountains. That was clear practical proof that training at that time did not work as it should.

* * *

Maktab al-Khadamat's training fortunes soon improved when Abu Burhan al-Suri, a Syrian with military experience, took over the management of training at the Sadda camp and began his efforts to improve the quality of training offered.

* * *

MH: The arrival of the Syrian officer Abu Burhan in the summer of 1986 resulted in a transformation in the level of training of Arabs at Sadda. Abu Burhan was one of the two most important individuals who affected the course of Arab-Afghan training after 1985 when volunteer numbers began to increase. The other person was Ali Muhammad, an Egyptian American who worked with Tanzim al-Jihad and al-Qaeda, and we will talk about him later.

Abu Burhan was former Ikhwan Muslimin and among those who emigrated from Syria after the armed revolution against Hafiz al-Assad's regime in the early 1980s failed. Abu Burhan was a tough military man. I remember the shock I felt one day when I saw him smiling and on another occasion when he was caught hiding his concern for me when he argued against me assuming leadership of a major operation with the Arabs in Gardez in 1992. Abu Burhan argued against me leading the operation at a meeting he attended along with Abu Abdullah, Abu Hafs and Abu Ubaydah al-Banshiri among others. I misunderstood his stance in the beginning, but he explained in a sincere way that he was concerned for my safety. I did not expect that from him. He said to me that he argued to the others I should not lead the operation because, 'It is difficult to replace him if he is lost!' No one had shown such concern for me at any time during the war, with the exception of Haqqani once in 1979 and again in 1991.

The most important work Abu Burhan did outside of the training was his compilation of the 'Afghan Jihad' encyclopaedia, which Maktab al-Khadamat printed and distributed. The encyclopaedia included most of the training courses studied in the camp, or that should have been taught, had circumstances allowed. It was a unique work, and no work of its kind or anything similar appeared for that stage of the jihad in Afghanistan between 1979 and 1992.

Abu Burhan's participation stretched from 1986 until 1993. Although he stopped working in 1992, he continued for a year giving consultation to the young people who took over the management of the Khaldan camp in Khost, where training moved after the Sadda camp was closed. On his advice, the camp moved inside Afghanistan when Pakistan began to harass the Arabs and capture a few of them. After that, Abu Burhan left for Sudan.

Abu Burhan did not participate directly in the famous 1987 Jaji battle, but his students from Sadda participated. He also travelled to Jaji to provide some training there before the battle. Abu Burhan's students trained on some important weapons such as mortars and the rocket launcher, BM 12, and they received lessons in topography, which made them more skilled in surveillance and direct artillery fire. Although they were few in number, their participation was vital in that battle.

* * *

The establishment of Sadda camp reportedly caused significant concerns among some governments, particularly after explosives training was introduced. Later, Palestinian volunteers trained in explosives use and subsequently returned to use this knowledge in attacks against Israeli targets.

* * *

MH: Arab governments were attempting to block the emergence of any serious military training for young Arab volunteers, because they feared these youths might carry out armed activities when they returned to their countries. Saudi Arabia had the greatest fear of this occurring, and because it had a great influence on the government of Pakistan and Afghan organisations, it was able to block early attempts to train Arabs in special camps. The establishment of the Sadda camp came as a shock to the Saudi regime, because it could not monitor activities at Sadda as closely as it could at Pabbi in Peshawar where earlier efforts at training had been conducted. The Saudi regime had not expected this 'red line' would be crossed.

LF: Although training became more sophisticated under Abu Burhan's leadership, the mismanagement of Maktab al-Khadamat continued to impact upon the Sadda camp, and was among the reasons bin Laden sought to establish an independent training location. His attempts to do so in 1986 were repeatedly opposed and he also failed to find a suitable location. I wonder whether opposition to bin Laden's plans to establish an independent training location—one attempt at which was to try to start his own camp in the Sadda area—was in part because his doing so was essentially a reform effort, which might cast others in a bad light.

MH: In the beginning Abu Abdullah's efforts had a strong reform focus, but this came after he saw for himself the conditions at the fronts, and that the money that was being received by Maktab al-Khadamat was not reaching where it was needed inside Afghanistan. After he saw the fronts, Abu Abdullah's first priority was making sure the money reached there rather than establishing a new training camp. He wanted to separate his work from Maktab al-Khadamat and to work inside Afghanistan himself because that way he could make sure the money and the resources reached where he thought they were needed.

LF: This was when bin Laden went to work for Sayyaf and started on some construction projects to improve the conditions near the front? And this took place after his visit to the area, where he saw for himself how poor the conditions were?

MH: Yes.

LF: Bin Laden doesn't seem to have given up on his desire to start a separate Arab grouping though, which he subsequently did in an area of

Jaji that later became known as al-Masadah. I am just wondering how much the issue of corruption and squandered resources factored into his separation from Maktab al-Khadamat, and also how much it factored into resistance from some against him separating from Maktab al-Khadamat. It seems to me that corruption, initiatives at combating corruption and efforts to resist reform initiatives had a significant impact on the course of the jihad. Corruption seems to have played a major role in the establishment of several groups, not only Mawlawi Mansur's Taliban, but also Maktab al-Khadamat, which itself was inevitably corrupted.

MH: Yes, corruption played a very big role in the jihad and in the history of Arab and Afghan groups in the war against the Soviets, especially in Peshawar. It also played a very big role in Abu Abdullah's separation from Maktab al-Khadamat, because separating from the corrupt yard was one of the reasons al-Qaeda was established after the victory at Jaji.

5

JAJI AND THE ESTABLISHMENT OF AL-MASADAH

The Jaji region is a mountainous area close to the Pakistan border inside Afghanistan's Paktia province. Jaji became famous because of a battle in 1987 at a small base called al-Masadah, which bin Laden had established on a mountaintop in the area in late 1986. Against all odds the mujahidin at al-Masadah under bin Laden's command repelled a Soviet Special Forces-led attack. By doing so, they changed the course of history. As a result of this battle, bin Laden became the leading Arab-Afghan, and conditions were made ripe for the emergence of al-Qaeda as a splinter group of Maktab al-Khadamat.

How and why al-Masadah was established

We noted in Chapter 3 that bin Laden's earlier efforts to establish a training base separate to Maktab al-Khadamat came to nothing because of opposition to his plans, and his inability to find a suitable location. But in 1986 an opportunity to establish a base at Jaji presented itself while bin Laden was overseeing construction work for Sayyaf in the region. Bin Laden's construction work had begun after his seeing the poor conditions of the mujahidin in the area on an unsupervised visit, after which he decided to become more active inside Afghanistan. These direct engagements in projects at Jaji and elsewhere in Afghanistan resulted in bin Laden further distancing himself from Maktab al-Khadamat and its

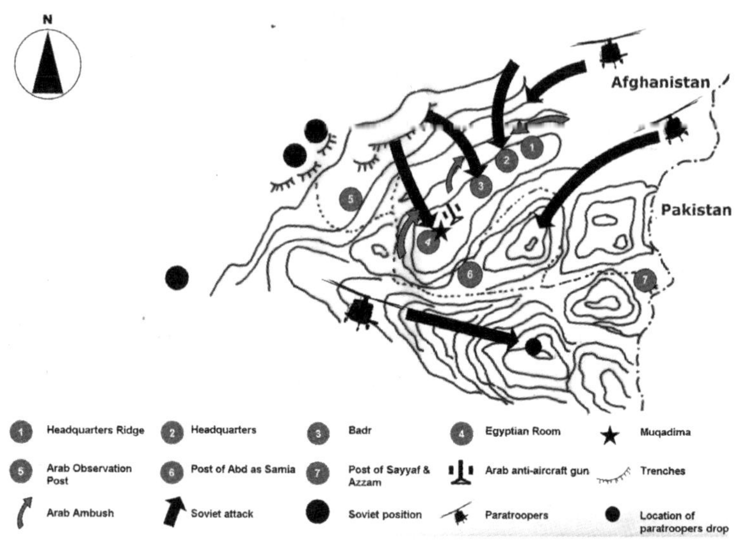

Fig 7: The battle of Jaji, 1987

mostly Peshawar- and Sadda-based activities, which he also ceased funding around this time.

Al-Masadah was identified after some youths working with bin Laden on the construction projects in Jaji became frustrated at their lack of involvement in military activities. These youths, some of whom were still in their teens, had mostly been direct-recruited by bin Laden and were anxious to see combat instead of working in construction. In order to placate them, bin Laden sent them on a scouting mission in the Jaji area to monitor enemy movements. It was on one of these missions in September 1986 that they identified a mountain site and surrounding area that would later come to be known as al-Masadah. At its peak, al-Masadah reportedly included several different sections or 'camps', although these were small and scattered in the surrounding area. Around seventy Arab-Afghans were based at al-Masadah, which was a significant population in view of the still low number of Arab-Afghans participating in the jihad.

Bin Laden's establishment of al-Masadah in October 1986—a month after the location was first scouted—was not without controversy. Many senior mujahidin were opposed to his idea of building a training base at al-Masadah with a permanently stationed force because of its exposed location and vulnerability to enemy attack. This did not deter bin Laden, who ignored their advice and ploughed his resources into building al-Masadah, which came under attack from Soviet and Afghan forces during Ramadan in May, 1987, resulting in one the most famous battles of the Arab-Afghans in the Afghan jihad.

* * *

MH: Abu Abdullah spent a large amount of money for Sayyaf in the Jaji area because at that time Sayyaf, as the head of the Union, was the legal amir for the Arab and the Afghan jihad, and because Abu Abdullah had seen the conditions of the mujahidin there on his trip to the area earlier in 1986. So Abu Abdullah started building a stronghold for Sayyaf in the area of Jaji near the border of Pakistan. He was making big tunnels for storing ammunition and weapons; he even made a good hospital, I heard.

When Abu Abdullah sent a group to scout the area, they found a mountain, a very strategic one. From this mountain, they could observe the valley and the garrison of Jaji. After they found the place, they went back to Abu Abdullah very excited, saying they had found a place that covered all the area. They told him, 'if we take this as our base we have a good position, and we can fire at every place and not just several places', and that was true. Abu Abdullah liked the site in Jaji from the first moment, just as he did in Tora Bora the first time he arrived in that area in 1996.

* * *

Bin Laden's own account of Jaji shows his liking for the site and belief in its utility. He told Basil Muhammad the 'brothers returned with the video … and I found it was as they described … the enemy's locations were exposed … every individual could be observed … we went there and I was really surprised as … it was overlooking … movements of the enemy's soldiers, tanks and supplies … I asked: why do the mujahidin not stay in this region? I was answered that the region was isolated and bombed many times last year … the Russians left it … because of the strong wind … the roads leading to this region become blocked by ice in the winter making it difficult to get supplies.'[1]

* * *

MH: The conditions at al-Masadah were exactly like Tora Bora, which was where Abu Abdullah retreated after the American invasion in late 2001. Al-Masadah was isolated, difficult to supply, and strong winds and ice blocked the roads leading to the region. In both instances, Abu Abdullah's selection of locations put his men in a trap.

LF: Yes, there are some striking similarities between the two locations from that perspective. It seems that although al-Masadah offered an excellent vantage point, it was very vulnerable as a location for a permanent camp. I think you may have said that it was ideal for guerrilla warfare, but not for a permanent base.

MH: Yes, although I should add I was referring to the back base, not the front mountain where they wanted to build the camp.

LF: You were referring to al-Arin?

MH: Yes, although some people came to refer to the entire area as al-Masadah. Anyway, Abu Abdullah was thinking about this area in terms of conventional warfare and it was very unsuitable for this type of warfare.

LF: Indeed. Bin Laden apparently sent a message to Sayyaf and told him the location had great military importance and he wanted to construct a road with trenches to protect the mujahidin from bombardment. He seemed to have an enduring fascination with building trenches and truly believed they worked. I remember him recommending the mujahidin in Iraq use trenches, which I thought was not the most well thought out advice in the face of uncontested US airpower and the geography of much of Iraq.

It seems that when bin Laden had his unlikely victory at Jaji, it reinforced his belief in the effectiveness of using trenches, which as we know, and will later discuss, had bad consequences when he tried to do it again at Tora Bora in late 2001. When bin Laden offered his advice to the Iraqi mujahidin, he mentioned how the Tora Bora battle was a success because of the trenches. It seemed to me to have disastrous results. It did not achieve what he wanted, there were huge supply issues, people died or were captured trying to retreat and, unlike at Jaji, he did not stay and fight, he left.

MH: Yes, Abu Abdullah liked the idea of trenches—at Jaji, Jalalabad, Kabul and Tora Bora. This trench idea of his was not even conventional warfare; it was out-dated World War I-style tactics. Of course, even in guerrilla warfare there is a use for digging and concealment. As the Sun Tzu saying goes, 'The general who is skilled in defence hides in the most secret recesses of the earth; he who is skilled in attack flashes forth from the topmost heights of heaven.' Digging played a big role in Afghanistan—especially the caves and also the trenches.

Trenches are useful but you should not design your entire defence around them, or dig a trench and sit in it and occupy it. In Afghanistan, it was not the kind of warfare where there were two lines. Trenches were useful for concealment or supply networks, or for firing posts, but not to hold and defend positions. Abu Abdullah wanted to build trenches for holding and defending positions, and he wanted to build a base on the highest place where he could see the entire valley. But of course, the enemy would want to take his base, especially since after the Arabs finished constructing the base, they brought some guns and heavy machine guns, which attracted the enemy's attention. In fact, this is what happened; they attracted attention, and in 1987, the battle came.

Many of us also thought the mountain base should not be permanent, but instead the rear area should be used for guerrilla attacks, because the location where they chose to establish the al-Masadah base could not be effectively protected on a permanent basis, without a huge effort. To do so would take up valuable resources that were needed elsewhere.

The Jaji adventure ended up costing Abu Abdullah millions of dollars; not rupees, but dollars! For something that was eventually abandoned for the very reasons everyone warned; millions of dollars on what? In Paktia, three years earlier the mujahidin were budgeting for 3 million rupees for a month. It was a waste of money.

LF: I did not fully understand the extent of the waste until you told me the amount spent at al-Masadah compared to what it would have cost to support an entire campaign for a month in Paktia. I wonder if this perhaps explains some of the 'corrupt' Afghan practices that annoyed Abu Hafs and Abu Ubaydah so much during the Battle of Jaji. If the Afghans saw Arabs wasting money, perhaps this encouraged them towards these practices. I read also that the waste of resources angered Abdul Aziz Ali and he spoke of how some Afghans were annoyed.[2]

MH: Yes, and if you remember from the interviews given to Basil Muhammad from this time, Abdul Aziz Ali commented that he thought Abu Abdullah was 'throwing his money into dust'.[3]

LF: Yes, Basil Muhammad quoted him as saying so, and Amin al-Haq, who I think eventually came to provide very important support for al-Qaeda, told Basil Muhammad that the Afghans looked at what bin Laden was doing at al-Masadah as 'an example of someone who takes money and throws it into the sea'.[4]

From Amin's account, some Afghans were not happy about all of the equipment going to al-Masadah. The Afghans knew the area could, as it had before, easily fall into Soviet hands and the equipment would be lost. Some believed that the Arabs 'had money and ... wanted to have fun', saying, 'let them have fun with their money and dig into the mountains'.[5] Apparently, quite a few Arab mujahidin had a similar view.[6]

MH: Yes. It was not widely supported, but when Abu Abdullah got an idea into his head there was little anyone could do, because unlike everyone else he had the money to just go ahead and act as he wished, even if there was opposition to his plans.

* * *

Opposition to bin Laden's establishment of al-Masadah

Opposition to bin Laden's decision to establish a base at Jaji came from both military and financial perspectives. Abu Hajr al-Iraqi, commenting on this some years later, remarked: 'The people around him did not agree, and told him that: you came here to make tunnels to protect the Afghans ... so you do not have anything to do with the military operations.'[7] Despite such opposition and the military inexperience of most of the men with him at that time, bin Laden was determined to push forward with establishing a permanent base at Jaji.

* * *

LF: What is your recollection of efforts to convince bin Laden to rethink establishing al-Masadah because of the danger it posed? It is my understanding that the main objections were both financial and military. It was thought al-Masadah did not have the strategic value bin Laden claimed, particularly not in terms of the cost of building infrastructure at the base, and defending it when many of the youth were not adequately trained. As a result, some figures lobbied bin Laden to send people for basic training at Sadda before they were dispatched to al-Masadah, because some had no training and could not even defend themselves.

Is it correct that bin Laden kept arguing the main priority was to build the base because it was overlooking enemy territory, and since his primary focus was on construction the youth did not need training? Were you among those who tried to convince bin Laden to work elsewhere, and to put his resources in places where they were more needed?

MH: I was. They actually asked our group at Khost to join them, which at that stage included Abu Hafs al-Masri—although Abu Ubaydah was already with Abu Abdullah. They were asking people to come to participate and Abu Khalid al-Masri called us in Miranshah and asked if we would come. Abu Hafs initially agreed to go—but my friend Abdul Rahman and I said we would think about it. We decided not to go; we were worried that everyone was rushing to join them but there was no planning, no strategy and very little organisation. We spoke to Abu Hafs about it; he said he would go but come back if the conditions were not suitable. We knew he would not come back.

LF: I find it fascinating Abu Hafs stayed despite his objections to having a permanent base there. He was not alone in this either. Abu Khalid al-Masri, who had called Abu Hafs to come, and Abdul Aziz Ali and others all had objections, and in fact meetings were convened in Islamabad to discuss how to convince bin Laden to stop this project, and how to minimise the damage he could cause.

MH: Many Arab-Afghans tried to convince Abu Abdullah to reconsider his project in Jaji and more than one meeting was held about it in Islamabad. It was not that we thought the area was worthless, but most of us were concerned about establishing a permanent base on the mountain. Guerrilla warfare was the only thing suitable for that area on a long-term basis—and ironically, the use of guerrilla tactics is what won the Battle of Jaji under the command of the famous Qais camp graduates Abu Hafs and Abu Ubaydah. The two of them made use of the lessons they learned in the Zhawar battle they shared in 1986, which was that static defence is not enough and ambushes are necessary to defend the rear base of the guerrilla fighters.

LF: Yes, I recall reading what Abdul Aziz Ali had to say on the matter where he said the location was only suitable for experienced military men and for hit-and-run tactics, and that if bin Laden wanted to stay he should leave only a few men for hit-and-run attacks, not a large base full of men. According to him, bin Laden initially agreed to abandon the area as a permanent base but then changed his mind.[8]

MH: Even Abu Hafs and Abu Ubaydah thought the area was too difficult to defend on a permanent basis but that the area was suitable for guerrilla operations, particularly the rear area. They were not totally against having some position at Jaji. After all, they were students of the Qais camp and they saw the value of the location for guerrilla attacks. But they did not support permanently stationing forces there, or operating a training base in the area—which is what Abu Abdullah wanted to do. They, along with the other military men of experience, tried to convince him of this—but they failed. Instead, of course, they ended up staying there and becoming the founders of al-Qaeda, along with Abu Abdullah.

Here we are touching on a very important point, which helps us to understand how Abu Abdullah was thinking then, but also how he came to think later. Abu Abdullah became stronger in his will when he was opposed by the mainstream; this made him feel like he was right, and he insisted to continue his way. Jaji was a prime example of this, because most of the people around him told him it was not a good idea to establish a permanent base there but he insisted on continuing.

When they then won the Jaji battle in 1987, Abu Abdullah became certain of his way. He became more certain of ignoring advice after the Jalalabad disaster in 1989, when he followed the mainstream and he lost. Abu Abdullah came to believe that if he opposed the mainstream, he won. This is why he pushed ahead with 9/11 in spite of everyone from the old leadership opposing it. He was against the mainstream there too.

LF: Yes, it certainly seems that way. In the case of Jaji, some people were appointed to try to lobby bin Laden to change his mind about making the base there. Abu Hafs al-Masri was among them, and he later made the observation to Basil Muhammad that bin Laden just kept asking people for their opinion on the issue, until he eventually found someone who agreed with him on one part of what he was saying, and that is how he justified his position and staying.[9]

MH: Yes, I think Abu Abdullah used what some people had said about the rear area having value as an early warning position, or as a location for guerrilla warfare, to justify building a base on the front mountain. He would have done it anyway; as I said, Abu Abdullah liked to go against the mainstream.

LF: It doesn't seem that anyone could have really stopped bin Laden. Abdullah Azzam, who was also among those opposed to al-Masadah, had an interesting observation about bin Laden in relation to Jaji, when he said bin Laden's 'enthusiasm and money enabled him to do what he wanted to do'.[10]

MH: Yes, that is true. Abu Abdullah's money did allow him to do what he wanted. He was not the best commander among the Arabs, but he was the richest. Eventually that put him in front of everyone, even Abdullah Azzam, especially after the Jaji battle.

LF: With most experienced Arab-Afghans against the idea of a permanent base at al-Masadah, why did some of them go to Jaji? I remember reading a decision was made at one of the Islamabad meetings to try to minimise the damage bin Laden could cause.[11] Were you at that meeting, and do you think the others went to Jaji as a kind of damage control? Is that why Abu Hafs and Abu Ubaydah stayed? As I understand it, when bin Laden refused to leave al-Masadah, Abu Ubaydah al-Banshiri decided to try to help him, not because he supported the project, but because he was trying to reduce the damage, and that is how he became involved.

Abu Ubaydah asked Abu Hafs to join him because he was having difficulty with the volunteers at Jaji who were impatient to see combat and he needed Abu Hafs' help because discipline was a bit of a problem. I think you had a memo in one of your books from Abu Ubaydah after Jaji, which to me seemed to show that he was arguing for something like a broader disciplined training programme.[12]

MH: It is an interesting point. Yes, discipline was a serious issue but Abu Ubaydah and Abu Hafs did a very good job under difficult circumstances. They tried to control the youth and train them in the severe way that creates discipline. Then the youth would go to Abu Abdullah and he would be gentle with them, perhaps because he feared they might leave—and the work of Abu Ubaydah and Abu Hafs became harder. So in the circumstances they faced, they did a fantastic job. Al-Masadah would have fallen in the 1987 Jaji battle without their training and their leadership.

* * *

The Jaji battle and its aftermath

The Jaji battle took place in May 1987 when Soviet Special Forces supported by Afghan government forces attacked al-Masadah. Bin Laden had been repeatedly warned of the dangers of an attack on the area, and despite the best efforts of Abu Hafs and Abu Ubaydah to train the youth, the 'force' of fighters at the al-Masadah base was woefully unprepared. Nonetheless, against the odds, and with the help of other Arabs and Afghans, the attack was repelled.

* * *

MH: Al-Masadah was attacked by the Soviets with a combined group, but, mainly at the beginning, the Soviets sent their Special Forces to al-Masadah. After that the regime's Afghan troops came. The fighting was at very close range. Jaji was a fantastic battle and something very big happened there on the mountains. It was maybe the first and last time there was man-to-man combat between the Arabs and the Soviets during the fighting in Afghanistan.

The engagements of the Arab 'foot soldiers' led by Abu Hafs and Abu Ubaydah, and their face-to-face fighting with soldiers from the Soviet Special Forces at and in the areas around al-Masadah, were dazzling victories, the likes of which had not previously occurred and were not repeated with the Arabs in the rest of the war. They in fact stole the light from the rest of the Arabs' military participation in the Afghan war.

The contributions of those Arabs who worked in heavy weapons and surveillance were no less important than the foot soldiers, although they were less spectacular in terms of media coverage. It is enough that one of them gained a title that remained with him for the rest of his life because of his skill in using the rocket launcher in that battle. This was Abu Abdul-Rahman al-BM, who was killed along with most of his family by an American drone strike in Waziristan. But Abu Hafs and Abu Ubaydah were the true heroes of that battle. Abu Hafs killed one soldier in hand-to-hand combat and his and Abu Ubaydah's group killed five or six Special Forces troops in one ambush. Abu Hafs and Abu Ubaydah led the battle and did a truly excellent job under the flag of Abu Abdullah, who also shared in combat.

Once, Abu Abdullah was sitting there on the mountain with a small group when he found the Russians a few yards away from him approaching through the trees. They fought against each other for some time, and I think this was the first and last time Abu Abdullah fired his weapon in combat in Afghanistan. After this battle, Abu Abdullah became first among the Arabs. He, Abu Ubaydah and Abu Hafs became the heroes, and from that they started to form their own organisation.

LF: It is often assumed Azzam participated in the Jaji battle and sent forces from Sadda to support bin Laden. Apparently, Sayyaf and other senior Afghan leaders like Hekmatyar also provided support to the battle. What was Azzam's role and how much support did the Afghan leaders provide?

MH: There were other Arabs and Afghan mujahidin who did participate in the battle, but the main role was played by the Arabs at al-Masadah. Azzam did not directly participate in this battle. He was up in the mountains with Sayyaf, watching; although he did dispatch people to support Abu Abdullah once it became clear that he was not going to leave the area. In the beginning, Azzam, like others, did not support Abu Abdullah forming anything in Jaji. He was against establishing the al-Masadah camp, he was against the Battle of Jaji, he was against it all, but when the battle came, he supported it. It was like what happened in the war in 2001. Everyone was against Abu Abdullah doing something because of the consequences it would bring, but when the consequences came, they all supported him.

LF: Why? Why would people like Azzam and the other Arab-Afghans support someone who had not listened to their advice and whose activities had endangered people? And again on 9/11, which I am sure we will talk about later.

MH: This question was facing us at the time of Jaji. I think it was because Abu Abdullah was a very honest man and very religious and he gave up everything. He was very rich but he came by himself to Afghanistan and he did not need anything from jihad. Everyone came to trust him, and people thought that they could not leave him to be hurt alone, and so they could not leave him. Then, of course, there was another element too—people thought they should keep near to him because he was a source of money. Tanzim al-Jihad was the most honest about this. They said, 'Abu Abdullah needs men, we need money', and so they thought they should keep close to him. In fact, they tried to influence him but he ended up influencing them, which really means that money is stronger than anything else.

As for 9/11, it was very important. Everyone was asking this question to themselves, but the answer was the same for almost everyone. What everyone was afraid of had already happened: the war had started, which was what we all feared. There was no use for questioning who was responsible because the war had already come, and there was a need to stand united and fight, and that is what happened in most cases.

A higher standard of unity came among the Arabs after the war started in 2001. But people did not understand this war would be different. Everybody was imagining it would be in the style of the war against the Soviets; they thought they could sit and make camps like they did in Afghanistan during the first war, and fight from there. They thought they were going to repeat this experience; that they could go any place and fight like before, and there was only one person who was angry and thinking the opposite.

LF: I presume this person was you?

MH: Yes. I was very sad and I created some problems at that time and we will talk more about this later. To return to our talk about Jaji, some people did come to 'support' Abu Abdullah, but most of it was symbolic support. Azzam, for example, stayed up on the mountains with Sayyaf, whose role in Jaji was not good. In fact, after Jaji, Sayyaf became weakened because the battle made clear to all the Arabs that Sayyaf was rubbish; that he was a betrayer.

LF: How so?

MH: Abu Hafs and Abu Ubaydah saw first-hand the corruption of Sayyaf and the other leaders. All of them were in Jaji; the main one was Sayyaf, but the others like Hekmatyar and Rabbani were there, and they were also very corrupt and had a very negative impact. They did not co-operate with the Arabs. Hekmatyar and Rabbani did not share in the battle: they only provided a little support. Mostly, they just sat there watching and waiting for the Arabs to discover that Sayyaf was not the leader they thought he was. Sayyaf tried to betray the Arabs and make their efforts fail. He tried to control the times of the operation; he promised he would provide them with artillery cover and did not; he promised he would supply them with ammunition and he did not; and he tried to give the orders of the battle, which Abu Hafs al-Masri, who was one of the main commanders, hated. Abu Hafs was very stubborn about this and very severe.

LF: Yes, I remember reading about what Abu Hafs had to say—particularly when Sayyaf attempted to take control over the kind of groups Abu Hafs was trying to dispatch.[13]

MH: After Jaji, Abu Abdullah shifted his trust from Sayyaf to Hekmatyar, who did provide a little support in the battle. He wanted to shift to Khost to co-operate with Hekmatyar, who he thought was a big leader and senior Ikhwan person. It was a serious mistake Abu Abdullah made.

Exclusion of the Afghans

LF: Is the behaviour of the Afghan party leaders part of the reason why Afghans were excluded from Jaji, and later from al-Qaeda? Bin Laden and the Arabs at al-Masadah expelled a Shia Afghan commander from Jaji; why was it that Afghans were excluded?

MH: After Jaji, something bad did come in the thinking of al-Qaeda towards the Afghans, especially Abu Hafs al-Masri and Abu Ubaydah al-Banshiri, because they suffered a lot in the Jaji battle and saw some Afghans behaving very poorly. Some of the Afghans were traitors, some of them were spies and some of them left the battle at critical moments.

LF: Obviously after Jaji there were some issues of trust, particularly in relation to the leadership, but I am just wondering why lower-level training also excluded the Afghans?

MH: After the Jaji battle Abu Abdullah, Abu Hafs and Abu Ubaydah started to make their own training camps for the Arabs; it was their first time to do that. What Abu Abdullah wanted to do was to make his own training camp because previously the Arabs were in the Badr camp with the Afghans, which was an unsuccessful effort, or they trained by themselves under Azzam in the Sadda camp. But it doesn't mean that Abu Abdullah's intent was to push the Afghans out.

LF: I noticed Abu Ubaydah's memo did not mention the Afghans in his training outline—except as guards for the camps.[14] If memory serves there were few if any Afghan members of al-Qaeda, except perhaps for Amin al-Haq.

MH: In the beginning, before the Battle of Jaji, Abu Abdullah wanted to recruit the Arabs to join him and unite to fight together because they were scattered everywhere. There were many organisations and he wanted to gather them and form one group to fight together. In this point, he was correct. It was one of the main issues that made him a strong figure within the Arabs. He wanted to build a strong military force that would fight together with the Afghans; to form it with the Afghans, to fight together, and to teach them together. It was thought at that time that doing so would give more benefits to the Arabs and to the Afghans.

This changed after the Battle of Jaji when al-Qaeda was formed. Abu Abdullah's focus changed to building a training camp or a training institute and its training focus was for outside Afghanistan, not inside. Al-Qaeda turned radically towards training and away from combat and field involvement, which when it took place was treated more as a training exercise.

In al-Qaeda's camps, thousands of young Arabs trained, regardless of whether they had joined al-Qaeda. The Afghans, who were still fighting to liberate their country, did not have a share in al-Qaeda's camps, which were restricted to Arabs and some al-Qaeda allies who joined it from the non-Arab groups—although their numbers were very limited. Al-Qaeda did hire a number of Afghans in logistics, but it did not include Afghans in its membership. Among al-Qaeda's staff were countless Afghans who were very close to its leaders, and because of this, they saw themselves as honorary members of al-Qaeda.

LF: But how about the Shia Afghan commander who had previously been based at Jaji and was asked to leave the area? Do you know why this happened?

MH: That was Abd as-Samia. It was not Abu Abdullah's idea to push him out, but the Arabs around Abu Abdullah said: 'We do not need Abd as-Samia here.' It was not a nice thing to do; he was a good figure, a strong figure but he was Shia. This caused some of the Salafi youth in al-Qaeda to argue against his presence in the area and unfortunately Abu Abdullah let a good part of his leadership at that time be dictated by the youths around him and a fear of them leaving him.

On leadership and lessons: the dangers of the Jaji success

LF: Your mention of bin Laden letting his leadership be dictated in part by the youths around him is similar to his own relationship with Arab-Afghan figures, and the leaders of some Afghan groups in Peshawar. Those leaders were fearful of bin Laden leaving them and saying negative things about them, which is why they tolerated his activities or agreed to his plans—even when some of them were dangerous. Bin Laden was young and impetuous and wealthy, which meant there was probably more reason for the leaders in Peshawar to let their leadership be dictated by his whims.

In that context, I find it fascinating that once bin Laden had followers at Jaji, despite his still young age and his significant wealth and influence, he too ended up letting his leadership be influenced by the youth. He feared them thinking badly of him, or leaving him and then saying negative things about him, which would harm his project. To me, this indicates that a fear of the youth and a fear of reputational harm or loss of status in some ways transcended financial power because on the bottom line we find the same thing: the young, brash and impetuous youths were ultimately shaping the decisions that were made in the Arab-Afghan jihad.

It also seems that because of this fear there was a tendency to cover up negative issues, or problems, which meant advice from more pragmatic and experienced leaders was being drowned out if what they had to say was not popular. So, advice that urged caution and restraint, and planning and strategy—things not so popular with the young and impetuous—was often drowned out. In fact, it seems a lot of good advice and initiatives were ignored or side-lined out of a fear of the youth's reaction and their negative sentiments making their way back to funders and potential new volunteers in the Gulf. I think we can see this too in the aftermath of Jaji, because it seems to have been presented as a battle with no flaw.

From what I have read, there was no discussion afterwards on what had gone wrong at Jaji, or what could be fixed, or improved. This might explain, I think, how the Jaji victory became the stuff of myth: unquestioned and unquestionable, and how it led bin Laden to believe that the ability of his forces at al-Masadah to withstand and defeat the Soviet assault changed the course of the war. In fact, it seems bin Laden came to believe his drawing in of the Soviets and defeat of them at al-Masadah was among the reasons the Soviets decided to withdraw from Afghanistan.

What are your thoughts on this?

MH: This is similar to what they also said about how they succeeded to draw America in to be involved in Afghanistan and Iraq. 'We succeeded,' they said, which was completely wrong. They said the same thing at al-Masadah: 'We succeeded and because of that the Soviets ran from Afghanistan.' This is rubbish and it led Abu Abdullah to believe that he could win the war against the Americans in small battles in the trenches of Tora Bora Mountain, as he believed he had defeated the Soviet Union in the trenches of al-Masadah in Jaji. Al-Qaeda's contribution to the huge war against the Soviets and their allies, which lasted for more than thirteen years, can be regarded as modest. In the Battle of Jaji there were fifteen Arab martyrs, and not all them were followers of Abu Abdullah because al-Qaeda had not yet formed.

I think after Jaji in 1987, the danger of success became clear. It was a great success; no one can challenge that. But this great success also had the seeds of failure and defeat within it because there was no review of the good and the bad from the battle. Nobody from the Arabs there analysed the battle; it was as if analysis was given up, even though there were some shortcomings in that great success.

I wrote about them; I tried to put it in front of the leaders and I tried to discuss it with some of the rising generation, but they were not ready to hear it. The leaders said, 'You can't talk about mistakes while the people feel they defeated the Russians. Nobody is even ready to listen to you.'

So I think you are right about the fear of negativity. The problem was these mistakes went unchecked and they got bigger and bigger, and in Jalalabad there was a huge disaster and defeat. Abu Abdullah could not even believe that he was defeated and he lost a group of his best followers at that time. I was very angry, because some of those who were lost in the battle were my friends from Khost and they were marvellous. They were gone for nothing. They were gone because no one wanted to challenge this success story and learn from their mistakes.

As for a fear of the youth, I will give you another example of this with Abu Abdullah, which also had very severe consequences. When Mullah Omar asked me to reach out to Iran to discuss opening new routes, Abu Abdullah also spoke with me about al-Qaeda investigating routes through Iran. Then the youth reacted because they were against Iran and Abu Abdullah told me 'remove it from the page', because he was fearful of the youths' reaction. He meant, 'let's not ever speak of this again'.

Of course, it turned out that al-Qaeda desperately needed such routes after the Americans invaded in 2001 and many people were captured because these routes had not been developed. You know, the Americans have listed me as a terrorist because I supposedly arranged the military co-operation of al-Qaeda with Iran about such routes! It never happened because Abu Abdullah was too afraid of the reaction of the youths who were against Iran. He let his leadership be guided by the views of these Salafi youths.

LF: Yes, I agree with you. Regarding the transit routes with Iran—you are right about al-Qaeda not having developed routes of its own in that period. A few years ago I developed a little fascination with mapping them for a research project I was doing for my thesis and it was very clear the routes al-Qaeda used were built and controlled by another Arab-Afghan network, which al-Qaeda was forced to use in the period up to 2001 because it did not have its own. But we will talk more about that later.

Returning to Jaji, it seems so much of both bin Laden's personality and leadership traits were solidified in that battle or in its aftermath, and also a lot of his thinking. Bin Laden's belief that his victory at Jaji was in large part responsible for driving the Soviets out of Afghanistan meant he did not look at the shortcomings of this battle, and led to the hubris surrounding his involvement in the failed Jalalabad campaign, as well as the future strategies he put in place against the United States.

I want to ask what you think would have happened if Jaji had been a big defeat instead of a victory? If bin Laden, Abu Hafs and Abu Ubaydah were heroes because they had an unlikely victory in spite of the opposition to building the base, what would have happened if they had lost? Do you think this would have affected their credibility to the point that history would be very different?

MH: It would have been very different. There would have been no al-Qaeda, at all. Al-Qaeda was made from the battle of Jaji. The start of al-Qaeda was in Jaji, and its downfall was in Jalalabad, and that is the real history of al-Qaeda. After that, it was something else. After Jalalabad al-Qaeda became something meaningless; it became a football at the legs of the Americans in a global game and new world order and Abu Abdullah lost control of everything. He lost the initiative in everything but this battle at Jaji, which was fantastic. But they did not learn from it.

LF: I agree with you about the failure to draw lessons. It seems to me the Jaji battle made bin Laden even more convinced that a military approach was the solution and there was no need for politics or religious education or aid, which made the differences between him and Azzam even greater. So much so that in some respects I have come to see al-Qaeda as a splinter group of Maktab al-Khadamat, because after Jaji all bin Laden seemed interested in was the military aspect of jihad. He seemed to forget jihad was more than just fighting.

MH: Yes, Abu Abdullah was focused on fighting. After the Jaji battle, and its great success, he initially thought about making a platform for gathering the Arabs together for a big strike force or a big *tanzim*, a multinational *tanzim*, where he would train the Arabs and push them to the battlefield.

6

CONFUSED ORIGINS

AL-QAEDA'S POST-JAJI EMERGENCE AND THE ARAB ADVISORY COUNCIL

The platform bin Laden wanted to make for gathering Arabs together evolved to become al-Qaeda—an organisation he founded, funded and over which he exercised absolute authority. In essence al-Qaeda was a splinter group of Maktab al-Khadamat—even in the brief period it focused on training Arabs for battle in Afghanistan before changing direction to focus on preparing trainees to participate in activities outside of Afghanistan. Al-Qaeda grew from the Jaji battles, but following a disastrous defeat at Jalalabad in the summer of 1989 it all but disintegrated—after which time another incarnation of the group took form. This has led to significant confusion as to al-Qaeda's actual origins, size, evolution and early direction, as well as who was involved in its initial establishment.

* * *

LF: The stories of how al-Qaeda was founded differed widely until the 2001 trial by the United States of the suspects in al-Qaeda's 1998 African embassy bombings. Jamal al-Fadl was a key witness at the trial, providing information about al-Qaeda's early structure and activities. He left al-Qaeda in the mid-1990s after being caught stealing money, and then approached the United States for protection in return for information. His testimony, along with the discovery in 2002 of digitally archived paperwork that appeared to document al-Qaeda's founding, forms the basis of much of what is publicly known about al-Qaeda's early years. The paperwork was discovered in a raid of the Sarajevo office of the Benevolence International Foundation, a charity staffed by and with long-standing links to a number of veteran Arab-Afghans.

Not all of the material seized in the raid related to al-Qaeda, but a folder called 'Tareekh Osama' (the history of Osama) had minutes from a series of meetings that investigators concluded showed the founding of al-Qaeda. These minutes also appeared to support Jamal al-Fadl's testimony, and since American prosecutors admitted them as evidence in the January 2003 trial of Enaam Arnaout, they have been widely accepted as marking the beginnings of al-Qaeda.[1]

However, these documents do not cover al-Qaeda's earlier activity in the period 1987 to 1988, following the Jaji battle. They have also done little to stop the widespread belief that Abdullah Azzam was involved in, inspired or even directly instigated the establishment of al-Qaeda. As a result, a great deal of myth still surrounds how, when and why al-Qaeda was formed.

The how, when and why of al-Qaeda's formation

LF: In my view the official interpretation of al-Qaeda's alleged 'founding documents' has contributed to the confusion about al-Qaeda's origins. These documents were alleged at trial to have been al-Qaeda's 'founding documents':

- 'Finding Aid: Tareekh Osama 122–123', containing notes from an 11 August 1988 meeting and which I refer to as Document One;[2]
- 'Finding Aid: Tareekh Osama 127–127a', containing notes summarising meetings between during 17 and 20 August 1988 and which I refer to as Document Two.[3]

There are other documents relevant to al-Qaeda's history, which to my knowledge were not included in the evidence presented at trial. Document Three is called 'Finding Aid: Tareekh Osama 128–135', and contains the minutes of meetings among the Arab-Afghans on 17, 18 and 20 August 1988.[4] Document Four is called 'Finding Aid: Tareekh Osama 91' and Document Five 'Finding Aid: Tareekh Osama 93'.[5] They are of unknown authorship but contain an outline of issues relating to the Arab-Afghan yard.

In Document One, the government translation shows Abu Rida al-Suri and bin Laden talking in an 11 August 1988 meeting about the establishment of 'new military work', but in the translation 'work' has been crossed out and the word 'group' written in.[6]

MH: In the Arabic copy it does not say 'new military group', it says 'new military work'; it means new military work.[7]

LF: So the discussion is not about establishing a new organisation but rather new military work. That is a significant difference, particularly viewed in the context of Documents Two and Three, which show an Arab-Afghan Advisory Council was formed to distribute the military work in Peshawar.[8]

In Document One, the translation also records bin Laden as saying, 'we have not started an organisation', and he and Abu Rida talk about how much progress had been made in the military work.[9] This comment seems to lead people to assume the military work bin Laden and al-Suri discuss is in fact a conversation about establishing the al-Qaeda organisation.

It has since been claimed by Wael Julaydan who was a leading figure in Maktab al-Khadamat that Abdullah Azzam, Abu Hafs Abu Ubaydah, Abu Hajr and Sayyid Imam also attended this 11 August meeting and that he was there too.[10] The author to whom he indirectly made those claims (the conversation was conducted via an intermediary) contends that the meeting was called specifically to form a new organisation—al-Qaeda.[11]

MH: To my knowledge this meeting in 1988 was not to form al-Qaeda, because the organisation was already in the process of being established. It was to form a joint Arab Council to oversee the work in the Arab-Afghan yard, which at that time had a number of issues relating to mismanagement and disorganisation, as well as disagreements as to who should be in charge of what.

LF: Yes, that was my interpretation too, particularly since bin Laden's remark looks to be part of a conversation about the performance of the Arab-Afghans: how time had passed and things were still not organised and goals were not met in the military work. In that context, the conversation looks to be about solidifying what was already in place for al-Qaeda, and streamlining training and membership selection processes, as well as planning and coordinating the work.

This becomes clearer when looking at Documents Two and Three, which show discussions being held not for establishing a new organisation, but for an Advisory Council to divide up the military work between the Arab-Afghans at Sadda, among others.[12] This work was to be overseen by the Advisory Council's Military Committee, and al-Qaeda's own programme.[13] Both Document Two and Three appear to show an Advisory Council with an oversight role operating at that time, and comprised of members of Maktab al-Khadamat and al-Qaeda members.[14] Its role was to coordinate the military work of the various Arab-Afghan groups in Peshawar.[15]

It this way, the Advisory Council seems to have represented a 'new distribution in Peshawar', of work and possibly also groups, while at the same time overseeing this distribution—at least on paper.[16] Document Three shows some issues with leadership and authority within the Advisory Council.[17]

MH: The pages are not in order in Document Three.

LF: No, but when you put the pages of Document Three in order you can see an interesting discussion about 'no group without an amir' and talking about 'obedience to one'.[18] This is then followed by the note 'One amir not two opinions', which seems to indicate there is some sort of leadership problem.[19] The document also shows a number of problems pertaining to the Arab-Afghan situation.

MH: Yes, there were many issues at that time.

LF: Document Two is a summary of what took place at the Advisory Council meeting—as well as some additional notes relating to al-Qaeda's work. In the document it is written: 'work of al-Qaeda commenced' on 10 September 1988, 'with a group of 15 brothers, including nine administrative brothers', who are named.[20]

The 'General Amir' is listed as Abu Ayoub, and the 'Military Supervisor' is Abu Usama al-Jazairi.[21] There is no mention of bin Laden, Abu Hafs or Abu Ubaydah in this list—despite Abu Ubaydah being referred to in the document as Commandant.[22] As I understand it, this was a common title for the head of al-Qaeda's Military Council, which, according to an al-Qaeda list of members, Abu Hafs later used when he assumed the position.[23] Abu Ubaydah was very clearly already the amir of al-Qaeda's Military Council at that time, which is not reflected in the list. This leads me to think it is not the first list of al-Qaeda members, but rather a personnel list for a subsequent project, or possibly a camp.

I can see how at first sight these documents do appear to show the establishment of al-Qaeda, especially if that is what someone is looking to find. But in addition to what I have just outlined, I doubt these are al-

Qaeda's founding documents because al-Qaeda was already operating in late 1987. My research—part of which comes from your books and other first-hand accounts—shows al-Qaeda was a functioning organisation well before its alleged 10 September 1988 establishment.

Al-Qaeda had a Media Council that was already issuing a magazine. It had a Military Council commanded by Abu Ubaydah. A new training camp had been established in Zhawar, and Ali Muhammad the Egyptian-American military trainer was already teaching Tanzim al-Jihad and al-Qaeda trainees. The establishment of the Advisory Council seems to have been misinterpreted as the establishment of al-Qaeda, and the military work the Council was tasked with coordinating and overseeing, misinterpreted as al-Qaeda's military programme.

In Document Two, you can see that while al-Qaeda has outlined a testing and selection programme it plans to pursue, a programme is also listed for the Arab-Afghans of Sadda, which was overseen not by al-Qaeda but the Advisory Council.[24] Also, the mention of Abu Ayoub in the second document seems to suggest al-Qaeda was establishing a military training programme with him.[25] As I understand it, Abu Ayoub was involved in training work and was active in the Jalalabad region around the time the minutes were written.

Taken together, it seems the establishment of the Advisory Council and its committees have been mistaken as the formation of al-Qaeda. What are your thoughts?

MH: You have raised some interesting points, but to address them we need to first go back to the idea of starting al-Qaeda as a *tanzim*. This idea came from Abu Ubaydah directly after the Jaji battle when thousands of people rushed to join Abu Abdullah because he and his group were the heroes.

LF: The name al-Qaeda started before the Battle of Jaji, didn't it?

MH: Yes, it traces back to when Abu Ubaydah was trying to convince Abu Abdullah to use the al-Arin area as a base of guerrilla warfare; as you know this was the area behind al-Masadah. Abu Ubaydah said, 'It is good if we turn this area into a base of guerrilla warfare.' So, the name Qaeda started before the Jaji battle because in Arabic this 'Qaeda' meant a military base. Then, after Jaji, Abu Ubaydah suggested the making of a *tanzim*, and suggested calling it al-Qaeda al-Ansar or something like that.

The impressive victory at Jaji was the main cause of al-Qaeda's emergence as a separate organisation, and its rapid growth. The second reason it became so successful in such a short time was Abu Abdullah's financial strength, because almost everybody else was lacking money. Although many people rushed to join this victorious group, as an organisation al-Qaeda really only took shape when military training began at Jaji and Zhawar. This came from Abu Ubaydah's efforts to push al-Qaeda towards a more practical and organised training path. In fact, military training was the most important and continuous activity in al-Qaeda's history.

LF: Just to clarify: the group existed before the training started on this practical path Abu Ubaydah wanted, but it was not fully organised?

MH: Yes, as I said, after Jaji people rushed to join al-Qaeda; it was not prepared for this and it took some time for the work to be organised, especially in the training.

More than a move: al-Qaeda's relocation to Khost and its turn away from Afghanistan

MH: Al-Qaeda's first training camp was in Jaji, but this was only temporary because immediately after the Battle of Jaji, Abu Ubaydah's plan to transfer 'Al-Masadah' to Khost was approved.

LF: Really? I thought they stayed at al-Masadah and in the Jaji area for a while.

MH: They continued to use it but the main base was moved—although it did take some time to move everything. The move away from Jaji was very significant, because it was not just a move to another location; it marked al-Qaeda's move away from Afghanistan. Why? After Jaji, al-Qaeda stopped focusing on helping the Afghans to win against the Soviets and establish an Islamic state. Instead, al-Qaeda focused on working outside and using Afghanistan as a training base and a location for gaining combat experience.

This was a very big change, and it came about because of the experiences of al-Qaeda's leaders during the Battle of Jaji. We spoke earlier about how Jaji was one of the most corrupt yards in the Afghan jihad. As a result of their experiences in the Jaji battle, Abu Hafs and Abu Ubaydah came to believe that because the Afghan yard had become so corrupted, an Islamic state was not possible. They thought the focus should turn to working outside Afghanistan to liberate Arab lands.

This change in their thinking was very important. It had significant consequences for later; for why al-Qaeda had almost fully disintegrated when it left Afghanistan in 1993—and was still in this state when it was forced to return to Afghanistan in 1996; for why Abu Hafs was so unhappy to return to Afghanistan when there were no alternatives; and finally, for why Abu Ubaydah did not return in 1996, but instead resigned from al-Qaeda. Abu Ubaydah was also unhappy about Abu Abdullah's lack of support for the Egyptian cause.

Al-Qaeda's training activities were heavily affected by this change of thinking; training became focused on what was required for outside work and al-Qaeda grew sensitive about keeping training away from public view. In the corrupt Jaji yard, it was not possible to keep things private, and this was why al-Qaeda turned to make a training base in Khost.

Zhawar, in Khost, was the first place chosen to make a camp because Abu Hafs had participated in battles in this area and knew it well. The camp was located in an area that belonged to Haqqani, and it was at this camp that Ali Muhammad carried out training in late 1987 and early 1988 for Tanzim al-Jihad and al-Qaeda members. But there were problems with this camp because al-Qaeda's trainers did not feel comfortable with Haqqani's brothers Ibrahim and Khalil, who in turn did not feel comfortable about al-Qaeda's presence in the area.

We spoke earlier about the conflicts between the Afghans and the Salafis over their different religious practices. It was a problem in Zhawar too because the uncompromising *fiqh* of some members of al-Qaeda put it in constant tension with any Afghan centre, such as Haqqani's, which in this case was attached to them and in fact hosting them.

LF: Zhawar was also a relatively public location, wasn't it?

MH: Yes. Because after the historic 1986 Zhawar battles many foreign guests, including Pakistanis, Europeans and Americans, visited the area. This caused problems for al-Qaeda, whose leaders wanted more privacy for their training work. Another reason the camp at Zhawar stopped was because of a training accident in July 1988, which caused the death of twelve people, including eight Arab trainees. Some of them were from al-Qaeda and Tanzim al-Jihad.

After training stopped in Zhawar, the search began for another location in Khost. One was found at Jihadwal, which was an area under the control of Hekmatyar. As I mentioned earlier, after Sayyaf's fireshow at Jaji, Abu Abdullah placed more trust with Hekmatyar, and so al-Qaeda rented land from him and established a camp in the area of his base. This was in early 1989, and al-Qaeda called it Jihadwal. So, to respond to your first comment, yes, al-Qaeda's training activities had started before the date of these minutes.

In fact, to try to better manage its training activities during this 1987–8 establishment period, al-Qaeda formed a number of councils to oversee the conduct of business, including Military and Media Councils, as you noted. These councils did not last long because the Battle of Jalalabad erupted in March 1989 and soon afterwards al-Qaeda mobilised all of its resources to fight in this battle. Everything stopped to focus on this battle.

LF: One thing I noticed was absent from accounts of al-Qaeda's early organisational structure was a Political Council. Since al-Qaeda had no real goals or strategy I am not surprised it was operating without one. I am also doubtful about the claims al-Qaeda had a Religious Council (Shariah Council) at that time. Jamal al-Fadl in his testimony alleged Abu Qotada and Sayyid Imam were both on al-Qaeda's Religious Council.[26] Aside from a discrepancy with the dates, where al-Fadl seems at times to be referring to al-Qaeda's organisational structure in the time frame of 1992, to my knowledge neither Abu Qotada nor Sayyid Imam were ever al-Qaeda members.

Jamal al-Fadl also lists a number of other Arab-Afghans as being on al-Qaeda's Shurah Council, among them Abu Burhan, which seems to me to reflect some confusion again, between the Peshawar Advisory Council Shurah and al-Qaeda's own internal Shurah Council.[27] I wonder if this is also the case with the Religious Council he reports. Or is it possible that since al-Fadl did not join al-Qaeda until very late in 1989 or early 1990, by then another structure was in place because after the 1989 Jalalabad battle al-Qaeda essentially had to reconstitute itself?

MH: With no Political Council al-Qaeda was like a three-legged horse. While the youth were running to join Abu Abdullah after the Battle of Jaji, the absence of a political focus did not have a big impact, but later it meant al-Qaeda developed with no strategy, no real goals and no set direction. You can see the impact of this by the time it left Afghanistan in 1993; al-Qaeda was an organisation that had almost fully disintegrated.

As for the councils, they all stopped when al-Qaeda involved itself in the Jalalabad battle. Sayyid Imam and Abu Qotada were never part of al-Qaeda or any al-Qaeda Shariah Council as far as I know. Abu Burhan was to my knowledge never part of al-Qaeda or on its councils.

LF: That is what I thought too. I agree with you that the absence of a Political Council significantly weakened al-Qaeda, and the impact of it operating without one can be very clearly seen, all the way through until al-Qaeda left Afghanistan in 2001.

MH: Here is another point we should consider. In its history, al-Qaeda never produced its own in-house scholars. Those who were scholars all joined from the outside. No religious scholars grew from within al-Qaeda. It was a very big problem for them; in some discussions I had, some of its own members privately admitted this but it was a problem that despite their efforts they never really fixed.

LF: Yes, it is a striking absence. I also noticed al-Qaeda did no aid work, unlike Maktab al-Khadamat.

MH: Yes, al-Qaeda was created exclusively as a military organisation. It did not involve itself in Islamic preaching like the religious groups, and did not have the political efforts of other revolutionary groups, or perform any aid work. Even its media activities were restricted. In 1988 al-Qaeda began publishing a magazine that was distributed in Peshawar, but this only lasted a few months. Abu Abdullah ordered it stopped after its publication in Peshawar caused him problems.

LF: I didn't realise the magazine caused problems.

MH: Yes, it had included some strong opinion pieces that were published alongside the news clippings.

LF: Was this magazine published by Abu Musab al-Reuters, the reported head of al-Qaeda's Media Council at that time?

MH: Yes, but Abu Abdullah was often away during this period and had not seen these articles. They caused him a lot of embarrassment because they made many people angry and stirred controversy in the Peshawar yard. He stopped the magazine and did not let al-Qaeda publish anything externally under its name for a very long time.

In fact, many things took place during periods when Abu Abdullah was away. From al-Qaeda's establishment in 1987 until Abu Abdullah returned to lead the organisation into battle at Jalalabad in May 1989, Abu Hafs and Abu Ubaydah enjoyed broad powers and authority in al-Qaeda. Under their leadership, al-Qaeda grew rapidly; in only a few months it grew to exceed 10,000 people from among the foreign volunteers in Afghanistan.

LF: 10,000? Those numbers are huge. I thought the actual 'members' of al-Qaeda got to around 300–400 people before they began to decline in the period 1990–1992. Are you including the several thousand who joined for the fighting and followed al-Qaeda's combat instructions, but never became 'members' of al-Qaeda?

MH: This number came direct from the man who was tasked with keeping the register, as he told me, but here I should add a point: people would come who led their own groups and they were asked by al-Qaeda how many people they had under their command and so their answer was added to this number. For example, some Bengalis joined al-Qaeda in this way, several hundred of them in fact. But you are right the number of members was smaller. The number of people staying for a long time in the region, or permanently, was small. If you count only the Arabs, the number at al-Qaeda's peak was no more than 500 and not all were al-Qaeda cadres, or members, and later it got very small until there were only around fifty cadres who were in al-Qaeda when it left Sudan.

In the early days many people joined and most of those rushing to join al-Qaeda were attracted because it had enjoyed a fantastic victory at Jaji. They wanted to join the action. They did not know that al-Qaeda was in fact formed to turn away from the action inside Afghanistan and to focus on working on the outside. When they came to know this, many did not stay with al-Qaeda, especially after the defeat at Jalalabad when al-Qaeda withdrew almost completely from action inside Afghanistan and just became a big training institute. They left to go elsewhere to fight on the many fronts that had opened, made their own groups or simply went home.

Changing focus: Arab-Afghan efforts to gain bin Laden's support and al-Qaeda's resources

MH: When al-Qaeda first formed—when it had manpower, money and influence—many people were trying to get Abu Abdullah to put al-Qaeda's resources towards their own national causes. This intensified as more groups began to arrive in Afghanistan. Some of these people seeking to convince Abu Abdullah were inside al-Qaeda. For example, it was Abu Hafs and Abu Ubaydah who said, 'We should prepare for the Arab countries.' That was exactly the idea of Tanzim al-Jihad for Egypt, which had arrived on the Afghan scene in 1986. By 1987, Gamaah Islamiyyah had also arrived on the scene, and these two Egyptian groups were in competition.

Some North African groups also arrived around 1988, the first of which was the Algerian group of takfiris led by Dr Ahmad al-Jazairi, and then later we heard the Libyans had arrived. Each of these groups had its own process of organising and training its personnel but Tanzim al-Jihad and al-Qaeda were especially close because Abu Ubaydah was a member of both of them. He was the head of the Military Councils of both groups.

LF: I find Abu Ubaydah's joint membership fascinating. How did that work? Was it because he was important to both groups and they needed him? In al-Qaeda's membership guidelines, being a member of another group was not allowed.[28]

MH: In the beginning it was allowed—especially for Abu Ubaydah. He had high responsibilities in both groups, and they both needed him. Also, in the early beginning of Tanzim al-Jihad's time in Afghanistan it had effectively merged into al-Qaeda. Many members of Tanzim al-Jihad were members of al-Qaeda. Al-Qaeda needed al-Jihad's training expertise because they were so heavily focused on training, and al-Jihad needed money from al-Qaeda.

Abu Hafs initially joined al-Jihad, then left al-Jihad totally and joined Abu Abdullah. Abu Ubaydah stayed in both, and it was when he was military leader of both organisations that Tanzim al-Jihad wanted to take all of the momentum from Jaji to Egypt. Tanzim al-Jihad wanted Abu Abdullah to put al-Qaeda's resources with them and support them in a campaign against Mubarak's regime.

LF: It is my understanding that Abu Hafs joined Tanzim al-Jihad after he arrived in Afghanistan. Is that correct?

MH: As far as I know Abu Hafs was not in any *tanzim* when I first met him in 1984; neither was Abu Jihad al-Masri. Abu Ubaydah was in Tanzim al-Jihad before he came to Afghanistan and he had earlier spent three years in jail in the case of Sadat's assassination.

Abu Hafs joined Tanzim al-Jihad after the discussions we had in Islamabad about advising Abu Abdullah on his plans for building a base at Jaji. Our committee had discussed sending people to talk with Abu Abdullah. Abu Ubaydah and Abu Hafs were very close friends and they met Abu Abdullah, and instead of listening to their advice, he convinced them to join him. They agreed together to join him, but then Abu Hafs retreated and instead joined al-Jihad for a few months, before he changed his mind and joined al-Qaeda.

The funny thing is Abu Ubaydah was a member in Tanzim al-Jihad and also joined al-Qaeda, and Abu Hafs retreated from Abu Abdullah and went to Tanzim al-Jihad. It was a mess: who was al-Qaeda and who was Tanzim al-Jihad? Because of this, many people were thinking Tanzim al-Jihad had kidnapped Abu Abdullah to their agenda.

LF: I've noticed that by the time al-Qaeda left Afghanistan the two groups appear to have separated a little, a process that seems to have started after the disaster at Jalalabad, when al-Qaeda started to refine its membership processes and become a more defined organisation.

MH: Yes, after Jalalabad the two groups started to be more separate. Al-Qaeda really lost many members. I saw this for myself in 1990 when I complained to Sayf al-Adl about al-Qaeda not sending me enough men to help us for our campaign against Khost Airport in July/August of 1990. He said, 'I sent you most of our cadres.' I could not believe it because the number was small.

LF: The numbers did drop dramatically, didn't they?

MH: Yes, and they decreased very early.

LF: Returning for a moment to Tanzim al-Jihad wanting to take the momentum from Jaji to Egypt, I did not know Abu Hafs and Abu Ubaydah played such a huge role in trying to convince bin Laden. Most accounts stress the role of Ayman al-Zawahiri, and do not say much about Abu Hafs and Abu Ubaydah. How much influence did Ayman have?

MH: Dr Ayman was at his peak at that time, although Dr Fadl was the amir of Tanzim al-Jihad. Abu Abdullah respected them both, and he also had a lot of respect for Abu Ubaydah and Abu Hafs. So this group of four strong people pressed hard on Abu Abdullah to go to Egypt.

LF: Despite intense lobbying Tanzim al-Jihad was unsuccessful in its efforts to convince bin Laden to put al-Qaeda behind its cause. It seems al-Qaeda did not really join the struggle anywhere or have any publicly declared focus. This 'outside work', the future projects and the purpose of al-Qaeda's training are so undefined even in its documents; yet people still joined the group. I initially wondered if this was because bin Laden's mind had already turned to Yemen, although this seems to have been a somewhat private focus for him.

MH: The Egyptians wanted Abu Abdullah to focus al-Qaeda's resources on Egypt—but no one could get there, and so Abu Abdullah said no. Yemen was open, anyone could go, and he wanted to start jihad there. Abu Abdullah was thinking Yemen could be another copy of Afghanistan. He did not make this specific focus on Yemen public for fear it could cause splits in al-Qaeda. As I mentioned earlier, at that time everybody was focused on their own countries. To his close inner circle, Abu Abdullah spoke of Yemen, but to the youth Abu Abdullah spoke about focusing on the outside and doing external work, but he was never really specific.

I was very much against this external focus. Since the beginning I had said, 'If we do not succeed in Afghanistan we will never succeed anywhere because we have all the facilities necessary to succeed: the manpower, the money, the weapons, the land and the fighting field; and we can build our experience, and build our leaders.' I argued, 'We can make a big success in Afghanistan and defeat the Russians, and this country will be ours.' By 'ours' I did not mean for the Arabs, but for the Muslims. Many times I said, 'Either we die here or we live here, we should not leave Afghanistan, they will chase us, they will kill us, they will never leave us to live freely after having this experience in war. If we succeed, they will see us as their enemy and a danger for them.' Unfortunately, this happened exactly as I said.

Al-Qaeda and the Arab-Afghan Advisory Council

LF: I am a little confused about where the Peshawar Advisory Council fits into the picture. I was wondering whether it was formed to try to shape bin Laden's focus and keep him involved in Afghanistan, because people thought it would affect Saudi funding for the jihad if he moved his attention away from Afghanistan.

I know for example that Tamim al-Adnani, who was a member of this Council and was initially with bin Laden at al-Masadah before leaving to join Azzam, did not like bin Laden's changed focus and approach. He was unhappy bin Laden's focus had shifted away from helping to win the war in Afghanistan and establishing an Islamic state in the country, to essentially using Afghanistan as a training location and a place where trainees could be 'bled' in combat. Tamim al-Adnani said he and Azzam 'believed the youth should be directly assembled with the Afghans and in the service of Afghans', before remarking, 'Abu Abdullah may have thought that the Afghan cause may be useful to us in training … as if he wished to make us benefit from Jihad.'[29] The implication of al-Adnani's words as I understand them were that bin Laden was seeking benefit from the jihad, rather than giving benefit through jihad.

MH: Tamim al-Adnani was right in many ways, although some benefit did come—at least indirectly—through improved training. Although, here too there were some problems, because while al-Qaeda's training became more sophisticated, it also focused more and more on tactics not useful for Afghanistan. That was because of Ali Muhammad, who came to train Tanzim al-Jihad, and he also trained al-Qaeda.

Fig 8: Tamim al-Adnani

But, yes, the activities of the Peshawar Council were interesting. We should look at why the Advisory Council was formed, and the relations between Abu Abdullah and Azzam and among the Arab-Afghans more generally, and the different approaches they had to the Afghan jihad.

First, to return to your initial comments about al-Qaeda, and your point about the Advisory Council, I can add something important here. What they were trying to do was to put together a new body to arrange the work of the Arabs in every aspect: combat, training, *dawah* and helping the Afghans.

LF: Just to clarify here, this body was not al-Qaeda, correct?

MH: It was not al-Qaeda; it was something different. It was a committee or a council of Arab-Afghans that was formed as an effort to try to move the approach of Abu Abdullah and the approach of Azzam together in one platform.

LF: I see. This explains the separate military programmes that are outlined in the Advisory Council meeting documents: one of long duration for al-Qaeda and one of short duration for Sadda.[30] It seems the Advisory Council meetings were an effort to ensure these programmes did not conflict and instead tried to cooperate. Cooperation does appear a little one-sided though: al-Qaeda seems to be trying to take recruits from Sadda's recruit stream. Did these efforts ever amount to anything?

MH: As far as I know, al-Qaeda did not access Sadda's trainees the way it was outlined, because at that time it had its own trainees. Maybe for a short time, but this was in the period when people were still rushing to Abu Abdullah. They were still going to al-Masadah, trying to join with the victorious group, although by then al-Qaeda had moved its important training and its main base to Zhawar.

This Council, as a coordination and support initiative, did not move very far forward, and came to little. I know because it had its own military committee to coordinate and support activities, and this committee was meant to support my project in Khost in 1988. In fact, it was meant to support the programmes of all Arab-Afghans. My project was the first one they considered. They interfered with it and they spoiled it very badly. The Council's activities soon stopped when the Jalalabad battle started. Everything was stopped to focus on this.

In reality, Arab-Afghan councils such as these did not work because Abu Abdullah followed his own programme—al-Qaeda's programme. He did not listen to advice. It was the same for Azzam, who was also very strong financially. He did not listen to advice either. Even with Maktab al-Khadamat, Azzam had a very good group around him, despite the corrupted ones from Jordan. For a time, there was a good group like Abu Abdul Rahman al-BM and Abu Hajr al-Iraqi (who both later joined al-Qaeda) and others, but all of them failed to change the ways of Azzam in his work. He suffered from the same problems as Abu Abdullah. Initially, Abu Abdullah was more willing than Azzam to pay attention to the military work. But both of them had shortcomings: both had absolute individual leadership, and marginalised the role of the Consultative Council and made it non-binding, and both of them had a habit of intervening in everything.

Abu Abdullah could follow his programme and not the one outlined by the Council because he was stronger and he had his own money so he could go his own way. He could get money any time he wanted. Azzam had money too, but he had to go and ask this man and that man, whereas Abu Abdullah just put his hand in his own pocket. Also, Abu Abdullah was a commander in battle, especially after Jaji, while Azzam was more interested in *dawah*. Abu Abdullah had no time to take sermons and that gave him credibility with the youth. He was a practical man. He was a rich man. He was a fighter who was going to the battlefield by himself and so the youth followed him because they thought he would lead them to the action. Because of that, he won in Peshawar; he won.

LF: This seems to be another example of people following the leader and not the idea. When the youth joined al-Qaeda, they did not really know what they were joining but they knew, or they thought, that bin Laden was the leader who would help them see combat, and possibly attain martyrdom. It certainly wasn't an 'idea' they followed since al-Qaeda didn't really have one at that time; it had no real stated goals or strategies, it did not have much of anything—except training.

MH: Yes, they followed Abu Abdullah because at that time he was the most popular. They thought if they followed him, they would get to join the action on the fronts. They thought it would be like what they read about the al-Masadah battle, which received huge amounts of publicity.

LF: When you speak of bin Laden winning, I presume you are talking about his appointment as amir of the Arabs, which was in reality the position of amir of the Peshawar Advisory Council.[31] When was bin Laden appointed amir of the Arabs? Was it at those advisory meetings in 1988, or was it earlier? All I know is that bin Laden was amir of the

Arabs, while Azzam was appointed amir of Sadda and Wael Julaydan was made amir of Peshawar activities. From what I read in your books Abu Ubaydah was the head of the Peshawar Council's Military Committee, and other members included Abu Hafs al-Masri, Abu Hajr al-Iraqi and Issam al-Libi.[32]

MH: Abu Abdullah's appointment as amir of the Arabs occurred in early 1988, although it may have been made formal a little later. It stretched from after Jaji until Jalalabad because it was in this time that Abu Abdullah was first among the Arabs, after his victory at al-Masadah and before his defeat at Jalalabad.

LF: What are your thoughts on whether bin Laden was allowed to 'win' this position as amir of the Arabs to keep him engaged in Afghanistan at a time when his attention was starting to turn away from the country? It seems to me it would have been disastrous for bin Laden to become unhappy and go back to Saudi Arabia and criticise the jihad in Afghanistan, particularly after Jaji because it could have affected the willingness of others to finance the jihad. This is where I thought the title of amir of the Arabs came from, and that it was more an honorary title than a position with any real authority. Bin Laden was not in charge of all the Arabs, correct? He wasn't, for example, your amir, or the amir of any other Arab-Afghans who were not in al-Qaeda?

MH: He was not my amir. He was not an amir to anyone outside of al-Qaeda and he had no authority over Arabs outside of his organisation. There were many reasons the Advisory Council was formed. The main one was to try to unite these two currents of Azzam and Abu Abdullah. Its purpose was 'to distribute the specialisations and organisation' of the Arabs' work and 'to coordinate action with the understanding it prevents conflict'. Its establishment was also about protecting funding because if there was conflict, funding would be affected.

LF: What are your thoughts about claims bin Laden was made amir because the Saudis wanted a Saudi in control? It has also been said there were Saudi concerns about Azzam being affiliated with Ikhwan, and so bin Laden attained this role because people wanted to make sure the Saudi funding did not stop. Azzam's son-in-law, Abdullah Anas, has said Azzam told him bin Laden's appointment took place because the Saudis did not want him (Azzam) in charge because he was Ikhwan, and because they wanted a Saudi in charge.[33] I am not sure about this because bin Laden was at one stage Ikhwan and the Saudis never seemed to have a problem with that, or with his funding of the Ikhwan Muslimin in Syria for example. It also doesn't seem the Saudis had a problem with Azzam being Ikhwan, since a lot of Saudi funding went to Maktab al-Khadamat, despite it being close to Ikhwan.

MH: Remember it was the Saudis who sent Azzam to Islamabad in 1983, and when he was there, his neighbour was the Saudi military attaché. Relations were good between Saudi Arabia and Azzam. I do not think it was because Azzam was Ikhwan, at all. But, yes, of course the Saudis would have preferred a Saudi in charge.

LF: I was wondering whether the Saudi view of Azzam had begun to change as a result of the training taking place at Sadda, which you said shocked them because the camp was established away from where it could be monitored, and also because training on explosives was taking place. I wonder if this had any bearing on the Saudis' desire to perhaps see bin Laden in charge—although by then Ali Muhammad was training al-Qaeda in explosives too.

MH: This may have been a factor, but the main reason for the Council being formed was to try to bring the approaches of Abu Abdullah and Azzam together because they were growing too far apart both in activity and in intent.

Azzam wanted the Arabs to go to the fronts to fight to raise the spirit of the Afghans and to share in this way but on a small scale. That was it. Abu Abdullah was talking all the time about the fighting outside the area. Although his thoughts were toward Yemen, he did not publicise this because as I told you earlier this would cause problems—because everyone was thinking about their own country.

Even Azzam was thinking about his own country. While he was talking about helping all Muslims by establishing an Islamic state in Afghanistan, he was really focused on Palestine. By 1988 he had brought Palestinians and Jordanians to Sadda and trained them to carry out operations inside Israel. This was while Afghanistan was still not prepared, while there was still no Islamic state, but he brought these people to Sadda and launched attacks in Israel when the situation was not ready for that. This led to Azzam's assassination because Israel became crazy—it threatened the Saudis, the Saudis threatened the Pakistanis; the Pakistanis asked everyone they knew to tell the Arabs not to train the Palestinians and they also said 'don't train the Arabs on explosives'.

Meanwhile, Abu Abdullah was just training in the camps. While Abu Abdullah was talking about working in the international atmosphere, he did not make anything international. He also did less in Afghanistan, and then after the 1989 Jalalabad defeat al-Qaeda stopped all of its combat work inside the country, except small-scale activity in Paktia, which served as a form of training. Generally, after Jaji, al-Qaeda just did its own training. I do think one reason people accepted Abu Abdullah as amir was his popularity with other wealthy merchants and financiers who supported the Afghan jihad; and they were probably fearful that if he left Afghanistan or criticised the jihad there they would lose funding.

LF: Azzam's comment about how bin Laden's money allowed him to do whatever he wanted comes to mind here, again. When you and I spoke about this earlier you made the comment that Azzam did not support bin Laden or al-Qaeda's agenda at that time, but he could not stop bin Laden doing as he pleased because of bin Laden's extraordinary financial strength at a time when everybody was hunting for money, support and supplies.

MH: Yes, so you can see that there were two big approaches in the area of Arab support for the Afghans, one for Azzam, another for Abu Abdullah. Azzam's approach to Afghanistan was to help the Afghans directly in every field of work by giving the aid to them: directly for the front, for the refugees, for education, for everything—even for political training.

For Abu Abdullah, the focus was on military training of the youth from every place. While in the beginning this idea for training was to send the youth inside to fight, it soon turned to training for outside work—even though al-Qaeda did not do any at this time. Abu Abdullah's approach of sending the youth to the Afghan fronts—it was not to fight to win and establish an Islamic state, but to fight to train. This is what Tamim al-Adnani was talking about when he spoke of seeking benefit from the jihad instead of giving benefit to the jihad. It also caused a big gap between al-Qaeda and me and we were always having discussions about that.

The Arab-Afghan yard: disagreements, arguments and power plays

LF: Speaking of discussions and arguments, another element that is often tied into the story of al-Qaeda's creation is the account of a 'Shariah Court' being held where Azzam was reportedly tried. According to one account by Wael Julaydan, there was a Shariah Court where bin Laden had to intervene to help Azzam because he had become so weakened.[34]

I know an incident did take place and a 'court' of sorts was formed to resolve a matter with Abu Abdul Rahman al-Kanadi who was a Canadian of Egyptian descent. I did not think this had anything to do with al-Qaeda's formation, but was a dispute between Abu Abdul Rahman and Maktab al-Khadamat. I am interested to hear your thoughts on this: what happened and was it linked to al-Qaeda's formation?

MH: Well I think we first need a bit of background on Abu Abdul Rahman's role, which was very important. Abu Abdul Rahman al-Kanadi did excellent work during the jihad against the Soviets but it has not been well recognised, especially the military work he did in Logar province. As you know, Logar is in between Paktia and Kabul. Abu Abdul Rahman al-Kanadi trained at Sadda and was at Jaji with Abu Abdullah; he and Abu Abdul Rahman al-Surahyi did a fantastic job with their observation work and giving guidance for the Arab activity. When the enemy discovered their hiding place, the jets bombed the area very heavily but they were not hurt.

Neither of them joined al-Qaeda. They kept themselves isolated and built their own projects in Afghanistan. Abu Abdul Rahman al-Kanadi did try to work with Maktab al-Khadamat, but this did not go well: he had a huge confrontation with them and Azzam. Maktab al-Khadamat offered to cooperate with Abu Abdul Rahman on his charity project, because at the time he was doing some important charity work. Sometime after they had agreed to cooperate and the project had started, Abu Abdul Rahman returned to Canada for a visit and to raise funds. When he came back to Afghanistan, he found that Maktab al-Khadamat, working with some others, had taken everything and claimed it as theirs and evicted him from his own project.

Maktab al-Khadamat basically tricked Abu Abdul Rahman and took his project and everything with it; they took it all. It was a very bad argument between him and them. He went to this group of scholars, and some of them made a ruling that Azzam and Maktab al-Khadamat should return everything to Abu Abdul Rahman and they did. Afterwards, he went to Canada to get support for his project, called 'The Challenge Project'.

Other Arab-Afghans were maybe jealous because Abu Abdul Rahman had his own financial support network from Canada and elsewhere. He was independent and did not depend on Saudi aid, and he had strong leadership and a strong personality, and good relations with Hekmatyar. This may have caused problems with the other Arab-Afghans and the

Saudis because while Sayyaf was the choice of the Saudi government and the most famous and rich, Hekmatyar was the choice of Pakistan's government and was stronger.

With his own financial support networks, Abu Abdul Rahman did some excellent work in Afghanistan. He was the first among the Arabs to directly help inside by establishing schools, hospitals and clinics. He did a fantastic job. This incident with Maktab al-Khadamat and the Saudis had nothing to do with Abu Abdullah's selection as amir of the Arabs, or with al-Qaeda's formation.

LF: It did take place around the same time the Peshawar Advisory Council was operating, which might account for the confusion. Abu Abdul Rahman's issue was resolved later in 1988 when a ruling was made his project should be returned to him.[35] I noticed the ruling went against Wael Julaydan who was involved in taking Abu Abdul Rahman's project and part of the group who was forced to return the project and Abu Abdul Rahman's belongings.[36] His omission of his involvement along with some other discrepancies—particularly in relation to how and why al-Qaeda was formed, and his views on the role of some Egyptians—has given me cause to reconsider information he has provided.

It appears there were many power plays going on at the time and it was quite common for groups to try to take the projects of others. The Afghans tried to take each other's projects and al-Qaeda, especially later, was quite active in trying to gain control of other groups' projects. I had not heard much about Maktab al-Khadamat doing that and didn't realise this is what they were trying to do with Abu Abdul Rahman. The only incident I knew of was when they tried to take over Abu Harith al-Urduni's project.

MH: The case of Abu Harith al-Urduni is an interesting one, but there is a difference. Maktab al-Khadamat basically tricked Abu Abdul Rahman in order to take his project, but they threatened Abu Harith al-Urduni. I did hear that Maktab al-Khadamat also threatened Abu Abdul Rahman, but they threatened Abu Harith in a much more severe way.

LF: I know that Maktab al-Khadamat wanted Abu Harith to join it but I do not know much beyond this because although many people fought on Abu Harith's front there is very little written about him.

MH: I first met Abu Harith in 1986, when he visited our house. There was a rumour going around Peshawar that a journalist had a secret library that contained secular books that were anti-jihad. They were in fact books

Fig 9: Abu Harith al-Urduni and Mustafa Hamid

about guerrilla warfare, and other things, which Abu Harith found out when he visited. He arrived and went straight to our library on the second floor. I left him to read, and after a while he said 'the mujahidin need to know this', and after that we became friends. Abu Harith had military experience in Jordan and when he arrived to join the fight in Afghanistan, he initially worked with Azzam. Abu Harith's father was a big man in Ikhwan, and so Abu Harith came first to work with Azzam.

At that time, Azzam wanted to put Maktab al-Khadamat in the picture of what was happening in Khost, which was the location of some very sensitive and important work. After my friend Abdul Rahman was martyred in May 1988, which was partly the fault of the Peshawar Advisory Council's Military Committee ruining our project, Khost became empty of Arabs working in the military field.

We were the main group working there helping our Afghan friends, and we really consisted of just a few people; Abu Jihad al-Masri and Abu Ubaydah and Abu Hafs sometimes joined us but usually it was just Abdul Rahman and me. We had this idea that the Arabs would operate separately as a group but that this group would work together with the Afghans. In this way, we were able to make a big disturbance against the enemy in Khost. Around that time, Abdullah Azzam sent Abu Harith to Khost to be a centre for Maktab al-Khadamat; to be near Haqqani, to know about his plans, and what supplies and support he might need.

LF: Was Maktab al-Khadamat laying claim to Abu Harith by dispatching him to Khost, or was he already working with them before this?

MH: Abu Harith did not join any party. Abu Harith would not join anyone, or follow their orders: not Ikhwan Muslimin, not Maktab al-Khadamat and not any Arab Jamaat. He had a good relationship with Azzam and Maktab al-Khadamat, but at the same time, he was against them because of their focus on Peshawar, and them not caring much about the fronts.

But, yes, Maktab al-Khadamat wanted to claim him. They tried to make him as one of their group and he refused. It was usual for Maktab al-Khadamat to think, 'If we send you, you are ours; you represent us and should follow our position, and you should work with our instructions.' Little by little, Abu Harith became independent and refused this. Then Maktab al-Khadamat wanted to throw him out because they were working in the game of Sayyaf and not the game of jihad. Maktab al-Khadamat was under the influence of the Saudis of course, and all of this meant they wanted to weaken Haqqani.

Abu Harith worked closely with Haqqani, and he believed in him and trusted him. Haqqani felt the same. Although Abu Harith was independent of Haqqani's group, he was reliable and so he and his group were part of Haqqani's battlefield planning. Abu Harith played an important role in guarding Torghar Mountain after its 1990 capture. Earlier, in 1984 when Haqqani first captured Torghar Mountain, he left it to some Afghan groups to guard and they sold it to the Afghan regime because they were people of the mountain who were mobile and had no sense of the land. When Haqqani captured it again in 1990 he gave Torghar to Abu Harith's group to protect, because he knew the Arabs would never sell the mountain to the regime and that they were brave and never withdrew at all. This was a very good thing and a very bad thing in the Arab military work, because the Arabs did not trust the manoeuvre of withdrawal or hit-and-run tactics.

Anyway, because Abu Harith was not joining any party of the Arabs or the Afghans, people began to come to his front. Abu Harith's group was not constant: there were only around a dozen or so people who were permanently in his group. They were independent people of various Arab nationalities and he also had two of his brothers working with him. Some Jordanians and Palestinians were relatively constant in staying with him, and one or two from Sudan also. Even if they did not stay long, most of the independent people came to Abu Harith and here he introduced a new approach in the Arab activities by being independent.

LF: Abu Harith must presumably have had his own funding sources that allowed him to do so, or was this why he had a falling out with Maktab al-Khadamat?

MH: Abu Harith had his own way of behaving, which helped him to raise funds for his project, and this was one of his strong points. He could go to the office of Maktab al-Khadamat, and when they would not supply him, he would curse them. Of course, this made all of Peshawar gather around the office to hear him. He would say he was going to tell everyone they were corrupt and they were cowards sitting in Peshawar.

LF: So Abu Harith employed the strategy of making such a loud noise that Maktab al-Khadamat would give him money and supplies just to get him to stop?

MH: Yes, and he was doing these things with everybody. He would go to the aid agencies and do the same thing, saying, 'I go to the front and you are sitting here wasting your money in Peshawar giving it to refu-

Fig 10: Jalaluddin Haqqani talking to the media at Torghar Mountain in 1990 after its capture. He tasked Abu Harith al-Urduni with holding and protecting the territory after its capture. Photo by Mustafa Hamid

gees while the front is lacking and the refugees have many supplies and the front does not.' He would say such things, and he was very good at saying them. Also, the people who had been to his front began to send money directly to him after they returned home because they liked this kind of work with him and this kind of activity. His base was marvellous; he was very accurate in fighting and very successful.

LF: Okay so that is how he got his money. Wouldn't that have put him under pressure when Maktab al-Khadamat wanted him to fall under its authority? How did he deal with that?

MH: Maktab al-Khadamat wanted him to leave his work with Haqqani. Because Abu Harith's father was a big man in Ikhwan Muslimin they went and complained to his father about him, and his father came and tried to control him, and bring him out of Haqqani's area. Abu Harith refused. Even when Ikhwan Muslimin said to him, 'Sayyaf is the leader' and 'Haqqani wants to make the power for mullahs and ulama; leave him,' Abu Harith would not leave.

LF: Abu Harith did not offer training, did he? Where did the people who joined his front train?

MH: Abu Harith only accepted people who had already trained, usually at Sadda and then later at Khaldan when Sadda closed, because these were the only places where independent training outside of an organisation was conducted. In fact, most of Abu Harith's people trained in Khaldan with Abu Burhan because they did not belong to any group and the only place to train for those independently minded people was Khaldan. Although Sadda and then Khaldan were run by Maktab al-Khadamat until 1992, they were not training camps for any one group.

LF: Before we talk some more about training, I was just wondering whether Maktab al-Khadamat tried to control bin Laden the way they tried with Abu Harith al-Urduni and Abu Abdul Rahman al-Kanadi?

MH: Maktab al-Khadamat did not try to take control of Abu Abdullah or cheat him in the same way because of his financial power. They initially tried to keep Abu Abdullah away from the fronts, but give him the picture that the mujahidin were making great victories so he would keep funding them. This happened for a few years until Abu Abdullah went to the front, and saw the real conditions. As we spoke about earlier, when Abu Abdullah realised none of the aid was reaching the fronts he became very upset and made a revolution inside the work of Peshawar. He said, 'the work here is corrupted' and decided to go inside Afghanistan and do the work himself. Then he found al-Masadah and the rest is history. They never tricked or threatened Abu Abdullah.

What is interesting, and we should pause to discuss this, is that Abu Abdullah and Azzam both cooperated to get Abdul Aziz Ali's training programme cancelled. Abdul Aziz Ali, if you remember, trained Fatah's Ikhwan Muslimin faction in Jordan, which included Abdullah Azzam. He was very experienced and he was one of the people who supported the initiatives that we put forward, which eventually led to Maktab al-Khadamat's establishment.

In early 1988, Abdul Aziz Ali started a training programme at the Warsak camp. Abu Abdullah and Abdullah Azzam were there and dominated the first session. They prepared the camp, chose the trainees and attended the camp themselves. Then they cancelled it after only one session, because Abdul Aziz Ali was talking about how the Afghan party leaders were thieves. On both their orders, the camp was closed. They stopped it because Abdul Aziz Ali was talking about the hidden political aspects of the jihad and the corruption of the Afghan parties.

Training

LF: So with the Arab and Afghan yards being environments where rivalry, power plays and corruption were going on, this must have affected the quality of the training offered. If Abdul Aziz Ali's programme stopped, what else was left? Sadda was still running and al-Qaeda's camp at Zhawar was working. Were they the only two real locations for Arab-Afghan training during this period? I am thinking this meant that neither Sadda nor al-Qaeda would have been short of trainees if they were the only two options available.

Al-Qaeda at that time was quite selective in terms of whom it accepted into the group, as I understand it—although it would accept anyone for training and combat. Its courses at Zhawar were famous for being very severe.

MH: Yes, although al-Qaeda would accept anyone for training, in the beginning it was very hard to join al-Qaeda and later it became easier and easier and then too easy after that.

LF: Yes, I read Abu Jafar al-Kandahar's account of failing to get into al-Qaeda, and it seems it was quite difficult.[37] Likewise, Fadil Harun has also told of what he heard about the early al-Qaeda training and then it becoming easier.[38]

MH: Yes, Abu Jafar was unlucky.

LF: Speaking of training, I believe you gave some lectures at al-Qaeda's Jihadwal camp when it opened in early 1989, and got into a very big argument with Abu Hafs about the camp's location and safety.

MH: Yes, al-Qaeda had a camp in an area that belonged to Hekmatyar; they rented a piece of land from him in a bigger area that he had bought from the Goboz tribe, on which he built his base known as Jihadwal. Al-Qaeda built its camp there, which was called by the same name, and opened in January 1989. The first session there was one for the Yemeni youth of al-Qaeda. By this time, the pace of al-Qaeda's recruitment had increased, as had the flow of young people who came after hearing about their training programmes, which did not require membership of the organisation to participate.

LF: I seem to recall you and Abu Hafs argued about the location of the camp and its vulnerability to airstrikes. When you arrived and saw it was in an exposed location and had large white tents that could be seen from the air, you became angry. You said to the trainees when you arrived, 'Either an ignorant person carried this out or a person who intended to commit murder.'[39] Then you asked them which it was before someone told you bin Laden had personally selected the location and Abu Hafs had established the camp on bin Laden's orders! That must have been a little awkward.

MH: Yes. I was very angry at that time. The camp was very exposed.

LF: You and Abu Hafs had another disagreement because he would not move the camp, and you left. Some Yemeni trainees followed you, asked you to come back and asked how they could learn about such mistakes if you would not teach them. You gave them the task of finding more suitable locations for camps, and that is how locations for some new camps were found.[40] Is that correct?

MH: Yes, that is correct. I liked those boys; I remember them. They did an excellent job selecting the best places in the area. At one of these locations they selected, al-Qaeda opened a new camp, not far from Jihadwal, and called it al-Faruq. It became the most popular Arab camp in Afghanistan, both in the Soviet war era and until the Americans attacked it with cruise missiles in 1998.

During the Soviet war era, al-Faruq had the largest training operations for the Arabs, especially those coming from Saudi Arabia. After a while there was a dramatic decline in the number of people who lasted through the training. The severity of the programme was a shock to trainees who had anticipated leisurely training. Some ran away from the training and hard work and left al-Faruq, and even al-Qaeda. In the beginning, it was easy at al-Faruq, compared to the severity of Zhawar, but later as the training programme changed, it became harder.

LF: Is this why membership restrictions were lifted and it became easier to get into al-Qaeda? What about the 'testing camps'? Was the training at these camps the Ali Muhammad training programmes?

MH: For those seeking greater privacy and seriousness in training, al-Qaeda opened very small camps to the north-west of Jihadwal. The first of these was named al-Saddiq, and the second called Khalid bin Walid. This chain of camps in Khost made al-Qaeda the most important training centre during the Afghan–Soviet war in terms of not only size but also technical elements of training.

LF: So it is fair to say that most of this technical expertise came from Ali Muhammad, whom Abu Ubaydah contracted to do training for its members, and his decision to bring Ali Muhammad had a lasting impact on al-Qaeda and its history?

MH: The programmes introduced into these camps marked a fundamental point of change in the course of training the Arab-Afghans, not just al-Qaeda because they were offensive training programmes that went beyond guerrilla warfare, and they spread far beyond al-Qaeda. Some of the people Ali Muhammad trained left and went and became trainers in other camps and groups. There is no doubt that Ali Muhammad had a very important role training the Arab-Afghans.

As I mentioned earlier, the first training session Ali Muhammad conducted was in the winter of 1987–8 and it was attended by a number of cadres of al-Qaeda and Egyptian Islamic Jihad. The most prominent of those attending the session was Abu Hafs al-Masri. Ali Muhammad's participation in training saw a big jump in the quality of the programmes, especially as he transferred his experience in guerrilla tactics that he learned with the American Army in the countries of Latin America and not his officer training in the regular Egyptian army, which is what other Arab officers like Abu Burhan al-Suri had done. On the training in the use of weapons, Ali Muhammad did not offer anything more than what could be gained at Abu Burhan's Sadda camp.

Ali Muhammad's most important training additions were useful tactical work in the area of guerrilla ambushes and raids. In fact, apart from his work on guerrilla ambushes, most of Ali Muhammad's teaching materials were not needed by the Arab mujahidin in Afghanistan, such as hijackings and kidnapping individuals, encryption, monitoring and surveillance within the cities (which took place in Pakistan). This was offensive training, which was of little use for guerrilla warfare inside Afghanistan.

The courses taught by Ali Muhammad graduated several dozen trainees, who then transferred that new knowledge to a broad sector of Arab youths in Afghanistan. Even in camps other than al-Qaeda, some of his students started teaching the courses they had learned from him. Ali Muhammad's students had a significant influence on the international situation; their participation was evident in later attacks made by al-Qaeda against America.

Al-Qaeda's first attack against America—the bombing of two US embassies in Kenya and Tanzania—was carried out directly by the students of Ali Muhammad and he also did reconnaissance of these targets with them a few years earlier. It is not an exaggeration to say Ali Muhammad is the actual founder of the 'terrorist' organisation al-Qaeda. He, and not Abu Abdullah, is also the founder, after the Cold War, of the conflict of the West with the Islamic world under the slogan 'Islamic terrorism'.

From an analytical point of view, I would say that Ali Muhammad's injection of this unnecessary training into the courses was deliberate and it was associated with the American security services, whose goal was to equip a new enemy and a replacement for the Soviet Union. That enemy was later termed 'Islamic terrorism' and the biggest symbol became al-Qaeda, which was trained by Ali Muhammad.

LF: I don't agree with your observation, which I think is part of your argument that al-Qaeda was a football in the hands of others, but I imagine as we move along we will be returning to discuss this again!

MH: Yes.

LF: You made a very interesting comment in a recent discussion we had that al-Qaeda was the *tanzim* of three battles: Jaji, Jalalabad and Tora Bora. Obviously, al-Qaeda was one of many groups who fought in the Jalalabad battle, but it seems the battle had a huge impact on its evolution, and the history of the Arab-Afghans more generally.

The history of al-Qaeda we have just discussed was the al-Qaeda that emerged before the alleged 1988 founding minutes of the organisation were written, before the 1989 Jalalabad battle and before people like Jamal al-Fadl joined. This al-Qaeda was inundated with people wanting to join the organisation and accepted anyone for training but had begun focusing on putting more rigour into the way things were done. To do so, al-Qaeda moved its main base with what I guess were its early testing training sessions, to Khost.

What remained at al-Masadah was the entry point for new arrivals, who were kept there until the serious candidates could be identified and then dispatched for more advanced training at Khost, away from public view. Many people who were with al-Qaeda at that time seem to have just floated around at the fronts, until the Jalalabad battle, after which time most left al-Qaeda.

This first version of al-Qaeda, which lasted until the Jalalabad defeat, started off very big. It was not well organised, with two levels of people within it—newly arrived trainees and combat groups who were not formal members, and then the much smaller number of actual al-Qaeda members. Although there were committees operating at that time it all seems to have come to a halt when bin Laden made the ill-fated decision to join the Jalalabad battle. The al-Qaeda that was left after the Jalalabad defeat was a fundamentally different organisation.

MH: Yes. The impact of the Jalalabad defeat on the history of al-Qaeda cannot be overstated—and on the Arab-Afghans more generally.

LF: Before we move on to the Jalalabad battle I wanted to quickly revisit the Arab-Afghan training climate at this time—for those who were outside of al-Qaeda. One area we have not touched upon is the South East Asian group, Jamaah Islamiyyah. The group essentially spent its founding years in Afghanistan and trained at Sayyaf's Pabbi Military Academy and later at Sadda, close by to the Arab camp.

According to Nasir Abbas, Jamaah Islamiyyah members attended Sayyaf's academy for a period of three years, where they had their own classes and instructors, although some training was shared with the Afghans.[41] I found it interesting Sayyaf limited the access of Jamaah Islamiyyah members to the front lines just as he did with the Arabs—despite the fact that their training programme was much more rigorous than that of the Arab camps.

Some Jamaah Islamiyyah members also trained in Arab camps but most trained in Sayyaf's academy or the camp near Khaldan until they established their own camp at Torkham in an area between there and Jalalabad.

MH: Sayyaf's military academy trained mostly Afghans, although it did also train a few groups. It improved little by little, because some Arab-

Afghans came and helped in the training. It is not a surprise to me to hear that Sayyaf restricted Jamaah Islamiyyah because he had no real organised group inside Afghanistan. The people he trained, he kept in Peshawar. This was deliberate.

Gulbuddin Hekmatyar was also training his own people. He made a group called Lashkar Ethar, trained them and put them in the field. When he did he found something very strange; when those boys went to battle and started to engage with the enemy and deal with other mujahidin, they began to ask Hekmatyar's party to do something which was not in the policy of the party—to coordinate with the others to plan for attacks. Because of this, Hekmatyar stopped the group. He scattered them in every place and brought the leaders near to him in Peshawar to work in the offices and he finished the group.

From the beginning Sayyaf did this deliberately, but Hekmatyar first put his group inside Afghanistan until he discovered it was very dangerous for him because then leadership would be coming from inside. If he left his group this way they would have the weapons, and the people, and they would be inside making decisions, leaving him alone in Peshawar.

LF: The Indonesians, it seems, managed to stay away from many problems like this in the training and deployment scene, and so they avoided the pressure that came on other groups.

MH: Yes, particularly in the period 1987–1989, which was when some 'prohibitions' or 'red lines' in the training emerged. These came mainly from Saudi Arabia, which had a huge influence in Peshawar because of its financing of the Afghan parties and Arab-Afghan organisations. Saudi Arabia was also the main funding source for Maktab al-Khadamat and its projects—including the Sadda camp.

Saudi Arabia also monitored very closely the activities of its citizens in Afghanistan and Pakistan and it had a large network that collected information about them. It did not favour the existence of training camps, especially for the Arabs, but these camps justified their existence by defending the Arab participation in the jihad.

The Saudis were shocked when Maktab al-Khadamat opened Sadda camp and when it began operating at a level of sophistication they had not anticipated, and so they sought to put three reservations or prohibitions in place. These were in the areas of explosives, politics and governance.

LF: If I can interrupt here quickly: why were they shocked at Sadda's establishment and not at al-Qaeda's?

MH: Because at that time al-Qaeda was just a combat organisation or so they thought. At that time, the training with Ali Muhammad, or the turn to focus outwards, was not clear. Later, when it became clear, the Saudis also put pressure on Abu Abdullah.

LF: Okay, I imagine they might have thought they could control one of their own better than Sadda and Maktab al-Khadamat, which had nationalities and interest groups not perhaps so inclined to listen to Saudi guidance.

MH: Yes, they were a little worried about Azzam, but he was very hesitant in two things, the involvement of Arabs in serious fighting inside Afghanistan and the conduct of high-level military training. Azzam avoided involvement in these things in order to avoid angering the Saudis and losing huge amounts of official and private funding coming from there.

Azzam's avoidance marked a fundamental difference in views with Abu Abdullah. This, along with errors in administration and corruption inside Maktab al-Khadamat, caused Abu Abdullah to withdraw his funding and to personally implement his own vision of work in Afghanistan, which was opposite to Azzam on these two points. Abu Abdullah originally wanted to see direct and wide combat participation for the Arabs in Afghanistan and to pursue a large training agenda so that they could perform well in battle.

So began the march of Abu Abdullah from Jaji to al-Qaeda, but as usual he changed his objectives, and his plans were always seasonal or even momentary. In the beginning Abu Abdullah tried to take into account the position of his country's government and its warnings, but because he was in Saudi Arabia most of the time, his two work deputies, Abu Ubaydah and Abu Hafs, and with them the young enthusiasts working in the management of the camps, often crossed the red line. From time to time, they retreated under pressure coming from Saudi Arabia, but in the words of Abu Abdullah 'at the earliest opportunity these violations emerged again'.

LF: Was that the only type of pressure Saudi Arabia put on al-Qaeda? How did it feel about al-Qaeda's magazine, for example? You mentioned earlier it caused bin Laden problems in Peshawar. Did these problems reach back to Saudi Arabia?

MH: Saudi Arabia's pressure was dropped once and forever after al-Qaeda's disastrous efforts to issue a newsletter and several publications, which were distributed in Peshawar and contained the views of its Media

Council. These publications were unstable in standards and wild, and they angered everyone, especially Ikhwan Muslimin and the Afghan parties in Peshawar. In fact, the *fiqh* and political views expressed in the newsletter embarrassed Abu Abdullah and al-Qaeda, and defending it was extremely difficult. As a result, he sent strict orders from Saudi Arabia to close the newsletter. This was al-Qaeda's first and last attempt in the field of press work until late 1998 and 1999, when Abu Abdullah was trying to write his memoirs; his secretary was writing his memories, but I don't know where these things are now, maybe the Americans took it.

LF: What were the prohibitions in governance the Saudis tried to put in place? I take it you are referring to them trying to control the emergence of the takfiri current.

MH: Yes. They were also more generally on politics and governance, because political talk was very common in the atmosphere of Peshawar, which was the first stop for young Arab fighters. The talk was mostly about the politics and relations of Afghan parties, and stretched to the policies of countries related to the problem. The opinions were not deep because the area was largely free from specialists on this topic, but yet the Saudis panicked, especially when the political views marched towards the restricted area, which was Saudi policy and its relationship with American policy, especially in Afghanistan.

Takfiris had also proliferated within the Arab-Afghan community, especially from the North African countries but also from Saudi Arabia and Yemen. The result was people began mixing their political conversations with religious fatawa, especially in the theme of '*takfir*'. Soon some Arab-Afghans were making *takfir* of all rulers, including the rulers of Saudi Arabia, and so the government of that country pressed with all its intensity to stop such conversations in the camps and guesthouses.

This ban continued to be in effect most of the time, but the talk began to grow again, especially after the formation of the second Afghan Interim Government in Peshawar in 1989, when some Arab-Afghans made *takfir* against the leader, Mujaddidi. This reached most or all of the leaders of the Afghan parties. Some Arab-Afghans also continued to make *takfir* against the rulers of Islamic countries, with Saudi Arabia at the forefront. The result was that armed jihad against the rulers of these countries began to rise to the top as the primary interest for trainees and Arab camps.

LF: How effective was the Saudi pressure? To me, it does not look to have been very effective. While al-Qaeda's media work may have been closed down, this seems to have been as much because of local reasons than Saudi pressure; and training at the camps, appears to have continued unabated. The *takfir* current also grew during this period, despite attempts to limit its influence.

MH: For training there was a small impact. In some cases, the training became more secret. For example, even the lectures I gave in the camps were shrouded in secrecy, but after the trainees left, news of what was said spread to Peshawar and even the homelands of the trainees. The subject of my lectures was the theory of guerrilla warfare for the Afghan experience, which was a subject that was by its nature political and military at the same time.

I think for the groups and the camps, their training became more secretive, particularly when they began their work in explosives. The training of the youths on explosives was an important and highly sensitive issue for Arab security agencies, and stronger for Saudi Arabia.

This kind of training became common and it was a source of competition between the camps to attract new members to the organisations who ran such courses. Training notes on explosives and other topics proliferated to the extent that they were sold in photocopy centres in Peshawar. The owners of these shops were holding their own copies—without the knowledge of the owners of the notes—and then sold them to young Arabs. The copies they held included various types of notes, papers and books. One day, in a moment of humour, one of the Arabs said, 'Young people are taking photocopies of everything that falls into their hands, even a copy of the Qur'an.'

In 1988, the year before Abdullah Azzam was assassinated, the Sadda camp crossed the barrier of training on explosives. Azzam's enthusiastic religious speeches about the Afghan jihad had attracted a number of Jordanians of Palestinian and Chechen origin to train on explosives and other skills to carry out operations inside occupied Palestine.

One of these operations was very painful to Israel, more than what was broadcast and it sent a strongly worded threat of a strike against Saudi Arabia if Azzam's activities did not stop in the Sadda camp. The Saudi government, facing Israeli rage, turned to Pakistan, and forced them to take steps that resulted in Arabs no longer receiving training in the Sadda camp. My friend Haqqani told me the story of the Israeli threat and Saudi pressure on Pakistan.

Initially, the idea of manufacturing ammunition and explosives faced stiff resistance among the Arabs and the Afghans. I experienced this first-hand when, after the Battle of Urgon, I proposed to Afghan leaders to manufacture ammunition for small arms and explosives in anticipation of a siege against our campaign in Paktia. But in 1987, some Arab volunteers appeared who were chemists and they transferred their experiences of manufacturing explosives into the Arab-Afghan training camps. Several names became known in this field and the most important of them was Abu Khabab al-Masri. He was a chemical engineer who initially worked with al-Qaeda before resigning and working instead as an independent trainer moving from one camp to another, which earned him wider fame.

This type of training on explosives was not to help with fighting inside Afghanistan, it was mostly for outside. Some of the Arab trainers also discussed unusual issues such as the preparation of poisons and toxic gases. Progress in these areas was very limited, for many reasons, because of the level of scientific research required and the lack of technical equipment.

The main result of the arrival of these chemists was that from that time onwards sessions on the manufacturing of explosives became part of the training programme in many Arab-Afghan camps. These sessions were unregulated because there were copies in the libraries of Peshawar photocopy shops, which were taken from the lessons and available to those who paid.

LF: So in the end, these training prohibitions do not seem to have been very effective at all.

MH: Well, they were when compared to what happened with the training storm that took place after the defeat of Jalalabad, which was beyond the control of everybody.

LF: True, that is a very important point. They do not look too effective until you see what comes later. Before we move on to discuss Jalalabad and the training storm, I am curious to hear your views on the types of training conducted and the prohibitions in place.

MH: Since the early days I had heated and long-term debates with the founders of al-Qaeda (especially Abu Ubaydah and Abu Hafs), as well as Tanzim al-Jihad and others who were interested in the subject of training Arabs in Afghanistan. I believed the training provided in the camps did not meet the needs of the Arab fighters in Afghanistan, and that training should help them to carry out tactical duties assigned in the field. The work of the Arabs was not linked to their own strategy or compatible with the Afghan strategy, if there even was one for the Afghans.

Most of the training was unsuited for work inside Afghanistan, and as time went on, it became more focused on outside work.

There was a great proliferation in training and all kinds of courses were offered, and trainees were given as many as possible of them, yet only a few were of any practical use. This type of activity was a waste of money, time and effort. Despite all these courses, there was a great shortage in political education, which should have been included alongside military training. A guerrilla fighter needs to have an awareness and knowledge of politics: this is one of the fundamental differences between him and regular forces, or militias or mercenaries. Political knowledge is what determines the direction of his military activity from the lowest to the highest levels. This was lacking in nearly all of the training.

Religious training was also limited, and what was offered was confined to the Salafi direction, which was alien to the majority of the population in Afghanistan and the Arab and Islamic world. A guerrilla fighter should be familiar with the common religious practice in the country in which he operates, or the enemy will be able to make a barrier of alienation and perhaps hostility between him and the people. In Afghanistan, we saw many cases where the enemy's propagandas focused on doctrinal differences between the Afghans (Hanafi) and Arabs (Salafi).

The shortages of courses in these areas stand in great difference to the numerous courses offered in other areas. In many camps, training was open to anyone, and trainees were encouraged to take all possible courses, whether they were needed, or not. This took place under the broad and strange banner of 'Preparation of the Ummah'. Only those certain people in the camps received this training. But a nation is prepared by countless means, and military training is only one of them, and received by individuals dedicated to the issue of defence.

LF: I imagine with your list of critiques, you had some interesting debates. You mentioned 'Preparation of the Ummah'; this current rose up strongly in the aftermath of the Jalalabad battle, and was a big part of what you have called the training storm.

MH: Yes, it began earlier in some small groups but after the Jalalabad defeat it became very strong and caused huge damage.

7

JALALABAD AND THE ARAB-AFGHAN TRAINING STORM

Muhammad Yousaf, a former Pakistani ISI figure tasked with helping the mujahidin, observed that the Afghan jihad was never the same after Jalalabad.[1] While the impact of the Jalalabad defeat on the Afghan mujahidin and on the course of Afghanistan's history has been well covered, little has been written about its effects on the Arab-Afghan jihad, which were equally, if not more, significant.

The impact of the Jalalabad defeat and the training storm that rose from it, culminating in the Jalalabad School or School of the Youth, not only shaped the history of the Arab-Afghan jihad but also continues to play a significant role in today's jihadi landscape. This is most evident in recent events in Syria, and in particular the conflict and competition between the various Salafi jihadi groups and schools, most notably al-Qaeda and the Jalalabad School, the origins of which can be traced to the Arab-Afghan jihad.

In mid-February 1989, the Soviets left Afghanistan after a phased withdrawal that began shortly after the April 1988 signing of the Geneva Accords. Afghan mujahidin, anticipating the speedy collapse of the Kabul regime after the Soviets' departure, had already formed an Interim Government comprised of representatives of the major mujahidin groups, with Sigbatullah Mujaddidi to be president, and Sayyaf prime minister. Buoyed by the Soviet withdrawal and anxious to install themselves in power, members of this interim body were already jostling for position in the belief the regime would soon fall and they could assume power.

The new Afghan government was to be initially seated in Jalalabad, following a major mujahidin assault to take the city, which it was believed would pave the way for the liberation of the rest of Afghanistan.

While taking Kabul directly was well beyond the capabilities of the mujahidin, a more hubristic assessment prevailed of their capacity to take and hold Jalalabad. In reality, the Afghan mujahidin were woefully unprepared and under-resourced to transition to, and launch, the type of conventional attack needed to take Jalalabad. Nonetheless, a few weeks after the Soviet withdrawal, the Afghan mujahidin had gathered a force together for an attack on Jalalabad. Many were untrained and some even lacked weapons.

* * *

MH: People were taken straight from the Afghan camps; some without guns and sent directly to Jalalabad to fight for its liberation. Thousands of them died.

* * *

The battle began on 5 March 1989 when bin Laden was still in Saudi Arabia. The Afghan mujahidin and the Arabs who fought alongside them enjoyed some early success, and were able to push forward and force the Afghan Army to retreat from Samar Khel Mountain, which had previously housed a garrison for the Afghan Army after the Soviets had withdrawn. Taking Samar Khel allowed the mujahidin control over the surrounding area.

* * *

MH: Samar Khel Mountain had good visibility, even to the Jalalabad airport. You could also see almost to the border of Pakistan, as well as into surrounding desert. The international road coming from Torkham to Jalalabad was at the bottom of the mountain, and so this too could be controlled.

Initially, the Afghan Army did not have a reliable alternative defence line. Their withdrawal from Samar Khel nearly turned into a defeat as the mujahidin quickly followed and were able to push forward to Jalalabad airport, which was several kilometres south of Jalalabad city. Another group came from Kunar and approached from the east through the farmland and cultivated areas, which they were able to take with little resistance, and which offered them good cover. In these early days, it appeared that the city would soon fall into the hands of the mujahidin.

LF: Were any Arabs involved at this stage?

MH: Yes, but they were not with Abu Abdullah because he did not arrive until May. At the beginning of the Jalalabad battle, the Arabs joined the Afghan parties, especially Sayyaf's, but they discovered he was not strong in the area. Sayyaf did have a strong commander there from the Kuchis; he was called Shammali and some Arabs joined him. Some Arabs also joined Khalis, who was stronger because he was from Jalalabad.

* * *

Despite the early success, the position of the mujahidin soon faltered as shortcomings with planning, coordination, supply and logistics began to emerge. Although they had managed to push eastward, moving closer to encircling and capturing Jalalabad, their plan of attack was soon changed, and the battle moved to the desert areas south-west of the city. This change of plan was reportedly on the direction of the ISI and made the mujahidin vulnerable to the massive aerial bombardments the Afghan regime directed at them in the form of airstrikes and Scud missile attacks. It also placed them directly in the path of the Afghan Army's tanks.

* * *

MH: It was at the time when the mujahidin were pushing eastwards that Pakistani intelligence sent one of its officers to them, and asked them to withdraw from the farms and join with the rest of the mujahidin to besiege Jalalabad from the desert. I heard this from someone who was there when this Pakistani official gave the direction. The mujahidin changed their positions, which was a huge mistake because the farms in which they were operating were impossible for the Afghan Army to seal off, and their entrances reached deep into Jalalabad city's outskirts. Also, the Pakistani intelligence officers did not direct the mujahidin to close the road from Kabul to Jalalabad, so the Afghan Army's supplies flowed into the city without any serious obstacles.

LF: I thought the mujahidin seized the road but internal coordination problems among them meant that convoys were able to slip through.

MH: It was a very big mistake to fail to secure the supply route coming from Kabul because in a situation like that before you attack a city you should isolate it. You should not attack while leaving the supply lines open. The supply route came through a very tough road in the mountains: how could they leave it like this? What occurred in Jalalabad was a betrayal.

LF: Why was it a betrayal?

MH: It was a betrayal because the Pakistanis did not want the Afghans to win and so they gave them very bad direction. It was the idea of the ISI to teach the mujahidin a lesson: that they could not take the cities. This would force them to the negotiation table to make a coalition government from among the mujahidin and the communist parties.

* * *

By May it was clear the mujahidin were in trouble. At that time, bin Laden returned from Saudi Arabia to rally the troops and join the fight in Jalalabad. He ordered all of al-Qaeda's available resources into battle. Bin Laden's enthusiasm was ignited by the early gains the mujahidin had made, but he, like many others, did not realise—or disastrously overlooked—the potential for the mujahidin to be entrapped. While by late May it was clear to many that the mujahidin were already defeated, and could not take Jalalabad, bin Laden continued to push for others to join him in battle.

* * *

LF: I'm curious why bin Laden decided to enter the war at a time when many thought it already seemed lost. Did he think he could turn it around?

MH: One of the main limitations in Abu Abdullah's thinking—and it was repeated several times after Jaji—was that he had a way of behaving where he thought he was the hero, and he could come like the musketeer on his horse, and win the battle by himself. Later, this behaviour became even bigger when he declared war on America thinking he could liberate the Ummah by himself.

In Jalalabad, this is how it was; Abu Abdullah came suddenly from Saudi Arabia and rushed directly to Jalalabad, without consulting anybody. He was like a speeding locomotive, and he took over direct command from Abu Ubaydah and Abu Hafs, who were in charge in his absence.

LF: How did the leaders in al-Qaeda feel about this?

MH: Abu Ubaydah was enthusiastic while Abu Hafs was opposed to the idea of battle and the great interference of Pakistan in all of the details.

Abu Hafs had shared in the early battle for Jalalabad airport, which was unsuccessful. Muhammad Makkawi was also there and famously called it 'a goat fight'. At that time, Abu Hafs realised the Pakistanis had their own agenda and the campaign could not be won because of their interference. When Abu Abdullah returned, Abu Hafs refused to go again into battle. Instead, Abu Hafs withdrew and went to Peshawar and carried out administrative and logistic work in the service of al-Qaeda, which was very disorganised.

LF: Did Abu Hafs speak out against al-Qaeda getting involved in this battle? As we all know, changing bin Laden's mind once it was set on something was virtually impossible, but did Abu Hafs try?

MH: Yes, Abu Hafs did speak, but not publicly. He did make statements among the Arab volunteers in Peshawar that Pakistani intelligence was the real leader of the Battle of Jalalabad. This raised the anger of Abu Abdullah, but Abu Hafs' statements were right.

LF: Abu Hafs was criticised heavily in Peshawar, as I understand it; was this because he was the 'only' face of al-Qaeda there, and so the criticism was directed at him?

MH: Yes.

LF: Why didn't Abu Hafs speak out more?

MH: This is a question I asked him myself, because I was very angry at the loss of life in Jalalabad. Abu Hafs said to Abu Abdullah, 'It is a disaster, stop.' It was very good he said that but I was very angry with him at the time and asked him, 'Why did you not say this publicly?' He said, 'I am in the *tanzim*, I cannot.'

LF: So, basically, he could not, or would not, go against the leader of his organisation?

MH: Yes, and Abu Abdullah was pressuring people to join the battle. He made a very big momentum for the war; it was a little quiet before he came.

LF: Was it quiet because by then people were thinking the mujahidin had been defeated?

MH: The Afghan Mujahidin Interim Government played a very negative role in that battle. The mujahidin were in miserable conditions: there was no equipment, no training, no plan, nothing at all. What happened was the Afghan Army had withdrawn from a big area and abandoned it. The mujahidin rushed to the area to collect war spoils when the Afghan Army was withdrawing, and that made the army exceed its withdrawal plan and it withdrew more than was planned. Some thought the Afghan Army was going to lose Jalalabad, but this was not correct.

When Abu Abdullah arrived, he gathered all of al-Qaeda and the Arab-Afghans outside of al-Qaeda to join him in pushing forward into the desert as the ISI had asked.

LF: So what was this trap? Was it encirclement out in the desert?

MH: Yes, the mujahidin overextended past what they could defend and supply, and soon they were sitting too far out in the desert under massive aerial bombardment with the Afghan Army forces coming towards them, and they had to very quickly withdraw. They were lucky to escape. This cost them dearly and they lost many people in that battle. If the mujahidin had continued with their campaign approaching from the east before the Pakistani interference, the story would be very different.

LF: Why did the Arabs push forward into the desert areas and not the Afghans? Was this bin Laden's choice?

MH: The Afghans encouraged the Arabs to fight and push forward, because they saw the Arabs as a good way of getting war spoils. In fact, it was in Jalalabad this appeared: the Afghans would let the Arabs fight and then take all the spoils the Arabs won and keep them for themselves. It became a race between the Afghans to bring the Arabs with them, let the Arabs fight, get the war spoils and take it for themselves. It was very corrupt, and when the Arabs sometimes said they wanted a share in these spoils, because they needed supplies and weapons, the Afghans refused.

There was nearly a fight over this matter between the Afghans and al-Qaeda and the other Arabs who were with them. At the beginning of the battle, Abu Abdullah's people took war spoils; some weapons and maybe one or two tanks, but the Afghans refused to give it to them. The boys with Abu Abdullah were angry and it was a big problem that came between al-Qaeda and the Afghans. Abu Abdullah stopped it. He said, 'No. Leave everything.' So the Afghans kept the spoils.

Anyway, Abu Abdullah, al-Qaeda and the Arab-Afghans who followed him made a deep incursion chasing the retreating forces and seeking war spoils. But they went too far forward into the desert and established positions they could not hold, and with nothing behind them to support their rear and their flank. Of course, then the Afghan Army came and Abdul Rashid Dostum's militias made a crushing blow against the Arab-Afghans, forcing a withdrawal that resulted in Abu Abdullah nearly being captured.

Before the Battle of Jalalabad, I told them: 'If you are going to join the Afghans in large attacks do not work in the infantry; concentrate on the artillery and the tanks.' They refused. I told them: 'You are not the people of the infantry; the Afghans are, because in the infantry there are a lot of things you as foreigners cannot deal with.' This is what happened. Al-Qaeda received a very heavy blow from an attack by Dostum's group and the Afghan Army. Abu Abdullah lost many of his followers; some of them were from al-Qaeda and some of them were volunteers from other Arab-Afghan groups.

Another problem was that Abu Abdullah trusted the ISI and its guidance. In fact, al-Qaeda was happy because after that battle and maybe during it, they received weapons from the ISI like any other mujahidin party. Before that, Abu Abdullah had put his own money towards weapons without external support, but then he started to receive weapons. As far as I know it was not during the early advance he made during the Jalalabad battle, but afterwards. Also, Abu Abdullah along with many Afghan leaders wrongly believed that they could field a military force—an infantry force—that could fight conventionally in the desert, with no cover and under massive bombardment. There were many mistakes.

LF: Al-Qaeda stopped nearly everything to fight at Jalalabad, the councils/committees were stopped and the training was stopped. Is that correct?

MH: Al-Qaeda's projects were stopped when Abu Abdullah decided to join the Jalalabad battle. Everything: training, committees; anything that had been agreed, stopped. All of al-Qaeda was with Abu Abdullah in Jalalabad and many Arab-Afghans followed him there. He poured money into the Jalalabad battle, purchasing weapons, ammunition, cars and he himself went to battle. He said, 'Anybody who wants to come, come.' That raised a lot of energy among the others to go and join him.

LF: How many Arab-Afghans joined? What about those at Sadda camp, did they join in too? Abdullah Azzam was a big supporter of the Arab-Afghan campaign at Jalalabad, as I understand it.

MH: I think everybody in Peshawar went to the battle because Azzam was shouting about it very loudly in Jalalabad. In his *Al-Jihad* magazine, he made pages about the *shuhada*—those who were killed in battle. He was supporting the campaign very heavily and bringing attention to it and this attracted people from outside Afghanistan to come and join. They didn't read anything about the weapons or the battle even, they only read about the martyrs, and they came to join to be martyrs.

I don't know the numbers exactly but hundreds of Arabs went and many more non-Arabs. For example, 300 Bengalis fought with Abu Abdullah in this battle.

LF: So a large number of people joined bin Laden. Outside of Abu Hafs, and yourself, was there much opposition among the Arab-Afghans to the war?

MH: Only a few Arabs were fundamentally against the idea of the Jalalabad battle itself. I think I was among the strongest in this field, but there were also others who were against being there such as Abdul Aziz Ali and Muhammad Makkawi, who as I mentioned earlier was so angry at the early disorganisation he called it 'a goat war'. It was no better organised when Abu Abdullah joined the battle. When I met with Abu Abdullah, he had a tactical map with many movements, but no strategic view at all.

LF: I don't know much about Arab-Afghan opposition apart from what I have read in your accounts, but there is a very famous quote by an Afghan mujahidin commander, Abdul Haq. He said the year before the Jalalabad battle, when the Russians had still not withdrawn but when the mujahidin wanted to attack Jalalabad, that it would be stupid to try to take the city, because 'it would be stupid for 10,000 people to die' and that 'the Russians would bomb the shit out of us'.[2]

Obviously, the Russians had left at the time of the Jalalabad battle, but by the statistics of the Afghan military's aerial campaign against the mujahidin, it seems they did as Abdul Haq predicted the Russians would. An astounding number of Scud missiles were launched, and I think in the period 1989–1992 Afghanistan was the location of the largest aerial bombardment since World War II.

MH: This was Abdul Haq of the Hizb i Islami of Yunis Khalis? He was against Jalalabad but at that time, he had no real authority. It was a grave mistake for the mujahidin to try to fight conventionally in the desert, especially under such heavy bombardment with little cover, and no rear support. They did not have the capability to do so. They had no real heavy weapons, although some did arrive on the Jalalabad scene very late.

I will tell you a story to show you how comical the war was: the heavy weapons and the heavy anti-aircraft guns: do you know where they came from?

LF: I guess from Pakistan.

MH: Well the ISI brought them into Afghanistan, but they came from the Americans: from Iraq and Kuwait, they were the spoils of the Gulf War!

LF: From the Gulf War?

MH: Yes.

LF: How on earth did they get to Afghanistan?

MH: Some Afghan mujahidin joined the Americans directly against Saddam Hussein in liberating Iraq. They went directly to Saudi Arabia, and they were financed heavily and there are photographs of them. They said it was something temporary.

LF: The Afghan mujahidin?

MH: Yes, some big leaders of the Afghan mujahidin were there and took money to join. After Saddam Hussein was defeated and left Kuwait, the Americans gave them a prize: they took arms from the Iraq Army that were taken from Kuwait and they took some heavy equipment—heavy machine guns, artillery pieces—and they sent it in a convoy, crossing Peshawar to the front of Jalalabad. My dear friend Abu Zayd al-Tunisi told me the story because he was there in the front line when this equipment came and he was watching what was going on. He was very angry. He said, 'They came, these Pakistanis from the Intelligence, and put the guns in one line and fired on Jalalabad. They kept them there for a day or two and then they took them back. They took everything and went back. They did not leave anything at the front.'

LF: I thought Afghan participation in the Gulf War was the stuff of myth.

MH: No.

LF: So did any weapons from the Gulf War stay in the hands of the Afghan mujahidin?

MH: The ISI took the weapons back but later they claimed that they had provided heavy weapons in Jalalabad. They also gave some of these weapons from the Iraq war spoils to Haqqani. His relations with the ISI had worsened so they gave him some Iraqi anti-aircraft guns. It was a trick to keep Haqqani close to the ISI and reliant on them, because they did not supply much ammunition and it was not available at the tribal markets. They knew Haqqani would need it from time to time and would have to ask them for it, and so this 'gift' would tie him to them. For other Afghan leaders, the ISI gave the spoils as a reward for sharing in the war with the Americans against Saddam in Kuwait.

LF: So, weapons seized by the Americans in Kuwait and Iraq ended up in Pakistan and were shipped into Afghanistan for use in Jalalabad and given as gifts. I thought the Jalalabad battle did not last that long. How did Abu Zayd al-Tunisi see this? Why was he in Jalalabad if al-Qaeda had withdrawn from the area?

MH: The battle, or the siege as it turned into, went on for a long time. But before this, there were very limited heavy weapons, which contributed to the mujahidin's defeat. Al-Qaeda was defeated very badly in July of 1989, and after this it did not participate any more as an organisation. But that does not mean its members did not visit the fronts and run training camps for a while, and try to be close to watch the others' activities. At last, though, al-Qaeda left Jalalabad totally. In my book, I called the whole campaign 'a big folly', and it was.[3]

One reason it was such a disaster was because many people who supported the campaign did not think in military terms. They did not think about things like needing heavy weaponry. I remember arguing with some of the Salafis from the organisations about why being involved was a bad idea. I told them, 'This battle is a disaster. It is a big mistake.' They said, 'You are a politician not a Shariah man. It is correct in Shariah.' I said, 'Stop. It is not the right place to fight the communists.' They ignored my advice that it was the wrong battle. Exactly like Abu Abdullah ignored advice on 9/11.

LF: Speaking of groups, you commented earlier that bin Laden raised a lot of energy among the Arabs to join him in this battle. Did they think he could repeat the victory at Jaji and this time they wanted to be a part of the action?

I have always wondered why so many groups joined, particularly those that had not earlier really joined in the action, like the Egyptian organisations. Did they follow along because they wanted to keep close to bin Laden? Did they think if they did not participate he might stop giving them money? I find their case particularly curious since they were among the loudest critics of the Afghan Interim Government because it was headed by Sigbatullah Mujaddidi, who I think some of them even made *takfir* against. Why did they fight when, if they won, someone they had publicly made *takfir* of would be the head of the Afghan government?

MH: All the groups went to Jalalabad because they were afraid of being left out of the big victory that was expected to come. Yes, some went to stay close to Abu Abdullah and they ran to join al-Qaeda and to be partners in this victory. They were looking out for their own interests. What they got instead was a heavy defeat that had disastrous consequences for everyone.

* * *

An inglorious defeat

Although the Jalalabad conflict dragged on until April 1992, when the regime finally fell, the forces of bin Laden and the Arab-Afghans who followed him were largely defeated over a two-day period in July 1989. They were forced to withdraw under heavy attack from the Afghan Army and Dostum's militia and lost all of the territory that had been gained, including Samar Khel, at a great loss of life.

The defeat came as a shock to the Arab-Afghans who had expected victory. In its aftermath, bin Laden and others like Azzam who had supported his campaign were singled out for criticism.

* * *

LF: I read in Mustafa al-Yamani's account of the Jalalabad battle's aftermath that bin Laden refused to address the criticism directed at him, or to answer questions from people about the defeat.[4] What about Abu Hafs and Abu Ubaydah? You had some strong words to say to all three of them. You said you would try them in a court.

MH: During the battle of 5–7 July 1989 I said if 'I had the power I would put them on trial' because of the waste of lives of the youth in a battle that was clearly a trap, which they had been warned against. It was like 9/11: they were warned not to do it and they did it.

During al-Qaeda's preparation for Jalalabad, I gave Abu Ubaydah my paper about the defects of the campaign and why it was a terrible idea to join the battle. At the time, Abu Ubaydah said to me he thought it was logical, and he took it to Abu Abdullah in Jalalabad. When Abu Ubaydah came back, I asked what the result was and he told me, 'I saw something different there on the battlefield. I wanted to throw your paper to the wind.'

LF: Did they address your criticism or the criticism of others in the aftermath?

MH: No, not really. Criticism of Abu Abdullah was very heavy, especially from among the people who had warned him about involving him-

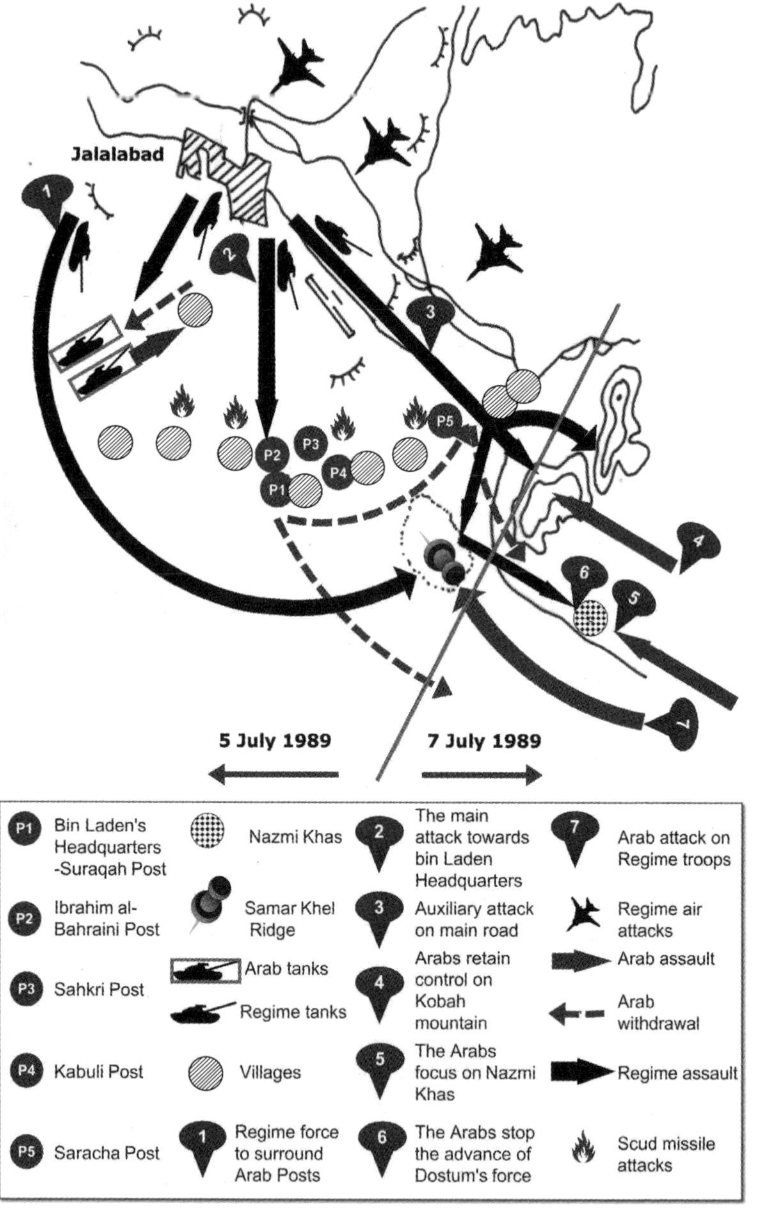

Fig 11: Map of the Battle of Jalalabad

self in the Jalalabad battle but whose advice he had ignored. I made some very strong comments because Abu Abdullah came rushing to the Battle of Jalalabad. He was not organised: there was very little planning, and in the space of a few hours he managed to lose what had been gained in weeks and weeks. A lot of people died; for what? Many very good people died; some were my friends from Khost. But here I should add Abu Abdullah was not the only one criticised. Abdullah Azzam was also heavily criticised.

LF: Why did Azzam receive criticism? Was it because he was calling for people to join the battle?

MH: Yes, Abdullah Azzam had raised a lot of publicity calling for people to come and join and he failed to notice any of the traps of the battle for the Arabs and Afghans. Hundreds of youth came from outside because of Azzam's articles.

LF: It seems to me while the Jaji battle showed the role a victory plays in group formation and making leaders of men, especially bin Laden, the Jalalabad battle shows us the opposite. It shows how defeat affects leadership, but more importantly, it shows how defeat caused more factionalism in the Arab-Afghan yard, and the creation of new groups who no longer wanted to follow the leadership of bin Laden or Abdullah Azzam.

MH: Yes, the role of victory and defeat in forming these groups is very significant. The success at Jaji made unity around the successful leader and the outcome of this was al-Qaeda and the rush of people to join with Abu Abdullah. After Jalalabad, the opposite happened. It was an unsuccessful war, and people left and the Arabs separated and divided into many groups. So, from Jalalabad we can clearly see the role defeat played in forming the new groups that emerged after Jalalabad.

Also, the defeat damaged relations within al-Qaeda. After that battle and its very negative results, the cohesion between the three great leaders of al-Qaeda—Abu Abdullah, Abu Ubaydah and Abu Hafs—was damaged and it never fully recovered.

LF: We can also see the role failure played in shaping al-Qaeda's organisational development and direction after Jalalabad, namely that it disintegrated, which is something you've written quite a lot about in your books. After the failure at Jalalabad, there were a few phases of this disintegration. First, the groups who fought with bin Laden, or made allegiance to him before the Jalalabad battle, left. Was the defeat why so many of them stopped being a part of al-Qaeda? We spoke earlier about how there were many non-Arabs in al-Qaeda. Did the Jalalabad defeat affect their willingness to follow bin Laden and al-Qaeda?

MH: Yes. There was a great loss of life in Jalalabad; not only from al-Qaeda but also from the other organisations that had pledged allegiance to Abu Abdullah, or followed him as temporary allies in the Jalalabad battle. In fact, their losses were much higher. The Battle of Jalalabad cost Abu Abdullah more than the Battle of Jaji because it lasted longer and extended into larger areas with longer supply lines that were exposed to the enemy.

Unlike Jaji, Abu Abdullah did not emerge victorious, and so those who had wanted to follow him when he was successful no longer wanted to follow him, because as the leader he was responsible for the defeat. We should also note that some groups only joined al-Qaeda for the battle, so their allegiances were temporary, and when they were defeated, they left.

LF: When these groups left, al-Qaeda's numbers were greatly reduced.

MH: Yes, and it happened very quickly.

LF: It seems there were more departures from al-Qaeda too, from among those who remained with the group but then became frustrated because after Jalalabad al-Qaeda basically withdrew from combat in Afghanistan and stayed in its camps. For those who joined al-Qaeda seeking action, this change of direction meant they were not, as they had imagined, on the fronts fighting but instead in the camps, and so they left. In this way, the failure at Jalalabad seems to have caused al-Qaeda's priorities to shift to training, and the result was a loss of members.

MH: Yes. The best example of this is Abdul Majid al-Jazairi. He was initially a part of al-Qaeda but he left because he was dissatisfied with al-Qaeda's new 'work' of training. He then set up his own group in Jalalabad. This group of Algerians later became involved in the events in Algeria in the 1990s, which were very bad.

LF: I read in your book that after bin Laden left, and Abu Ubaydah and Abu Hafs were again in charge, they focused their attention on making al-Qaeda the leading training institution.[5]

MH: Yes.

LF: But al-Qaeda had some competition for this goal by then because Ikhwan Muslimin had become active and established a camp and other organisations had established their own camps. A number of new groups had also been established, including some by former al-Qaeda members like Abdul Majid.

It seems to me that not only had the Arab-Afghan yard become much more competitive, but al-Qaeda no longer had the 'gloss' it once had after Jaji, or the authority, or level of respect. It essentially had to rebuild itself and recruit from among trainees in the camps it had.

MH: Al-Qaeda withdrew after this disastrous defeat and had no future strategy for what was left of the organisation after the battle. Abu Hafs and Abu Ubaydah worked to make a strong group of highly trained, highly equipped men, but after Jalalabad they stayed in the camps!

Those boys in the camps wanted to go out and fight because there were no real activities in the camps while there was real fighting going on everywhere. There were very few of them after Jalalabad. When I asked al-Qaeda to give me some men to help in our 1990 Khost Airport operation, they only gave me a small number. It was under ten people, and I was angry, thinking they were not helping, but Sayf al-Adl told me they gave me nearly all of their trained people.

It is important here to note why al-Qaeda had so few people left, and it is a reason you missed in your explanation. When I talked with Sayf about why al-Qaeda could not give me more people to help at Khost he told me that the reason they had so few people left was that Tanzim al-Jihad had separated from al-Qaeda. This is a very important point.

Tanzim al-Jihad separated their people because they were already planning to go to Sudan. Tanzim al-Jihad's leaders thought they should relocate there because an Islamist regime had come to power and it was very near to Egypt. They could work there because they met many Sudanese doctors in Afghanistan who returned to work in the Sudanese regime at a high rank. Tanzim al-Jihad was the first to think to shift to Sudan, and because of this, it withdrew its force from al-Qaeda. This is why by 1990 al-Qaeda had very few people left.

Al-Qaeda's numbers did grow a little after that because of the efforts of Abu Hafs and Abu Ubaydah and others to build up their force. In late 1991 through 1992, they built a good group; well equipped and highly trained. When I asked al-Qaeda to support my programme in Gardez in 1991, they agreed to give me this group, which at that time numbered around sixty. It was good because those boys were highly trained, but they were just sitting in the camps. They were very happy when they came to know I was going to take them to the Gardez front. We began preparing for a campaign from October 1991 to April 1992, but then Gardez surrendered and there was no fight.

Abu Hafs and Abu Ubaydah worked hard to make al-Qaeda the leading training academy and to bring new people and groups towards them, but they faced many challenges in this work, and al-Qaeda remained a small organisation.

LF: Yes, it seems so. From the account of Jamal al-Fadl, it was during this time al-Qaeda was recruiting from its camps, trying to raise its numbers.[6]

Would it be fair to say that there were almost two al-Qaedas during this time? First, the combat organisation, whose numbers were large and with a large number of non-Arabs, but which essentially dissolved after the Jalalabad defeat. Then, the smaller post-Jalalabad al-Qaeda, focused on training and outside work.

MH: Yes. When Abu Abdullah left for Saudi Arabia after the defeat at Jalalabad, al-Qaeda lost many members. Then Tanzim al-Jihad took its members and began moving to Sudan. Then, of course, al-Qaeda lost members when it retreated to the training camps, and abandoned almost entirely any fighting in Afghanistan, leaving the boys in the camps with nothing to do.

We should note here there is an irony in al-Qaeda withdrawing to the camps to focus on training, because al-Qaeda, despite its military character, did not know how to produce military leaders. During the Afghan jihad its military names were confined to two people: Abu Ubaydah al-Banshiri and Abu Hafs al-Masri, who led the Battle of Jaji, which was al-Qaeda's only military achievement during this time.

LF: Some other al-Qaeda members like Khalid Habib did distinguish themselves in battle though.

MH: Yes, but no military figures appeared after the Afghan jihad and al-Qaeda did not have any more military achievements in Afghanistan. After Jalalabad, al-Qaeda almost disappeared from the combat arena in Afghanistan; it only participated several times in a very symbolic way.

If Abu Abdullah had won in Jalalabad, I am sure everything would have changed, but he did not, and after that battle, al-Qaeda did virtually nothing in Afghanistan. Al-Qaeda fell down very fast after Jalalabad. It was badly damaged.

* * *

The defeat at Jalalabad resulted in Azzam and bin Laden's status becoming weakened in the eyes of the volunteer youth. Previously treated with a degree of reverence, both men were heavily criticised in the aftermath of Jalalabad. Azzam remained in Peshawar, while bin Laden retreated to Saudi Arabia.

* * *

MH: After leaving the front Abu Abdullah went very quickly to Saudi Arabia because everyone was angry and the youth and other leaders criticised him. Azzam also lost his credibility and even the youth in Peshawar began to criticise him.

LF: Bin Laden's retreat to Saudi Arabia appears to have been prompted by the criticism levelled at him following the Jalalabad defeat. Mustafa al-Yamani's account of the aftermath of Jalalabad is very revealing. He said when he and others were trying to talk to bin Laden about the failure that bin Laden refused to address their questions.[7] Do you think bin Laden's departure further weakened his standing among people, because he did not stay and answer his critics?

MH: Abu Abdullah could not believe he was defeated at Jalalabad and he lost a big group of his best followers at that time. I was very angry because some of them were my friends from Khost, and they were gone because of bad leadership. Abu Abdullah did not stay long before leaving to Saudi Arabia, which weakened his and al-Qaeda's standing, and Arab morale in Peshawar. Azzam was left alone among the angry and disappointed Arabs.

LF: Do you think bin Laden left because people like Mustafa al-Yamani were asking him hard questions?

MH: Yes of course.

LF: Before I read Mustafa al-Yamani's account I didn't know the Yemenis were so angry at bin Laden, and they too were demanding answers.

MH: Yes, many people were angry.

* * *

Anger at bin Laden and Azzam within the Arab-Afghan community was such that it essentially created a climate of insurrection among the youth—where they were less likely to follow the guidance of these two men. Adding to the increasingly fractured environment were the loud voices of a growing takfiri movement that influenced a number of the youth, many of whom were seeking to establish their own group and undertake training. This resulted in the rise of a preparation current and the militarisation of the Arab-Afghan yard.

Azzam's 1989 assassination removed the last counterbalance to this rising current—although it is doubtful whether either he or bin Laden had the clout in the aftermath of Jalalabad to challenge the current rising among the new generation of volunteers. It also meant the Sadda camp found itself without a leader of Azzam's calibre, and many of its members dispersed into newer groups, who were establishing camps for themselves in the Jalalabad region, most in the area along the road between Torkham and Jalalabad. The entrance of Ikhwan Muslimin into the fray further complicated the already crowded and increasingly competitive scene. The group had previously remained on the sidelines, but around the time of Jalalabad and in its aftermath, it became more active.

* * *

Ikhwan Muslimin enters the fray

MH: Ikhwan Muslimin was very far from the fighting in Afghanistan, but in Jalalabad something significant happened. During the Jalalabad fight in 1989 and in 1990, strange comments were coming from Ikhwan Muslimin circles in Peshawar. They were giving warnings to the leaders of al-Qaeda. They said, 'We will never let Abu Abdullah be the leader of the Arabs, or the hero of the Arabs, which he tried to build himself as when he went to Jalalabad. We will never allow that.' They said they would not allow Abu Abdullah to become a hero of the Islamic nation. The leaders of al-Qaeda learned of the warning but it was not spread among Arabs in Peshawar. It was the first time for Ikhwan Muslimin to say something like that very strongly.

LF: What did bin Laden say in return? Anything?

MH: He was not there at that time; he had left.

LF: Did he hear about it?

MH: Of course he heard, of course. I did not hear directly from him what he said, but I was told he made a comment about horses that are retired from the race, and said that there was only one horse running in the race. I knew Abu Abdullah meant Ikhwan Muslimin was the horse that was out of the race now and he was the only one running.

LF: But al-Qaeda was not very successful in getting control over the other groups either. I may have this wrong, but I thought al-Qaeda was vulnerable to the efforts of Ikhwan Muslimin who saw the power vacuum left by Azzam's assassination and bin Laden's absence as an opportunity to get control.

MH: They sent a few cadres to Jalalabad, mostly from among the Iraqis. Later, in 1990, and for the first time in the war, the Iraqi Ikhwan Muslimin came and established a camp. This was in 1990. The second thing was that Ikhwan Muslimin increased their pressure on Abu Harith al-Urduani to come under their influence and he refused very strongly.

At that time, Ikhwan Muslimin was unable to control all of the Arabs, even after Abu Abdullah's departure from the Afghan yard and Azzam's death. This is because Ikhwan Muslimin had stood to the side during the Afghan jihad and they only joined in the smallest way in Jalalabad, and after the battle finished.

All of the Arab mujahidin in the field knew Ikhwan Muslimin had just been sitting in Peshawar doing relief work helping the refugees. The Arabs knew Ikhwan Muslimin had nothing to do with fighting because they were afraid governments in Arab countries would think they were preparing themselves to launch a military campaign in their countries. Ikhwan Muslimin stayed out of the Afghan jihad because it was very keen to show the governments that it did not intend to field any military force.

LF: How about the camp set up by the Iraqi Ikhwan Muslimin?

MH: In 1990, some Ikhwan Muslimin from Iraq appeared in Jalalabad and set up a training camp for themselves. The war was nearly over and Jalalabad had turned into a protracted conflict for both sides—although the communist government's control of the city remained constant. Abdul Hadi al-Iraqi came and trained in that camp, and as you know, he later played a role in the fighting inside Afghanistan after the American invasion.

Ikhwan Muslimin mainly entered to prevent Abu Abdullah becoming the leader of the Ummah and making an international-jihadi platform that would compete with Ikhwan Muslimin. But by this time, and although he had been defeated at Jalalabad, Abu Abdullah had more combat experience.

Ikhwan Muslimin's combat time in Palestine was very short. The Afghan jihad was longer and bigger. Abu Abdullah was younger and more revolutionary, and so Ikhwan Muslimin became afraid that there was a threat coming from Afghanistan by the name of Abu Abdullah with his al-Qaeda organisation. Because of Abu Abdullah's organisation, Ikhwan Muslimin did not follow him or support him. It was not because they hated violence; after all, they supported the mujahidin in Syria in 1982. It was not a case of them being against violence or killing people; it depended on the benefit they saw in supporting a movement or an organisation and what they would gain from it. In fact, this is similar to what Ikhwan Muslimin has done in the revolutions in the Arab world: it did not share in the initial efforts, but after the people had risen up and occupied the streets then it came to be involved because it saw benefit in doing so and thought there was something to be gained.

LF: It certainly appears that way. With the youth not following Ikhwan Muslimin and essentially insubordinate to Azzam and bin Laden and al-Qaeda's commanders, the climate after Jalalabad had no real authority structure. This created a dangerous vacuum allowing for the rise of the Jalalabad School.

The rise of the current of preparation and the Jalalabad School

LF: In your books you wrote about the aftermath of the Jalalabad defeat precipitating what you called the current of 'Preparation of the Ummah' (*Idad al-Ummah*), which revealed a 'dangerous disaster in the intellectual and practical structure in the Islamic work'.[8] It is my understanding this preparation current was heavily influenced by Sayyid Imam's book *Al-Umdah* and the teachings of the Salafi-takfiri movement more generally. By the time the book was released, a number of leading figures from the Salafi-takfiri movement were based either in Peshawar or in the camps. Some groups within this current established camps in the area around Jalalabad, namely Gamaah Islamiyyah and Tanzim al-Jihad.

Azzam's speeches show he made some attempts to counterbalance this current, but he was already weakened, and by the end of 1989 had been assassinated. There was little to stop the current gaining influence. Al-Qaeda was essentially paralysed and it lost leadership status among groups who may not have been takfiri but were looking for action outside of Afghanistan. It seems it really was a power vacuum open for the taking, which led to the formation of many different groups, and had very significant consequences on the Afghan-Arab yard. I think what formed in this environment were not really groups but rather a School of Jihad that was ultimately exported to other countries.

MH: Yes. We should note this aftermath of Jalalabad, this training storm, continues to affect the world today because the Jalalabad School of jihad that grew from it still exists. In fact, today it is the strongest of all the Schools, and the one that appeals most to the youth because of its focus on action without attention to consequences—despite the fact it has brought nothing but disaster.

The Jalalabad School started without any leadership, strategy, or political thoughts; without belonging to a nation or homeland. It was and still is characterised by impetuous youth with extreme Salafi thoughts and a careless approach; they did not care or did not think about the consequences of their actions. This Jalalabad School, or School of the Youth as I sometimes call it, spread and infiltrated what was already established in the Arab-Afghan yard. It infiltrated the School of Abdullah Azzam, and Maktab al-Khadamat and Khaldan. At last, it infiltrated the School of al-Qaeda, when Abu Abdullah was encouraged by the kind of shiny operations that had no strategy and no political vision and the peak of all of that was the operation of 9/11. Now, these two schools are in conflict for influence and control, as we have seen in recent events in Syria, and which we will talk about later.

LF: Yes, training storm is certainly a fitting description, especially since it spread beyond Jalalabad, and as you note still continues today. For this reason I think it is important to delve deeper into the training storm that grew into this school and to clarify what it is we are including in these terms. When I talk about this training storm coming from the camps of Jalalabad, or growing into the Jalalabad School or the School of the Youth, I mean the camps around Jalalabad, but also Khost, with al-Qaeda's group of camps, and the moving of the activities of the Sadda camp to Khost where a camp was established and became known as Khaldan. Because of Khaldan's links with a number of the camps and key figures operating in Jalalabad, I consider it a part of the Jalalabad School, particularly since what remained from the Jalalabad camps appears to have merged into Khaldan when most of the Arab-Afghans left the region in 1992–3. This left Khaldan and al-Qaeda's Jihadwal in Khost as the major dedicated training camps for foreign volunteers. Do you agree?

MH: Yes, but here we should add there was also Hekmatyar's Yarmuk camp in Logar, although that did not start until after the civil war began in 1992, and the Arabs who trained there fought with him. It was not like Khaldan or al-Qaeda's camps, which were more independent and open for all.

LF: When did the Sadda camp move from Pakistan to Khost? Was it after Abdullah Azzam's assassination?

MH: The camp transferred the main activities after Abdullah Azzam was martyred and the Pakistanis had started to chase the Arabs. Pressure had come on Sadda after its training of Palestinians in explosives. Because of this, Abu Burhan al-Suri recommended the transfer of training to a camp in the tribal area of Khost. At that time, he was still working with Maktab al-Khadamat.

Khaldan became one of the landmarks of Arab training and at times competed with al-Qaeda. They formed most of the history of the Arabs training in Afghanistan, and each of them had many impacts on world events after the liberation of Afghanistan. Today, they are both influential, and fighting each other for influence and control in Syria. But now I think al-Qaeda is weaker and the Jalalabad School is winning.

LF: Yes. Both have a living legacy we might say, and one that continues to this day. To me, this makes understanding the history of these groups-turned-Schools all the more important. Khaldan's history has always fascinated me, partly because it has remained so misunderstood and underestimated as an influential player in its own right and as part of the Jalalabad School, which is as you note now the dominant school. The dynamics of the camp changed quite significantly after the move into Afghanistan. As I understand it, Abu Burhan soon left and Khaldan started operating under 'new management', which was more independent from what remained of Maktab al-Khadamat, and more extreme—particularly in terms of welcoming Salafis and takfiris. Here, I am talking of Ibn Shaykh al-Libi, who took over from Abu Burhan. Later, Abu Zubaydah joined Ibn Shaykh in the management of the camp and its guesthouses in Pakistan.

MH: Abu Burhan had prominent students who took over military training after he departed to Sudan following Pakistani threats against him. These students took a tighter doctrinal approach and a political path that was more violent in nature. The methodology in that camp was very strange.

LF: It was takfiri I thought, or at least that is the account from some other groups who were initially working in the camp, like the Uyghurs from East Turkestan.[9] I know the Indonesian group Jamaah Islamiyyah, which was itself quite doctrinally strict, stayed away from Khaldan. When Sadda shut, instead of going to Khaldan in Afghanistan like other groups did, they moved to Torkham, and when they needed to close that camp they went to the Philippines.

MH: Yes, Khaldan was strange with the different groups it supported. Most of them were North African and the main group was the Algerians. The North African camps in Jalalabad, and also later Khaldan, provided the Islamic Group in Algeria with trainers, and contributed to a damaging and violent military campaign that changed the face of Algeria.

Khaldan began forming close working relationships with the Algerians even when they had their own camp in Jalalabad, which was the 'Abdul Majid al-Jazairi camp'. Abdul Majid had been a former member of al-Qaeda but he split with them and formed his own camp for the Algerians; because of that, he shared in responsibility for the disaster in Algeria and he was killed there.

LF: Khaldan also had close links to Ibn Khattab and Osama Azmarai's groups. Both these men initially had their own camps. After these camps closed, people wanting to join their fronts went by agreement to Khaldan. These two men were, if memory serves, part of the youth who refused to follow bin Laden or Abdullah Azzam, and instead set up their own groups.

MH: Yes, in that period it was the first time for training camps for the youths of Saudi Arabia to appear. Khattab led the most prominent of these and later became famous because of his role in Chechnya, which severely affected the course of events there. Khattab worked for a time on the Tajikistan case and fought behind the Amu Daria River attacking Tajik and Russian Army positions on the other side. Among Khattab's friends was Azmarai, a courageous fighter during his time in Afghanistan, who later worked against American targets in East Asia until he was arrested there.

LF: Azmarai has always interested me. He worked closely with Khalid Shaykh Muhammad and his cousin Ramzi Yousef, who were also very active in the Jalalabad scene and later, at Khaldan. As you know, Ramzi Yousef carried out the first World Trade Center bombing, and Khalid Shaykh orchestrated the 9/11 attacks; and together with Azmarai they had plotted to bring down many American aircraft in Asia in the mid-1990s.

It has always been assumed that Azmarai was influenced to target the United States by al-Qaeda, but he was from the earlier current that emerged from Jalalabad and Khaldan and argued for attacking America.

Fadil Harun claimed in his book that you were responsible for encouraging the anti-American current and pointed to some meetings held in 1991 at which he claimed you argued for the need to attack America.[10]

MH: In 1991, there was the Gulf War and it was widely known America was a big enemy and destroying the Arabs. In ten years, over 1.5 million people were killed from America's actions, and most of them were children. America became the enemy because of its actions, not me.

Also, I should point out it was after Jalalabad that the Western media started to call us terrorists. It was the first time we heard the expression 'the Arab terrorists in Afghanistan' and it came from the secretary of NATO. This was the start of the change of the mood of the West towards us.

Pakistan of course followed, and they started to pressure us, and some people from its intelligence services said to us frankly, 'You should leave before we move, we can't withstand American pressure on us for much longer.' Then they started to chase the Arabs, and by 1993, they had finished and nearly everybody was out. Just before this, there were some American investigators who came to investigate the Arabs, including one lady who interrogated them very roughly and she hit them and she was under very good, very strong protection from Pakistan's authorities. One of our friends saw this during the interrogations and so everybody came to know that the Americans were behind Pakistan's pressure on us. I did not convince them: it was very clear for everyone. America gave the evidence itself and everyone came to know.

What Harun said about this meeting is not true. Harun was not there at the time. This is guesthouse gossip. I did not convince anyone. It is my old personal thoughts and still my thoughts until now. It is a permanent case. I consider the actions of the American regime as those of an enemy; for me, and for my people. Here, I mean America, the regime, not the American people. But considering something an enemy does not mean to fight—or at least not fight at that moment, and I didn't ask anybody to attack America. It was a very stupid idea for anyone to attack America. It is suitable now for the Taliban in Afghanistan because America is there occupying the country. But even the Soviet Union during all of its period did not attack America and it was the main opposition to America and its biggest enemy. This is because the Soviet Union knew any attack would not be in its favour. Also, I should add that at that time Abu Abdullah was focused on Yemen, Sudan and Saudi Arabia. He did not decide to target America until much later, although of course he was very angry at the occupation of Saudi Arabia by American armed forces during the Gulf War.

LF: One reason I doubted the stories about Azmarai being a part of al-Qaeda, or being influenced by its agenda, was your account about meeting Azmarai, and how when he initially thought al-Qaeda was supporting your Tajikistan project, he became angry. He thought this was directing attention to the wrong area and that America should have been targeted as a priority.

MH: Yes, he was angry at al-Qaeda; thinking they were supporting me and not focusing on attacking America, until he came to know Abu Abdullah had not approved al-Qaeda supporting my Tajikistan project.

LF: It has always perplexed me why links were drawn between Khattab and Azmarai and al-Qaeda, especially when a close look at their origins and setting up of independent camps in Jalalabad reveals that from the beginning they refused to come under the historical leadership of either Azzam or bin Laden. Nor did Khattab and Azmarai follow the same programme.

MH: No, they represented two different currents. Khattab was focused on fighting at the fronts. Azmarai seemed to favour attacking America, which was not done on an open front.

LF: Both would have been threatening to al-Qaeda. Although, I imagine at that time Khattab, as a Saudi taking young men to train for combat on open fronts, was seen as the greater threat by bin Laden because a significant number of Saudi and Gulf mujahidin followed Khattab. He was attracting the people al-Qaeda was seeking to recruit.

MH: Khattab was a big threat and he refused many attempts by al-Qaeda to draw him in; from the beginning at Jalalabad, all the way through until after al-Qaeda formed the World Islamic Front in 1998.

LF: Azmarai was also Saudi and had his own camp in Jalalabad but he never seems to have secured as many followers. Although, we could say he had a bigger impact in some respects because the 1993 World Trade Center attack, the Bojinka Plot in Asia and possibly the attacks on American interests in Saudi Arabia in 1995 all trace their origins to his Jalalabad camp, and later to Khaldan. I think you have also made note of the origins of some of these plots being in the Jalalabad School of jihad. Since then a number of other attacks and plots have emerged whose origins also trace to Khaldan and the Jalalabad School.

MH: I made note of how the attack in Saudi Arabia was not al-Qaeda but came from the Jalalabad School instead.

LF: I can trace a lot more to this current, particularly after 1996, which we will discuss a little later.

Returning to the aftermath of Jalalabad, what is striking is that every group seems to have had a desire for immediate action, and operated under their own programme, with their own understanding of jihad and preparation of the Ummah, and a strong belief that everyone else should follow them. I think we can see now with events in Syria and the competition and infighting among the Salafi jihadi groups that history is repeating; it is like Jalalabad all over again. Do you think a reason the groups were not willing to follow the historical leadership of bin Laden and Azzam after Jalalabad and formed their own organisations was because of the *Al-Umdah* book and the current around it—even for people like Azmarai and Khattab, who were not takfiris?

This current seems to have made popular rejecting traditional leadership by arguing that performing jihad essentially meant one did not need education or religious knowledge, because knowledge and purity were gained through jihad. The consequence of this was that anyone who had fought could claim authority: not only as a mujahid, but as a leader, gaining some form of religious authority solely by virtue of their participation in jihad. As a result, the groups that emerged from the training storm, and the Jalalabad School of jihad that developed, all claimed religious authority for *Idad al-Ummah*—preparing the nation—usually based on their participation in combat.

MH: None of those groups had strategic goals, agendas, or programmes. They all seemed to follow that shiny slogan '*Idad al-Ummah*', but very few really understood what that meant. They were all very disconnected from the Ummah, in fact. These new groups that rose up had people in them who were not representative of their people. Most members were middle class, and few were from the poor. The principles adopted by these groups were Wahhabi and Salafi/takfiri, which caused deep divisions between them and their people, who were, in their eyes, either *mushrikin* or infidel.

As I mentioned earlier, the features of the Jalalabad School and the Khaldan camp that still exist in today's Salafi jihadis are that they operate without leadership, political vision or strategic planning, and do not care about the consequences of their actions. They do not care about the Ummah; sometimes they do not recognise it and other times they are hostile towards it. This is because they target the internal Islamic line, and even when they do turn outside—to targets outside the Ummah—they quickly return to internal engagement, and fighting, which we can see now in various places following the Arab Spring.

After gaining experience in Afghanistan, some movements focused on combat but still they remained far from their people, even in their combat work, because it damaged the majority who did not benefit from such action. They also had no alternative plan, or action, or goals beyond religious slogans, which could not address the urgent needs of the people. Moral advice did little to help against the structural oppression the people faced within their home countries, and which forced them to deviate to survive. So, these groups remained far from their people, instead of working for them and with them.

Al-Qaeda was no exception, but suffered more as a multinational organisation, which did not focus on the requirements of a particular region or people. It compensated for this by focusing exclusively on military training, but the kind of training it offered took the youth away from their nation. It made them lonely, aggressive, more militant and dependent on the gun to solve everything.

Even so, there was a very big gap of experience between these new groups of the Jalalabad era and the older groups of al-Qaeda and Maktab al-Khadamat, especially in political experience and in matters of method. It was made worse by al-Qaeda withdrawing from fighting because the youth 'leading' these new groups, like Khattab and Azmarai, wanted action, they wanted to continue fighting, so they chose to fight with Sayyaf.

They were eager to fight but they did not know anything about the political situation in the Jalalabad area and the corruption and they did not know the role of Pakistan. They also did not know that Sayyaf wanted to take advantage of this group and use them to help persuade other Arabs to stay in Jalalabad, because he feared they would all leave and go to Khost and join Haqqani. Azmarai and Khattab stayed in Jalalabad and did not go to Khost, like al-Qaeda and the others. This is why these two came to have so much influence among the Jalalabad youths.

LF: Speaking of influence, in the period 1986 to 1989, a number of senior Salafi figures appeared in Pakistan and on the Peshawar scene and were influential in the emergence of the current of *Idad al-Ummah*. Among them were people who were trying to rebuild organisations like the Egyptian Gamaah Islamiyyah and Tanzim al-Jihad, which both established camps in Jalalabad. But their influence did not bring the groups together. Instead they were operating separately to a number of other groups who emerged or arrived around this time from Indonesia, Somalia, Bangladesh, China, Libya, Algeria, as well as groups like Khattab's and Azmarai's. I remember reading a comment in your book where you wrote all of these groups were 'like a rainbow of different currents that could not be brought together'.[11]

It seems to me that an environment of factionalism, competition and insurrection grew in the surrounds of Jalalabad. I wonder how much of this was from the takfiri influence? Or was the weakening of bin Laden and Azzam more of a factor? I know Azzam tried to reduce the takfiri influence, but did he try to unite groups before he was killed or was he too weakened by this point? Did anyone try to bring them together? I thought al-Qaeda's leaders tried, although I assume this was difficult to do when bin Laden was not there. Again, I am struck by the parallels with what is taking place in the jihadi milieu in Syria.

MH: Abdullah Azzam could not control all of them, but he could control a good number of them. After he died, many of those who were under his influence went to other groups, or fell under the influence of the takfiris. The leadership vacuum gave everyone from these new smaller groups the chance to be a leader. Even though they were not capable, this did not stop them. They would say 'we are in the battle and we are battle leaders, and we are training and fighting', and so they thought they were the leaders of the jihadi movement. And yes, here there are strong parallels with what is happening in Syria.

After Jalalabad, al-Qaeda's leaders did try to gain control over these new groups or at the least tried to influence them, but the defeat in Jalalabad as you said resulted in the spread of insurrection among the Arab youth. It was directed against Abu Abdullah and al-Qaeda, but also against Azzam and Maktab al-Khadamat. The youth criticised Abu Abdullah and Abdullah Azzam—the two highest-ranking Arabs—and no longer listened to their advice, or followed them or their deputies. This resulted in the emergence of a large number of groups led by relatively new and inexperienced young people who were extremist in their thinking and behaviour and refused the historical leadership of Abu Abdullah and Abdullah Azzam. They wanted action and were impetuous and could make their own training centres, and formed groups because they all found funding from the same old areas of Saudi Arabia and the Gulf region.

Meanwhile, al-Qaeda's leaders had concluded that this battle was fruitless and it was full of corrupted people and they were going to lose the youth. On the one hand they thought they should withdraw entirely. But on the other they did not want to leave the Jalalabad area because it was full of camps of these youths, and al-Qaeda thought if they continued the way they were they were going to make a disaster.

Initially, al-Qaeda established camps in the Jalalabad area to try to influence them. Al-Qaeda spent a lot of money providing good food and supplies not only at its camps but also for these new groups to try to draw them in, but they failed. After around a year of running training camps there and trying to draw the youth in, al-Qaeda's leaders said, 'it is a waste of our money and time'. None of these groups listened to them, none of them respected them, and none of them followed its advice or obeyed them. So they left the area and returned to Khost.

These groups could continue at Jalalabad, and then Khaldan because although there was a power vacuum there was not a financial vacuum. Even without al-Qaeda's or Maktab al-Khadamat's help, these new groups could get money easily because it was still flowing from the Gulf merchants. Anyone who wanted money—even the takfiris—found it from the Saudis and the Gulf. Because of their funding, they contributed to this current of preparation that emerged in the aftermath of Jalalabad, and which has until now given nothing but failure.

Most of the groups today, when I hear about their actions or what they say, or I read what they write, I think they are from Jalalabad. The School of Jalalabad still exists: it even infiltrated al-Qaeda. What is happening now is not al-Qaeda; this way of thinking and behaving is the School of Jalalabad, and it has brought nothing but disaster.

Even the Afghans could not control these groups. In 1992, when Mujaddidi was the president in Kabul, the first action of those who were extremist came from some people who were settled in a camp near the Torkham entrance to Jalalabad, around 80 kilometres from the city, which by then was full of camps on both sides. They attacked a United Nations convoy and killed one person and said, 'It is our way of jihad; we do not allow the United Nations to come to the land of jihad.' Abdul Qadir, the governor of Jalalabad, arrested them for a few hours, but he could not keep them for a long time because most of the mujahidin were sympathetic towards them. The impact of Jalalabad was very big and much more than anyone can imagine.

LF: I think it is important here to note that we are talking about a big impact from what was comparatively a small group of people. Often, when the word 'camp' is used people have an idea that the Arab-Afghan camps inside Afghanistan were large like those of the Afghan Mujahidin, which were more bases than camps. None of the Arab-Afghan camps were that large. Khaldan reportedly could accommodate around 100 people at a time and it is my understanding that al-Qaeda's al-Faruq camp in Khost was possibly the largest but its capacity was under 200 people.

This idea that the camps were quite big has led to inflated numbers and estimates of how many people actually trained there. For this reason I think it is important to look at the size issue, because ultimately we are talking about a current of people who, for their collective size, had a massive impact on national and international politics, and in my view, still do.

For example, if I were to list all of the Arab-Afghan camps of Khost and Jalalabad it would read like this. In Khost, there were al-Qaeda's al-Faruq, Jihadwal, al-Saddiq and Khalid bin Walid camps. Then there was the Khaldan camp.

MH: Don't forget you also had the Salman al-Farsi and Badr camps where Pakistani groups were training.

LF: Then we have Jalalabad and al-Qaeda's three camps: two camps on farms along the road, reportedly called Badr al-Kubra and Badr al-Sughra, and the Abu Shahid al-Qatari camp. Tanzim al-Jihad, Gamaah Islamiyyah, Khattab and Azmarai all had camps there too.[12] Jemaah Islamiyyah from Indonesia had a camp and Abdul Majid al-Jazairi had a camp for his group. Did I miss any?

MH: You have forgotten Jamil ul-Rahman's camp in Kunar, which was a camp for the Salafis, until he was assassinated in 1990, but he was not part of the Jalalabad School.

LF: Yes, I am sure I have probably missed others, but my point is this: if you imagine the camps to be big, a list like this would look like large numbers of people were trained. But many of these camps were not big, and not all operated for a long period of time.

MH: I did not visit all of them, but I did see some.

LF: While we are on the subject of numbers, we spoke about the Gulf War earlier. When Iraq invaded Kuwait bin Laden called for all available Gulf mujahidin in the Arab-Afghan camps, except for the trainers, to travel to Saudi Arabia to defend the country. Did many people from the camps heed bin Laden's call to go to defend Saudi Arabia?

MH: When Saddam Hussein invaded Kuwait Abu Abdullah called for his people in Afghanistan to join him to defend Saudi Arabia and he began preparing places for a secret war in the desert. He purchased many weapons, ammunition and cars. He was preparing cars with additional fuel tanks to go longer in the desert. He worked hard at that time but the war ended the way we have seen.

Before Saddam Hussein invaded Kuwait, the Saudi government had a good relationship with Iraq and with Saddam Hussein. They financed him against Iran for ten years or more. During those days, Abu Abdullah was against Saddam and gave speeches where he said, 'Saddam is very dangerous for the Gulf and very dangerous for the Saudis and we should stop supporting him.' But the government of Saudi Arabia stopped Abu Abdullah from talking like this and treated him very roughly.

When Iraq invaded Kuwait he said, 'I told you this would happen, I said that before.' The Saudi government left Abu Abdullah to do his preparation activities until Saddam was defeated and had left Kuwait. Then they told Abu Abdullah to stop everything. We should look at this disguise because the government left him to do these activities. He and his followers had ammunition, they had secret places, they had guns and they put supplies in the desert and the towns preparing for a secret war.

Abu Abdullah was true in what he said at the beginning about Saddam and true at the end. Because of that, the government held him, and put its hand over his mouth to stop him from talking; to stop him meeting anyone, to stop him from doing anything.

LF: The American presence in the Saudi heartland is often argued to have been the turning point for bin Laden and al-Qaeda and the reason he decided to target America. But bin Laden didn't make *takfir* on the Saudis for hosting the Americans and he didn't declare war against America either. I think you wrote in your book that Abu Musab al-Suri objected to bin Laden's call for the youth in Afghanistan to go to Saudi Arabia because he thought that bin Laden was preparing to fight alongside the Americans.[13] Bin Laden did not openly rebel against the Saudi state at that time, or the religious establishment. He was still following the religious establishment and would not act without religious endorsement. Doesn't this mean that bin Laden wasn't very loud against America and wasn't very loud against the Saudi regime like he was later?

MH: No, no, he was 100 per cent against the Saudi government about that, but he could not say so in a loud voice because he was between the hands of this government. Many of the ulama had taken money from the government and closed their mouths. Most of the ordinary people in Saudi Arabia are rich and living comfortably; they do not care what is going on; they have a lot of money and a leisurely life. The youth themselves were not ready to do anything, and security was very heavy and strong. It was not the time for Abu Abdullah to speak up, and so he kept silent. Even though he kept silent the Saudi government still held him until he found a way to trick them and return to Pakistan.

8

THE AFGHAN CIVIL WAR AND ARAB-AFGHAN FLIGHT

Short on options: bin Laden's journey from house arrest in Saudi Arabia to Pakistan

In April 1991, after tricking the Saudis into issuing him a passport, bin Laden arrived back in Pakistan to a very different scene from the one he had left in July 1989.

* * *

LF: Not all the Afghan mujahidin leaders welcomed bin Laden's return to Pakistan, and it seems he thought he might be assassinated. Who did he think was trying to assassinate him and why did people he had previously fought alongside not welcome him?

MH: The Saudis were very angry with Abu Abdullah, and many Afghan mujahidin groups still received funding from Saudi Arabia. Some did not want to lose Saudi Arabia's support, and since Abu Abdullah could no longer provide them with money, they chose a side, the Saudi side. For this, they did not welcome him back.

What was not noticed at the time was the Saudis, Pakistanis and Americans were already preparing for the next phase after the fall of the Kabul regime. Although this did not happen until nearly a year later—in April 1992—they were already discussing how to form a coalition government in Afghanistan between the communists and the mujahidin. They knew Abu Abdullah might obstruct this and so they did not want him to stay.

LF: Does this also include some Afghan parties?

MH: Yes, some Afghan parties were not happy Abu Abdullah had returned because they were preparing to share power with the communists and Abu Abdullah did not agree. They thought he might gather the Arabs around him, along with some Afghans who were against such an arrangement, and make a disturbance. They thought Abu Abdullah still had the influence to do so, but in reality, he was not thinking about this at all.

Nobody tried to assassinate Abu Abdullah, but there was a fear in some circles he would be assassinated. People were warning him about this. They thought the Saudis or someone from Pakistan might assassinate him, because after Azzam was killed everyone was thinking Abu Abdullah would be next. When Abu Abdullah was in Saudi Arabia the Saudi regime could jail him but not kill him; when he returned to Pakistan, they could. This was the fear in some circles.

* * *

Al-Qaeda changed significantly during bin Laden's absence. The large organisation he left in 1989 was long gone, having disintegrated in the bitter aftermath of Jalalabad. Upon his return, bin Laden found a weakened and smaller al-Qaeda.

* * *

MH: By the time Abu Abdullah returned in 1991, al-Qaeda was very small. I do not know the full numbers, but I do know in late 1991/early 1992 al-Qaeda agreed to give me most of its trained group to help with the campaign to capture the city of Gardez. As I mentioned to you earlier, this trained group was around sixty people.

LF: Was returning to Pakistan something bin Laden wanted to do, or was it his last option other than remaining in Saudi Arabia?

MH: He wanted to leave Saudi Arabia because the government had placed many restrictions on him. To leave, Abu Abdullah contacted his friend whose father was the defence minister, and asked for his help. He said, 'I have a lot of money in Pakistan and I have to get it myself; give me a passport for one visit and let me go and get my money.'

Abu Abdullah travelled to Pakistan, and then after a while he escaped to Sudan. By this time a lot of his money, which was around 30 million dollars in total, and some of his people had already shifted to Sudan. When Abu Abdullah arrived in Pakistan, he took what was there and moved it to Sudan. There was very little money left for activities in Afghanistan; when we asked for some to help the mujahidin in a campaign they said they had none.

LF: Al-Qaeda's cash shortages do not seem to have been made public.

MH: Al-Qaeda's people in Pakistan and Afghanistan had less money transferred to them because everything was being sent to Sudan. Even when Abu Abdullah was still in Saudi Arabia, he could not transfer money to Pakistan because the government was watching him.

At that time, al-Qaeda's presence in Afghanistan was already weakening. There were not many people in its camps or practising on the battlefield; training was at a very low level. Al-Qaeda's leaders kept the shortage of money quiet because they feared this becoming public would make their situation worse. At that time, al-Qaeda was not focused: it had one leg in Sudan and one in Afghanistan.

LF: Was bin Laden involved in any other activities when he returned to Pakistan? It seems he stayed away from the Afghan parties, especially since not all of them were happy to see his return.

MH: By the time Abu Abdullah arrived back in Pakistan, the decision to shift to Sudan had already been made, and they were in the process of transferring everything. In Sudan, there was supposed to be another programme but nobody was sure what it was.

LF: So it was basically a pack-up-and-leave operation?

MH: Yes, although al-Qaeda did want to maintain some kind of connection with the Pakistanis and the Afghans—they did not want to cut everything. There were very few people willing to stay in the region to maintain these ties.

LF: Why was that? Was it clear by then the Afghan mujahidin would not unite and that a civil war was coming?

MH: The clear civil war did not come until Kabul fell in April 1992, but many people had already lost hope an Islamic state could be established in Afghanistan. While the civil war was a shock to Arabs away from the Afghan and Peshawar field, it did not shock the people who were there to anywhere near the same extent because they had seen it coming.

LF: So there was a sort of sense of inevitability about this?

MH: Yes, and those who had long believed this would happen did not want to stay in the region.

* * *

The fall of the Kabul regime, Afghanistan's descent into civil war and Pakistan's crackdown on Arab-Afghans

Afghanistan's civil war began in April 1992, after the Afghan mujahidin groups began fighting among themselves for power. Its descent into civil war meant the religious rulings—fatawa—declaring participation in Afghanistan's jihad obligatory, no longer applied because fighting had descended into civil conflict.

* * *

LF: What happened to the Arab-Afghans when the civil war broke out? We know some groups like al-Qaeda and Egypt's Tanzim al-Jihad were already in the process of leaving for Sudan, but how about the other Arab-Afghan groups, especially those who had established themselves in the surrounds of Jalalabad?

MH: Some groups did remain in Jalalabad for a time because the situation there was stable, although it did become much harder to enter the area. The Pakistanis were making difficulties at the Torkham entrance, which was the route used to come from Pakistan to Jalalabad. But some groups who had camps in Jalalabad were already looking elsewhere.

LF: Yes, it was around that time Khattab was thinking to go north, first to Tajikistan, and then to Chechnya, where he remained until his 2002 death. Gamaah Islamiyyah soon became heavily involved in events in Bosnia. The Algerians returned home or moved to Khaldan. What about Azmarai? I know he had already begun to focus on striking targets in the West and America in particular. How long did his Jalalabad camp last? I was under the impression he essentially merged his operations into the Khaldan camp. Was Khost, where Khaldan was located, easier to access than Jalalabad?

MH: I do not know exactly how long Azmarai's Jalalabad camp lasted, but Khost was easier to reach than Jalalabad, so he may have transferred to Khaldan. The first time I met Azmarai was around the beginning of 1994; we were asking him to join us in the al-Furqan project. He was very angry about this project. He said, 'We are concentrating on America.' He was angry with Abu Abdullah because he thought al-Furqan was an al-Qaeda project and al-Qaeda should be focusing on America. He said, 'me and my group are going to focus on America'.

He did not trust Abu Abdullah and he did not come to work with us in al-Furqan. He was very nice with me when he came to know that al-

Furqan was an independent project and not an al-Qaeda project. He was a very nice man and a famous fighter. He was a Saudi with an Uzbek background who was married at that time to an Afghan lady.

LF: After 1992 there seems to have been a greater incidence of conflict between Arab-Afghans in Peshawar, which reportedly included some shootouts. I was wondering if this was a result of people coming back to Peshawar as conditions deteriorated in Afghanistan?

MH: Few stayed long in Peshawar because there was little to do there. In fact, I think the absence of things to do was one of the reasons problems grew in Peshawar: there was no battle to take the attention of these people. The conflict among Arab-Afghans in Peshawar was mostly because of the extreme fringe; one group called Jamaah al-Khalifah chose a khalifah and they turned to become takfiris. This group said, 'We will attack anyone who does not make an oath to our khalifah.' This meant they would attack anyone who would not give their leader an oath of allegiance. At that time, this group was based in the tribal areas and they said this to the Arabs in Peshawar. They made some big problems in Peshawar; they would come in, conduct night raids, steal property and make threats.

LF: What happened to Maktab al-Khadamat? Did it close because of Pakistan's growing pressure? I know even Khaldan, which operated the most freely of all the groups, came under some pressure. Abu Zubaydah, for example, was arrested and spent some time in jail.

MH: Maktab al-Khadamat continued to operate until the early 1990s; we heard they were closing and they stopped the magazine. I do not know why Abu Zubaydah was arrested, because Khaldan managed to escape much of the crackdown despite Pakistan's pressure on the Arabs.

The people working for Khaldan were usually able to move in Pakistan the same way they had during the Soviet time. They worked in Karachi and other locations, where they received people arriving, mostly from Algeria, and put them in guesthouses before transferring them to Khaldan. The rest of the Arabs, especially those of us still in Afghanistan, we faced great difficulty even visiting Pakistan. I think Khaldan was under the influence of some agencies concerned with the Algerian conflict, which was a kind of struggle between France and America over that important country.

LF: Some Arab-Afghans remained in Afghanistan after the civil war began and joined with Hekmatyar?

MH: Yes, they joined him at a camp he had started in Logar province, called Yarmuk, in Mes Aynak.

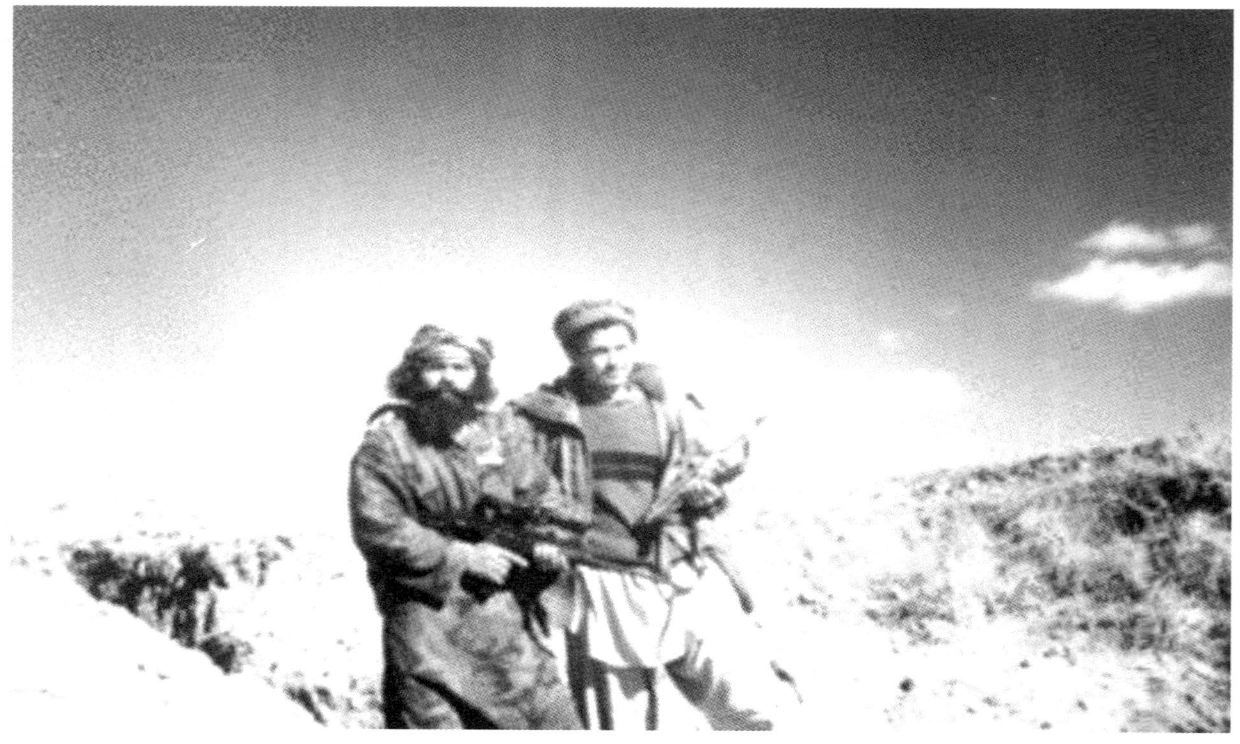

Fig 12: Right, Abu Musab al-Zarqawi

LF: The Arab-Afghans who joined Hekmatyar were helping him to fight against the mujahidin government in Kabul?

MH: Yes, he was against the government. Hekmatyar's party was very strong during the war against the Soviets because he had the support of Pakistan's intelligence services. Once the Soviets left and the communist government in Kabul fell, Hekmatyar lost most of his support. Many Afghan fighters left because in their view the jihad finished when the Kabul regime fell.

After this, some Arabs joined him and they became the backbone of his strike power. They were mostly youth who had received Abdullah Azzam's inflammatory literature relatively late, but were motivated to come to Afghanistan. When they arrived, they joined Hekmatyar's camp. Among the famous names in Hekmatyar's group was Abu Musab al-Zarqawi, who won international fame in Iraq for his work against the Americans for al-Qaeda. Abu Musab had earlier been among the new members of Abu Harith al-Urduni's group, but he later joined almost as a whole to Hekmatyar's group.

MH: Here we should note the Yarmuk camp was also helped by the efforts of American Muslims of Arab origin. Among them was Abu Rouda al-Suri, the owner of the idea of the camp, who was frequently going between America and the Yarmuk camp in Logar province. The Yarmuk battalion disintegrated after Abu Rouda was killed in a military operation on the border of Kabul. The battalion's deputy was not competent and changing alliances between the Afghan parties meant the Arabs found themselves fighting beside those they had earlier been fighting.

LF: Just to clarify, this was Abu Rouda al-Suri, not Abu Rida al-Suri, who we talked about earlier when we discussed the alleged minutes documenting al-Qaeda's founding?

MH: It was Abu Rouda al-Suri not Abu Rida al-Suri and Abu Rouda was killed in Kabul.

* * *

With the environment in Pakistan becoming increasingly inhospitable, and Afghanistan wracked by civil war, a large number of Arab-Afghans returned to their homelands. Many, however, looked elsewhere for another jihad. Choices abounded.

By the early 1990s, opportunities for jihad were present in Algeria, Chechnya, Somalia, Bosnia, Yemen, Indonesia, the Philippines, Burma and elsewhere. Several fronts, such as those in Bosnia and Chechnya, received fatawa endorsing jihad from prominent religious figures in the Gulf. As a result, money previously sent to Afghanistan began to flow there instead.

* * *

LF: We spoke earlier about how groups from Jalalabad began to look elsewhere as new fronts opened in the early 1990s. Al-Qaeda does not seem to have participated in a combat role in any of these fronts, with the exception of Somalia, although Fadil Harun claimed al-Qaeda sent people to Chechnya.[1] Did al-Qaeda have emissaries in Chechnya who worked alongside the Arab-Afghans operating on this front?

MH: Harun was talking about Abu Islam al-Masri. Abu Islam was already leaving al-Qaeda. You know how those people in al-Qaeda were thinking? Abu Islam had decided to go to Chechnya because he thought the jihad was finished in Afghanistan. Al-Qaeda's procedure was to say 'okay, go; you are our person there', even though he was leaving anyway regardless of what they said. Then, when any of the youth wanted to leave and go to Chechnya, al-Qaeda could say 'okay go to Abu Islam'.

Khattab was the leading figure in Chechnya; he went first and he had experience in fighting. He was feared as a commander; more than anybody in al-Qaeda. It was not an al-Qaeda plan to send Abu Islam to the Chechen front because he was leaving to go there independently, and it was not organised. Al-Qaeda had no strategic plan for anything, not even for Somalia.

LF: So this was a way of letting Abu Islam go but still keeping claim on him and maybe drawing Khattab in towards al-Qaeda?

MH: Maybe al-Qaeda wanted Abu Islam to coordinate with Khattab, but this did not work because Khattab did not like al-Qaeda. They exchanged a few letters but that was it.

Khattab was the victorious one. He did not need al-Qaeda. His front was more popular. Even later, after 1996, when the young people came to Afghanistan to join Abu Abdullah, they found him fighting in Afghanistan against other Muslims. They were confused about this fighting: it was a big debate about fighting other Muslims. This problem did not exist in Chechnya; it was clear for everyone to understand. The Chechen front had heroes and stories of victory, and Khattab, and money and supplies. This made it attractive to the youth. Also, I should correct a very important point for you. In Somalia, al-Qaeda did not participate in combat activities against the Americans.

LF: I know there is a lot of misinformation about why al-Qaeda went to Somalia. Many people think al-Qaeda went to fight the Americans even though it was there well before the United Nations intervention began. But I thought from the claims al-Qaeda later made that its members were directly involved in combat against the American forces in Somalia, and the United Nations contingent more generally?[2]

MH: Here we should go back to the beginning of this story, because you are missing another important point and one that relates to why al-Qaeda was in Somalia. One of al-Qaeda's main activities in Somalia was training the Somali groups, which was arranged well before the American invasion, but the other was transferring weapons from there to Yemen.

LF: To Yemen?

MH: Yes, but let's start from the beginning.

LF: Can I ask that we please start with Yemen first, because clearly I have this all wrong. I thought bin Laden's jihad efforts in Yemen failed. However, if there were weapons being transferred from Somalia to Yemen, then clearly these efforts did not completely fail.

My understanding of bin Laden's activities in Yemen comes mostly from Abu Musab al-Suri's account of trying to convince bin Laden to start a jihad there. He said bin Laden made several attempts to start a jihad in Yemen, but they all failed.[3] He also wrote that bin Laden hesitated to get involved in jihad in Yemen without getting endorsement from leaders like Abdul Majid al-Zindani, who I understand was the leader of Ikhwan Muslimin in Yemen.[4]

MH: Yes. Abdul Majid al-Zindani visited Afghanistan during the war against the Soviets, and many years later, after al-Qaeda had returned to Afghanistan, he came to visit Abu Abdullah.

LF: According to Abu Musab al-Suri, Abdul Majid al-Zindani refused to support bin Laden's desire to start jihad in Yemen.[5] Do you know why?

MH: No, I do not know the specific reasons. During the time of the Afghan war against the Soviets, there were many meetings about Yemen and what to do there, and how to get rid of communism. I met two influential leaders from the south of Yemen in a meeting in Peshawar in early 1988. Abu Abdullah and Ayman al-Zawahiri and others also attended and we were talking about how to fight in Yemen and discussing what kind of war could be fought there.

Fig 13: Abdul Majid al-Zindani, on the right, and Abdullah Azzam, back to camera, during the first Afghan jihad[6]

LF: Considering how much enthusiasm there was in Arab-Afghan circles for jihad in Yemen it is odd it never really happened. From what Abu Musab al-Suri says, one reason for this was Yemen's president put in place a very successful strategy of buying the loyalty of many religious and tribal leaders, and even Arab-Afghans who had returned to Yemen. He says bin Laden spent a lot of money funding people to start jihad

Fig 14: Al-Zindani, firing weapons with bin Laden and others, while on a visit to Afghanistan in the Taliban era[7]

after the 1990 re-unification between North and South Yemen, but Yemen's president essentially out-spent him.[8] The result was that senior people who had earlier supported bin Laden's jihad efforts turned against him, with some, like Moqbil al-Wadi, apparently going so far as to publicly call bin Laden 'the root of sedition in Yemen'.[9] This was where I thought bin Laden's attempts for jihad in Yemen ended; but from what you have recounted it seems bin Laden remained undeterred.

MH: I think Abu Abdullah's Yemen project did not stop like Abu Musab al-Suri thought; it was going smoothly from the underground. It was not a big project and it started after 1990. In preparation for jihad in Yemen, Abu Abdullah was arranging for weapons transfers from Somalia to Yemen. During the time of Ziad Barre in Somalia, the Somali army had been well equipped because it was supplied by the Soviet Union. Abu Abdullah's men obtained and shifted weapons and ammunition from Somalia to Yemen.

Yemeni jihadists from Ikhwan Muslimin and the people of al-Qaeda started to make bases in Yemen's south to receive the weapons smuggled from Somalia. One of the al-Qaeda people involved in this, Abu Omar al-Yamani, was my friend and had earlier worked with me on my Khost project. There was a very nice group there in Yemen who had been in Afghanistan previously. They were a small group, but they did a very good job.

LF: It is complicated to keep track of events because several significant developments took place in the same period. There was bin Laden's focus on Yemen and attempts to start jihad work there with Arab-Afghans; the dispatch of al-Qaeda people to Somalia and their transfer of weapons to Yemen; and the outbreak of the Gulf War, when Saddam Hussein invaded Kuwait. We spoke about bin Laden's efforts in Saudi Arabia earlier, and you mentioned that he bought a lot of arms and had secret hiding places in the Saudi Arabian desert. Given the time frame, I was wondering whether the weapons bin Laden gathered and hid in Saudi Arabia in case Saddam Hussein invaded were the same ones that were shipped from Somalia to Yemen?

MH: There were many weapons available in Yemen and most weapons in Saudi Arabia came into the country from Yemen. I do not know if they were the same weapons that originally came from Somalia.

LF: Clearly, there were people in Somalia a lot earlier than is commonly thought, if al-Qaeda was shipping arms from there to Yemen. I just want to revisit the history of how al-Qaeda came to be involved in Somalia. Is it correct that Abu Ubaydah first negotiated providing training for the Somalis after he met a group in Peshawar?

MH: Yes. During the Afghan war the Somalis trained in some of Sayyaf's camps, and a few of their leaders came. I met some of them in a guesthouse of al-Qaeda. They were talking about Somalia and the situation there. After they trained and saw everything, they formed a group and I heard they called it Al-Ittihad because at that time they very much admired Sayyaf; but I am not sure if this is true.

I do know they wanted some more training in their own country and al-Qaeda agreed to help. This is how al-Qaeda came to be in Somalia a few years before the Americans. In the beginning, al-Qaeda did excellent work in Somalia. By the time the Americans arrived, they had already trained plenty of people.

LF: Was al-Qaeda the only group there? I thought some other Arab-Afghans went with funding from bin Laden, which is curious if bin Laden was having financial problems at that time.

MH: The other Arab-Afghans arrived very late. It was after al-Qaeda had already moved out of Somalia, which caused a vacuum inside the country. Some people contacted Abu Abdullah for assistance to go to Somalia. They were mainly the people who had been involved in the fighting in Bosnia and were looking for another place. They went to Abu Abdullah, and he supported them. It was not a lot of money.

Al-Qaeda's numbers in Somalia were never very big, but for a small group they did good work. The boys who were in charge in the beginning, like Sayf al-Adl, they did excellent work tactically. That was because Abu Abdullah or even Abu Hafs was not there above them, ordering them.

LF: It is interesting how in any organisation, some bosses are always a problem and often when they are absent things tend to run a little more smoothly.

MH: Yes. In this case the boss had uncontrolled power in the organisation and that led, at last, to big failures.

LF: It seems fairly universal; it doesn't matter what type of organisation.

MH: Many organisations are like that and I can say all the Arab groups were like that.

LF: It seems the absence of leadership did have some negative points for the al-Qaeda people on the ground. Letters from al-Qaeda members in Somalia back to their leaders show they were asking for support and guidance. They do not appear to have received much of this from bin Laden or other senior al-Qaeda leaders.[10]

MH: This is also because Abu Abdullah did not have much free money. He put the money he managed to get out of Saudi Arabia into investments in Sudan. The big plans they had for Somalia were not something he could fund, although he could have done more. There was also a lack of political guidance from al-Qaeda's leaders. It was a big flaw in the organisation and it had been there since the beginning.

LF: I would add the absence of a strategy seems to have been equally problematic and was lacking from the beginning.

MH: Yes, there was no strategic plan; not for Somalia, not for anywhere.

LF: Regarding al-Qaeda in combat, you have said al-Qaeda was not involved in combat against American forces in Somalia. What about the stories al-Qaeda members shot down American helicopters in Mogadishu in 1993?

MH: The helicopters were shot down by the Somalis; by Aideed's group, who America was fighting. Abu Hafs al-Masri was very close to the battle, but he did not participate. He and the others were hiding in a house with the Americans everywhere around them, but they were not preparing to do anything. They kept themselves out of the battle, which was very fierce all around them.

LF: Really?

MH: It was completely Aideed's group. Al-Qaeda did nothing in direct combat against America. It did do some excellent tactical work on the ground; leading the troops it was training from place to place, and by doing so, making disturbances. The United Nations troops retreated from any place where there were forces led by the Arabs.

LF: Bin Laden intimated al-Qaeda shot down those helicopters.[11] I think he may have been a bit economical with the truth.

MH: I do not remember what Abu Abdullah said, but I am sure of what Abu Hafs told me, which is what I told you. There was no fighting or shooting by al-Qaeda against the Americans. Aideed was secular; there was no way for him and al-Qaeda to work together. Maybe al-Qaeda's allies from among the Somalis went and were involved in the fighting, and because they were their allies, al-Qaeda claimed they did it. But I heard from people who were there that they did not get directly involved.

LF: What strikes me is that even if al-Qaeda's men on the ground did claim to be fighting the Americans and having successful engagements, it did not earn them any extra support from al-Qaeda's headquarters. Around a year later, bin Laden ordered everyone to leave and return to Sudan, despite some al-Qaeda people protesting their activities in Somalia were yielding success. Before bin Laden ordered a withdrawal from Somalia, you wanted to link up your work in Central Asia, which was not under al-Qaeda's control, with the group operating in Somalia, to form a combined programme. Did this ever come to fruition?

MH: Yes, it was my dream. It was just a dream. It was not even a project, it was a dream of a project; but it never happened. Al-Qaeda of course left Somalia. I was very angry that they left; I was always angry with them. If they went to a place, I was angry; if they left, I was angry. In the beginning, I was against them going to Somalia; this is true. But they went and a big victory occurred while they were there. They shared in that victory without fighting, and their allies were very strong and they were very influential in the area, so why then leave? It was just like Afghanistan; after we had a big victory there they left, and they did not make any benefit from the victory. It was stupid.

* * *

On bin Laden's orders, al-Qaeda withdrew most of its forces from Somalia in 1995. This left the organisation with only its Sudan base, and a small group at Jihadwal in Afghanistan who remained behind when al-Qaeda left for Sudan.

* * *

LF: You stayed in Afghanistan and heavily encouraged other Arab-Afghans to stay, despite the conditions in the country. Why?

MH: Yes, I did not leave and I did not want the others to leave. I told them not to leave from the beginning, and I told them again after the capture of Gardez in 1992. I said, 'The most happy men, the happiest fellows from among us are the martyrs. If we are killed, we are happy. If we are not killed, we will suffer. They will chase us everywhere; they will kill us one by one. They will put us in jails and make us criminals.'

Why did I say that? Because, it has been our historical experience; since the Palestine war of 1948 this has occurred. I told them, 'This is the regime; this is the way they will deal with us, like the 1948 mujahidin in Palestine.' Can you imagine that until that time most of the mujahidin were still alive but could not return to Egypt, because they were wanted because they fought in 1948? Those from Ikhwan Muslimin who fought in this war, by this time they were around sixty or seventy, but if they came to Egypt they would be put in jail.

LF: So you thought everyone should stay in Afghanistan?

MH: Yes, I told them, 'Don't return home. Don't leave Afghanistan. We opened this country. We should stay.' Also, you know, we had offers to stay. The Afghans, especially my friend Haqqani, he said 'settle here in Gardez'.

It was the day we captured Gardez in 1992. Haqqani and I were sitting in what had been the Afghan Army's camp in Gardez. He told me, 'You are our partner in this success; you have the same rights according to Islam. You have the same rights as us in Afghanistan because both of us, we opened it.' He wanted to give land to the Arabs who had fought with the Afghans. He said, 'We can give land to you.' I told him, 'We have families, where will we settle?' He said, 'Settle here. Settle in this area. You see this land; we can give it to you.'

At that time Haqqani was the most powerful leader in Paktia province. He said, 'If you need a training camp take this.' He gestured to the Afghan Army camp we were sitting in. It was a very big one with barracks, and was completely furnished. Haqqani said, 'Take this and do your training because we need training if we are going to build an army from the Afghans.'

It was something fantastic, you can't imagine it. I told him, 'Okay, we can settle here.' He was happy. He said, 'You can train the Afghans here; you can make your society here.' In fact, we had very good Arabs with us to do so: doctors, engineers, instructors, everyone. We had the skill set to stay and do something good for us and for the Afghans.

I told the people with influence among the Arab-Afghans about his offer. I told them, 'We should stay. Please do not move. If you go outside they will chase you, they will kill you, they will put all of you in jail, they will never let you live in peace.' I told them, 'After you have shared in the success of the defeat of a superpower they will start to make you their enemies.' But nobody listened.

LF: Still they all wanted to leave?

MH: Yes, they wanted to leave. They believed the Afghans would not establish an Islamic government, and so they left and the result it is like what you see now.

LF: Bin Laden obviously was among those who did not want to stay in Afghanistan. But why did he choose Sudan?

MH: I do not know exactly what he was thinking, but Abu Abdullah built his thoughts and programmes in a sudden way, which nobody expected. I think he surprised himself; he certainly surprised the others. He committed a huge mistake leaving Afghanistan after the victory. Some way or another he shared in this victory. He contributed a massive amount of money from his own pocket, from his family pocket. He spent a lot of time, he exposed himself to great danger and he simply left. This was an error in strategic thinking. If you share in a battle for several years, you do not just leave the place and go, especially if you are successful. Our side had been successful and we had an offer to stay. But he did not listen.

LF: I presume you said something similar in the January 1992 meeting you had with al-Qaeda's leaders at its Jihadwal camp where you presented a project proposal to maintain a training capacity in Khost in Afghanistan?

MH: You are speaking about the proposal I wrote for training a Tajik force. I wanted al-Qaeda to help with this Tajikistan project, which I came to call the al-Furqan project.

LF: Al-Qaeda did not accept your plan.

MH: No, it was not approved by the al-Qaeda people in Afghanistan, and soon after Abu Abdullah ordered the closure of al-Qaeda's camps because the *tanzim* was moving to Sudan.

LF: Why was it not supported?

MH: They held a meeting about it at Jihadwal, about the Tajikistan project. Abu Hafs al-Masri attended, along with Sayf al-Adl and a few other al-Qaeda people. I was out of the room, because this was a meeting for al-Qaeda discussions. They refused to support the project and one of my friends who was in the meeting told me they rejected it because it came from outside al-Qaeda, and not from inside al-Qaeda. He told me, 'This made the others feel like their dignity had been harmed.' So they refused to support the project.

LF: Dignity? That is interesting; I would have thought it was more about control.

MH: Well it was that also. They did not like to support things they could not control.

LF: Sayyid Imam, the former amir of Tanzim al-Jihad, made a similar observation in relation to al-Qaeda's tendency to seek control, in particular bin Laden's desire to maintain control.[12] I understand this was part of the reason al-Qaeda did not become involved in Bosnia or Chechnya, because it could not control things there.

MH: Yes, it was a very big shortcoming and because they would only fund things they thought they could control, al-Qaeda missed many opportunities.

LF: You wrote that not everyone was happy about al-Qaeda's relocation to Sudan; there were accusations that al-Qaeda had deviated and was no longer supporting jihad.[13]

MH: Many people and groups were unhappy about al-Qaeda going to Sudan. The exception was the Egyptian groups. The Egyptians wanted to base themselves there because they could go through Sudan to Egypt, and they could gain the support of Sudan's government because at that time it was against the Egyptian government. The Egyptians were really the only ones. Most others did not accept the regime in Sudan was Islamic because its leaders were Ikhwan Muslimin, and so it was not trusted.

Within al-Qaeda, some people were unhappy too; although they were not only unhappy at being in Sudan, but also because at that time al-Qaeda had no direction. In Sudan, al-Qaeda was 99 per cent a construction and agricultural company. About fifty people stayed with Abu Abdullah in al-Qaeda, and they were civilian workers in his companies in Sudan. It was no longer the al-Qaeda of before. In fact, there was no real al-Qaeda during the Sudan period; it only started to be al-Qaeda again after they returned to Afghanistan in 1996 when they had nothing to do but make some kind of jihad.

LF: It seems to me that both the Bosnian and Chechen conflicts took recruits away from al-Qaeda because it could only offer up administrative work in Sudan. What impact did this turn towards 'civilian work' have within al-Qaeda?

MH: It caused a rupture in the organisation because when they followed Abu Abdullah to Sudan people did not imagine they would become civilian workers in his companies. In the end, al-Qaeda was letting the boys go to Somalia to keep them satisfied. They were going on their holidays to Somalia to do some shooting, train some people or be trained on a refresher course.

LF: So this kind of holiday jihad was a way of keeping people in the organisation?

MH: Yes. It was a reward for loyalty.

LF: While al-Qaeda was doing civilian work in Sudan, bin Laden did continue to fund some groups. You drew a chart that showed that funding was provided for a while to Algeria's Jamaah Islamiyyah and Egypt's Tanzim al-Jihad. In the chart[14] you wrote that bin Laden stopped funding the Algerians after they threatened him.

MH: In the beginning, Abu Abdullah tried very hard to help the Algerians. Al-Qaeda tried to open a branch there and open a smuggling route to the group in Algeria. Then the Algerian group split into two factions, and one faction came to Sudan and threatened Abu Abdullah. They said, 'If you supply money to the other faction we are going to do something against you,' and so he stopped at once.

LF: Were they the group who tried to kill him?

MH: No. They threatened him, but the group who tried to kill Abu Abdullah in Sudan were mostly Saudi and Sudanese takfiris; they were multinational, but mainly guided by Saudis.

LF: Why did this other group want to kill bin Laden?

MH: The Sudanese authorities investigated them and al-Qaeda's security people attended this investigation, but their reason was not clear.

LF: The other group your chart shows bin Laden funded was Egypt's Tanzim al-Jihad. He stopped funding them too, and Tanzim al-Jihad was not very happy about this?

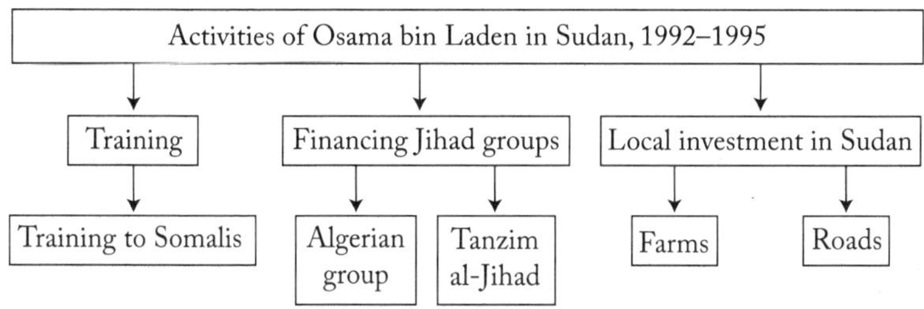

Fig 15: Activities of bin Laden in Sudan, 1992–5

MH: Yes, Abu Abdullah stopped funding Tanzim al-Jihad at a very critical time in its operations in Egypt. Because of this, Ayman al-Zawahiri was angry with him and their friendship was severed. It was not repaired until Dr Ayman arrived in Afghanistan in mid- to late-1997.

All of the work had stopped. Abu Abdullah had stopped funding the Egyptians, stopped funding the Algerians and withdrawn most of his cadres from Somalia. The Yemen project also finished in 1994 after Yemen's civil war ended and the country re-unified, and al-Qaeda's members there found themselves without a programme.

LF: Bin Laden's campaign against the Saudi regime did not stop. From 1994 until 1997, he wrote many letters to the Saudi king and the Saudi regime.[15]

MH: Yes, Abu Abdullah was concentrating heavily on his country and giving advice to the king to make reforms, because for the first time there was an opposition movement within the kingdom.

LF: You are referring here to the Awakening Movement, which took place in the mid-1990s.

MH: Yes. Some of the people who were involved in the opposition escaped to London and started to issue statements against the Saudi regime. They formed the Advice and Reform Committee, which was very famous at that time in Saudi Arabia. Through this committee, Abu Abdullah started issuing statements. The Saudi government became crazy, and America, of course, also became crazy. From that point, they started to press the Sudanese government to silence him, but Abu Abdullah did not agree. Then, later, the Sudanese government made an agreement with the Americans to expel Abu Abdullah to Afghanistan, as was said by Qutbi al-Mahdi, Sudan's intelligence chief.

LF: Bin Laden was under pressure from the Saudis in al-Qaeda at that time too.

MH: Yes he had big problems because the Saudis who were with him wanted to make al-Qaeda a Saudi organisation. They came and told him, 'Every country has his own organisation. We want al-Qaeda to be only Saudi.' They said, 'We don't need other nationalities; we don't know these Egyptians who are dominating al-Qaeda,' like Abu Ubaydah and Abu Hafs. Abu Abdullah refused. So these Saudis left and went to Saudi Arabia and surrendered to the government.

LF: Okay, so he had a few problems then.

MH: There was another problem too. One of Abu Abdullah's very good men surrendered to the Saudi government. He was married to Abu Abdullah's niece, and was his secretary at the time. He knew every secret in al-Qaeda, and he told the Saudi government everything. The government of Saudi Arabia sent him to America to be interrogated and then he was sent back to Saudi Arabia. That means al-Qaeda was completely open to the Americans. They knew every small secret about al-Qaeda. They knew Abu Abdullah at that time had no power, no money.

When they knew al-Qaeda was no longer doing enemy work, they made an agreement with Sudan's government to send Abu Abdullah to Afghanistan, and that is what happened. Abu Abdullah had no money at all because his 30 million was frozen in Sudan, and most of his other money was frozen in Saudi Arabia. Sudan gave Abu Abdullah some of his money one or two times, and then they stopped giving him anything.

This was al-Qaeda in that miserable place Sudan until it returned to Afghanistan in 1996 and started another phase in its history.

* * *

It was in spite of bin Laden that al-Qaeda had camps to return to in Afghanistan: on his departure from Pakistan in 1992 he had ordered everything to be liquidated and moved to Sudan. A small group of al-Qaeda members did, however, end up staying at its Jihadwal camp until the group's return from Sudan 1996.

The forgotten men on the mountain: the Arab-Afghans who remained in Khost

When preparing to leave Pakistan in 1992, bin Laden ordered the liquidation of all remaining al-Qaeda camps and equipment in Khost.

Among the camps he ordered to be liquidated were Jihadwal and al-Faruq, but an intervention by Sayf al-Adl saw this process halted. A small skeleton staff of al-Qaeda remained at Jihadwal, where equipment from the other camps was transferred. Al-Faruq was handed over to Mustafa Hamid who, along with a few friends, remained in Afghanistan to undertake an independent project training Tajik volunteers from al-Nahda, which he called the 'Al-Furqan project'.

* * *

MH: I thought the Tajiks had good potential and al-Qaeda had the capacity to help, but they did not help. Sayf al-Adl managed to save al-Faruq from being liquidated, so we were able to use that camp to train the Tajiks. For our Tajik project, we initially hired some of Sayyaf's trainers but they only stayed a month or two because we did not have money to pay them. Abu Atta al-Tunisi, the amir of al-Qaeda's members in Khost, helped me. He and his friends at Jihadwal helped train the Tajiks. I relied on our friendship, and the al-Qaeda people at Jihadwal were willing to help me because we were friends—even though they did not have permission from al-Qaeda in Sudan to help in this project.

At that stage there were only around ten of them in Jihadwal and they were in a very poor position. They could not even protect themselves or their livestock, which were regularly stolen by the tribes in the area! Because of this, we supplied them with a security contingent made up of our Tajik trainees to guard Jihadwal.

They even had to borrow money from shopkeepers in Khost because there was no money coming from Sudan. In fact, nothing came from Sudan. It was very rare they received instructions or assistance. I told Abu Atta, 'I use you as trainers, use your ammunition, use your old camp and still Abu Abdullah refuses to support the Tajik cause while I do everything by your instruments. I am fooling you.' Later, the people at Jihadwal opened a small camp around 500 metres away, called Salman al-Farsi. I call it a camp but it was made up of two tents! One tent was for the boys, and another for the equipment. The camp was for the special training; for fighting inside the towns, for guarding important people.

Here, I should add something else important about the Tajik project. All of the Afghan parties who were fighting in Kabul in the civil war; initially they all supported the project in one way or another, even Dostum. You can't imagine: Dostum helped us, Hekmatyar, Masud,

Haqqani; they all helped us. Even the government of Kabul as a whole, it gave no objection and allowed us to pass with our weapons. It was very strange at that time to have everybody supporting us and welcoming our Tajik trainees and their party, al-Nahda, to Afghanistan. Of course, it did not last long, and soon many forces turned against our project.

LF: You attempted to take the Tajik group trained at al-Faruq north into battle in Tajikistan, but the new military leader of Tajikistan's al-Nahda party blocked you. Did your friends from Jihadwal go north with you?

MH: No. They helped with the training but they did not travel north. Our group at al-Faruq took about seventy or eighty well-trained Tajiks north to Takhar in 1994 to start the project. We were not able to cross the river and because of the situation with al-Nahda's new military leader, who at the time was not supporting our presence there, and some assassination threats against us, we had to return to Khost.

LF: When you were in the north, you met with a member of the al-Nahda Shurah Council, Tahir Yuldashev, who would go on to form the Islamic Movement of Uzbekistan. Many people assume this group was formed by or with the support of al-Qaeda, and that it started in 1999.[16] It seems from your account neither of these assumptions are correct and the group has a much earlier, more distinct and independent history.

MH: Yes. I did meet Tahir Yuldashev in Taloqan in 1994. We met and from that time we became very close friends. In fact, he was the one who told me the news that some people were planning to assassinate me on the road further to the north, and it was because of this I decided to go back to Khost.

LF: At that time, Yuldashev was already thinking about forming his own force to undertake jihad in Uzbekistan, and you discussed them receiving training at al-Faruq.

MH: Yes. The history of the Uzbeks is an interesting story. Tahir's decision to form his own group came out of events in Tajikistan with al-Nahda, which I witnessed, because the same events that ruined our Tajik project at al-Faruq also caused Tahir to establish his group.

LF: The events, I presume, are those surrounding the change of leadership and direction in the al-Nahda party, whose members were training at al-Faruq for jihad in Tajikistan while al-Qaeda was in Sudan?

MH: Yes. As you know when I met Tahir he was on the Shurah Council of al-Nahda.

LF: Why was an Uzbek on al-Nahda's Shurah Council?

MH: In the beginning, al-Nahda was presenting itself as a group for all Middle Asian Muslims, but when the problems came in Tajikistan, the Iranians, the Russians and the Saudis told the leader of al-Nahda not to talk internationally or regionally. Al-Nahda's leader then decided it should be a Tajik-only group, with no programme in Uzbekistan or other countries, and so al-Nahda then became more nationalist.

Tahir resigned and spent about two years building another Islamic movement for Uzbekistan. He made a big tour of Middle Asia and he was depending to some extent on his networks in Turkey, because many within his group had Turkish blood. He also depended on the group he sent to be trained at al-Faruq. They played an excellent role in the movement. All of them became instructors and organised the military side in Tahir's work. In fact, Tahir and all the al-Nahda leaders appreciated the positive way the boys had changed after training at al-Faruq, and so did their families.

LF: Had you left Afghanistan before the Uzbeks arrived for training? They arrived around the same time some Chechens also arrived to get some training. Shamil Basayev, a senior leader of the mujahidin in Chechnya, was among them.

MH: I was still there when the Chechens came to Peshawar. Shamil was their leader; he did not share in the training. I snuck into Peshawar to meet him in the Tajik house, because at that time the Pakistanis were chasing the Arabs. He was very interested to learn about the role the caves in the mountains played in the Afghan jihad. He had heard they played an important role towards the end of fighting, which was true. I told him, 'I will take you to the main caves and you can see how they were used, and how this was a different kind of digging and fighting style than the trenches.' He planned to come but something happened and he left quickly to Chechnya. I didn't meet him again after that.

LF: A small group from Chechnya did come to train at al-Faruq sometime after Shamil's trip.

MH: Yes. I think it was around six members. All of them became influential commanders when they returned to Chechnya, and played an important role in the fighting. When I asked about them a few years back, all except one had been martyred. I think he is a Shahid now too. The Chechens, Uzbeks and Tajiks were the best trainees I had ever seen: everybody loved them, even the Afghans in Khost.

LF: Khaldan also trained people for Chechnya. There was a back channel from Khaldan through to Turkey and then to Chechnya, via the links between Khattab, Abu Zubaydah and a Kurd based in Turkey who worked with both of them. The al-Faruq training seems to have been before then.

MH: The group who trained at al-Faruq were the first from Chechnya and they had a senior position in the fighting. Khaldan was mostly training Arab volunteers for Chechnya, although some Chechens may have trained there later.

LF: It has been alleged that Abu Zubaydah, who remains detained at Guantanamo Bay, provided training at al-Faruq in addition to his work with Khaldan.[17] There exists a great deal of misinformation about Abu Zubaydah's role and the role of Khaldan more generally, with many people assuming his group and Khaldan were part of al-Qaeda when, for much of their history, they were competitors.

MH: Abu Zubaydah did not train anyone at al-Faruq. He helped us for a short time; mostly in logistics from Peshawar because most of us were being chased by the Pakistanis and could not go to Peshawar. Very few people could come and go from Peshawar, and Abu Zubaydah was one of them because he was Palestinian, and so they were not chasing him. But he became angry with us, and stopped helping us very early.

LF: Why was he angry?

MH: Because he did not like the way things were organised. At al-Faruq at that time, power was not centralised—leaders were told what was required of them and allowed to make their own decisions. That confused many Arabs because they wanted the amir to do everything; to give all the instructions, which is a very stupid way of working.

LF: It seems the tendency to follow the leader among Arab-Afghans was very strong.

MH: Yes, and many of them did not like the more independent way of work at al-Faruq, but I think this way was very practical and gave very good results. Many times communication between groups was cut for one reason or another; if the group did not know from their amir what their mission was and what was required of them, they could not make a decision. In the beginning, people were not accustomed to this decentralised way of working, but then they became accustomed and they did a very good job.

LF: What about Jihadwal at that time? Were the al-Qaeda people there doing any training of their own?

MH: No, they were not—except once, when a few Pakistanis came to be trained secretly. After a few days, they divided and claimed *takfir* against each other and even against al-Qaeda. Abu Atta who was the amir of al-Qaeda in Khost dismissed all of them.

LF: You have written before about how the al-Furqan project was important to developing relations with the Taliban as it began to gain power, and you were one of the first to meet the Taliban as it came to power.[18] Can you tell me about what was happening as the Taliban became active and started to take territory? I know the Taliban also had some contact with the people at Khaldan, but there were some deep suspicions between the two.

MH: I think I was the first among the Arabs at our Khost camp to make contact with the Taliban. This was when they were still fighting in-between Kandahar and Kabul. They had reached the borders of Kabul but they had not yet reached Khost. The first meeting was in al-Faruq camp, and a very nice young man called Abdul Wakil came and visited us. He was an Uzbek Taliban, and as you know there were Uzbeks, Tajiks and Hazara all in the Taliban. He was very happy to see Uzbeks coming from the other side of the river to train with the Tajiks, with the Arabs and with the Afghans. He visited the camp several times, bringing news of the Taliban and watching the activities in al-Faruq.

Even then, I liked the Taliban, because for many years during the Soviet war I had said an Islamic movement would come from Afghanistan to repair all the defects, deviations and corruption that was taking place. It was clear this was what the Taliban was doing. Once we came to know Abdul Wakil, we offered the Taliban training because at that time it did not have any special camps for training its fighters, but the Taliban refused. This was in 1995, and the Taliban were still very sceptical of the Arabs because earlier that year when Taliban forces arrived in Wardak province (which neighboured Kabul province) they found themselves confronted by Hekmatyar's forces.

The Afghans among Hekmatyar's forces were reluctant to fight the Taliban—to shoot the youth who are from the students of the Holy Quran—but the Arabs with Hekmatyar's forces did not have these concerns. They fought the Taliban fiercely and inflicted heavy losses of life. The Taliban movement also feared the Arab trainers' impact on their youth, especially because Arabs were notorious for their rigid doctrinal way of Salafism, which strongly criticised the practices of many of the Afghans and their beliefs.

LF: How about the Taliban's early relations with Haqqani? He was in charge of Khost: what happened as the Taliban approached Khost?

MH: When the Taliban finally reached Khost, there was about to be a fight between Haqqani and the Taliban in that area, because Haqqani was not from the Taliban. The Taliban had reached Gardez, and Haqqani's brother Ibrahim had welcomed them and given the area without any fighting, like many other commanders had done. But the Taliban came and started to behave very roughly; they took everything from Ibrahim and left him only one Kalashnikov, four guns for his guards and one car.

Ibrahim became very angry because he had many followers around him and because he was in fact protecting the area. But they said: 'We are here now so there is no need to protect the area.' It became a very big argument between Ibrahim and the Taliban and a bad situation because then Jalaluddin Haqqani became angry and of course all the Zadran tribe became very angry asking, 'Why are they treating Ibrahim like that?' Ibrahim was a very important commander; he fought from the beginning to the end of the war against the Soviets.

Ibrahim, Khalil and Jalaluddin Haqqani and all the Zadran elders had a meeting in Khost to discuss if they were going to let the Taliban into Khost. A route the Taliban had to pass was very difficult, and controlled by Haqqani and the tribes of the area. If Haqqani did not agree to let them pass and decided instead to block them and fight them, the outcome would have been very bad. It would have been a huge fight, and hundreds of Taliban would have been killed, maybe thousands, because Haqqani and his tribes were very experienced in fighting in this area.

Because of this, I was very upset. I went to Haqqani several times. I told him, 'Mawlawi Sahib, avoid the fight between you and the Taliban. The Taliban are your sons. You know them well. They are good people. They are coming and organising the country.' He was very angry, and he was replying in a very short manner with me. It was the first time Haqqani had talked to me like that. He said, 'Tomorrow we are going to hold a meeting and I will make a final decision.'

LF: You were worried, how about your al-Qaeda neighbours at Jihadwal?

MH: We were all worried about what would happen and that severe fighting would come. When we came to know the time of the meeting Haqqani was holding, a group of us, including my friend Abu Atta, went by car to hear for ourselves the outcome.

About an hour before the meeting, I went to talk to Haqqani. At least 500 elders had gathered for the meeting. Haqqani told me, 'Don't worry, I am not going to fight them.' I knew that if Haqqani decided not to fight the Taliban and to let them pass, then all the elders would agree with him, so I felt some relief. At last the meeting finished. Haqqani said, 'No fighting.' The elders said, 'Okay, no fighting Mawlawi Sahib.' So they allowed the Taliban to pass the road to come to Khost.

LF: How did your earlier relations with the Taliban develop after that?

MH: The man who was in charge for the Taliban in the area also came to Khost. He was Mawlawi Ihsanullah, one of the best Taliban leaders. We became friends very quickly, as if we had known each other for a very long time. He was maybe the third man in the movement, and he and I had many discussions about the Taliban situation. So I became very near to the Taliban at that time.

LF: You left Afghanistan shortly after this. Why? Had your project ended?

MH: I ended my al-Furqan project because events had changed and I had no money to continue. I had started writing my first book, and continued writing. I was mid-way through my third book when I left to Sudan on my way to my family in Yemen.

LF: Did everyone leave in 1995? Did al-Qaeda close its camps and return to Sudan? I know there was a lot of talk of people leaving but it seems some remained.

MH: All of the al-Qaeda members remaining in Afghanistan wanted to leave as soon as possible. After I ended my project, they closed al-Faruq and transferred what we had left to Jihadwal, which remained operating with a small staff. The Salman al-Farsi camp continued for a short time and the person who did the training there was an Iranian.

LF: Salahdin?

MH: Yes, Salahdin. He was very good trainer. We were good friends.

LF: He was al-Qaeda, correct?

MH: Yes, he was from al-Qaeda, but he, in fact, did not like al-Qaeda. He criticised the Arabs, and worked with the Arabs in Afghanistan.

LF: So, he was Iranian—a Sunni Iranian, who was in al-Qaeda but did not like al-Qaeda: how does that work?

MH: Well, he was my friend, and because I criticised al-Qaeda all the time he would come and sit with me and criticise al-Qaeda too. He liked that I worked independently. He knew that I did not like the way the others worked, but I liked them as friends.

After I left, Salahdin continued to train the Tajiks because al-Nahda sent him groups to train as bodyguards for them, or to work inside Tajikistan. They sent a few groups, maybe five or six times. Every time the training took two or three months. Salahdin trained them at Salman al-Farsi, and Jihadwal was running with around ten Arabs and they let the Tajiks come to help them guard the camp. I think some Pakistanis came to train in Jihadwal, but they came with their own instructors and really only just used the space at Jihadwal.

They eventually closed Salman al-Farsi and al-Faruq and took the things to Jihadwal. I was away but when I came back from Sudan with Abu Abdullah he was very happy the camps were still there because otherwise he had no base in Afghanistan.

LF: So Jihadwal was still there and still operating when you returned to Afghanistan, but with a skeleton staff of only a few people?

MH: Yes. The Pakistanis were there, they had kept the camp busy; and although they made their training away from al-Qaeda, they were loyal to al-Qaeda. Abu Abdullah was very happy the camp had not been closed. All the time I was fighting him, 'don't close the camps, don't close the camps', even after I had to leave. When he returned to see Jihadwal working, he started to energise it again.

LF: Did bin Laden actually believe Sudan's government would expel him? As I understand it, you, Abu Hafs and a few other people warned him his security was in jeopardy if he stayed in the country.

MH: No he did not. Abu Abdullah tried until the last minute to stay in Sudan. He contacted all his friends in the regime, but most of them were helpless and nobody could change the situation because Sudan was under heavy pressure from the outside.

LF: I thought Sudan came under pressure to expel bin Laden because of what the Algerians, the Egyptians and the Libyans were doing, and because bin Laden had been linked with these groups he came under pressure.

MH: No. Many people think like you; it is a common idea. But it is not the whole story. Abu Abdullah had stopped financing Tanzim al-Jihad and Dr Ayman had already left with his bodyguards and close friends. When Dr Ayman left Sudan, he was very angry with Abu Abdullah. The entire world knows Jamaah Islamiyyah in Algeria threatened Abu Abdullah and the takfiris tried to assassinate Abu Abdullah. The Libyans were separate from Abu Abdullah and had nothing to do with him. They had good relations with the West because the West supplied them with everything against Gaddafi and did not chase them. Everyone was chased except the Libyans, Syrians and Palestinians. For what reason I do not know, but Abu Abdullah had nothing to do with them.

For myself, I concluded America wanted to send Abu Abdullah to Afghanistan because they had a certain programme for Afghanistan; and do you know that among themselves some Taliban came to hold a similar theory about Abu Abdullah and his actions in their country? They said 'this man came to damage our movement'.

9

THE ARAB-AFGHAN RETURN AND THE RISE OF THE TALIBAN

Al-Qaeda was the first Arab-Afghan organisation to return to Afghanistan. Bin Laden and fourteen other al-Qaeda members, as well as Mustafa Hamid, arrived in Jalalabad on 18 May 1996, and remained there for close to a year before relocating to Kandahar. On their arrival, Jalalabad was still under the control of the Rabbani-led Kabul government; although a little over four months later the city surrendered to Taliban forces. In Jalalabad, bin Laden and the Arabs with him initially came under the protection of Yunis Khalis, and several former mujahidin commanders in the area, among them Saznor, Dr Amin, and Engineers Mahmud and Mujahid, who were well-known figures from the Soviet jihad.

Al-Qaeda's return to Afghanistan was an unwilling one, but despite repeated efforts to stay in Sudan bin Laden was powerless to stop his expulsion, or to extract the money he had invested in the country. As a result, he was, for a time, reliant on his protectors' hospitality and assistance from ulama in Pakistan. Not all of al-Qaeda followed bin Laden to Afghanistan. Some members chose to leave the organisation and/or remain in Sudan, including senior figures such as Abu Hajr al-Iraqi, Abu Hafs al-Mauritani and Abu Ubaydah al-Banshiri, who drowned in a ferry accident barely days after al-Qaeda had arrived in Afghanistan. As a result, al-Qaeda returned to Afghanistan with less than fifty men remaining in the organisation. Most were married with children and the men and their families settled in Jalalabad in what came to be known as the Arab village.

Al-Qaeda is often thought to have arranged its own sanctuary in Afghanistan, negotiating with Jalalabad area commanders to host bin Laden and provide protection to the group. In reality, the move was arranged by a figure in the Sudanese regime who had helped al-Qaeda with its move to Sudan. This figure contacted the Jalalabad commanders, and arranged for the transport of bin Laden and fifteen other Arabs to Afghanistan on an official Sudanese government plane. He also accompanied them on the journey to Jalalabad, via Shiraz in Iran, where a refuelling stop was made.

* * *

LF: You were on that plane with bin Laden and some other members of al-Qaeda. Was Iran aware of who was on the plane when you stopped for refuelling in Shiraz before continuing on to Jalalabad?

MH: The Sudanese government arranged the travel and there was a government official on the plane with us; he dealt with the officials in Iran when we stopped to refuel. He went out of the plane and told the officials in Shiraz the passengers were a diplomatic group. The Iranians did not know Abu Abdullah was on the plane and they did not enter the plane because it was an official one, and they were told it was a diplomatic envoy travelling to Afghanistan. But it was a very nervous time while we waited, and until we were in Jalalabad.

LF: Did al-Qaeda have much input into its relocation back to Afghanistan?

MH: No. It was all arranged by Sudanese officials. The ones who arranged it knew a number of leading Afghan mujahidin figures because they had fought in the Afghan war. They arranged for Abu Abdullah to be hosted with some people they knew. We also knew these people.

An unhappy return to Afghanistan

LF: Was everyone in al-Qaeda unhappy about returning to Afghanistan?

MH: Abu Abdullah and most of al-Qaeda did not want to leave Sudan, although not everyone knew the organisation was being expelled to Afghanistan. Some of the men in the plane were shocked when they came to know we were flying to Afghanistan because they thought we were going somewhere else, and when they found out, they became very sad.

LF: When did the rest of al-Qaeda's members arrive?

MH: They came several weeks later and brought their families as well as the families of those of us who came with Abu Abdullah. There were two planes. Can you imagine: two Russian pilots on Ukrainian planes hired by the Sudanese government?

LF: Abu Jandal claimed that on the plane Sayf al-Adl sat next to the pilot the whole way.[1] I don't know if it is true.

MH: It was not on this trip. Maybe it was inside Afghanistan, because they did not trust the pilots there, and they did sit behind those pilots with their guns. Coming from Sudan was different; we were on an official plane. For the families, the government arranged to hire planes from a private company to transport them to Jalalabad.

LF: How did you come to be on the plane? You mentioned earlier that you said to bin Laden you would not return to Afghanistan unless you had something to do there. How did he convince you to join him?

MH: Yes, I told Abu Abdullah this in February 1996 when I was in Sudan because my Tajik project, al-Furqan, in Afghanistan was over and so I went to Sudan and was intending to go from there to join my family in Yemen. I went back to Afghanistan because Abu Abdullah asked me to travel with him and the others. I was their reference point for the groups and activities in Afghanistan. I had been there the longest, I knew many people there and had knowledge of what the Taliban was doing. I also knew the position of the Afghan parties, and external parties like Pakistan and Iran, and what they were doing, and the activities of the Tajiks and the Uzbeks from the north. So he asked me to return with him.

* * *

The politics of al-Qaeda's return were complicated. Despite being under the protection of Yunis Khalis and a number of other powerful mujahidin commanders in the Jalalabad area, not all Afghans were happy to see al-Qaeda's return. The then governor of Jalalabad, Hajji Qadir, a former mujahidin commander loyal to the Kabul regime, was one of those unhappy about al-Qaeda and the Arabs' return.

* * *

MH: Hajji Qadir did not want Abu Abdullah and al-Qaeda in Jalalabad—despite knowing them well from the war against the Soviets. But he did not resist their presence, because Mawlawi Yunis Khalis along with the four big commanders from the Jalalabad area were protecting Abu

Abdullah and the Arabs with him. Hajji Qadir kept away from Abu Abdullah and kept silent to be balanced between these men and the Arabs, and the government of Kabul.

LF: Some of the people who agreed to protect and host bin Laden became subject to assassination attempts?

MH: There were a few assassinations. Saznor and Engineer Mujahid were assassinated in Peshawar, and Engineer Mahmud was assassinated in Jalalabad, near Torkham Gate.

LF: They paid a high price for protecting bin Laden. Dr Amin, the only one who was not assassinated, went on to have a long history with al-Qaeda and became one of bin Laden's close friends as I understand it.

MH: Yes. Dr Amin was a very good friend to Abu Abdullah. He was also a very good commander during the Soviet war in the area of Tora Bora, which was close to his village. In fact, in 2001 Dr Amin tried hard to convince Abu Abdullah not to establish himself in Tora Bora. He was right too; setting up in Tora Bora was a stupid idea. Dr Amin fought there against the Soviets and so he knew it was not the best place. But Abu Abdullah did not listen to him. Can you imagine that? Abu Abdullah did not listen to a very good commander who had fought in that area for several years, and instead he did what he wanted?

LF: Yes, I can, because one of the most enduring things about bin Laden seems to be his not listening to advice. In accounts, memoirs and documents released over the years, many figures from both inside and outside al-Qaeda complained about this, which I initially found quite surprising.

In 1996 you advised bin Laden against staying in Jalalabad and Tora Bora, and so too did Abu Hafs. Why did he want to stay there?

MH: Abu Hafs did not like Jalalabad after the defeat there in 1989. When we returned in 1996, I was not in favour of staying in Jalalabad; I thought we should go to Khost. I told Abu Abdullah, 'Go and start in Khost; sit in the camps. They are very good and there are very strong relations in the area.' But he refused. He fell in love with Tora Bora from the time of seeing it on his first visit. He said, 'I am going to stay here. We will bring everything here.'

LF: Bin Laden's first wife and his son, Omar, wrote about their dismay over the living conditions on the mountain.[2]

MH: Abu Abdullah and his family lived on the mountain. For a time they lived in a cave. It was hard living, but Abu Abdullah liked it. I also lived on the mountain with my family in two tents for a short while. You know the conditions in Jalalabad were also very bad and this is why some people moved up to the mountain. In Jalalabad, it was very hot and there was an outbreak of malaria.

* * *

From Tora Bora a declaration of jihad

While living in Tora Bora bin Laden wrote his now infamous Declaration of Jihad against the United States, which was reportedly released on 23 August 1996. The declaration was issued by bin Laden after several months of consultation and dialogue within al-Qaeda and with the Arab-Afghans around him.

* * *

LF: There seems to be a great deal of myth surrounding why and when bin Laden made the decision to release this declaration. Sayf al-Adl wrote the idea of declaring jihad came after al-Qaeda returned to Afghanistan and it was intended as a way of regaining experienced personnel lost over previous years.[3] I wonder about the logic of that because al-Qaeda had nowhere to house people if they came to join, although the declaration was probably useful as a fundraising tool.

I thought the declaration was about gaining control over the developing jihad movement in Saudi Arabia, which evolved independently of bin Laden, particularly since it was issued shortly after the June 1996 Khobar Towers bombing.

* * *

The Khobar Towers attack targeted housing facilities for foreign military personnel. It followed an earlier November 1995 attack against the Office of the Program Manager, at the Saudi Arabian National Guard complex in Riyadh, which also accommodated foreign military personnel.

* * *

LF: You were against bin Laden issuing the declaration, and spoke at length with him about his decision. Can you clarify why he declared jihad at that time and how well supported his decision was inside al-Qaeda?

MH: There are many important parts to this story, but first let's focus on Saudi Arabia. Abu Abdullah was worried about what was happening inside Saudi Arabia. We all were. There were new fighting songs circulating among the youth that just urged people to kill and explode things, and they were gaining popularity like they had in the camps of Jalalabad.

LF: I thought these songs came from Algeria, and that an Algerian influence was seeping into Saudi Arabia?

MH: No. They were like those circulating in Algeria, but they came from Saudis inside the kingdom. Abu Abdullah was worried, and his fear this current would cause great harm in Saudi Arabia was one of the main reasons he issued his declaration—to master it before it became like Algeria.

LF: It was a pre-emptive move to stop this movement gaining power?

MH: Abu Abdullah thought if there was command over the situation in Saudi Arabia, and a reasonable leader, then a disaster could be avoided. By that, he meant to protect Saudi Arabia from what this current was preparing, which would be disastrous. We discussed this in Tora Bora before he issued the declaration.

LF: Where was this current in Saudi Arabia coming from? Was it influenced by the Jalalabad School and people who had gone to fight in Algeria and Bosnia coming back to Saudi Arabia radicalised to more takfiri ideas?

MH: All of this played a part, but the people who went to Algeria to fight did not stay for long. Not only were the takfiris there crazy, and doing things that had nothing to do with Islam—killing people, raping women, taking the property of the people—they were also killing Arabs who were fighting there. They did this to prevent the Arabs telling others about the unlawful things happening there and making a bad reputation for the Algerians.

LF: So basically, bin Laden was concerned about the emergence of a growing movement beyond his control, and the harm it could cause inside Saudi Arabia.

MH: Yes, the two attacks—one in Riyadh and the other in Khobar—were done by people completely away from al-Qaeda, and were both against the Americans. One of the people involved in the Riyadh attack was in the Jalalabad camps, and he took the fighting songs from one of those camps. Nobody from al-Qaeda knew this man from that time; nobody knew he was an expert in making explosives.

Despite having been involved in jihad for many years, and training thousands of people in his camps, Abu Abdullah found himself away from the game. He had nothing in Saudi Arabia, because he did not support attacks inside the country. We should note this point because it is an essential one. Since establishing al-Qaeda, Abu Abdullah was against fighting inside Saudi Arabia. But when he found the people rising in Saudi Arabia and explosions starting to occur, he announced jihad, and one of the reasons was to handle this emerging current.

LF: To control it?

MH: To prevent it doing damage and causing Muslims to fight Muslims. Abu Abdullah wanted to focus attention on attacks outside Saudi Arabia. I think he insisted on making big operations outside Saudi Arabia to avoid violence inside Saudi Arabia. In fact, this is when Abu Abdullah came up with his theory of the three operations: three operations and he will get America out of Saudi Arabia. I discussed this with him at length and told him he was wrong. He said, 'You see what happened in Lebanon when they blew up the marine headquarters.' I explained, 'This is not a reference for anything; it is Lebanese affairs, which are very different to Saudi affairs.'

LF: It seems fairly clear at that time al-Qaeda lacked the men and money to do much of anything at all.

MH: Al-Qaeda was in a bad situation. Abu Abdullah was borrowing money from the ulama of Pakistan because he had to provide for the families of his fighters, and for the Arabs who were beginning to return to Afghanistan and join him. Conditions were poor in Jalalabad and the situation in Afghanistan was not stable.

LF: Speaking of the return of other Afghan-Arabs, many people think Ayman al-Zawahiri influenced bin Laden's decision to declare jihad against America. When bin Laden authored his declaration Ayman had not yet returned to Afghanistan and it is my understanding relations between them were not repaired until Ayman arrived in mid-1997.

MH: Dr Ayman was very focused on Egypt, and at that time he was away from Afghanistan and still angry with Abu Abdullah for withdrawing funding for Tanzim al-Jihad in 1995. He had no influence on this at all.

LF: A lot of accounts about al-Qaeda and bin Laden's history seem to assume bin Laden fell under the influence of others, whether it was Abdullah Azzam during the Afghan jihad, or Ayman al-Zawahiri during the late 1990s. It strikes me no one was able to influence bin Laden, especially if he had made his mind up on something. If anything, bin Laden seemed to influence others.

What has always interested me is that bin Laden had no real stance to speak of until he wrote his 1996 Declaration of Jihad. Although he wrote letters about Saudi Arabia and other topics, he had not really outlined a solid position, or a strategy or doctrine. The 1996 declaration was his first statement of an ideological or doctrinal position, but even it lacked detail. For example, the declaration announced an intent to wage jihad, but offered up no plan for how it was to be done; instead, it called for consultations. This may explain why so few people joined al-Qaeda after the declaration was released.

MH: There were consultations going on for six weeks. Many people tried to advise Abu Abdullah before the declaration, and after it was released. Abu Abdullah did not have a strategic focus, because he was not fond of long-term work. This is why al-Qaeda lacked strategies and its goals often changed.

Here we should also note Abu Abdullah's declaration was written in reaction to events in Saudi Arabia; it was not intended to be a detailed plan for the future. He wrote it to make clear what was and was not good for jihad and to focus the jihad work outside the kingdom, but he did not outline a programme or strategy.

LF: I thought the declaration's purpose was to put a claim to leadership over the emerging jihadi current in Saudi Arabia; to step in and take control because this current was basically a competitor, and al-Qaeda's legitimacy was at stake. It strikes me the declaration had less to do with America and more to do with controlling this current and rebuilding al-Qaeda—at least in the short to medium term.

MH: Of course it had to do with America and its occupation of the Arabian Peninsula! This is what caused those other people to carry out attacks inside the kingdom. Abu Abdullah did want to influence these groups and to do so early. He thought if he left it until later, they could cause great damage, which would result in a deeper level of American occupation of Saudi Arabia. He also thought if he delayed trying to influence these groups he would face difficulties unifying them later.

LF: Were these reasons discussed at length in the consultations bin Laden held? As I understand it, there was opposition to his making such a declaration.

MH: Abu Abdullah made the decision to issue the declaration by himself. Al-Qaeda's people in Tora Bora agreed with him, but later he ignored advice from people outside the *tanzim* who had concerns about the consequences of making such a declaration. Opposition to the declaration was not because he was targeting America, but because al-Qaeda had no capacity to do so, and also no plan or strategy.

LF: You were among those arguing against his jihad project. Why?

MH: I was not against the idea of making America leave the Arabian Peninsula and all the Arab countries. But I thought the project was too big for al-Qaeda and that it had not created a programme for how it would conduct jihad against America. A project like this required a grand strategy. It required broad participation—at a much greater level than just al-Qaeda's fifty men, who of course did not have the capacity to build a programme at this level. A successful project could not be a one-man show, or even carried out by one *tanzim*.

LF: So your view, essentially, was that bin Laden was treating America like a paper tiger, believing he could defeat the country all by himself and that little effort was required?

MH: We had big discussions at Tora Bora and later on in Kandahar. Abu Abdullah thought America would withdraw its forces very quickly if it sustained just three big hits. He talked a lot about the 1993 helicopter incident in Somalia and the bombing of the US barracks in Beirut in 1983. A few of us tried to convince him that circumstances were different. We said, 'If you go to fight America now the entire world will be against you. You will be absolutely alone and you are not ready.' I told him, 'If you fight America now you are very weak, and if the Americans find an enemy very weak they eliminate them totally. They will finish you; you and your group.' In fact, that later happened.

LF: Bin Laden had a tendency to seek out support for his opinion rather than listen to those who cautioned him, as some of his own staff even noted; was this one of those instances when bin Laden pressed ahead anyway?

MH: Yes, people tried to convince Abu Abdullah that declaring jihad on America would involve more than just a few operations, and that it was dangerous to declare jihad without a strategic plan, when nothing had been organised. Doing so would harm not only al-Qaeda but the jihad cause.

LF: I think Abu Musab al-Suri made a similar argument, saying that all talk and threats with no action would undermine the cause of jihad.[4]

MH: I was probably among the strongest because I argued al-Qaeda should be dissolved if Abu Abdullah wanted to do this project. I said to

Abu Abdullah, 'It is a vast undertaking and requires an entirely different way of organising and programmes of action that are beyond al-Qaeda.' It needed to be a project focused on rallying the Ummah, because the Ummah had to support the project in order for it to be successful. I said, 'Let the Ummah wake up and fight with the whole Ummah.'

LF: How did bin Laden take this advice?

MH: He did not accept it. By then, Abu Abdullah was accustomed to running al-Qaeda as his own organisation and he was in a hurry to fight. He did not even accept the advice we gave about not making his declaration, a declaration of just one man against an entire country.

LF: I remember reading your account of this.[5] Bin Laden was warned against issuing the declaration by himself because it would cause difficulties convincing others to join the cause, especially when al-Qaeda was an organisation run and funded solely by him.

MH: Yes. By declaring war all by himself, Abu Abdullah made himself vulnerable to being isolated and defeated if the Ummah did not support him. But Abu Abdullah, like he had at Jalalabad and Jaji before, could not resist being like the lone warrior who came to the rescue.

LF: You wrote bin Laden saw himself as one 'who came wielding his sword to save the Two Holy Mosques, and teach the Americans a lesson'.[6] Did he think the Ummah would come to support him after he attacked America? It seems to me that rather than build a programme to wake up the Ummah, bin Laden thought attacking America first would do the job for him: that he could use attacks as the way to convince people to join him.

MH: That is true. He thought he had the historical experience and if he started first, even alone, then everyone would come later and follow him.

LF: As I understand it, the declaration failed to attract people to join al-Qaeda. I did notice both Abu Musab al-Suri and Khalid Shaykh Muhammad approached bin Laden after his declaration, which had called for consultation and preparation for the American jihad project.

Khalid Shaykh approached al-Qaeda for support for his idea to hijack planes inside America, after earlier approaching Abu Zubaydah—who told him he had no capacity and referred him on to al-Qaeda. After approaching al-Qaeda, Khalid Shaykh was told the plan wasn't feasible, but bin Laden did ask him to join the organisation. Khalid Shaykh declined and continued working with Abu Zubaydah and his group, among others. It seems al-Qaeda was doing a good job hiding its financial problems if people were coming with or referring propositions like this to al-Qaeda.

Abu Musab al-Suri also approached al-Qaeda after the declaration was issued. He too declined the invitation to join al-Qaeda. Abu Musab later wrote he found many positives in bin Laden's declaration against America, and although he was hopeful it would work, his hopes were ultimately dashed.[7] Abu Musab took issue with al-Qaeda's lack of capacity, strategy and programme.

Beyond these two figures, it seems people were wary of signing up to bin Laden's project. Some were fearful of surrendering their independence if they joined al-Qaeda, or thought the work was disorganised or unrealistic. Others were focused on jihad at open fronts like Chechnya, which were supported by fatawa and offered the opportunity for combat, while targeting America did not. Or they were focused on overthrowing regimes and did not want to surrender this goal for targeting America. They did not accept bin Laden's argument that America was the head of the snake and must be dealt with first.

MH: Yes, people were cautious for many reasons, and other fronts and groups were popular. But we should note at that time routes to Afghanistan were very dangerous, so this also affected the flow of people joining. Al-Qaeda still had financial problems, but only a few in the close circles were aware of this; it was not public knowledge.

* * *

The Taliban gain a controversial guest

Bin Laden's 1996 declaration of war was issued a day before the Taliban took Jalalabad. The declaration came as a shock to the Taliban, who at that time were yet to have direct contact with bin Laden.

* * *

LF: How did the Taliban feel about gaining a house guest who had just declared war on the world's remaining superpower?

MH: When Abu Abdullah announced jihad against the Americans, Kabul had not yet fallen to the Taliban and was still under the control of the Rabbani government. Abu Abdullah's declaration was released a day before the Taliban entered Jalalabad, and by the time they entered the city the whole world had begun to talk about Abu Abdullah and his declaration of jihad against America. It was a big disturbance.

A few weeks later, the Taliban captured Kabul and announced Mullah Omar was the 'Amir al-Muminin'. I told Abu Abdullah, 'Now everything has changed. There is a new leader and a new regime in Afghanistan; you should recalculate everything, your thinking should be revised, your role in Afghanistan should be revised.' I said this because if Abu Abdullah wanted to attack outside, permission was needed from Mullah Omar because he was the Amir al-Muminin. But Abu Abdullah did not revise his position and he began giving media interviews. I did not support Abu Abdullah carrying out media work during such a sensitive time for the Taliban.

LF: Bin Laden gave a number of interviews in the remaining part of 1996.

MH: I do not know the exact number, but the result was the Saudi ambassador came from Islamabad and put a lot of pressure on Pakistan and the Taliban. In fact, a large number of envoys came to the Taliban after it came to power, including many from the West. A lot of them raised the issue of Abu Abdullah. The Taliban began to complain saying, 'Who are these nations? We don't even know their place on the map.' They were very unhappy and said 'the entire world wants to talk about Abu Abdullah', and they wanted Abu Abdullah to stop his interviews because it was causing them problems. They said, 'Please let him stop talking.' That became the crisis between Abu Abdullah and the Taliban for all their history.

LF: Did the Taliban raise this issue with bin Laden directly? The accounts of their dealings are a little murky.

MH: They tried but Abu Abdullah would not see the Taliban's leaders in the beginning. He asked me to go instead! The prime minister of the Taliban became very upset about Abu Abdullah's media interviews and sent an envoy to call him to Kabul. Abu Abdullah thought it would be a big crisis, so he did not go to see him; instead, he told me to see the prime minister! Abu Abdullah said, 'Abu Walid, please go and meet him.' I said, 'Why? Why should I go?' Abu Abdullah said, 'You know them, you know us; you should interfere to cool the situation down to avoid any crisis.'

The prime minister came to Jalalabad, stayed for two days, and then left to Kabul saying, 'Send Abu Abdullah to me.' This was when I went to meet him. First, I went to meet the minister of justice in Jalalabad; I talked with him and he said, 'You should go to the prime minister in Kabul.' I went to Kabul along with Abu Hafs al-Masri and Abu Jihad al-Masri, who was from Tanzim al-Jihad, and among the first of them to return to Afghanistan. We sat and talked with the prime minister for several hours. I think they asked me to go because I have white hair, and the Afghans respect people who have this white hair! Also, I had been in Afghanistan the longest.

So then I met the prime minister, and I talked with him and he asked me, 'Abu Walid what is wrong with Saudi Arabia and America?' I explained in detail about their relationship and the oil, and the spread of the American bases in Saudi Arabia after Iraq's invasion of Kuwait. He listened intently, and at the end he said, 'Just wait to give us a chance to settle everything in Afghanistan; we are facing a lot of problems every day. All our neighbours interfere inside Afghanistan; outsiders come and interfere. Please give us a chance. Please stop him (Abu Abdullah) talking,' and so on.

At the end of our meeting the prime minister said, 'You are foreigners, you are our guests, you are mujahidin and we want to help you.' Then he went out of his office and brought back a sack full of Afghan money. I said to him, 'Why?' He said, 'It is for the people in your village.' The Afghans were very sad because the Arabs had arrived and were living in mud houses in very crowded conditions; they had not seen Arabs poor before.

We tried to convince him that everything was alright and we could manage, but he said, 'No. Take this money.' So we took it. It was around 3,000 dollars' worth of Afghan currency. As we said goodbye to him there were tears in his eyes. He was a very nice man. When we reached the Arab village, Abu Hafs and Abu Jihad took the money and gave it to Abu Abdullah. But after two days a big explosion happened in the Jalalabad ammunition depot and some Taliban died. Abu Abdullah took this money and gave it to the families of the Taliban who were martyred.

LF: So what did bin Laden say about being asked to be quiet? Did he listen?

MH: No, and it was not the last time I had to mediate between the Taliban and Abu Abdullah. From time to time, I had to go and mediate if there was a problem from Abu Abdullah meeting someone, or making a statement. Abu Abdullah would say, 'Abu Walid you have to go and mediate.'

LF: Did you ever consider saying no?

MH: The position of the Arabs was very weak at that time. I disagreed with Abu Abdullah, but I went to mediate because without the Taliban, the Arabs and their families would have been in a very bad situation. In fact, it was already dangerous enough because not all the Taliban were happy with the Arabs being in Afghanistan. One day I was in Kabul with an Afghan friend attending a large conference with the foreign minister. At the end of the day, they were going to pray and the foreign minister did not know there was an Arab in the room. He said, 'In fact we do not need these Wahhabi Arabs in Afghanistan; they create problems for us and they make *takfir* on us.'

This was how I came to know there was a big fault-line within the Taliban over the presence of Arabs in Afghanistan. It was very dangerous because it was a very strong and influential current within the Taliban. The moderate Taliban like the prime minister begged, 'please tell Abu Abdullah not to talk'. That meant the moderate wing did not like Abu Abdullah to talk, or the Arabs to be in the country, but they kept quiet about this. The hardliner wing did not want the Arabs in Afghanistan.

LF: What do you think caused the current to be so strong so early on? I knew it was there towards the end, but I didn't realise it was so strong at the beginning of al-Qaeda's time in Afghanistan.

MH: I should mention there was another fault-line among the Taliban on the matter of Abu Abdullah and al-Qaeda, and how the Taliban thought about the politics of the situation. One person from the Taliban came to me because I was nearer to the Taliban than other Arabs. They said, 'Some influential Taliban think the Americans sent Abu Abdullah to spoil our movement and create problems for the Taliban in Afghanistan.' I said, 'No, please don't think like that. This man is honest; I know him. He fought for a long time during the Soviet war and he gave his money for the cause. He could not do something like that.'

I defended Abu Abdullah against these allegations. The people who thought this did not show themselves; just in secret meetings, but I knew their current inside the Taliban was strong.

LF: When did bin Laden meet Mullah Omar, and did he ask bin Laden to be quiet? There are many conflicting stories about their meetings.

MH: Mullah Omar sent for Abu Abdullah while the Arabs were still living in Jalalabad. It was November 1996. He sent a helicopter with some armed men who arrived, and said they had instructions from Mullah

Omar to 'go and bring Abu Abdullah'. The helicopter arrived at the airport and the armed men came saying, 'Abu Abdullah is wanted in Kandahar by the amir.' That is all they said, and they said it with very grim faces that were so serious I thought, 'Oooh, they are going to execute him.' Truly, I thought this. It was very serious that Abu Abdullah was wanted by the amir in Kandahar—especially since they had not met before.

LF: At this time, bin Laden was continuing to give media interviews?

MH: Yes, he had not stopped. Abu Abdullah also became very worried when these men arrived and summoned him. I was with Abu Abdullah when they came to get him. Straight away Abu Abdullah asked for Abu Hafs. He came and Abu Abdullah told him, 'I am going to Kandahar, and I may not come back.' Abu Abdullah gave Abu Hafs advice about what to do if that happened and appointed him amir. He was giving advice because he truly thought he might not come back.

Then Abu Abdullah said to me, 'Abu Walid, please come with me.' I said, 'What? You want me to be executed with you?' I knew that he would use me as protection for him, because I had this white hair the Afghans respected, and I knew some Taliban. Abu Abdullah never listened to my advice, but in times of danger like this, he always wanted me to go with him.

LF: Did you go?

MH: Yes, I went with him, and Sayf al-Adl came too, along with five bodyguards for Abu Abdullah. It was impolite to go to meet the Amir al-Muminin and take your bodyguards; the Afghans did not like this. We went to the helicopter and travelled to Kandahar airport, and then a car took us to the building where Mullah Omar was working. It was a very long meeting, and he told Abu Abdullah, 'Please don't talk. Keep quiet. We are in a dangerous position here now. Everything is against us. We have troubles everywhere, from every place. We have a lot of problems. We have no money.' Mullah Omar explained everything. He said, 'Please wait; we are going to help you and help all the Muslims. But wait.'

Mullah Omar was as tall as Abu Abdullah, and he was crouching on a military bed for the soldiers. We were sitting on the ground in front of him in two rows—us and the Afghans—and he said frankly, 'Look I can't help you now. I am just like this,' and he motioned to how he was crouching. He said, 'I am not sitting and not standing; and this position is a very hard position. Leave things until I stand or sit.' That was a good example from him, and it was clear he expected Abu Abdullah to be quiet and not make any problems until the Taliban's position was stronger.

Mullah Omar was very strict with Abu Abdullah in the meeting, and he wanted to end the meeting positively. To be polite he said to Abu Abdullah, 'You are in your country; you can do whatever you want.' He only meant it to be polite, but Abu Abdullah caught this, and after we had left said, 'Oh, you see, he said I can do whatever I want.'

I became very angry. I said, 'Abu Abdullah don't play this game. Mullah Omar said that to be gentle with you after spending several hours telling you don't do this or that. He said that just to be polite.' Abu Abdullah said, 'No. Mullah Omar said, "Do whatever you want."' And Abu Abdullah started to behave like that; as if Mullah Omar had told him to do whatever he wanted. This was the first meeting between Abu Abdullah and Mullah Omar.

* * *

The situation of the Arabs in Jalalabad remained tenuous for reasons other than bin Laden's public announcements. The Taliban's position was still weak, and in late 1996 through early 1997 it nearly lost Kabul after Masud and Dostum's forces launched a strong attack seeking to re-capture the city. The near-fall of Kabul in this battle worried the Arabs.

* * *

MH: Kabul went very close to falling and it would have without Haqqani, whose forces saved the city. At that time I said to Abu Abdullah, 'Dostum is coming; we should go and fight in Kabul.' If the Taliban were defeated in Kabul, Jalalabad would be next and Dostum's forces could very quickly be in our village. I said to Abu Abdullah, 'We cannot fight here in our village; we have the kids and the women, and if they are captured it will be a disaster.'

A group of us decided to go to the front to see how the things were, and to talk to the Taliban and tell them we wanted to help. I went with two other Arabs, Abu Tariq al-Tunisi and Amir al-Fateh. We talked to the Taliban and said 'we want to come and fight' but they said 'no'. At that time, despite their situation, they were still very suspicious of Arabs. This was because the Arabs were a part of Hekmatyar's force that fought the Taliban in Wardak in 1995. Among them were famous Arabs like Abu Khabab al-Masri. In that battle, the Arabs killed many Taliban and the Taliban did not forget this.

Many of the Arabs who stayed in Pakistan or Afghanistan during the Afghan civil war period, were initially against the Taliban. Abu Abdul

Rahman al-Kanadi was one of them. Because of this Arab history against the Taliban, some of its commanders north of Kabul would not meet with us; and they refused to allow us to fight alongside them. This was at the end of 1996. The invasion of Kabul ended in the first week of 1997 when Haqqani pushed Masud and Dostum's forces out of Kabul to the Salang Pass.

LF: It was around the end of 1996 that a group of about thirty-six Arabs, most of whom had previously been in Bosnia, arrived in Afghanistan, and some ended up joining al-Qaeda. It is a curious story because apparently this group, which was mostly made of Gulf mujahidin, came to Afghanistan keen to go to Tajikistan for jihad. Instead, many ended up joining al-Qaeda, and fighting to defend Kabul a few months later in mid-1997 when Masud and Dostum again attempted to take the city.

Apparently, the group was told there was an open front in Tajikistan and this is why they travelled to Afghanistan. It seems from the account of one of those involved that bin Laden was trying to draw this group close to him by saying al-Qaeda had a front in Tajikistan.[8] I thought the Tajik jihad never materialised, and was certainly not an al-Qaeda project as bin Laden is alleged to have claimed?

MH: This was around the time Abdul Hadi al-Iraqi joined al-Qaeda. Before that he had worked with me on my Tajik project and he continued working with the Tajiks after I left. Once Abdul Hadi joined al-Qaeda it claimed his work as its own. But al-Qaeda did not have a front there or a project.

LF: The group went north to Taloqan but could not enter Tajikistan. After their effort failed, they reportedly met with bin Laden and some other leaders who asked them to join al-Qaeda. From their travels north, the group apparently acquired the name 'The Northern Group'.[9]

Some were reluctant to join al-Qaeda because they had travelled to fight and al-Qaeda had no open fronts, just training in its camps. One former member claimed many in The Northern Group were also unsure about bin Laden's jihad project against America, and it took a great deal of effort by bin Laden and other senior figures to convince some of the group to join al-Qaeda. As part of these efforts bin Laden argued there was a three-day right of hospitality and the group should stay with him for three days.[10] Can you tell me about the three-day right of hospitality, as I have always wondered about this?

MH: It is an old Arab habit. When a guest comes from far away to a place you live and you don't know him, you leave him three days. Nobody asks the guest who they are or where they come from. The guest is given food and hospitality for three days and then asked. The guest's right is for three days, after that, you can ask him and see what he wants.

LF: So does that also mean that if bin Laden argued for a three-day right of hospitality, he could talk to them that whole time and they had to listen?

MH: They could talk as they liked, but under this rule, he would have had no right to ask them any questions before they spent this three-day period.

LF: It must have worked because it was apparently after this some of the group decided to stay, and later completed training and became al-Qaeda members. Their doing so gave bin Laden a new generation of militarily experienced cadre, and most importantly added some more Gulf Arabs to al-Qaeda's ranks. Until that time, al-Qaeda had few Gulf Arabs, which presented it with a legitimacy problem, especially since bin Laden's declaration was about liberating Saudi Arabia, and the Gulf more generally, from the Americans.

What particularly interests me is that the members of The Northern Group who did join al-Qaeda were convinced to do so as a result of them spending time with bin Laden. Proximity to him seems to have been very important to al-Qaeda's recruitment efforts, perhaps more than anything else.

MH: This is a very good point because after they stayed with him the people from the Gulf started to build a very close relationship with Abu Abdullah. The result was that they did not follow anyone but him. That made Abu Hafs, Abu Muhammad al-Masri, Sayf al-Adl and other elders in al-Qaeda angry, because these youth did not follow the command system.

LF: Al-Qaeda's efforts at that time also appear to have been focused on recruiting experienced people; those who had already been involved in jihad, like The Northern Group. I wondered if that was one of the reasons bin Laden's declaration of jihad contained so little in the way of religious justifications, and was not supported by a fatwa? If he was trying to attract people who were already mujahidin, perhaps he thought he did not need to educate them, or present them with a fatwa because they were already committed to jihad.

MH: Ready-made mujahidin.

LF: Yes, exactly; but it seems bin Laden miscalculated. As his efforts with The Northern Group reveal, less than half joined al-Qaeda and within this group some members reportedly put a condition in place that they would join al-Qaeda but would leave if a better-sanctioned jihad started and a new front opened.[11]

Even though the whole Northern Group did not join, the extra manpower from those who did become members must have been welcomed by al-Qaeda. Around the time they joined, in early 1997, there was an assassination attempt made on bin Laden, which caused al-Qaeda and the Arabs to move from Jalalabad to Kandahar and for security procedures to be tightened.

MH: Actually, it was not just an assassination attempt on Abu Abdullah. It was to be an attack on the whole Arab village. In early 1997, a large group came from Pakistan to attack the Arab village. The Taliban captured the group and found out it was led by the son of Hajji Qadir, the former governor of Jalalabad, and was financed by the Saudis and guided by Pakistan. The Taliban asked the Arab families to leave the village quickly. Within a few hours, all the families from the village—over fifty of them—were shifted in cars, buses and by plane to Kandahar.

LF: It was in Kandahar that Mullah Omar paid another visit to bin Laden. Why was that? I thought relations between the two remained a little tense.

MH: Relations between Mullah Omar and Abu Abdullah were still not good. Mullah Omar had consulted some Pakistani ulama for advice on how to repair the relationship. They suggested Mullah Omar visit Abu Abdullah and talk to him. They also suggested Mullah Omar marry a daughter of Abu Abdullah's because then the Arabs and Afghans would become like a big family and things would be smoothed down. This was traditional thinking in the region, and the Pakistani ulama thought it would work with the Arabs.

Abu Abdullah refused. He said, 'My daughters are still very young; they are not of the age of marriage.' A few months later, he gave his eldest daughter in marriage to one of the Saudi boys. That means he refused to give her to Mullah Omar.

LF: I doubt a family relationship would have stopped bin Laden.

MH: He would have continued. Abu Abdullah would not stop anything if he wanted to do it. This was his nature.

LF: When Mullah Omar visited were the Arabs still not allowed to participate in Taliban military operations? Did they discuss issues such as this when they met?

MH: Mullah Omar came to the Arab village in Kandahar with about fifteen or twenty of his men, and they came and sat with us. At that time, the Arabs were not allowed to be involved in the military affairs of the Taliban. It was a long meeting and many topics were covered—but not Arab participation alongside the Taliban.

Mullah Omar talked a lot about problems on the borders with Pakistan and Iran. At this meeting, I suggested he reach out to Iran to try to improve relations, and as a result, he ended up sending me there as an emissary.

LF: I thought you went on al-Qaeda's behalf too?

MH: Abu Abdullah and I discussed it. I said, 'You need to develop good relations with Iran because the route from Pakistan is very dangerous.' He initially supported doing so, but then some of the young Gulf people heard about it and began to complain. They did not approve of relations with Iran because it was Shia, and because of this Abu Abdullah told me to put what we had discussed 'in a drawer'. That meant he was telling me not to open this topic or do anything about this, and to never mention it again, so I did not. But yet, still the Americans accuse me of acting as mediator for al-Qaeda.

LF: Bin Laden's reaction to disapproval of the youth reminds me of what we spoke about earlier—about problems in Afghan jihad against the Soviets caused by the Arab-Afghan leadership reacting to the whims of the youth. It seems this trend was not just isolated to the Afghan jihad, but was also present in al-Qaeda.

MH: Yes, I had an argument with some people in al-Qaeda about letting the young generation guide the organisation. When Abu Abdullah let them do this in relation to Iran, he missed an opportunity to build his own routes into and out of Afghanistan. Later, al-Qaeda paid the price of this after the American invasion of Afghanistan in 2001 when many of its people were captured.

I went to Iran on behalf of the Taliban and Mullah Omar. It was a difficult trip. In Iran, I was with my friend Abdullah Nuri who was from the Tajiks. I was sitting with him and some Iranians around the time an incident occurred at Mazar Sharif in Afghanistan after the Taliban entered the city. The Iranians were very angry with the Taliban, and of course, angry with the Arabs. I was trying to explain things at this meeting and I found myself like a man between the bees. There were many people around who were angry, talking, talking, talking and I was alone. I tried on this trip to build relations but the results were not what we had hoped.

When I returned to Kandahar, I was expecting to brief Mullah Omar and spend time briefing him, but some serious events taking place in Kabul had taken his attention. A very dangerous situation had arisen. Ahmad Shah Masud's force had attacked the Taliban posts on Kabul's border, at the entrance to the Salang Passage, and pushed them back a few kilometres. The Taliban were again in danger of losing Kabul.

It was a shocking defeat for the Taliban forces at the Kabul front, whose defence lines collapsed. They said to Mullah Omar, 'Kabul is in danger of falling, please send some assistance.' Then Mullah Omar sent a message to the Arab village, 'Please send everybody who can fight to Kabul urgently.'

LF: The situation must have been desperate for the position of the Taliban on Arab military participation to be reversed.

MH: Yes it was, but also relations had improved a little after Mullah Omar's visit. It was just after Mullah Omar had sent the message that I reached Kandahar. Abu Abdullah came to me and said, 'Mullah Omar sent this message asking us for help. Can you please go and see the situation and tell us what we can do? You know the area and were watching it with Haqqani.' Abu Abdullah was very happy Mullah Omar had asked for assistance, and was excited for the chance to make relations stronger between the Taliban and the Arabs.

I went to the front with Abu Hafs al-Masri and a few others. When we got there, we found a disaster. It was a complete mess, everywhere. Everything was disorganised. It was a dangerous situation. Haqqani had left the Kabul area a few months earlier, and do you know why this miserable situation happened?

LF: Why?

MH: It was because the Taliban did not follow Haqqani's advice after he conquered Masud and Dostum at the beginning of 1997. Haqqani had seized the top of Salang Passage and his forces had come down a little on the other side. When he withdrew his forces, Haqqani told the Taliban minister of defence that he should keep forces at the top of the mountain, because Kabul was easier to defend with this under Taliban control. Some people in the ministry said no, and thought that keeping the entrance to the passage and not the mountain before the entrance was sufficient.

It was a stupid decision and the people who made it did not know anything about how to fight in mountains because they came from desert areas. As many famous military strategists have argued, you must hold the mountaintops; if you hold the mountain, your enemy must come up the mountain to fight you. Haqqani was very angry and upset at the time; he knew because of this stupid decision it would be very easy for Masud to come again and attack Kabul. In fact, this is exactly what was happening when I returned to Kandahar from Iran.

LF: If it was such a disaster from the outset, why did the Arabs participate in this battle?

MH: Because if Kabul fell at that time, the Taliban could have collapsed.

LF: The 1997 battle was a turning point for al-Qaeda and the Arabs who joined it in battle. How many of them fought? I thought it was around forty or so?

MH: It is unknown exactly. It was not a lot and because of that Abu Abdullah asked the Pakistanis to supply him with some manpower. They supplied a few hundred men but Sayf al-Adl was not content and Abdul Hadi al-Iraqi said that Pakistanis were consuming too much money and resources with little result. Then they separated and the Arabs worked as a separate group in a small number.

Abu Abdullah also sent for the Yemenis and The Northern Group to come and join this battle, but some of them were not willing to fight because the people they were being asked to fight were 'previous mujahidin'. They asked, 'Why should we fight against mujahidin?'

Here we should notice something very critical about the battle for Kabul. Most of the Arabs were Salafis and they did not like to fight other Muslims unless they were declared *kafir*, and it was a very big discussion at that time about the permissibility of fighting Masud's forces. Eventually al-Qaeda said they were *kafir*, but others said they were not *kafir*, they were Muslims.

LF: Al-Qaeda and the Arabs lost quite a few people in this battle.

MH: Yes, the result of the battle was very disappointing. The Arabs were upset that Taliban fighters abandoned their posts easily during battle and did not fight. It also became very clear the Taliban's situation was fragile and the situation in Afghanistan could change sharply at any time.

It could be just a matter of hours for everything to change if Masud came again to take Kabul.

LF: The attack was repelled, and al-Qaeda along with some other Arabs had fought with the Taliban. As I understand it, al-Qaeda's participation drew criticism, especially from the folks at the Khaldan camp. Abu Abdullah al-Muhajir, who headed Khaldan's religious institute, was an outspoken critic of al-Qaeda and the Taliban, and led the opposition to Arab involvement in the fighting.

MH: Yes, he did not support jihad inside Afghanistan at all.

LF: Abu Abdullah al-Muhajir had influence because Khaldan, unlike al-Qaeda, had its own religious institute, which he headed. Khaldan was more populated than al-Qaeda at that time. It had a steady stream of trainees and more groups were represented there.

Abu Abdullah al-Muhajir's viewpoint was also not in the minority. Most of the groups who had sought sanctuary in Afghanistan were takfiri like Abu Abdullah al-Muhajir. They did not support al-Qaeda's agenda, and they did not support the Taliban or fighting alongside it; at least at the beginning—although some later changed their views.

Around this time, a number of groups had begun to arrive in Afghanistan; among them, the Egyptian groups Tanzim al-Jihad and Gamaah Islamiyyah, and groups from the Maghreb. You wrote that they were 'disorientated fragments of destroyed organisations that were seeking sanctuary and to rebuild themselves in Afghanistan'.[12]

MH: Yes, although the Libyans did not initially base themselves in Afghanistan. Their doctrine was very strict, much stricter in fact than the Egyptian groups and they did not accept the legitimacy of the Taliban. In fact, initially they were among those who made *takfir* against the Taliban.

LF: Yes, there was quite an anti-Taliban movement there among some of the takfiris. What strikes me is that despite the vast doctrinal differences between some of these groups—for example between the Islamic Movement of Uzbekistan and the East Turkestan Islamic Movement, which already had a presence in Afghanistan, and were becoming more active, and the Arab groups arriving back into the country, there is one common thread. All of these groups were nationally focused and were not interested in al-Qaeda's global agenda. There were only two groups that had agendas similar to al-Qaeda's. Both were stubbornly independent and refused al-Qaeda's entreaties for them to join; they were Abu Zubaydah's group and Abu Musab al-Suri's group.

Another similarity is that few of these groups were interested in supporting the Taliban. The exceptions were the Islamic Movement of Uzbekistan and the East Turkestan Islamic Movement after it moved away from Khaldan, as well as Abu Musab al-Suri and the small group he later formed in Kabul. Despite none of these groups supporting al-Qaeda's activities, and few supporting the Taliban, it was the criticism from Khaldan that had the most impact. This is presumably because it encouraged other Arabs to also speak out and make *takfir* against the Taliban, and potentially those who supported it, like al-Qaeda.

Bin Laden reportedly made efforts to reach out to the people in Khaldan, but according to one report, he was denied permission to visit.[13]

MH: I have never heard about any visit being refused.

LF: Yes, it was an interesting account that came from someone who was close to Abu Abdullah al-Muhajir and was present at the camp. Khaldan, it seems, was standing in the way of al-Qaeda's expansion plans. A growing anti-American current had emerged, including Abu Zubaydah's group as well as Ramzi Yousef (the first World Trade Center bomber, who visited before he was arrested) and others.

Khaldan also posed a problem because the bulk of volunteers coming into Afghanistan were going there and not to al-Qaeda's camps. Khaldan was the location of choice for people wanting training for Chechnya, Algeria and elsewhere, and had an extensive recruitment network that stretched through Europe and Turkey. Via Abu Zubaydah and Ibn Shaykh al-Libi's networks, it also had a presence in South East Asia, in the Philippines in particular.

MH: Abu Abdullah lost a great amount of influence in the time between his leaving for Sudan and returning to Afghanistan. Because of al-Qaeda's limited activity, many people thought Abu Abdullah had retired from jihad work. Al-Qaeda had not been involved in Chechnya or Bosnia, while Khaldan was training and sending people to both these places. Al-Qaeda lost Algeria, and Khaldan became the training camp for the Algerians. So Khaldan had a history during this time that al-Qaeda did not.

When Abu Abdullah returned from Sudan, he found this small camp of Khaldan was more famous and stronger than his camps, which had been sitting idle doing very little training. At that time, al-Qaeda had no training projects of its own, and the little training that took place was by some Pakistanis who had their own trainers and really only used the land and ammunition.

LF: I don't imagine it helped things when Khaldan's Abu Abdullah al-Muhajir declared bin Laden's American jihad project illegitimate, while at the same time issuing his own guidance encouraging strikes against the West, which appears to be something Abu Zubaydah's group was actively working towards.

I always find it curious so much attention is paid to bin Laden's reported 'fatawa' and these being the first to target the West, or more specifically the United States, because Abu Abdullah al-Muhajir's Beliefs Battalion Institute at Khaldan already had a little department focused on attacking Western countries and taking their money. So bin Laden's focus on America and declarations were not necessarily unique, or first, although his use of international media was unique.

What I thought was significant was that Abu Abdullah al-Muhajir's issue with bin Laden's American jihad project was not with the choice of the target; it was with the programme, or in the case of al-Qaeda, its lack of a programme. This set up a rather interesting competitive dynamic between al-Qaeda and Khaldan, which Abu Zubaydah and others have since acknowledged.

MH: It was a matter of priority; the difference of priorities between the two groups.

LF: I think it was also an issue of competition for scarce resources, trainees and funding, at a time when neither group was particularly well financed. It seems this competition eroded relations between al-Qaeda and Khaldan, which were already troubled because Abu Abdullah al-Muhajir had denounced al-Qaeda's cooperation with the Taliban.

MH: Khaldan had a very strict Salafi *manhaj* at that time, especially in relation to the Taliban and the issue of fighting alongside it.

LF: There seems to have been a somewhat complicated situation in Afghanistan among the Arab-Afghans during this time, along with a fragile safety situation following the Taliban's near loss of Kabul. I imagine al-Qaeda's morale was low, particularly among those members who had not wanted to return to Afghanistan. It had few new recruits, lacked money and was being heavily criticised for fighting alongside the Taliban.

MH: Yes, here we should return to discuss the importance of the Kabul battle because you have missed a very important point that is more important than the one you raised about criticism of al-Qaeda and the Taliban. The Arabs who were there for that battle, especially the older al-Qaeda members, were very unhappy about the way it was conducted and the

Taliban's poor performance. They felt the situation in Afghanistan was not safe. They knew that if the Taliban fell, the Arabs would find themselves alone in Afghanistan. Because of that, they asked Abu Abdullah to find another place for al-Qaeda to move outside Afghanistan. Many people in al-Qaeda from this core who fought at Kabul wanted to leave Afghanistan.

LF: I didn't realise most of al-Qaeda wanted to leave Afghanistan at that time. I know quite a few people left al-Qaeda after the Kabul battle, so when al-Qaeda decided to do its African embassy bombings it had to draw from the remaining veterans of this battle. In particular, it had to draw from The Northern Group and the Saudi and Yemeni network around them because they were the only ones willing or able to be convinced to carry out a martyrdom operation.

Those who fought in the mid-1997 Kabul battle, among them the newly joined members of The Northern Group and their Yemeni and Saudi social network, were the main people involved in the African embassy, the *Cole* bombing and the first people selected for 9/11. If this network of people had not joined up with al-Qaeda, it could not have carried out its first two operations. Two of the three suicide attackers in the Africa embassy bombings came from this network, the *Cole* bombers came from this network, and so did the four operatives first chosen for the 9/11 attacks.

MH: There is something you should notice; those who fought in the Battle of Kabul, they were the core of al-Qaeda. They pressed very hard on Abu Abdullah to leave Afghanistan and eventually he said, 'Okay let us go.' But to what place? Chechnya? No. Bosnia? No. There was nowhere else but Somalia. He said, 'Let us go to Somalia. Send some people to see what the situation is like there.' But he also said, 'They can make a hit there if they find the Americans.'

LF: Was the order to make a hit, to carry out an attack if they could, meant to be a kind of morale boost, to change the fortunes of al-Qaeda?

MH: Yes, this was part of the reason. Al-Qaeda's leaders felt they were losing control over even the few dozen people in Afghanistan, and nobody would join al-Qaeda while it continued to do nothing and after the failure in Kabul. So they wanted to do something. But the thing is, if you go somewhere seeking refuge, you don't go and carry out an operation in that area.

Abu Abdullah sent a group of his men to Somalia, led by someone who had been there previously. It was this group, and from these very general instructions, that the African embassy attacks eventually came. Abu Abdullah gave this group the authority to behave separately and did not define anything 100 per cent; but the main idea was to hit Americans coming to the shores of Somalia or Kenya because it was known that from time to time the American marines would conduct exercises there. Al-Qaeda's leaders did not decide on the attacks. The group sent to Somalia decided by itself to bomb the embassies. It was not the decision of Abu Abdullah.

LF: But didn't bin Laden choose the people for a martyrdom operation?

MH: He personally picked them, but he did not tell them it was for the embassy attacks. The mission was hitting the American marines. It was an idea, just an idea. He said, 'If you find them, then attack.' One of my friends was among the group going there; he was talking about the American marines. He said, 'Every year they come and we may find them there.' It was not a sharply defined mission. I did not like this way of working. It was dangerous.

LF: If so many people wanted to leave Afghanistan for Africa, and an attack there would make al-Qaeda's position more dangerous, why was it done?

MH: I warned Abu Abdullah, 'Do not target the Americans in Africa or anywhere. Nobody is ready for the consequences.' I told him, 'Don't do it.' I knew it would cause severe problems in Afghanistan because the battle of 1997 in the north of Kabul showed that the Arabs and the Taliban were very weak and not even capable of facing Masud and Dostum and the farmers of that area. How to face America?

I warned Abu Abdullah, 'Don't do that. It is not the time. You can't do it.' I tried to explain to him that the situation would be very bad and an attack against America like that would be the first time anyone had struck them in this way without a guarantee from another force. After the end of the Second World War, nearly all the governments took sides; either the West or East. I said to him, 'Now you are going to face America and you have no support. The entire world is following America.'

I was sitting with Abu Abdullah; Shaykh Saeed al-Masri was there along with another man. I told Abu Abdullah, 'If those boys find something and carry out a strike against America, it will open the doors of hell on Afghanistan, and on you and al-Qaeda, and nobody is ready for that. The Afghans are not ready and you should not think you are ready either. If you fight against America, it is a very big project that needs the Ummah to rise up, or most of it. It is not something an organisation or even a group of organisations can carry out. It is a project that needs a long period of preparation work, and the fighting comes very late. It should not be a matter of an urgent project.' They did not like this kind of talking.

LF: What did they say?

MH: I was angry and I talked badly with Abu Abdullah; I raised my voice. I was angry and left the village in Kandahar to go and live in Khost. After that, I heard things from here and there but al-Qaeda's leaders did not come and talk to me the way they had before.

LF: When you cautioned them against attacking, what was their response? Did they say anything?

MH: No, Abu Abdullah did not accept it; he did not show any agreement. Later, he tried to give me something to do, just to make sure I kept quiet. I refused and kept to myself in Khost.

LF: He tried to give you a project to keep you quiet?

MH: Yes, to give me something to do; it was some lecturing work with al-Qaeda or with the Arabs. I refused. I know these tactics. I stayed away, and kept to myself in Khost. So my long argument with Abu Abdullah that it is not a battle of weapons, but it is a battle of mobilising people did not change his mind. He was interested in that point, but the result was not what I had meant, because Abu Abdullah then thought to use attacks as a way of mobilising people.

LF: Speaking of mobilising people, as I understand it, The World Islamic Front that al-Qaeda established was essentially formed for this purpose. To mobilise people and also, I thought, to create an authority structure for any future attacks. Forming the Front allowed al-Qaeda to claim an authority greater than its own for any attacks it might carry out. Yet, Afghan and Pakistani scholars authored the fatwa that was released. Al-Qaeda did not issue its own, despite opening its religious institute in October 1997, which was run by Abu Hafs al-Mauritani.

MH: The institute was academic. It taught mostly Shariat and Arabic for the Afghans. Abu Hafs al-Mauritani taught Arabic to many influential Taliban, which greatly benefited al-Qaeda. The Taliban he taught were near to Mullah Omar and became near to al-Qaeda, which was very useful for al-Qaeda at certain times.

LF: I found it striking there was no public fatwa issued by any member of al-Qaeda's institute in support of the Front, or in support of al-

Qaeda's attacks. I thought that might have been because Abu Hafs al-Mauritani did not have legitimacy in the international Salafist environment, and at that time, as far as I know, he was the most prominent scholar in al-Qaeda's ranks.

MH: Abu Hafs al-Mauritani was not a Salafi and this weakened his position among the Arabs because most of them were Salafis. Abu Hafs was *Maliki*, like the people of North Africa who mostly follow this *madhab*. I think this is why al-Qaeda did not issue a fatwa. I do not agree with this procedure of issuing a fatwa according to the need of the leader or the group. I do not give it much value.

LF: It really does seem that al-Qaeda needed the World Islamic Front as an authority structure for its jihad project. Did the other groups participating know al-Qaeda was planning attacks in the near future?

MH: The Front was nothing; it was just for propaganda. It did not have any practical effect. I had a big argument with Abu Hafs al-Masri and Abu Abdullah about the Front and for their press conference plans. Al-Qaeda held a press conference, brought many journalists to Jihadwal in Khost, and gave them interviews.

LF: You were angry about that press conference?

MH: Yes. A few weeks before the press conference, when the front for jihad against America was declared, I told them, 'It is nonsense.' Abu Hafs became angry with me because I told him, 'This is something for propaganda. It does not mean anything practical. It should not be done like this, it is very harmful.'

Then he started to talk with me about the press conference. I said, 'It is wrong because we are still suffering with the Taliban. Mullah Omar told Abu Abdullah, "don't speak". That means, "don't speak".' Then Abu Hafs and I and Abu Abdullah went to a place on the hill in front of the Jihadwal camp, where we could talk away from the others.

I told Abu Abdullah, 'Mullah Omar told you not to speak.' Abu Abdullah said, 'No. Mullah Omar said do whatever you want.' I said, 'Don't say that please. This is an insult to him. He is not a stupid man; he is very clever. Respect him as amir; don't think he is a weak person. Don't think that because he is polite with you it means he is helpless.' This was the truth, Mullah Omar was very polite, but he was also very tough and many people in jihad are like that. I said to Abu Abdullah, 'Don't misjudge the man.'

At that point, Abu Hafs left us to talk more severely to each other. I said to Abu Abdullah, 'We have been friends for a long time, but in spite of all of that, if I were Mullah Omar, I would put you in jail.' I asked Abu Abdullah, 'If you were in the place of Mullah Omar, would you accept someone behaving as you are?' Abu Abdullah said 'No, I would not.'

LF: Yet he still went ahead and held the press conference?

MH: Yes, and it made a big crisis. The Taliban became crazy asking, 'Why does this man not respect the Amir al-Muminin?' Mullah Omar was very angry and tried to keep everybody cool, but he was thinking all the Arabs were like al-Qaeda, as the outside world claimed. He thought all of us behaved like al-Qaeda. He thought this for quite some time, but after a while he came to realise we were not all like that.

LF: Was bin Laden aware Mullah Omar thought everyone was al-Qaeda or like al-Qaeda, and didn't correct it?

MH: Yes.

LF: Bin Laden met with Mullah Omar right before the attacks, as I understand it. At that time, al-Qaeda would have known the African embassy attacks were coming, I presume?

MH: They knew attacks were coming, but they did not know where or against what. I was there when they received that warning, and I became very angry and refused to go to the meeting they had asked me to attend with Mullah Omar for another mediation. I said, 'I will not go, because I know something will happen and I am not going to deceive this man.'

LF: How did you know something would happen?

MH: They told me they received a message from their people in Africa saying they were ready and something was going to come. Al-Qaeda did not know what the attack would be, they just knew something was going to happen. They did not know if it was one, two days, within this week or next, but they knew something was happening. Nobody knew what the target was.

Abu Abdullah did not choose the targets himself. Those boys were recruited to go to Africa but nobody knew what their target was. Abu Abdullah, Abu Hafs and Sayf al-Adl; nobody knew it was the embassies. They knew this from the radio, like Mullah Omar and me. Abu Abdullah did not choose the target, this is sure. The boys there did.

LF: Really? That is not what conventional wisdom holds.

MH: I don't care what anyone else says. I was there in Kandahar. As I told you, I had travelled to Kandahar for a meeting with Mullah Omar and then I refused to go to their meeting with Mullah Omar because they told me that a hit was coming. They told me that they had been told something would happen soon, but they did not know the target; they found out on the radio like the rest of us.

LF: At that point in time there were fifty people or less left in al-Qaeda, and, what, five to ten in Tanzim al-Jihad and Gamaah Islamiyyah each? Around ten of them were sent to Africa in support of an operation without knowing what it would involve, including an explosives expert. It strikes me as an extremely big risk to take with a significant portion of your experienced cadres, particularly since al-Qaeda's Kenya office was compromised in 1997.

MH: I do not know the answer to this. I am sure they told me nobody knew what the target was. They said 'we didn't know'; they said, 'we know now from the news broadcast'.

LF: But did they admit it was their boys who did it?

MH: Yes, of course, because their boys had been working for a long time; maybe six, seven months they were working for that.

LF: What was bin Laden's reaction?

MH: He was astonished and so were the others.

LF: I take it you, on the other hand, were angry?

MH: I was already very angry from when Abu Abdullah had told me a few days earlier that 'an operation is ready in Africa, it is very near'. This was because Mullah Omar was coming to meet with them. I was about to be crazy: 'What you are doing, what you are doing?' I seriously wondered how Mullah Omar would withstand all of this. I thought Abu Abdullah committed a mistake; he should not have allowed these events to take place.

LF: I always assumed the African embassy operation was in part because al-Qaeda was on the brink of failure and that it needed to do something to keep going. I still hold this view, but I must say I am surprised they were seeking sanctuary in Africa while at the same time carrying out attacks on the continent. It does not seem like a wise move to me.

MH: Well, they went and made an operation there, which meant they had to stay in Afghanistan for safety reasons, because Africa became hot. But how to stay in Afghanistan after you have gone and carried out an operation against America when Mullah Omar told you, 'Don't talk'? What about going and making operations against America?

Mullah Omar was begging Abu Abdullah, 'Please don't spoil our work in Afghanistan; we are not ready for this kind of battle against America.

We have our programmes; we need to do many things in Afghanistan.' Al-Qaeda did not keep quiet. Then they bombed the embassies and wanted to take refuge in Afghanistan, and in that meeting just days before the operation Abu Abdullah had behaved very badly with Mullah Omar.

LF: I presume this bad behaviour is when bin Laden told Mullah Omar he was seeking independent Shariah judgement about Mullah Omar telling him to stay silent? I read an absolutely scathing letter from Abu Musab al-Suri to bin Laden about this.[14]

Abu Musab was furious at what he thought was bin Laden's insulting and insubordinate behaviour to Mullah Omar, and at bin Laden more generally for activities he thought were making the situation of Arab-Afghans in the country vulnerable.[15] Like many others, Abu Musab was angry at bin Laden for holding the press conference in Khost, which jeopardised the training activities of other camps in the area.[16] He was also mad at bin Laden for making what he saw as empty threats against America.[17] Abu Musab thought empty threats harmed the cause of jihad, and also caused tensions between the Arabs and non-Arab groups in Afghanistan, which I presume were the Uzbek and Uyghur groups.

Abu Musab also threatened to tell the Taliban about the divisions among the Arabs and explain that al-Qaeda did not represent the Arabs. Abu Musab wrote, 'Do you want the Arabs here to have no other alternative than to tell the Taliban ... that Abu Abdullah only represents himself and his group of guards but not the Arabs and that we don't agree with his attitude and his position. This involves the obvious harm of hanging our dirty laundry for others to see or should the men remain silent and suffer the consequences with you.'[18]

After receiving this letter in the period between the press conference and the African embassy bombings, bin Laden does seem to have restrained his activities and kept a little quieter. Do you think he took a lesson from all this criticism?

MH: No, Abu Abdullah did not change; he was still walking his own path even though in that period there was a lot of criticism of al-Qaeda. The group sent to Africa had not shown anything, and nobody knew what was going on. Nobody knew the position of that group, what they were thinking or if they could do anything, and criticisms like al-Suri's and others' were continually coming. Then, of course, there was the very bad meeting between Abu Abdullah and Mullah Omar as I wrote in my book *Cross in the Sky over Kandahar*, followed by the embassy attacks, which caused an even bigger crisis.

LF: What was Mullah Omar and the Taliban's immediate reaction to al-Qaeda's attacks when they came?

MH: The Taliban did not believe al-Qaeda did it, especially since there had been a meeting with Mullah Omar just before the operations.

LF: Al-Qaeda was heavily criticised after the attacks, even within its own circles, for killing and injuring all those civilians, including many Muslims. How was that viewed inside al-Qaeda?

MH: Al-Qaeda used the same fatwa used by Gamaah Islamiyyah: if the enemy puts civilians on the front of his lines, you can kill the civilians to reach the enemy, which is wrong in fact. For them, it was something to say to make an argument.

LF: Ayman al-Zawahiri was apparently writing to a number of leading religious figures trying to get them to release a fatwa to support the killing of women and children in battle, so I was wondering whether there was more internal debate and criticism going on about those attacks and the killing of so many civilians?

MH: I do not think so. Tanzim al-Jihad and Gamaah Islamiyyah used the same fatwa in Egypt because their operations killed many Egyptians, and they were criticised by different wings of Islamic factions. So I doubt they objected to what al-Qaeda did because they had done the same thing before.

LF: Where did the criticism of al-Qaeda come from?

MH: Most of it came from some groups of Salafis in London, as well as some Saudis inside Saudi Arabia, including many Saudi ulama.

LF: What was your criticism?

MH: Al-Qaeda was behaving in Afghanistan as if they had an individual state inside Afghanistan: a state inside the state. That damaged everything in Afghanistan and eventually brought the Americans there. I told them many times, 'You are not a state; you are in a foreign state and you didn't obtain permission to do those things. You are not free to do anything without permission from the people who are running the state.' This was al-Qaeda's original mistake, which damaged everything, even the organisation itself.

LF: It seems to me this is the mistake every *tanzim* makes; if a group does not hold territory they do not really have the authority to act on, or to be claiming to act on, anyone's behalf. Because of this, they do not have the justification to be behaving as an army defending the people, or a leader of the people, as they often claim.

MH: Yes. I wrote about that. We should also note the difference between the Taliban and al-Qaeda on this point. Al-Qaeda has no land; they are foreign in every place; they continually changed their strategic focus, and eventually they damaged everything. They had no right to behave like that in Afghanistan or any other place. Nobody will allow them to do that in their land. This is a major mistake committed by al-Qaeda.

Now people have discovered how to use the power of a population against the regimes, and this is a good discovery for the Arab countries. But it needs some conditions to be successful, and it is not fully clear yet whether they exist.

LF: The Americans reacted to the attacks on their embassies with cruise missile strikes against al-Qaeda's camps in Afghanistan.

MH: It was something very strange because after the attacks against the Embassies everybody knew a reaction might come and it would be against the camps. Many people were saying this and arguing the camps should be evacuated. Instead, al-Qaeda made a very big programme of training the youth who had arrived and sent them to Khost. It was crazy to do that.

LF: Training had only just started when America launched its retaliatory strikes, and this was al-Qaeda's first formal training programme since its return to Afghanistan. As I understand it, there were seventy or so people in al-Qaeda's training programme when the missiles hit?

MH: Yes, there were around that number, but we should note it was not the first training to take place since al-Qaeda's return, but it was the first big training programme. The strange thing was that all the leaders of al-Qaeda were happy this training programme was starting. They did not protest it starting at this time, despite the dangers of retaliation. They felt they had won a battle against America.

LF: Bin Laden had reportedly thought the attacks would bring thousands of people to Afghanistan to join him, but this did not happen. You wrote that al-Qaeda received hundreds of messages of support but only a few dozen people arrived.[19] I presume they were among the trainees.

MH: That small number was because of the difficulties in the route. It was hard to enter Afghanistan at that time.

LF: I am sure that had some bearing on the number being small, but it seems there were also a few other reasons. Al-Qaeda's target audience was experienced mujahidin. Bin Laden wanted the attacks to attract people who had already fought in jihad, particularly those who had left al-Qaeda for combat elsewhere. For those people, jihad on the fronts was a way of life, and al-Qaeda still did not have a legitimate front of its own so there was little to attract them.

MH: This is true, even the new generation of mujahidin wanted an open and easily accessible front, and we should notice here that public opinion in the Islamic world was unsatisfied with Afghan internal fighting.

LF: Despite bin Laden's hopes, few people returned. Afghanistan was not popular as a site of jihad, nor was it widely viewed as a legitimate conflict. Al-Qaeda could not compete with the allure of Chechnya or other places where fighting was taking place without the issue of fighting other Muslims.

What is interesting is that a few people who already had exposure to al-Qaeda were reportedly drawn back because of its use of martyrdom attacks in the embassy operations. Abu Jihad al-Makki, a former Northern Group member, was a suicide attacker against one of the embassies, and his participation seems to have drawn a few other people from The Northern Group network, and their network of Saudis and Yemenis, back to al-Qaeda. Many of them had left Afghanistan after the Kabul battle. Curiously, the same thing did not happen in Gamaah Islamiyyah, which also provided an operative for the embassy attacks.

MH: The man from Gamaah Islamiyyah was involved because of America's jailing of Omar Abdul Rahman.

LF: It is interesting he was included as an operative in the attack; it seems this was done only after efforts to recruit Saudis and Yemenis had failed. Al-Qaeda seems to have had difficulties recruiting for these first martyrdom operations. I thought it may have been because most of its core membership was older and had families. There was not that youth bulge within al-Qaeda. Older members of al-Qaeda were less willing to be involved in a martyrdom attack when al-Qaeda's safety in Afghanistan was in doubt and its precarious financial position meant there was no guarantee their families could be supported after their death.

MH: Al-Qaeda's numbers were still small, and in fact that was one reason Abu Abdullah was moving to live in the camp in Khost. He wanted to be in the camps. He thought more youth would join if he was there, because he felt al-Qaeda's numbers were not big enough.

The day of the American strikes, Abu Abdullah was supposed to be in Khost; not only for supervising the training, but his supporters had also planned a big meeting in Zhawar to celebrate the wedding of one of the youth. The meeting was delayed and Abu Abdullah changed his plans. I think this initial information shifted to the Americans somehow and because of that they hit Zhawar with cruise missiles. Zhawar had nothing to do with al-Qaeda's programme at all. Nobody was in Zhawar; it was just a weapons store for Haqqani.

LF: Did the missiles strike where bin Laden was meant to live in Khost?

MH: Yes, in the Saddiq camp he had built four rooms, three for his wives and one for meetings; every one of those was hit by a missile. In Jihadwal, a number of people were killed, including one of the Egyptians from Tanzim al-Jihad.

LF: I understand most of the casualties were at al-Faruq.

MH: Yes, missiles directly struck the tents. The man who was in charge at al-Faruq was from Gamaah Islamiyyah, and he was inexperienced and did not have enough background for doing this work. Abu Atta al-Tunisi was the official in charge of all of al-Qaeda's camps in Khost and the amir of Jihadwal, but he had left to Kabul to warn Abu Abdullah not to come to the area because he felt an American strike was coming soon.

On the day Abu Atta left the strike came, so he returned from Kabul at once. Communication had been jammed for five or six hours before; even the small walkie-talkies were jammed. I wrote in my book if Abu Atta had been there he would have understood from the jamming that a strike was coming, but the man from Gamaah Islamiyyah at al-Faruq was inexperienced and did not understand the danger. Many mistakes were made.

LF: I think a similar thing happened at Jihadwal. Apparently, the person left in charge at Jihadwal was a Yemeni, and it appears he too did not understand the danger. He was a part of The Northern Group and it was later claimed the American missile strikes on the camps drove him to volunteer for the USS *Cole* operation, in which he was one of the suicide attackers.[20] I do not know if this story is true.

MH: I do not know about this story, but I am sure there were many mistakes made that led to a heavy loss of life among the trainees.

LF: The American retaliatory strikes seem to have had quite an impact on changing the direction of criticism initially targeted at al-Qaeda. For example; the Libyan Islamic Fighting Group reportedly criticised al-Qaeda for the African embassy attacks, but when American missiles struck in Afghanistan and Sudan, it criticised America.[21] So to me, one impact from the American missile strikes was that they stopped criticism of al-Qaeda from among its counterparts, and instead contributed to criticism being redirected towards America.

MH: Yes, it is true. I also think if America did not attack after 9/11, more criticism would have come from the Islamic world and the Islamic factions. Of course, America gave a strong military reaction and everybody then gave Abu Abdullah support.

Before the American retaliation after the embassy strikes, al-Qaeda's relationship with Mullah Omar was very poor. This was because of the meeting between Abu Abdullah and Mullah Omar the day before al-Qaeda's embassy strikes. But after American missiles struck Khost and hit the camps, the local people of the area became heavily in favour of the Arabs in the camps. They felt insulted that their guests were bombed on their land, so they showed sympathy with the Arabs, with Abu Abdullah.

This caused a problem for the Taliban. Mullah Omar was in a difficult situation after the Taliban discovered many people in Khost had become in favour of Abu Abdullah, because he had not made public the bad state of relations with Abu Abdullah and al-Qaeda. So even though the Taliban's relations remained poor with al-Qaeda there was little he could do—it was a very difficult situation for him.

LF: Was this part of the reason why Mullah Omar refused to hand bin Laden over to the Saudis? Turki al-Faisal has said that in June 1998 negotiations with Mullah Omar to hand bin Laden over to Saudi Arabia were progressing smoothly, but Mullah Omar reneged in September of that year.[22]

MH: No, this is not true. Those negotiations failed on the first day. It was a very hot discussion between Mullah Omar and Turki al-Faisal. I heard about it from someone who was inside the room.

LF: Why wouldn't Mullah Omar hand bin Laden over to the Saudis if he was unhappy with him and with al-Qaeda being in Afghanistan?

MH: Mullah Omar could not do this according to Islamic or tribal law. It would have been a historical shame for him; he said that clearly.

LF: Al-Qaeda seems to have received some unexpected benefits from the American retaliatory strikes against it, which in my view had a critical impact on bin Laden's thinking. Al-Qaeda benefited from the American military reaction in two key ways: its relationship with the Taliban was cemented despite tensions between the two groups, and the people who were criticising al-Qaeda instead turned to criticise the Americans.

The result was that bin Laden's thinking changed from attacking America with a view to directly expelling it from Saudi Arabia, to attacking America with a view to drawing it into Afghanistan—where it would be defeated like the Soviets. This change was because bin Laden realised that power came not from what he did, but from whether what he did caused an armed retaliation. The power of causing a retaliation in Afghanistan was that it stopped criticism of al-Qaeda and it caused other groups to rally behind it, or at least express support. This gave unity or, at the very least, the appearance of unity, and thus made al-Qaeda appear more powerful.

MH: Abu Abdullah benefited more from the American reaction to the operation than from the operation itself. The operation created some problems, and if America had not reacted, I think Mullah Omar would have acted more strongly against Abu Abdullah. Since America reacted, he could not, he could not stand with America strongly in one line against Abu Abdullah; so he could not do anything.

Most of the Taliban were proud that Abu Abdullah was now facing America as an equal. In Pakistan, many people were happy with Abu Abdullah because at last they found someone instead of Saddam Hussein who would stand against America. They were eager to find somebody to stand in the name of Islam against America.

The thing was, Abu Abdullah had no strategy in his work; to decide to take this and leave that. He took whatever was ready to be done and he went and did it, if he had the capacity. He was expecting a very short-term battle with America.

LF: Testimony from some of the people involved in the African embassy bombings reveals there were disagreements among the group about moving forward with the attacks.[23] People allegedly disagreed with attacking America at that time because of ill preparedness, but because bin Laden had requested they conduct an attack, the plans went ahead. What was the sentiment within al-Qaeda after the attacks, and the American missile strikes?

MH: Nobody agreed. But Abu Abdullah was the leader and they had to obey him, although they did not agree on these things. After the American strikes against the training camps in Khost, Abu Abdullah became first among all the groups, and many people from the Arab countries started to talk about him and support him.

Al-Qaeda's members were happy because the embassy attacks caused it to become a famous *tanzim*. People came to Afghanistan to see them and talk to them, and they wanted to join al-Qaeda and train with al-Qaeda. Al-Qaeda felt proud of that but they were affected too much by their own propaganda. They started to believe they were big heroes and equal to America, and that America was afraid of them. They started to believe this and they felt they were very strong; stronger than Ikhwan Muslimin, stronger than any *tanzim* in the world. They started to believe al-Qaeda was the only horse in the race and that all the other horses had either died or were weak and retired. Because of this, they believed that all the others should follow al-Qaeda.

So you see, there were two different viewpoints inside al-Qaeda at the same time. Everyone was proud and happy, but they did not agree with the way Abu Abdullah was taking al-Qaeda towards something horrible and uncertain. The two things were present at the same time among them.

10

STRONG HORSE, WEAK HORSE

ARAB-AFGHAN POLITICS AND AL-QAEDA'S REALPOLITIK

Arab-Afghan activity peaked in the period from late 1998 through to the withdrawal of the Arab-Afghans and Taliban from Afghanistan in December 2001. Between 1998 and 2001, the number of foreign organisations operating in, or established on Afghan soil rose to around fourteen, varying in size from just a handful of people to several hundred. During this time al-Qaeda expanded to include its highest number of members since its post-Jaji peak in 1988.

However, the Arab-Afghan population was never as large as is commonly assumed. The total number of Arabs in Afghanistan at the time of the American invasion on 7 October 2001 was 1,195, along with 600–700 Uzbeks and Uyghurs.[1] This number included not only members of organisations, but also those who had emigrated to Afghanistan but not formally joined any group. These figures do not account for Pakistani trainees or mujahidin whose numbers were not well documented owing to their constant movements across the border.

The Taliban also expanded during this period, taking more territory and strengthening its grip on power. Relations between the Taliban and the Arab-Afghans were not always harmonious, and divisions between the Arab-Afghans spilled over into the Taliban, creating factionalism within the movement on the thorny subject of their foreign guests, particularly al-Qaeda. Yet contrary to popular opinion, al-Qaeda's attention and activities were not primarily focused on external operations but rather on recruiting new followers and other groups in Afghanistan that it wanted to join under its umbrella. These efforts were not only restricted to groups operating inside Afghanistan; al-Qaeda also sought to attract groups and followers from outside Afghanistan to join it—most notably the Arab-Afghan grouping in Chechnya led by Khattab.

* * *

Bin Laden's invitation to Khattab

LF: It is striking that even after al-Qaeda's embassy attacks, the Chechen conflict's popularity outshone al-Qaeda and it continued to attract more attention and recruits than al-Qaeda, prompting bin Laden to attempt to convince the leader of the foreign volunteers in Chechnya, Khattab, to join al-Qaeda's programme. Abdul Hadi al-Iraqi alluded to this competition in a letter he wrote to al-Qaeda's leadership in 1999. He told them that if the youth in Afghanistan were allowed to leave for Chechnya, nearly everyone would go.[2]

MH: The Saudi clerics heavily supported Khattab. They did this because they knew Abu Abdullah had been against the Saudi regime for years. They thought that if Abu Abdullah was attacking, he was also going to attack Saudi Arabia because it was the main American base. The Saudis put a lot of effort into shifting youths to Chechnya so they would not go to Abu Abdullah.

But you overlook an important point here. Abu Abdullah asked Khattab to join after the Russians had pushed Khattab out of Dagestan and Chechnya to the mountains of Georgia. When this happened, Khattab sent some people to Afghanistan to see about returning there. At that time, Abu Abdullah was still strong in Afghanistan; he told Khattab's people to tell him to return to Afghanistan and work under him. Khattab did not accept this offer and continued working in Georgia.

LF: I can see how the Russians invading Chechnya and pushing Khattab out to Georgia weakened his position compared to earlier, but how was bin Laden strong? Al-Qaeda had less than 100 members. Its al-Faruq camp did not open until the spring of 2000, and all it had at that time was a small camp in Mes Aynak in Kabul and its airport complex in Kandahar—neither of which were doing regular training because there was no real recruit inflow. How does that make al-Qaeda stronger than Khattab?

MH: Khattab was no longer strong. The Russians had forced him to retreat to the mountains of Georgia. Although it was small in number, al-Qaeda was working freely in Afghanistan. Abu Abdullah had become famous after the embassy attacks; he was challenging America in places no one expected, and people thought he was the man who had come to solve the problems of the Muslims. If you compare it to Khattab, Khattab was broken at that time.

LF: Khattab may have retreated but he had to order volunteers who continued to try to travel to him to be diverted. Some of them were sent to Khaldan in Afghanistan, where they were to be trained, and, when conditions improved, sent to Khattab. Al-Qaeda had no real recruitment networks of its own and was still a small organisation struggling to get people to join. Most of the youth still wanted to go to Khattab.

MH: You forget about the international media. CNN and the others; they were all talking about Abu Abdullah. You know I met some people Khattab sent. One of them gave me a unique confession. He said, 'The same problems you face here with Abu Abdullah, we face with Khattab. They are very similar and they are making the same mistakes.'

By that, he meant Khattab and Abu Abdullah were leaders who held all the authority, all the money and all the decisions. They did not care if no one else agreed with them; they went and did what they wanted.

LF: I guess then Khattab and bin Laden were not likely to have worked well together.

MH: It would not have worked. Anyway, Khattab refused.

* * *

The Arab contingent in Chechnya was not the only group bin Laden wanted to attract to Afghanistan and to al-Qaeda. From late 1998 onwards, he also increased his outreach to Pakistanis.

* * *

Bin Laden's outreach to the Pakistanis

LF: Bin Laden's media work from late 1998 onwards seemed in part directed at the Pakistanis. He began making comparisons between Afghanistan and Kashmir and portrayed them both as Islamic lands under threat.[3]

MH: Abu Abdullah was also trying to convince the Pakistani authorities that he was an ally for them against India, and to leave him routes in Pakistan for his people. There was a lot of Pakistani interruption against the Arabs trying to enter Afghanistan.

LF: Bin Laden also called for Pakistanis to come and defend Afghanistan. This was in spite of Mullah Omar's warnings to him about the dangers of dealing with Pakistani groups.

MH: Mullah Omar had warned Abu Abdullah about this since first meeting him in late 1996. Back then he told Abu Abdullah, 'Don't trust the Pakistani way of working; they are raising slogans; they may seem numerous and their voice may be loud, and they are going on the streets, but they are nothing.' He warned him several more times about this issue.

* * *

Bin Laden called for Pakistani assistance to defend Afghanistan when he had still not given an oath of allegiance to Mullah Omar as Amir al-Muminin. At that time, providing an oath to Mullah Omar was not widely supported among the Arabs.

* * *

The politics among the Arab-Afghan groups about giving oaths to Mullah Omar

LF: You were the first foreigner to give Mullah Omar an oath of allegiance.

MH: I gave Mullah Omar an oath of allegiance on 2 November 1998. I was the only one to give him an oath; nobody else from among the Arabs was in favour of doing that. Even the Uzbeks—who were very close with Mullah Omar—had not yet given him an oath.

LF: Why did you decide to give Mullah Omar an oath if it was so unpopular?

MH: I thought if I gave an oath, others might come and give Mullah Omar an oath. If they did this, it would put an end to all the groups and divisions between the Arab and non-Arab groups inside Afghanistan.

You know I was in favour of dissolving al-Qaeda. Actually, I was in favour of dissolving all the Arab groups inside Afghanistan at that time. There was no need for them. They formed to work in the Arab countries and their causes had been lost; they were finished. What was the meaning of keeping a group with the name of Gamaah Islamiyyah or al-Jihad, when they have no base in their own countries and they were making too much of a disturbance in Afghanistan? I thought they should go and give an oath to Mullah Omar and just be Afghan; be in the society and help Afghanistan and help the Emirate. That was my idea.

LF: Some group leaders did give an oath, but they did not dissolve their organisation. The Uzbeks and the Uyghurs reportedly gave Mullah Omar an oath, and so did Abu Musab al-Suri—although he did not have a group, as I understand it.

MH: Yes, the Uzbeks followed maybe less than a month or so after I gave my oath. Tahir Yuldashev went and spoke to his Leadership Council and he said, 'We should do it, because it is the right thing to do. What is the meaning of sitting here, and not giving him an oath? He is the Amir al-Muminin.' I am not sure about the Uyghurs; I think they followed what Tahir did. As for Abu Musab al-Suri, his oath came later, in 2000.

LF: Bin Laden never directly gave an oath of allegiance to Mullah Omar—instead he gave a proxy oath through you sometime in 1999, as I understand it.

MH: Abu Abdullah did not want to put his work under the programme of Mullah Omar. Abu Abdullah wanted to put his programme first, even if Afghanistan was damaged. Giving a direct oath would have disrupted what Abu Abdullah was planning, so to keep space for manoeuvring he did not give a direct oath.

LF: Did you know this when you agreed to give his oath?

MH: I thought even an oath through me might mean he would join the programme of Mullah Omar and stop pursuing his own programme, which could cause harm to Afghanistan. I thought if he gave an oath, all the groups might follow.

LF: It seems bin Laden was hedging his bets. He did not want to be constrained by directly giving an oath, but needed to give some gesture because other leaders like Tahir Yuldashev—whose group was then bigger than al-Qaeda—had given Mullah Omar an oath.

MH: Abu Abdullah maybe saw Tahir as a threat, because he was nearest to Mullah Omar. Abu Abdullah pressured Tahir to join al-Qaeda but he refused and suffered many attempts from the Arabs, including some from al-Qaeda, to split his group.

LF: Bin Laden was trying to get the Uzbeks to join al-Qaeda at a time when many people think the Uzbek group had not yet formed. It is often assumed the group formed in 1999 because this is when it declared jihad against the Uzbek regime. In reality, it formed several years earlier. The declaration released by the group said it had completed preparation and was ready to establish the jihad.[4] Is that why it waited so long to announce it existed?

MH: Actually, their preparation was not complete, but they released the declaration because they had to; because Khattab had ruined things for them.

LF: How did Khattab ruin things? Wasn't he still in the Caucasus after refusing to come to Afghanistan to join bin Laden?

MH: It is a big story. We have already talked about how Abu Abdullah and Khattab were similar leaders and destroyed the areas in which they operated. When the Russians pushed Khattab out from Dagestan, and from Chechnya, he thought to make a big offensive in the centre of Asia and sent a few groups to carry out operations in Uzbekistan and Tajikistan.

In Uzbekistan, Khattab's people carried out attacks outside some official buildings and the government launched a campaign against Islamists all over the country. They captured some of Tahir's people. The rest of the group in Uzbekistan said to Tahir, 'We are going to fight because after this we will be captured, sooner or later.' They told him, 'We have weapons, we have people, we have no other alternatives; if you do not announce jihad from your place we are going to announce it from here. You will be out of the game, and we will take our chances here.' So Tahir consulted with his Leadership Council and they decided to declare jihad at that time.

LF: This has echoes of bin Laden's declaration of war—declaring jihad to influence an emerging situation outside the control of the group. Even after its declaration of jihad against the regime in Uzbekistan, it seems the bulk of the Uzbek group's work was in Afghanistan, most of which seems to have been focused on assisting the Taliban. The Pakistanis had more people in Afghanistan, but from all accounts it seems getting the groups organised into a fighting force was a bit like herding cats. As a result, the Taliban preferred working with the Uzbeks, particularly in the north.

MH: Working with the Pakistanis was difficult, as al-Qaeda discovered during the 1997 Battle of Kabul. There is also something else; the Pakistanis could not work well in the north because they were not liked. They were afraid of the north because they knew Masud's group hated them. The atmosphere of the people was against them and it was also against the Arabs. Both of them had greater difficulties working in the north than the Uzbeks.

The Uzbeks could operate better because there were many Afghan Uzbeks in the area and they had the advantage of speaking the language. Mullah Omar wanted Tahir's group near to him because they were his tool to infiltrate the Uzbeks of the north, many of whom followed Dostum. Mullah Omar wanted to convince the Uzbeks of the north to leave Dostum and join him because people were saying the Afghan Taliban was a Pashtun movement.

LF: After Tahir's Uzbek group helped the Taliban in the north they gave him a base.

MH: Yes, but this was not until 2000. The Taliban gave the Uzbeks a large area in Logar, where they built a village. Logar's governor was an Afghan Uzbek who was sympathetic and helped them. The Uzbeks helped the Emirate too by being organised and good in their work, so the Afghans liked them. If you compare the Uzbeks with the Arabs or the Pakistanis, there was a big difference. Because of that, the Arabs were very jealous of them.

LF: How much of bin Laden's decision to give an oath to Mullah Omar was because of such jealousy, or was it more to do with counter-balancing this emerging non-Arab bloc of the Uzbeks, and also, I believe, the Pakistanis and Uyghurs?

MH: The centre of this bloc was Muhammad Tahir and his Uzbek group. The Uyghurs were very close to the Uzbeks, and fought on the front north of Kabul with Tahir, and not with al-Qaeda and the Arabs. This was a good thing because before they had been at Khaldan and were very severe like the Salafis there. The second group in this bloc was the Pakistanis who were very close to Mullah Omar.

LF: I thought Mullah Omar was wary of the Pakistanis?

MH: Mullah Omar was wary about Abu Abdullah dealing with the Pakistanis and certain groups among them. But Mullah Omar came to trust some Pakistanis very much. Because of this, they came to know many things about the Emirate; more than the Arabs and more even than the Uzbeks. The Pakistanis also developed close relations with the Uzbeks, and were closer to them than al-Qaeda. They worked with the Uzbeks at the front. With the Pakistanis and the Uyghurs, Tahir's Kabul front was at least double the size of the Arab front.

This bloc, as you call it, was closer to the Emirate because of the help it could provide, its size and because some leaders had given an oath to Mullah Omar.

LF: The leaders of the Arab groups were reluctant to give an oath, and some sought advice from ulama outside Afghanistan on the issue, among them I believe was Gamaah Islamiyyah. As far as I can tell, no decisions on the issue were reached, and it does not appear any of these groups gave an oath.

MH: Gamaah Islamiyyah did not give an oath, because they had a group and they gave oaths to the leader of their group. They were thinking of Egypt not Afghanistan.

LF: As I understand it, Tanzim al-Jihad also did not give an oath.

MH: I am not sure.

LF: The North African groups; the Libyans, Tunisians, Algerians and Moroccans, were also cautious about giving an oath to Mullah Omar.

MH: Yes, especially the Libyans, who as we spoke about earlier, stayed outside Afghanistan for quite a while, basing themselves instead in Peshawar.

LF: So basically, no Arab organisations appear to have given a direct oath to Mullah Omar. Bin Laden gave an oath by proxy, and Abu Musab al-Suri was not associated with a group when he gave his oath. I have always wondered if his decision to give Mullah Omar an oath stemmed from his problems with al-Qaeda.

* * *

The politics between Abu Musab al-Suri and al-Qaeda

Abu Musab al-Suri and al-Qaeda had a long but contentious relationship that stretched back to the late 1980s, when Abu Musab was briefly a member of al-Qaeda. The relationship became strained again in the late 1990s when Abu Musab returned to Afghanistan, and rather than join al-Qaeda, instead attempted to set up his own group. This, along with Abu Musab's statements against al-Qaeda's actions, meant that the organisation came to see him not only as competition but also as a threat.

* * *

LF: Abu Musab al-Suri and Abu Khabab al-Masri were reportedly threatened by al-Qaeda after they began planning a training project together. Abu Musab al-Suri had not yet established his group in Kabul, and Abu Khabab was working mostly from Derunta and Khaldan. He was independent and charged money to train people.

MH: Abu Khabab asked for money because he had no group to fund him or pay his living expenses. He and al-Qaeda had differences that went back a long time. Like Abu Musab al-Suri, Abu Khabab was for a short time also a member of al-Qaeda in its early days. They became close friends and this is why they said those things about al-Qaeda threatening them. It was not a threat against them personally but against their public behaviour; al-Qaeda thought they were going to destroy relations between the Arabs and Mullah Omar and the Islamic Emirate.

LF: Letters between Abu Khabab and Abu Musab al-Suri do show them talking about al-Qaeda members threatening them.[5] Abu Musab al-Suri had contacted Abu Hafs about it.

MH: Really?

LF: Yes, they complained to Abu Hafs about threats they received from some al-Qaeda members. He did not know about it and apologised. It seems the threats were about the camp project they wanted to start together, which Abu Musab al-Suri seemed to be leading with Abu Khabab providing training support.[6]

Abu Musab al-Suri often presented his projects as being an attempt to correct deficits in the jihadist work, which seems in part directed at al-Qaeda. I imagine at the time of this incident with al-Qaeda, Abu Musab was not shy in saying this publicly, which would not have helped build good relations between them.

MH: Abu Musab was presenting himself as a leader of the first class, and saying that Abu Abdullah was not and did not deserve to be a leader. Al-Qaeda was very angry with him and some of its members criticised him publicly. Sayf al-Adl was very tough with Abu Musab al-Suri.

LF: Sayf?

MH: Yes, Sayf and Abdul Hadi al-Iraqi. They talked very strongly against Abu Musab al-Suri, but Abu Abdullah and Abu Hafs al-Masri were more diplomatic. Abu Musab al-Suri was very ambitious—he could talk very well and he could analyse very well. In the field, he could not work like Sayf or Abdul Hadi because he did not work on the front lines as they did.

When Abu Musab al-Suri formed his own small brigade for work on the Kabul front, it was with the support of, and under the command of, Sayfullah Mansur, who was a Taliban leader. I think Abu Musab began this brigade project when his planned work with Abu Khabab did not amount to anything.

LF: Why were the Afghans supporting Abu Musab al-Suri on the front at Kabul?

MH: It was the game of those within the Taliban who thought Abu Abdullah had too much influence, and that Abu Musab could balance this.

LF: I do not imagine al-Qaeda was pleased.

MH: No. It was not good for unity. In fact, I advised Abu Musab al-Suri not to continue with his project in Kabul.

LF: I thought Abu Musab al-Suri had a camp in Kabul or Logar—called al-Ghoraba.

MH: No, this was the name of the brigade he formed on the front line in Kabul.

LF: But what about the filmed lectures of him teaching trainees?

MH: He was giving lectures in his house. I have been there—these are pictures of lectures inside his house. Most of the 'camps' in Kabul were houses like this. The 'camp' for Gamaah Islamiyyah in Kabul was not a camp; it was a big house. These houses ended up being called camps if small groups of people came frequently. If people slept there, it was called a guesthouse, a *madhafa*. Abu Musab may have had a guesthouse.

LF: If this was the case, why did al-Qaeda see Abu Musab al-Suri as such a threat? Obviously, he had leadership ambitions, but it does not seem he was very successful if he had no camp and was giving lectures in his house.

MH: He was not successful because al-Qaeda made efforts to prevent him from being successful, and also because of his own faults and ambitions. Although Abu Musab worked on the Kabul front, what he really wanted to do was to set up a big movement in *al-Sham*; in the area of Syria, Palestine, Jordan and Lebanon. He wanted to set it up and lead it. And can you imagine, he wanted it to be an al-Qaeda branch?! He needed the slogan of al-Qaeda and support and financing from Abu Abdullah to build himself up. But nobody from al-Qaeda trusted him because they knew he wanted to be a leader.

LF: Abu Musab wanted to do this, all the while saying he was a better leader than bin Laden? That is not exactly a good way to go about getting support.

MH: Al-Qaeda of course did not support this, but Abu Musab continued in his efforts to work towards establishing a presence in *al-Sham*.

This is why al-Qaeda helped Abu Musab al-Zarqawi when he arrived in Afghanistan, because it did not want him working with Abu Musab al-Suri in this area.

* * *

Al-Qaeda's support for Abu Musab al-Zarqawi as a counterweight to Abu Musab al-Suri

The commonly held story about al-Qaeda's support for Abu Musab al-Zarqawi is that Sayf al-Adl reached out to him following his arrival in Afghanistan in the latter half of 1999, and after successfully lobbying bin Laden for permission, offered to assist Abu Musab al-Zarqawi, who went on to set up a training camp in Herat.

* * *

LF: When Sayf al-Adl wrote about assisting Abu Musab al-Zarqawi he said he was motivated to do so because it was time to put differences aside and the opportunity to establish a presence so near to Palestine should not be ignored.[7]

MH: This is all true about the assistance. But the main reason al-Qaeda helped Abu Musab al-Zarqawi was to stop him and Abu Musab al-Suri working together. Sayf himself went to work to support Abu Musab al-Zarqawi because he was very much against Abu Musab al-Suri. The potential for establishing a presence near Palestine was of course attractive, but it was something shiny on top of this other story, which is that al-Qaeda ran after Abu Musab al-Zarqawi to prevent him from working with Abu Musab al-Suri.

LF: So I guess I am wrong in thinking bin Laden approved Sayf al-Adl helping Abu Musab al-Zarqawi primarily because he wanted control over al-Zarqawi's activities.

MH: From the beginning, Abu Musab al-Zarqawi was very independent. I saw him in Herat; I saw his group. He had a guesthouse and he built a small camp in some mountains near Herat. He was not under the control of al-Qaeda at all, but he had a good friendly relationship with them.

LF: That is very interesting, especially since in reality Abu Musab al-Zarqawi was closer to the Jalalabad School and Abu Musab al-Suri's thinking closer to al-Qaeda. I always wondered why al-Qaeda put so much effort into supporting Abu Musab al-Zarqawi given his orientation more towards the Jalalabad School, especially at a time when it had not even finished establishing its own camp—al-Faruq—in Garamwak, which did not open until the spring of 2000. In light of the Abu Musab al-Suri issue, it makes a lot more sense, especially Sayf al-Adl's plan for Abu Musab al-Zarqawi's camp to train volunteers from Jordan, Palestine, Syria, Lebanon, Iraq and Turkey.[8] Al-Qaeda was basically trying to undercut any potential recruit base for Abu Musab al-Suri, and I guess it thought it could exert sufficient control over Abu Musab al-Zarqawi.

MH: It is interesting, although I do not think it covered Iraq and Turkey. It is the same strategy Abu Musab al-Suri made in Afghanistan; he arrived and said to Abu Abdullah, 'You are not alone in Afghanistan, you are not the only option here. I am here.' Al-Qaeda went to *al-Sham* with Abu Musab al-Zarqawi and said to Abu Musab al-Suri, 'We are here; it is not only you.'

LF: While al-Qaeda successfully cut out Abu Musab al-Suri, the coming together of Abu Musab al-Zarqawi with other key figures like Abu Zubaydah and Luay Sakka and the networks they controlled saw them become competition for the organisation. Basically al-Qaeda might have cut out Abu Musab al-Suri, but it could not stop the Jalalabad current coming together to cooperate on external operations. At that time, Luay Sakka, a Syrian of Kurdish origin who was based in Turkey, had been working with Abu Zubaydah and his Mujahidin Services Centre at Khaldan and supporting Khattab. Sakka would receive and send trainees to Chechnya and to Afghanistan, and in addition to acting as a facilitator also provided his own limited training.

When Sakka arrived in Afghanistan from Turkey and joined up with Abu Musab al-Zarqawi in Herat, you have the coming together of Abu Zubaydah's Khaldan-based Mujahidin Services Centre, Luay Sakka's network and Abu Musab al-Zarqawi's network. Between them, there were some very extensive networks for travel routes, safe houses and document forgery as well as an experienced cadre of people working with explosives. As a result, they came to be competition for al-Qaeda, not just in facilitation activities, but also external operations. Abu Musab al-Zarqawi, Abu Zubaydah and Luay Sakka were involved in the foiled Millennium Plot in Jordan, while Abu Zubaydah was also involved in directing an Algerian to launch an attack against Los Angeles International Airport, among others.[9]

At that time al-Qaeda's external operations had faltered. Its attempts to strike an American warship in Yemen in early 2000 had failed and its 9/11 project had stalled. Although the Hamburg group, who provided three of the four pilots for 9/11, had been recruited and trained, the plot was not moving forward quickly because of a lack of suitable recruits who could work as hijackers. Al-Qaeda's al-Faruq camp had not started and few other suitable recruits had been identified.

Khaldan and Abu Zubaydah's Mujahidin Services Centre had the most instrumental role in the Jordan and Los Angeles attack plots, and were also involved in planning or supporting other attack plots in Europe. As such, this grouping was a significant competitor to al-Qaeda. For this reason, I imagine al-Qaeda was probably very relieved when Khaldan closed its operations in the spring of 2000, hampering Abu Zubaydah's work and pushing volunteers freshly arrived in Afghanistan to al-Qaeda's newly opened camp.

Khaldan closes operations in Jalalabad

LF: Khaldan had been ordered closed before and had earlier moved from Khost to Jalalabad. While Ibn Shaykh al-Libi, the camp's amir, had always managed to negotiate Khaldan remaining open, in early 2000 he was in Syria looking for a bride to get married.[10] In his absence, Abu Zubaydah reportedly went to see bin Laden to ask for help in keeping Khaldan open.[11] He reported that bin Laden said, 'No, it is better that it is closed and all the camps be under one *Amir*.'[12]

MH: Who said so?

LF: A few people wrote about this, but this was also what Abu Zubaydah reported.[13]

MH: I remember the Pakistani army shifted inside the border of Afghanistan and took the hills near Khaldan when it was based in Khost. The Pakistanis were on top of the mountains and watching the Khaldan camp. The people at the camp were afraid the Pakistanis might raid them because there were smuggling routes running very near to Khaldan. At that time, there were many cars coming from the Gulf through Iran, through Afghanistan into Pakistan to be sold at very high prices without taxes, and the Pakistanis tried to close this route. The Taliban could not protect Khaldan and asked them to leave the border area. After that, they shifted to Derunta at Jalalabad.

LF: Yes. It seems curious to me that Khaldan was the only camp shut and that Algerians, Tunisians, Moroccans and Uyghurs all remained in Jalalabad and were active in that area, or in Tora Bora. It seems only Khaldan was closed. Perhaps this was because the group was not popular with al-Qaeda or the Taliban; its members had previously made *takfir* on the Taliban and its plotting of attacks in Europe and America put it in competition with al-Qaeda.

MH: No, all the camps were ordered to move and most did move to Kabul. Maybe some kept their houses and their families in Jalalabad.

LF: Okay, the details on the North Africans are a little blurry, but what is striking is that bin Laden seemed to tolerate Abu Musab al-Zarqawi's group remaining outside his control. He did not apply to Abu Musab al-Zarqawi what he said to Abu Zubaydah about how there should be only one group and one amir.

Bin Laden's focus on Khaldan had some very good and unexpected benefits for al-Qaeda. When Khaldan shut down, new arrivals instead went to al-Faruq, including some people who would become the 9/11 hijackers. A dozen or so of them were seeking to go to Chechnya and had arrived in Turkey, where Luay Sakka housed them. Khattab could not accept the group, so Sakka contacted Abu Zubaydah, and it was agreed to send them to Khaldan for training until Khattab could accept them when conditions improved. Some of the group arrived at Khaldan before it closed and trained there. Others arrived later and instead went to al-Faruq for training. They were recruited to al-Qaeda there, and in turn recruited the friends they had travelled with, who had trained at Khaldan before it closed. The group of a dozen or so who left Turkey for training at Khaldan in fact became the 'muscle' hijackers for 9/11.[14] They were not seeking to join al-Qaeda; rather they had been looking to go to Khattab and ended up in Abu Zubaydah's Mujahidin Services Centre network—before Khaldan was closed.

MH: Then you can say that during the four years where al-Qaeda was in Sudan it lost most of its capacity, while the Khaldan people were developing their skills and network. When al-Qaeda came to use this network then, it means the essential element was not al-Qaeda, it was some other people who played important roles and then those other people, really they began to run things. 9/11, for example, this was the Jalalabad School, primarily.

LF: Yes, I agree it was the people outside al-Qaeda who played critical roles. It seems to me most of al-Qaeda's history is actually like this:

innovation, ideas and people came from outside the organisation to inside. Things often happened by chance rather than premeditation, as was the case with the arrival of those who became the 9/11 'muscle' hijackers. This outside–inside flow, and the role chance played, is often missed because of the dominance of an assumption that everybody was al-Qaeda from the beginning. So much of what happened for al-Qaeda came about because of specific events outside the organisation—some events it influenced, others it had no control over. This has been missed, because people see al-Qaeda as a powerful group that was everywhere at all times, but were it not for events outside the organisation and the role of chance, history might have been very different.

MH: Most of the abilities of al-Qaeda came from outside the organisation. Even some of my old friends in al-Qaeda told me so; one of them said, 'We do not raise things, everything comes from outside.' He had noticed the same deficiency.

* * *

Al-Qaeda did attempt to raise its own cadres, establishing the al-Faruq camp in Garamwak outside Kandahar, which provided a range of training to new arrivals. However, the camp was only in operation for around eighteen months.

Al-Qaeda's training efforts in Kandahar and Kabul

Al-Qaeda's al-Faruq camp was established in Garamwak in the spring of 2000—although al-Qaeda had secured the land from the Taliban some time earlier and had held some meetings with the press there before the camp was fully constructed. Al-Faruq camp had around ten to fifteen tents, each of which accommodated between five and six people. New arrivals were sent to al-Faruq to complete a range of training courses, with more advanced training also carried out in al-Qaeda's Abu Ubaydah al-Banshiri 'camp'. It was located inside al-Qaeda's complex at Tarnak Farms, and allowed training to be conducted in private and away from new recruits.

Many volunteers at al-Faruq returned home to their country of origin after finishing training or went on to join the fighting on the Kabul fronts. Around eighty to 100 of the estimated 700 to 1,500 volunteers al-Qaeda trained during this period joined the organisation, bringing its total sworn membership to around 200 by the time of its 9/11 attacks. While much of al-Qaeda's focus was on building its training capacity, it also began efforts to expand its presence on the fronts of Kabul.

Al-Qaeda had its own front in Kabul under the leadership of Abdul Hadi al-Iraqi, where it would eventually have a force of around 100 or so men, many of whom had completed training at al-Faruq and participated in fighting against the forces of the Northern Alliance. Al-Qaeda also had guesthouses operating in Kabul to accommodate these fighters and other staff members working in Kabul. The number of al-Qaeda staff in Kabul increased in late 2000 when bin Laden sent some senior figures there to ensure leadership continuity in the event of airstrikes following the USS *Cole* attack, which took place in October 2000.

* * *

MH: Al-Qaeda also took some staff and started to offer some courses for the Afghans, and they tried to expand themselves with the Taliban. Gamaah Islamiyyah did this as well, and so did the Libyans, and also Abu Musab al-Suri.

LF: Some of these groups also had their own fronts in Kabul, or a presence on them.

MH: Yes. Because of this, had the Arabs stayed a few years more in Afghanistan, we may have divided the Taliban into as many separate factions as we had.

LF: Yet, even now the picture many people have of the situation at the time is one of unity; that all of the foreign groups supported al-Qaeda, or were aligned with it, if not a part of the organisation. The reality, of course, was very different, but despite the existence of a good deal of evidence and information showing the fractured nature of relations between the foreign groups, this myth of unity still exists.

MH: That is right. Unity did not happen until later, until after the American invasion, when everyone was in danger and had to cooperate. Even then, it was never unity in the way people imagined.

LF: And it did not last.

MH: No, it did not.

11

ARAB-AFGHAN UNITY EFFORTS AND 9/11

LF: In 2000–2001, several initiatives to build unity among the various foreign organisations and immigrants in Afghanistan were introduced by al-Qaeda, and later by the Taliban. Al-Qaeda's focus was on building and leading a unified military group, although the other organisations in Afghanistan were not easily convinced to join such a group, or accept its leadership. Al-Qaeda's first 'book', which was released around this time, promoted the issue of unity. Written by Abu Hafs al-Mauritani, and with a foreword by bin Laden, it was called *Islamic Action between the Motives of Unity and Advocates of Conflict*.[1]

MH: The book was intended to help al-Qaeda with its efforts to unify everyone under one group. Abu Abdullah was eager to make unity among the Arab immigrant groups inside Afghanistan because there were many groups not united with al-Qaeda and he held some meetings at Mes Aynak about this.

* * *

The 'Arab Council for Unity' was convened by al-Qaeda on an invitation-only basis, and met at the Mes Aynak camp. It focused on organising Arab efforts in Afghanistan and creating a unified Arab military brigade from among the handful of Arab brigades operating on the Kabul front. It also focused on forming financial and welfare committees to assist Arab families of group members and immigrants.

* * *

MH: Abu Abdullah called for the main Arab groups to join this unity project. After that, he called people to join who had no group and who were in Afghanistan in an individual capacity.

LF: I presume the individuals invited included Abu Musab al-Suri, Abu Khabab al-Masri and Abu Abdul Rahman al-Kanadi? Were you there?

MH: No, I was not; I wanted to stay far away from the politics of the Arab groups in Afghanistan, but I was told in detail about it by several people who were there from the various groups. I am not sure about Abu Khabab al-Masri. I do know that Abu Musab al-Suri and Abu Abdul Rahman al-Kanadi were part of these efforts, but only for a short time as they both had problems with al-Qaeda.

Abu Musab al-Suri wanted to join in the first circle of the groups who had been invited, but he had no group of his own and did not belong to one—although he had his own small brigade. Abu Abdul Rahman was invited in the capacity of a moderator and to convene the meetings, but this did not last long as Abu Abdullah was unhappy with Abu Abdul Rahman holding this position.

LF: Were the Arab groups wary of this project? As I understand it, only the four main Arab groups were involved—al-Qaeda, Tanzim al-Jihad, Gamaah Islamiyyah and the Libyan Islamic Fighting Group.

MH: Some of them had to get permission from their leaders outside before becoming involved. Gamaah Islamiyyah asked their leaders outside if they could join and were told it was okay as long as it related to work inside Afghanistan. They were not allowed to be involved in anything outside Afghanistan. There was concern al-Qaeda would use the Council for propaganda purposes for its outside work.

LF: I suppose groups were cautious after the World Islamic Front episode?

MH: Yes, probably.

* * *

The first 'unity' meeting was between al-Qaeda and the two Egyptian groups Gamaah Islamiyyah and Tanzim al-Jihad, and was moderated by Abu Abdul Rahman al-Kanadi. It was marked by discord, particularly among the Egyptians who, between the two groups, had around twenty or so members. At this time, Ayman al-Zawahiri was not the amir of Tanzim al-Jihad; Abu Samha was performing those duties. A key item for discussion was the contentious issue of forming one Arab brigade to fight on the Afghan fronts.

* * *

MH: At the meeting there were problems between Ayman al-Zawahiri and Gamaah Islamiyyah on the issue of fighting on the front. Dr Ayman said to Gamaah Islamiyyah's members at that meeting, 'You are not fighting on this front—to join us as an equal you have to fight.' Abu Abdullah tried to moderate with a solution in the middle, as he was keen for the project to work.

LF: Was Gamaah Islamiyyah allowed by its leaders to fight on the front? I thought some had already been involved in fighting inside Afghanistan.

MH: Members of Gamaah Islamiyyah had fought in the 1998 Murad Bek battle and some members, like Asadullah, commanded a unit on the front line. This was unofficial and in an individual capacity, because the official stance of the group had been against fighting on the fronts. I do not know exactly when their leadership changed position, but around the time of this meeting, they gave members permission to fight on the Kabul fronts.

* * *

The first session ended with no agreement, so a second session was convened with the Libyan group also in attendance, represented by Abu Layth al-Libi and others. Ayman al-Zawahiri, Abu Jihad al-Masri and Abu Samha from Tanzim al-Jihad, and bin Laden and Sayf al-Adl from al-Qaeda were also present. There was disagreement in the meeting over the presence of Abu Abdul Rahman al-Kanadi, whom bin Laden subsequently dismissed when word of the gathering leaked into Kabul and reached Abu Musab al-Suri, who had not been invited and started to criticise the initiative.

* * *

MH: Everyone in Kabul came to know all the secrets of the first session. Gamaah Islamiyyah claimed it had not said anything and said either Tanzim al-Jihad or Abu Abdul Rahman al-Kanadi must have said something. Abu Abdullah decided to dismiss Abu Abdul Rahman al-Kanadi from moderating the sessions. At the next session, Tanzim al-Jihad brought along Abu Abdul Rahman al-Kanadi, against the wishes of Abu Abdullah, who became angry and left the room. Following a long debate Abu Abdul Rahman was dismissed. After that, Abu Jihad al-Masri became angry and left for Kandahar.

Abu Abdullah took over running the session after Abu Abdul Rahman was dismissed. He then asked all the groups there to tell him their conditions for unifying. Tanzim al-Jihad had around nine or ten conditions, most of which were why they did not want Gamaah Islamiyyah to share in the Unity Council. The Libyan group also discussed their conditions with Abu Abdullah. Gamaah Islamiyyah said its only condition was that its name not be mentioned in the Unity Council and not mentioned in the international media, which was also a condition of the Libyan Group. Gamaah Islamiyyah said that although their leaders had previously objected to fighting in the fronts of Kabul, they no longer objected. Dr Ayman was shocked by Gamaah Islamiyyah's agreement about fighting, as this had been his main objection against it being on the Unity Council.

Dr Ayman was also angry the groups wanted to hide their names. He said, 'You should put your name like we put our name, why do you not declare your name? Suppose Mullah Omar asked me who is on the Council; should I lie and say you are not there?' The Libyans started to debate with him and Abu Abdullah stayed silent.

Both the Libyans and Gamaah Islamiyyah thought al-Jihad and al-Qaeda wanted to make this Council for international propaganda. They said, 'If Mullah Omar asks we will explain why we do not want our names publicly mentioned on the Council.'

The purpose of the Council was meant to be to assist Afghanistan. The Libyans and Gamaah Islamiyyah supported activity that gave benefit to Afghanistan, like a united Arab front in Kabul, but they were worried al-Qaeda and Tanzim al-Jihad would use the Council for propaganda for their work. They thought it would be used in a way that people outside would think Abu Abdullah was the amir of all Arabs in Afghanistan, and that they all supported fighting America. There was no benefit for Afghanistan in this, and no benefit for the Arab groups who each had their own cause and did not like to follow Abu Abdullah's or Dr Ayman's path.

So, Abu Abdullah found that the Council was divided, with al-Qaeda and Tanzim al-Jihad on one side and Gamaah Islamiyyah and the Libyan group on the other. He made a decision to defer the meeting and hold another one later, which in reality meant he realised that the project could not be achieved in the way he hoped, and had effectively ended.

LF: It seems there was a good deal of scepticism about bin Laden and Ayman's agenda and also a wariness of cooperating too closely with al-Qaeda, although this was not necessarily the picture presented to outsiders.

MH: No. Outside, the picture looked more unified, but inside, as many have said, it was not united at all. People were cautious about Abu Abdullah because of his tendency to act by himself without consultation, and those who did share with al-Qaeda were treated in a way that made them feel lower. At least, this is what I was told. Because of this, it became clear there was no tendency for unity or even joint organising among the Arabs in Afghanistan at that time.

LF: What I find interesting is most people assume al-Qaeda was at that time focused on expanding its presence outside Afghanistan, when in reality its focus was inside Afghanistan; on centralising its work, expanding its membership and convincing other groups to join it.

MH: That is right. As far as I know, Abu Abdullah sent very few people out. I guess he wanted to put everybody under his hand in Kandahar. Any time he needed to send people out he could, but he was not thinking of making branches everywhere outside, where people would sit and wait for his orders.

LF: Yes, it seems as if internal expansion in Afghanistan was his immediate focus. Bin Laden had not given up on convincing other groups to join with al-Qaeda, despite these efforts yielding little success. In fact, as we have debated many times before, in my view al-Qaeda's 9/11 attacks were primarily intended to incite an American response that would force unity among the Arab-Afghan groups inside Afghanistan, over which al-Qaeda sought leadership. Although this was obviously not the only purpose of the attacks, it became more important as al-Qaeda's other efforts to foster unity and gain leadership failed.

MH: I think Abu Abdullah was expecting a big war in Afghanistan. He thought he needed to have many elements under his control for that kind of fighting inside Afghanistan. So he tried to convince all the leaders of the factions to join him in Afghanistan to make a good strong group.

LF: Al-Qaeda's efforts were not just restricted to the Arab Unity Council and releasing its book. It also hosted several conferences in

Kandahar, the most famous of which was the Solidarity Conference held in the summer of 2000, which focused on the release of Omar Abdul Rahman and other prisoners. While Abu Hafs al-Mauritani's book was rather obviously an effort at encouraging unity, the conference was less obvious, but it does seem to have been held with this purpose in mind.

MH: Al-Qaeda's raising of the slogan of freeing Omar Abdul Rahman came because of efforts by his sons and Gamaah Islamiyyah to get al-Qaeda to pay attention. Al-Qaeda wanted to show the others that it gave attention to everything and did not forget anything.

LF: You raise an important point about al-Qaeda giving attention to everything. Al-Qaeda's releases and statements seemed to change quite significantly around this time. In addition to calls for Pakistanis to come and defend Afghanistan, there was the Solidarity Conference about freeing Omar Abdul Rahman and other prisoners. Then, after the late 2000 Palestinian intifada, bin Laden began focusing more on Palestine and defending the Palestinians. All of this was on top of talk of attacking the Americans and expelling them from Saudi Arabia. When talking of these issues, al-Qaeda failed to announce any kind of strategy or programme that explained what was given priority, when, why and how.

MH: Everyone was confused about what al-Qaeda was doing, because Abu Abdullah kept changing aims and targets. He used strategic aims as tactics just for making propaganda for his organisation.

LF: Yes, I agree. Al-Qaeda seemed to want to be everything to everyone in order to attract new recruits, and to convince other groups to join under its leadership, which can be harmful to a group's strategic efforts. I remember you writing to Sayf al-Adl years earlier about the dangers of having a universal slogan, which is exactly what it had at this time.[2] The consequences can be clearly seen in al-Qaeda's struggles to appear legitimate, and attract groups and individuals to join the organisation.

MH: It was hard for anyone to attract people to Afghanistan. The conditions were still very difficult to enter the country. Confusion about al-Qaeda's programme did cause some problems, but you forget the impact of the USS *Cole* attack. After that attack, people did come to join Abu Abdullah, and he found more donations arriving to support his work.

* * *

Al-Qaeda's attacks against the USS *Cole* did increase its membership numbers, and donations to the organisation also grew, both of which meant al-Qaeda found itself in the most stable operating condition it had experienced since its post-Jaji heyday. After the *Cole* attack, al-Qaeda issued a number of media releases, some of which presented the attack as being in defence of the Palestinians.

* * *

LF: Bin Laden's late 2000 focus on the Palestinian intifada is particularly interesting. He justified the *Cole* attack as being in defence of Palestine, but according to Abu Musab al-Suri, when a Palestinian group came to bin Laden seeking assistance he would not help them unless they gave him an oath of allegiance and joined al-Qaeda. Abu Musab al-Suri said he helped this group after al-Qaeda refused. Bin Laden also reportedly obtained Mullah Omar's permission to conduct attacks against Israel.

MH: Instead of saying concentrate on the holy land of Saudi Arabia, Abu Abdullah started to concentrate on the Islamic places in Palestine and Saudi Arabia. He joined Palestine to his cause. I do not know about the Palestinian group Abu Musab al-Suri mentions, but I do know Abu Abdullah asked for permission to attack Israel during the intifada. He first asked for permission to work against America. Mullah Omar said, 'No, we cannot give you permission. Pakistan will react against us and we cannot withstand Pakistan's reaction against us because of our situation. But I can withstand the reaction if you attack Israel.'

During the intifada, the Taliban youth had become very attached to the Palestine cause. Mullah Omar made a wrong calculation because he thought Pakistan would not work against the Taliban if an attack was made by al-Qaeda against Israel. Anyway, this was the permission given to Abu Abdullah but he did not follow it; instead, he made the 9/11 operation. He was not going to change his plans.

* * *

By this time al-Qaeda's planning for the 9/11 operation was moving forward, although all was not happy within al-Qaeda. The youth from the Gulf had become particularly close to bin Laden and were ignoring the chain of command, angering Abu Hafs al-Masri and other senior leaders who were increasingly dissatisfied about the influence of the youth over bin Laden. Abu Hafs was also unhappy at the direction al-Qaeda was taking, which he felt was dangerous.

* * *

MH: Abu Hafs asked me for my advice about leaving. I told him, 'No, don't resign. From the beginning you came to control this man and now you want to leave him at the point when he is going to spoil everything; it is too late to leave now.'

LF: I would have told him to go. At a certain point, people can take you down with the ship and you need to jump off, or you go down with it.

MH: Everybody sunk with Abu Abdullah: Afghanistan, the Arabs, al-Qaeda—all because nobody could stop Abu Abdullah or change him.

LF: Abu Hafs al-Masri did not resign and it appears relations between him and bin Laden repaired—as around this time he married his daughter to bin Laden's son.

MH: Abu Abdullah wanted to keep Abu Hafs close to him and having their children married was a way to do this. If their children were in one family and Abu Abdullah had been killed, Abu Hafs would have the authority. It was also a very big support for Abu Hafs and gave him more authority.

LF: By late 2000, an increasing number of Arabs were arriving in Afghanistan. It is tempting to credit this to al-Qaeda's *Cole* attacks, but just as many if not more were arriving because of Hamoud al-Uqla's fatwa, which was among the first issued by Gulf ulama sanctioning the Taliban's legitimacy and fighting alongside its forces.

Al-Qaeda did, of course, benefit from the new arrivals—despite their arriving for other reasons. The Taliban did not have the capacity to train newly arrived foreign volunteers, and the Kabul front was still shared by many Arab-Afghan groups, with no unified place for training. Consequently, most new arrivals went to al-Qaeda's al-Faruq camp for training, where some were recruited to join the organisation. Al-Qaeda's membership increase at this time was around forty people, bringing its total number to 100 or so members. To me, this shows al-Qaeda's appeal, legitimacy and influence after the *Cole* attack has been over-estimated, and was certainly hyped in media coverage.

MH: The *Cole* attack was one reason more people came to Afghanistan. The fatwa was another, but alongside this there was also another reason: a few groups came from Kuwait and Saudi Arabia to start a war against the Shia in Afghanistan. In fact, it was the Arabs in Bamian who started to kill the Shia during the time of the Taliban. They killed them for what? There was no fighting in this area, they were just farmers; they had surrendered. But the Arabs were pressing hard to make it religious fighting against the Shia in Bamian and in the north in Mazar Sharif. The Taliban tried hard to avoid this, and they were pressing Abu Abdullah on this, but Abu Abdullah could not do anything because these new volunteers were not his youth. He did not share their view, but doing anything about it was beyond his control, because the youths went directly to these areas and committed crimes. Most of the Arabs in fact were not happy about this, and although many of them hated the Shia they would not fight them because the Taliban refused to fight them.

LF: So, there were some in al-Qaeda who did hate the Shia.

MH: Yes. But they did not fight the Shia as the other Arabs did because Abu Abdullah would not allow it. Some of them did talk about it. I remember one time, a Saudi commander in al-Qaeda came up to me when I was visiting one of its guesthouses one day, and he asked me what I thought about fighting the Shia. I was sarcastic in my answer to him. I said, 'This is a good idea, but first you should finish the Shia in the eastern province of Saudi Arabia, and when you finish them, please come back and let us complete the job here.' Another time, when the subject came up with some other Arabs, I said, 'Let us put a programme together; let us stop fighting between us and the Shia for fifty years, because we have been fighting each other for centuries. If we fight together and instead of against each other we will win all of our battles and then we can return to killing each other without notice.' It was because of my sarcastic talking like this that a rumour spread that I was Shia or that because I had not renounced the Shia that I was *kafir*.

LF: I had not realised this element of the Salafi jihadis was so strong at that time. The focus tends to be placed more on the later activities of Arab-Afghans such as Abu Musab al-Zarqawi in Iraq. The early manifestations of the anti-Shia stance during the Afghan jihad against the Soviets, and again during the time of the Taliban, have been mostly overlooked. The rise in anti-Shia sentiment during the time of the Taliban seems to have coincided with more Saudi and Gulf support for Afghanistan and for the Taliban—I am guessing as a way of trying to encourage more of this focus. But it does not seem to have been very successful. Although there was a noticeable increase in the volunteers from the Gulf arriving, and among them a good number were seeking to fight the Shia, we are not talking about large numbers, either of these volunteers or of the persons who were coming to join groups like al-Qaeda.

MH: There were many different groups increasing at that time and there was the rise you mentioned of youth from the Gulf coming to fight Shia. But the numbers were not that big. Al-Qaeda did not increase in size too much. I cannot say a firm number but I can say 100 is the centre of everything; it had around 100 members, maybe a few tens more or a few tens less. But we should also note al-Qaeda was working hard to build up its front in Kabul and there it eventually had another 100 or so people.

LF: The people on al-Qaeda's front in Kabul were not all members of the organisation.

MH: That is right. Not all of them were from al-Qaeda.

LF: It seems part of the reason al-Qaeda increasingly focused on its Kabul front was to keep people who completed training at al-Faruq but did not wish to become a member of al-Qaeda, engaged with the organisation. If they were fighting on its Kabul front and under the authority of its commander there, there was still a possibility they could be recruited by al-Qaeda later. Al-Qaeda's Kabul front also gave it somewhere to accommodate people who were members of the organisation and had registered for its martyrdom brigade. If they were left in Kandahar, there was a risk of them becoming bored and leaving to find action elsewhere.

MH: Boredom was a problem, and of course, al-Qaeda wanted to keep those it had trained near to them.

* * *

Al-Qaeda was not the only group focusing its attention on Kabul during this time. By late 2000, many training camps were established in Kabul, or had, at the Taliban's request, relocated from other areas, such as Jalalabad. This brought the number of camps in Kabul to around eight.

* * *

MH: Tanzim al-Jihad and the Libyan group had camps in Kabul, as did a Tunisian group. The Moroccans, Abu Khabab and Ibn Shaykh al-Libi all moved their camps from Jalalabad to Kabul and began operating there. Abu Omar's Kurdish group also had a training camp in Kabul and so too did Abu Hamza al-Qaiti's group, which received finance from the al-Wafa organisation.

LF: How about Gamaah Islamiyyah? We spoke earlier about its 'camp' in fact being a house? Were these eight camps actually camps, or were they houses?

MH: There were no real camps, but just big Afghan houses on the border of Kabul, or a small place in Rishikor, or Mes Aynak, or similar places. If you call a house a camp then I guess Gamaah Islamiyyah had a 'camp' too.

LF: In addition to the camps in Kabul, there were the fronts of al-Qaeda and Abu Musab al-Suri. Abu Musab al-Zarqawi had his camp in Herat, and al-Qaeda had its camps at Garamwak (al-Faruq) and in the Kandahar airport complex (Abu Ubaydah al-Banshiri). There was also the Uyghurs who had their camp at Tora Bora, and some Algerians and Tunisians in Jalalabad. It is not clear if they followed Khaldan and later moved to Kabul. Finally, there were the Uzbeks in Logar.

MH: Many of the camps shifted to Kabul.

LF: It really does seem to have been a somewhat disjointed environment, with so many different foreign groups operating, and I would imagine there was competition for resources and recruits. It was around this time al-Qaeda's relationship with the Islamic Movement of Uzbekistan became strained, partly because of its efforts to ferment a split in the group.

MH: With the exception of the Uzbeks, all of the groups were careless about Afghanistan.

The Uzbek–al-Qaeda relationship and Mullah Omar's appointment of Uzbek military leader, Juma Bai, as amir of the foreign brigade in Kabul

MH: Al-Qaeda was not the only group trying to undermine the Uzbeks. Some Salafis who came from Saudi Arabia also tried to bribe the main figures around the amir, Tahir Yuldashev, but he stopped all of these things.

LF: Al-Qaeda's relationship with the Uzbeks fractured after an incident in which al-Qaeda offered sanctuary to two Tatar/Russian trainees suspected by the Uzbeks of being spies. You wrote about this in your book telling how the trainees had escaped Uzbek custody and sought sanctuary at an al-Qaeda guesthouse in Kabul, telling the amir the Uzbeks were persecuting them because they were Salafis. The amir of the guesthouse allowed them to stay despite requests from the Uzbeks for them to be returned. When the request was refused, the Uzbeks came to get them by force.[3]

MH: Yes, there were big consequences from this event because it destabilised relations between the two groups very badly. Abu Abdullah called for Tahir to be put on trial.

LF: Didn't Tahir apologise to bin Laden?

MH: Yes, he was ready to do so, but Abu Abdullah would not accept this and wanted a Shariah Council be formed to address what had happened. Al-Qaeda's members expected he would be jailed.

LF: I imagine tensions intensified when Mullah Omar decided to make all the foreign groups unite their forces into one multinational brigade to be based on the Kabul front and appointed a senior figure from the Uzbeks, and not al-Qaeda, as the leader.

MH: This decision, which Mullah Omar made in secret by himself, shocked many people—even the Uzbeks.

LF: I don't imagine it shocked Abu Musab al-Suri. He had been strongly encouraging Mullah Omar to promote the Uzbek role and had even submitted a research report to him about this.

MH: I do not know about Abu Musab al-Suri's report in much detail, but the story of how this decision came to be made and how all the groups accepted it involves him, despite his not being at that meeting.

Abu Musab al-Suri and al-Qaeda were at this time in heavy competition. Abu Musab was trying to recruit people to his brigade on the Kabul front, which al-Qaeda did not like. To reduce his influence al-Qaeda put up flyers for its brigade in all of its guesthouses, and also banned Abu Musab al-Suri from entering them. Abu Musab had earlier gone into al-Qaeda's guesthouses and recruited some youth who were working on its front under Abdul Hadi al-Iraqi. Abu Musab al-Suri convinced them to join him instead. This made al-Qaeda crazy.

LF: He was recruit poaching! He did not mention that in his account of this period.

MH: Yes. Abu Musab al-Suri contacted the Taliban about being banned from al-Qaeda's guesthouses and some other issues. Soon al-Qaeda and the other Arabs came to know that Abu Musab al-Suri had sent a proposal to Mullah Omar to re-organise the Arabs in the front lines of Kabul into one group.

Abu Musab had a good relationship with some people in the Taliban and he started to give them news about the Arab situation. He had a special relationship with Mullah Jaleel and they co-operated helping the Arab families in Afghanistan and to find them housing. Other Arabs who did not like the way of Abu Abdullah also supported Abu Musab.

Competition between al-Qaeda and Abu Musab al-Suri and between al-Qaeda and the Uzbeks and those who supported them became an increasing problem, which forced Mullah Omar to intervene.

* * *

Mullah Omar's early 2001 edict was focused solely on the problem of unifying the various groups operating on the Kabul fronts and Arab-

Afghan military work more generally. It came after relations became strained following the Taliban prime minister's attempts to order all camps and guesthouses in Kabul closed, which caused a storm of protest from the various groups.

* * *

MH: The Taliban instructed al-Qaeda to contact all foreign groups, including Abu Musab al-Suri, and invite them to a meeting in Kandahar. I did not attend the meeting because I was not part of any groups, but many of my friends from the different groups attended.

LF: Was Abu Musab al-Suri invited by al-Qaeda?

MH: No, he was not. The Taliban had said 'invite Abu Musab,' so al-Qaeda invited Abu Musab al-Zarqawi—although he did not have a presence on the front in Kabul—and did not invite Abu Musab al-Suri.

LF: That seems like a tricky manoeuvre; I imagine Abu Musab al-Suri was not happy.

MH: He was very angry at being left out.

* * *

With the exception of the Algerians who had a car accident on the way to the meeting, all of the invited groups attended. They included the Uzbeks, the Tajiks, the Uyghurs, the Pakistanis, the Egyptian groups, Abu Musab al-Zarqawi, the Libyans and other groups based in Kabul and Jalalabad.

No one knew exactly what Mullah Omar wanted to discuss. Owing to the controversies in Kabul between al-Qaeda and the Uzbeks, and the Taliban prime minister's ordering of camps closed, most people thought an order relating to their activities in Afghanistan was coming, and that Mullah Omar would appoint a leader of the Arabs.

* * *

MH: It was widely expected that Mullah Omar wanted to organise the situation. The Uzbeks were late in arriving, but all the other groups present in the guesthouse before the meeting talked among themselves and agreed responsibility for leading the foreign fighters would be given to Abu Abdullah. At this time, al-Qaeda had around 80 to 120 people on its front, the Libyans had eleven and Abu Musab al-Suri had between ten and twenty. The other Arab groups had only a handful of people each on the fronts. The non-Arab groups together had at least double the combined number of Arabs.

Before the meeting, Mullah Omar's secretary gave the groups a paper to fill out. At this time, the Uzbeks had still not arrived. The other groups were surprised they were late and decided they could inform them later of the meeting's outcome. They had all concluded the matter would be settled with Abu Abdullah's appointment to oversee the foreign brigade in Kabul. At that time, the problem between the Uzbeks and al-Qaeda had still not been resolved after the incident in the Kabul guesthouse, and no one imagined the Uzbeks might be given a leadership role.

The paper Mullah Omar's secretary asked the groups to fill in was a form where they were to provide the requested information, which included details on each group's chosen representatives and the number of members it had fighting at the Kabul front. On this form, the groups were also asked to list on whose front they would like to fight.

LF: Although Abu Musab al-Suri was not at this meeting, it does seem the option to choose a front was included to resolve the issue between al-Suri and al-Qaeda about who should lead the front. This is the issue that seems to have originated in the proposal Abu Musab al-Suri sent to the Taliban.

MH: Later that afternoon the meeting was held with Mullah Omar. Among the leaders of all of the groups in attendance were Abu Hafs al-Masri and Ayman al-Zawahiri from al-Qaeda and Tanzim al-Jihad respectively, while Abu Muhammad represented the Uyghurs, and Juma Bai (who by this time had arrived) represented the Uzbeks.

LF: Why did bin Laden not attend this meeting? Was he using the tactic commonly practised during the jihad against the Soviets of sending a deputy to avoid being bound by any decisions made at the meeting? Or was it more that bin Laden, along with everyone else, assumed he would be appointed leader and so there was no need to attend?

MH: Everyone was sure al-Qaeda would be appointed the leader of all the volunteers. If Abu Abdullah was not there, he had a chance to manoeuvre if anything went wrong and another decision was made. Before Mullah Omar started the meeting, he asked for agreement from everyone there to obey his decision. In fact, he asked for the groups to obey his decision at least three times in that meeting, which reflected the sensitivity of the issue.

Mullah Omar told the groups they would all remain independent and have their own relations with the Emirate. He reminded them if they had any external work activities they should consult with the Emirate separately. He told them everyone needed to be in one fighting group for the fronts, under one leader who would be responsible for anything connected to military work inside Afghanistan, even for details such as how group members travelled in cars with their firearms. Then Mullah Omar said, 'The person who will be your amir and commander, who you will listen to and obey is Juma Bai.'

LF: I imagine that was greeted with shocked silence, since everyone thought it would be bin Laden.

MH: Yes, the others at the meeting were shocked, especially Juma Bai who said 'no, no, no', and went to contact his amir. Juma Bai said to his amir, Muhammad Tahir, 'I have been made amir of all on the fronts, even the Arabs; I cannot accept, what can I do?' Muhammad told him he should accept and obey Mullah Omar. In fact, it was a very wise choice by Mullah Omar because Juma Bai was the most suitable in the community for such a job.

LF: Mullah Omar managed to side-step the issue of having to choose between bin Laden and Abu Musab al-Suri by appointing Juma Bai. Given al-Qaeda's relations with the Uzbeks at that time, I don't imagine his decision was popular.

MH: The decision went close to causing serious problems because of the unresolved issue between the Uzbeks and al-Qaeda. There was an expectation by some in al-Qaeda that Tahir would be jailed after it insisted on a trial being held after the Kabul incident. Abu Hafs al-Masri and Dr Ayman were so angry at Mullah Omar's decision that when they left they took the car they had arrived in and went straight to Abu Abdullah, leaving the other people who had travelled to the meeting with them left stranded in the street.

LF: How did Abu Musab al-Suri accept the news?

MH: I do not know, but I can imagine he thought at least al-Qaeda had lost leadership and that was good for him.

LF: I understand from some other accounts of this meeting that bin Laden hosted a meal later at which Mullah Omar's order was discussed.[4]

MH: Yes, some people from other groups went to see Abu Abdullah to advise him to accept Mullah Omar's decision, which he did. Although Abu Abdullah accepted the decision, other members of al-Qaeda like Abu Hafs al-Masri and Sayf al-Adl were initially very angry and upset. Abdul Hadi al-Iraqi threatened to withdraw his force from the front. So, if Abu Abdullah had not accepted Mullah Omar's order some serious problems might have occurred. But he accepted and he ordered Abdul Hadi al-Iraqi to work with Juma Bai, which he did.

Abu Abdullah said, 'We have two vital areas of work here; first to support the Emirate by fighting at the fronts and with financial support if we can, until they control all the country. The second work is against the Americans to liberate Saudi Arabia.' When Abu Abdullah spoke about the first work, he said, 'If the owner of the work does not like you, you cannot force him.' By this, Abu Abdullah meant targeting the Americans would be his priority, because Mullah Omar's decision meant he could not work on the front in the way he had wanted.

LF: I imagine this priority was also because al-Qaeda's 9/11 project was nearing completion, with the hijackers finishing their training and recording martyrdom videos in Kandahar before leaving for America. Bin Laden was also preparing to announce Tanzim al-Jihad joining al-Qaeda, so there were other projects to focus on.

* * *

The al-Qaeda–Tanzim al-Jihad merger

In the summer of 2001, Tanzim al-Jihad merged with al-Qaeda after lengthy negotiations, which ultimately caused a split in Tanzim al-Jihad.

* * *

LF: It is interesting to look back at the al-Qaeda–Tanzim al-Jihad merger with the benefit of hindsight and a lot of research! At the time it was announced, because of Tanzim al-Jihad's history and the media coverage surrounding it, the group appeared powerful. Moreover, it seemed that it had merged with another powerful group, al-Qaeda. The reality, as we all now know, was that neither group was as big as media reporting was suggesting.

Tanzim al-Jihad had around ten members in Afghanistan. Al-Qaeda had around 150 members, plus another 100 or so people on the Kabul front, and around fifty to seventy or so foot soldiers—most of whom lived in Kandahar. Documents taken from a computer in Kabul used by Ayman al-Zawahiri, who was then the amir of Tanzim al-Jihad, show the decision to join al-Qaeda was the subject of heated debates.[5] Nobody outside knew for many years that only five people from Tanzim al-Jihad joined al-Qaeda, and the other five or so refused to join, which reflects just how controversial the decision was.

MH: Yes, the decision was controversial, not only within Tanzim al-Jihad: some in al-Qaeda were also unhappy.

LF: I do not imagine long-standing al-Qaeda members were happy when five people joined their organisation, and the amir appointed one as his deputy and the others all assumed senior leadership roles.

MH: Some al-Qaeda people and Arabs outside of al-Qaeda did not think highly of al-Jihad and Dr Ayman. These people thought al-Jihad was just ten people who wanted leadership in the area and they did not deserve it because all they were doing was making propaganda. Sayf al-Adl was not happy—he said to some people, 'We are 250 of the 400 Arabs in Afghanistan; why should we accept to be led by a person from a group of ten?'

LF: So basically Sayf al-Adl, and presumably others, thought al-Qaeda had the people and power. In this line of thinking, Tanzim al-Jihad should come under al-Qaeda and its people should not come into the organisation in leadership positions, as they subsequently did?

MH: Yes, but not everyone was against it, and of course, Sayf al-Adl accepted the merger when it came. Some others thought if Tanzim al-Jihad had good cadres who were qualified to lead, they should take leadership—especially if al-Qaeda did not have suitable people. Sayf was more against Abu Musab al-Suri than he was against the Tanzim al-Jihad leaders assuming leadership positions within al-Qaeda.

LF: What happened to the other five members of Tanzim al-Jihad in Afghanistan?

MH: They did not agree to join al-Qaeda and so the group split—Abu Samha became the amir of the al-Jihad group who did not merge with al-Qaeda.

LF: Shortly after the merger, al-Qaeda gave a television interview in which threats were issued against America.[6] By then, most of al-Qaeda's operatives for 9/11 were in place in America, and rumours abounded in Afghanistan about a coming al-Qaeda strike. They were fuelled in part by bin Laden's speeches in the camps and the recruitment for al-Qaeda's martyrdom brigades, for which lists were being distributed encouraging people to register their interest. It seems around 120 people had registered on this list by the time the American invasion began.[7] You were very angry over the television interview and the threats that were made in it by al-Qaeda's leaders.

MH: Yes, because Abu Abdullah practically appointed himself as ruler of Afghanistan. It was some kind of coup; declaring war on behalf of the Afghan people and their amir.

Disagreement about al-Qaeda's upcoming (9/11) attacks

LF: When you heard the threats al-Qaeda had made in the television interview you went to see some of al-Qaeda's media people and had a strong discussion with them, because you thought the statements amounted to a declaration of war that would invite an American response. You argued al-Qaeda, as guests in Afghanistan, did not have the right to declare war against a foreign country and only Mullah Omar as Amir al-Muminin had that right.[8] You also argued al-Qaeda did not have the right to impose war on the people of Afghanistan.[9]

MH: I told them, 'You should not liberate Saudi Arabia by the blood of Afghans; it is a battle of the Saudis.'

LF: Bin Laden heard about your criticism and arranged to meet you.

MH: Yes, it was the last time we ever met.

LF: I found it interesting he brought along a Saudi leader who was visiting to plan work with al-Qaeda in the Arabian Peninsula, and who he used to rebut your claims about the Saudis not wanting to fight the Americans. Bin Laden also told you a large operation was coming.

MH: Yes, Abu Abdullah told me he had prepared a very big strike where casualties would be in the thousands.

LF: You pointed out America was a superpower that could absorb a big strike and still retaliate, and that attacking America, especially without the permission of Mullah Omar, would unite the world against Afghanistan. You asked al-Qaeda to reconsider and not give America 'the legal and moral reasons to invade Afghanistan'.[10] Ayman al-Zawahiri, who was also at the meeting, responded and said, 'The first to strike has the upper hand in war', and added that if war is going to happen it does not matter if al-Qaeda strikes first.[11] This just goes to show Ayman did not have a good grasp of military history, or strategy for that matter. You replied by saying that war is strikes, and continuous strikes according to a programme and a plan, and asked whether al-Qaeda had such things in place.[12]

MH: Yes. I told Abu Abdullah, 'The problem is not how to start the war but how to win the war.'

LF: Bin Laden responded that he had another 100 people willing to conduct martyrdom operations. His response shows while he wanted to draw America into Afghanistan, he seems to have fully believed he could continue operating in the country and planning more attacks. He seems to have been stuck in a Jaji-style mentality—or rather stuck in the last war, where the mujahidin had freedom of movement, which would not be available to al-Qaeda in the event of the large-scale American response bin Laden was trying to provoke.

What I find striking is that so many people tried to warn bin Laden against launching a big attack. Not only were your warnings ignored, but so too were the warnings from others inside al-Qaeda. People like Sayf al-Adl, Saeed al-Masri and Abu Hafs al-Mauritani. It makes me wonder exactly who did support the attacks: the youth probably, but there are few from among the old cadres who seem to have supported it.

MH: No one inside al-Qaeda from among its old cadres agreed. All of them opposed action against America at that time. Abu Abdullah and Dr Ayman were the only ones in favour.

LF: Yes, I was surprised to hear from Abu Hafs al-Mauritani's interviews after his release from Iran that even Abu Hafs al-Masri disagreed.[13] He played an important role in planning and support for the attacks.

MH: Yes, it was like all of al-Qaeda's history. They disagreed but they would not go against Abu Abdullah. But this time some people left; Abu Hafs al-Mauritani was one of them.

LF: Were you nervous about what you heard al-Qaeda was planning? Were others? The Taliban's deputy foreign minister was with you when you had the first discussion with al-Qaeda's media people. Were the Taliban concerned that something was coming? Perhaps their concern was forgotten a little when al-Qaeda assassinated Masud on 9 September 2001.

MH: Yes, it had been clear for a long time that Afghanistan was in danger. When I heard these things al-Qaeda said, I was worried about what would happen in Afghanistan and the damage that could be done there. Al-Qaeda had apparently worked on the Masud operation for a long time—maybe one year. The Taliban were very happy Masud was gone and they said very good things about al-Qaeda but then 9/11 came and everything changed.

Al-Qaeda's pre-9/11 preparations for an American retaliation and an absence of warnings

LF: According to Sayf al-Adl, al-Qaeda had around two weeks' notice for the 9/11 attacks, and during this time, preparations were made in

Kandahar.[14] It also seems preparations had begun in Tora Bora, but despite undertaking these preparations, al-Qaeda did not appear to have warned Arab-Afghan groups or the Taliban.

MH: No one outside al-Qaeda and even only a small group inside al-Qaeda knew details about the attacks. They did not tell the Taliban; otherwise, they would have made hell for al-Qaeda.

LF: It is clear bin Laden wanted to draw the Americans into fighting him in Afghanistan because in the late summer of 2001—once he knew the attacks in America were going ahead—he began calling people back to Afghanistan. No one was sent out—not even the women and children. But yet none of the other groups were warned—a warning that may have allowed them to arrange themselves better to join in with what bin Laden had planned—or to evacuate their families.

MH: Yes, Abu Abdullah called people back; even the big *ulama*, the old mujahidin who had fought in Afghanistan, and every capable person. After the attack I wanted the families to be evacuated, but even when it became clear America would invade Afghanistan, al-Qaeda was not evacuating the families. I tried hard to convince them they needed to do this but they would not.

LF: Why not?

MH: Even before the American invasion, I asked them to shift the families to Iran so they could concentrate on the situation in Afghanistan because it would be very hard. I told them, 'If you have your families here you cannot fight, you will leave your duties in the war, and they will be in danger.' I said, 'Send the families now and concentrate on what you are going to do.' They refused. Instead, they were going to put the families in a village fifteen minutes away from Kandahar. I became very angry when I heard that because doing so was pointless. No one would be safe there.

Al-Qaeda did not want to send the families out because they did not want the Afghans to think the Arabs were fleeing. I told them, 'Our situation is different. The Afghans can send their wives and children home to their villages and tribes.' They did not listen and by the time they eventually began to move their families it was very late and very dangerous, and some were killed while they were trying to escape the war.

LF: By Sayf al-Adl's account there were seventy-five people involved in al-Qaeda's preparation efforts in Kandahar before the 9/11 attacks.[15] While Sayf seems to have taken responsibility for preparation around Kandahar, bin Laden's efforts were focused on Tora Bora. He anticipated that when America came to Afghanistan he could lure them to Tora Bora, and defeat them in the same way he defeated the Soviets at Jaji.

MH: Abu Abdullah expected the American reaction to 9/11 would be a paratrooper operation by the Americans to capture him. His plan was to make a mountain stronghold in Tora Bora and lead the enemy there. He thought he could build trenches where the youth could hide and absorb the airstrikes that would come before the paratroopers arrived. He was organising himself in anticipation of this, and believed he could make big losses for the Americans. He thought and hoped it would be the same as Jaji.

LF: That amazes me, because clearly Tora Bora was not Jaji. For starters, unlike Jaji, the border was not friendly, nor was it at all likely the Americans would directly send troops to the area, given their preference for aerial strikes. The similarities that did exist were the dangers of both sites, like the poor supply routes and isolation.

MH: Also, the part of Tora Bora where the youth were was unsuitable for paratroopers to be inserted. There was heavy tree cover, which was good for the youth to avoid detection, but it meant that paratroopers were unlikely to be landed in that area; and the surrounding area was also not suitable for the Americans who were afraid of losing their soldiers.

In fact, the conditions at Tora Bora were ripe for a siege and heavy bombardment, not paratroopers. Abu Hafs al-Masri and Sayf al-Adl warned Abu Abdullah about this. Dr Amin and other local Jalalabad commanders also opposed Abu Abdullah's decision, and reminded him that in the winter Tora Bora would be surrounded with snow and even supplying a force there would be very difficult. They knew it would be easy to put Tora Bora under siege and the trenches were not numerous enough for the fighters and not strong enough. They also knew the Americans would not come in the way Abu Abdullah had hoped.

LF: Despite all the warnings, bin Laden still wanted to draw America in, and he seems to have thought it would be the same as the jihad against the Soviets.

MH: Yes. I heard that when the preparations for Tora Bora were being made a wireless radio was sent to the mountain and some Arab-Afghans advised Abu Abdullah against using this, saying, 'they will know your position is in Tora Bora'. He said, 'I want them to know the place to come.' But you know, it was not just Abu Abdullah who thought it would be the same as fighting the Soviets. Many people were thinking this way. They thought there would be fronts like the last time, and that they could come and go from them and have camps nearby. They thought they could keep their families close by, and visit the way they had during the jihad against the Soviets. They did not understand this war would be very different. Even the Algerians, Moroccans, Kurds and Tunisians who lived in Jalalabad, and who decided to help Abu Abdullah, they thought this way too.

LF: I find their cooperation interesting, because before 9/11 they had been fighting among themselves and kept a distance from al-Qaeda, but afterwards they seem to have put these differences aside.

MH: Yes, before 9/11 there were many differences among them. But after 9/11 when it became clear the Americans and the coalition forces were coming, they started to unify. They thought they should support Abu Abdullah, so they formed one group and made a *Shurah* Council, appointed an *amir* and formed committees to organise themselves and their military activities and to take care of the families.

They had around fifty fighters ready to send to work with Abu Abdullah, who at that time had around 120 people at Tora Bora. But they did not want to fully join with Abu Abdullah: they wanted to take a separate post for themselves, and for him to coordinate. They thought each group could have one or two posts in the defence plan, and that they could rotate their personnel because many were married and wanted to go with their families—whom they thought could stay in the area around Jalalabad. They failed to realise the routes they would use to come and go would be the same routes the enemy would use to attack them!

There was also an issue with supplies—getting food and weapons to the area was very difficult. Abu Abdullah had ordered his men to prepare food and weapons for six months but they did not have nearly enough notice to do so. The area had to be supplied by mules, and it took two to three hours for them to travel up the mountain from the nearest supply point and at least ten mules each day to supply even the small group that was there in the early stages at Tora Bora before the war. Some people who were there said that without the supply help of the Jalalabad area commanders the fighters at Tora Bora would have been in big trouble.

The American invasion

LF: Things were initially quiet in Tora Bora after the war began on 7 October 2001. This caused some problems with the youth who were keen for battle and to fight the Americans who never came.

MH: The area was bombed in the opening stages of the war but the bombing targeted old trenches from the jihad against the Soviets and did not reach the youth, who were in the new locations further up the mountain. After a week or so, the bombing instead was concentrated on Jalalabad and targets in the city, and the situation became quiet in Tora Bora.

This caused the youth to become bored and Abu Abdullah was not there at that time. He was intending to go, but the Arabs and Afghans advised him not to because the trenches were not ready, so he sat for one week in a secret house in Jalalabad. When the bombing in Jalalabad intensified, he moved to Kabul.

The youth in the mountain were restless and bored, and the extra trenches were not ready, so a decision was made not to accept any more newcomers, and to keep the number at around 150. The seventy or so youth who had heard Abu Abdullah was in Jalalabad and went there to follow him were told they could go and fight in Khost or Kabul.

LF: It is interesting they were not sent to Kandahar, which seems to have been operating almost as an independent unit, and which was also where most of the senior leaders of al-Qaeda were based.

MH: Some people felt they should go to Kandahar to help defend it because the Arabs had caused this invasion so they thought they should help defend the city.

LF: Following the fall of Herat and Kabul in the second week of November 2001, the number of Arab-Afghans in Kandahar increased. Around the third week of November, a meeting took place in Kandahar that has always fascinated me. It was held shortly after Abu Hafs al-Masri's death and was arranged to organise the defence of Kandahar, and to appoint a leader. Many senior leaders from the groups present in Kandahar attended, along with some Taliban figures. Among those I can place at the meeting are Muhammad al-Islambouli, Abu Jihad al-Masri and Sharif al-Masri from Gamaah Islamiyyah, and Abu Hafs al-Mauritani, Sayf al-Adl, Khalid Shaykh Muhammad and possibly Abu Muhammad al-Masri from al-Qaeda. Abu Musab al-Zarqawi, Abu Zubaydah and a number of others also attended, including members of the Libyan group, and some Yemeni and Saudi figures.[16]

At the meeting, Sayf al-Adl was appointed commander for the defence of Kandahar, and according to some present they also gave an oath of allegiance to al-Qaeda.[17] The giving of this oath was quite significant because at this meeting bin Laden achieved what he had always wanted—

the unification of groups under al-Qaeda's command, making it the leading group. It is rather ironic that he was not there. I also noticed the Uzbeks were absent.

MH: No, the Uzbeks did not go to Kandahar. People followed al-Qaeda because it was the strongest of the groups there. These oaths meant nothing—they were only for the defence of the city.

LF: I realise the oaths did not last, but bin Laden had tried for years to get all of these different groups together under al-Qaeda's command. He had tried to buy their support, he had tried to convince them to join under a front and he had tried to get their camps closed. He had really tried everything. In the end, he achieved it not through any of these means, or by having a programme that other groups found appealing, but by an attack that incited America to invade Afghanistan and in doing so forced everyone to come together and accept al-Qaeda's leading position.

After 9/11, bin Laden made a comment in a meeting that was videotaped and later found. He was talking about the attacks and remarked that people do not follow a weak horse, they follow a strong one.

MH: Yes, I know this saying. We first spoke about it together.

LF: Oh, then you will know how much it has been misunderstood, and in how many different ways it is misunderstood. I think much of this stems from an unawareness about the internal circumstances inside Afghanistan, and assumptions that bin Laden's focus was outside, which we spoke about earlier. It is in this outside context that bin Laden's comment is also often understood, particularly by Americans, who have assumed it refers in part to them, in the context of bin Laden referring to al-Qaeda appearing stronger against America.

Bin Laden's comment has also been interpreted in the context of al-Qaeda wanting to appear stronger in the eyes of the Ummah. But the comment was in reality about the internal circumstances, just as al-Qaeda's 9/11 attack was as much about projecting strength to make it the strongest of the foreign groups in Afghanistan as anything else. It seems to me this is what bin Laden thought the 9/11 attack would do for al-Qaeda—make it strong internally. He thought he could repeat Jaji by drawing American forces into Tora Bora. In this context, he was talking about how al-Qaeda's attacks made it the strong horse inside Afghanistan—the horse others would want to follow as they had done at Jaji many years before.

However, events did not unfold the way bin Laden had intended. Although around 250 new volunteers had arrived in Afghanistan in the period between late summer 2001 and the American invasion, the other groups in Afghanistan did not rush to follow al-Qaeda in the aftermath of its 9/11 attacks. Cooperation and unity only solidified in the face of an American invasion, and in most cases did not last beyond the withdrawal of the Arab-Afghans from Afghanistan a few weeks later. In this respect, Mullah Omar's order for the Arab-Afghans to withdraw was the death knell for bin Laden's jihad project. As I understand it, there were a series of meetings about whether the Taliban should withdraw and whether it should tell the Arabs to leave, and it took a week or so before the order was given?

MH: The first meeting about withdrawing took place on 8 Ramadan, which was around 23 November. The Taliban held a Shurah to discuss whether they should withdraw.

LF: The Arabs knew about this meeting, I presume.

MH: Yes, at that time, they were working to shift the families if the withdrawal order was issued.

LF: I find it astonishing women and children were left so long, and the men were prepared to leave their families in the same areas that were being bombed and where they were intending to fight. I just cannot fathom how you would or could deliberately expose your family to that kind of danger, when you had the choice and the chance to evacuate them.

MH: I spoke about this to al-Qaeda very early on and told them they should evacuate their families, but even after there was talk from the Taliban about withdrawing they still feared the Afghans would think they were fleeing from the battle.

LF: So they chose pride and 'honour' over their wives and children, until they were effectively ordered to leave after this Shurah.

MH: It was not like this; there was a lot of confusion, which made making a decision difficult. The Taliban also changed their mind. Most of the Taliban Shurah wanted to withdraw from Kandahar, but Mullah Omar, Mullah Mansur, Mullah Baradar and Mullah Abdul Razak wanted to defend the city, and these three supporting Mullah Omar gave him an oath to fight.

Mullah Omar tried to convince the others to fight but they said, 'We have no capacity to fight because of the airplanes.' Some of them were afraid for the Arabs, and told Mullah Omar he should ask them to leave Afghanistan. The Arabs had also decided to fight, and there were around

300 or so of them in Kandahar at that time. If they were to go, hundreds of families had to leave, and Lashkar i Taiba in Pakistan had said it was ready to help host them.

LF: Yes, Lashkar i Taiba helped, along with the folks from two Pakistani groups, one that came to be known as Jundullah from Karachi, and some people from Harakat al-Ansar. Abu Zubaydah and Khalid Shaykh Muhammad both had close links with all these groups and arranged a lot of the transportation and housing of families because of their good ties into these networks. Between them, they organised at least thirteen to fifteen safe houses where people stayed, before moving to other locations in Pakistan or on to Iran. Still, not everyone wanted to leave Afghanistan; it is my understanding that some wanted to stay and fight.

MH: Yes, this was a problem. Many Arabs were in favour of fighting inside Kandahar until the last man and bullet, and that reflects their irresponsibility; they were not attached to the land and did not care about the Afghan people.

LF: Or their own families for that matter.

MH: Some of the Arabs asked Mullah Abdul Razak to get an order from Mullah Omar, because according to Shariah they could not withdraw without one. Taheb Agha from the Taliban came and spoke to the Arabs. He was very angry, saying, 'We have lost the battle, we should confess that—we don't want to lose more blood, let the Arab families go out.'

LF: Even after the Taliban ordered a withdrawal some youth from the Gulf would not leave their positions, and some members of al-Qaeda's religious institute had to get on the short-wave radio and order them out because they wanted to fight to the death.[18] Once this order was issued, the Arabs began to withdraw their forces and most of the fighters left around 3 December, with the city emptied of those who could flee by 7 December 2001.[19]

The bulk of the leadership in Kandahar seems to have then travelled out of Afghanistan over several days, leaving via Zurmat and, rather astonishingly, together in minibuses; twenty-four of them travelled together in one of these conveys.[20] It seems they were able to do so because the focus of the coalition forces was on Tora Bora, which is interesting because contrary to the popular rumours about Tora Bora, bin Laden had left there by early December and was long gone before the mid-December battle.

Most of the leadership who left Kandahar along with their family members seem to have found their way to Zurmat and then across the border to Bannu in Pakistan. From there, they travelled through a series of safe houses in Karachi, Faisalabad, Lahore, Peshawar, Islamabad and elsewhere, which were those Khalid Shaykh and his colleagues had arranged with the help of Abu Zubaydah and others.

MH: As far as I know, Abu Abdullah left the Tora Bora region in the first week of December. Before that, some people from the Libyan group met with Abu Abdullah to advise him to leave the mountain and Afghanistan; they were among many who thought the military position was wrong. Ibn Shaykh al-Libi and Abu Ayman al-Yamani were present at the meeting and although they agreed, they kept silent. The Libyans made an agreement to evacuate the people from Tora Bora and from Jalalabad. Some were betrayed crossing the border into Pakistan and were arrested.

LF: Abu Musab al-Suri said al-Qaeda's jihad project was extinguished when America invaded Afghanistan. I think this period certainly marked the strategic failure of bin Laden's project in terms of what he thought it would achieve. In some things he succeeded, like most of the groups coming together with al-Qaeda to fight. But it did not last, because it was built around reaction to a threat, not support for a programme or agenda. When the withdrawal orders were issued and the Arabs left, so too did any hopes for unity and any other benefits bin Laden had anticipated as coming from the 9/11 attacks.

MH: The way of Abu Abdullah in leadership spoiled everything inside al-Qaeda, and everything in Afghanistan.

LF: What is striking to me is that nearly all of al-Qaeda successfully escaped Afghanistan, most certainly the bulk of its leadership escaped. I do not know as much about the Taliban. So while the project was a failure in terms of meeting bin Laden's objectives—it was not a defeat of al-Qaeda in the sense its force was decimated. In fact, I'd argue what challenged al-Qaeda in the few years following, was when bin Laden began to reassert some control—particularly over al-Qaeda's external operations. He ordered people and plots activated and many of al-Qaeda's operatives were compromised.

Sayf al-Adl wrote to Khalid Shaykh about bin Laden's orders, resulting in the compromise of al-Qaeda and a loss of operatives, and urged him to stop, and to talk to bin Laden.[21] Once Khalid Shaykh Muhammad was captured in March 2003 and Abu Faraj al-Libi took over, al-Qaeda started training again, and became more active in dealing with its overseas members, some of whom had activated a branch in Saudi Arabia. At that time, bin Laden's role became more distant for reasons appearing to relate to his movements and restrictions. I think around the same time al-Qaeda began re-building, the Taliban had also begun similar efforts, following its collapse in the final days before the withdrawal of its forces to Pakistan in early December 2001.

MH: Strategically, the Taliban made a big mistake in their calculations. They did not think the Americans would come and bomb them in the way they did and they did not factor this in when they decided to send forces to the north to finish off Masud's Northern Alliance. They also miscalculated the anger of the north about Masud's death, and their anger towards the Taliban and Pashtun more generally. There were no good routes into and out of the area either. They lost Juma Bai and nearly all of the foreign volunteer force when they sent him to an area between Kunduz and Takhar. After his death, there was a big collapse in the morale of the fighters.

Perhaps the biggest miscalculation that both the Taliban and the Arabs made was thinking the war would be like the last war against the Soviets. The Taliban did not imagine the role the American Air Force could play. By the end of the jihad against the Soviets, the mujahidin knew how to face them, how to defeat the helicopters, how to fight effectively. But the American Air Force with its heavy bombing with accurate bombs dropped from high altitudes was something new and a great shock for the Taliban. They lost all their battles because of the jets and their targeting.

Not only did they lose their military battles but they lost the people. The Taliban made a mistake in their political calculations because the Afghans did not support the war—they were wary that it was Abu Abdullah, al-Qaeda's and the Taliban's war, not Afghanistan's war—so they remained spectators rather than participating. It took the Taliban two years to rebuild its position. It was a very hard two years to reconstruct its relationship with the people. To convince them what happened was a mistake, and to rectify that mistake with a hearts and minds campaign through social work and not just military work, and also to build effective new strategies and make good use of the American mistakes, which in fact helped the Taliban a lot.

LF: The Taliban's support for the Arab-Afghan groups in Afghanistan was nothing short of a catastrophe for the movement and its own programme. The Taliban obviously made a mistake allowing these groups to operate on its soil—and it is quite clear from what you and many others have said that there were misgivings and concerns among the Taliban from the outset. Why then did it continue to allow groups to settle and stay in Afghanistan, if these concerns existed? The Taliban has not spoken out about its experiences with the Arab groups. Instead, they have stayed quiet. Has the experience of losing Afghanistan caused the Taliban to rethink future support for such groups if it again comes to power in Afghanistan? You have said on many occasions that such groups would not be welcomed, but cooperation continues between the Taliban and a number of these groups who operate in the Pakistan–Afghanistan tribal areas.

MH: Abu Abdullah was already present in Jalalabad when the Taliban came to power in 1996. Although his relationship with the Taliban was troubled at times, the Taliban came to need the assistance of all of the Arabs in Afghanistan in 1997 when Kabul came under threat from the forces of Dostum and Masud. Most of that support came from Abu Abdullah's group because the people at Khaldan did not support the Taliban at that time and there were few other Arabs in the country. Because the Arabs helped the Taliban to defend Kabul, their presence was appreciated. It was also thought the presence of Arabs gave the Taliban religious legitimacy. In fact, the religious link was the strongest reason the Taliban allowed the Arabs to stay, in addition to the tribal customs which prohibits the abuse of one's guest or handing them over to the enemy, especially since the Arabs had been the guests of the Afghan mujahidin and had fought alongside them against the Soviets.

As for the Taliban not speaking of its negative experience with the Arab groups, the Taliban spoke about these problems in closed circles, but everybody outside was, and still is, attacking them; so they were afraid to talk about these things openly. This is understandable, but it is not permanent, and it should not be permanent. The Arab groups will not be allowed to operate in Afghanistan the way they used to; the Taliban will not allow this. Nothing that has the possibility of creating a disturbance among the Afghans will be allowed because Afghan society needs to be protected from outside interference in its many forms.

Anyway, most people from the Arab groups have returned to their countries. There are a few of them left, but they will not be welcomed in Afghanistan as organisations or groups. No military groups will be allowed—not even political groups. They will not be allowed because their activities cause disturbances in society. In fact, the Taliban has become more firm on this after events in Waziristan since the war of 2001, where the Arabs have caused very serious problems and made big disturbances among the tribes.

LF: Do you think the Taliban has also watched what has happened in Syria among the various Salafi jihadi groups?

MH: Yes, and I think they will know too how much of what is happening had already started to happen in Afghanistan before the war started, and they do not want that to happen again in their country. What is happening in Syria will only make them more firm in this position.

Even Wahhabism will not have a strong case in Afghanistan. As for al-Qaeda, dealing with that group will be very different to the past. There are many reasons for this, but with the disappearance of Abu Abdullah, al-Qaeda will be treated as foreigners. Before it was hard to do, because Abu Abdullah had a good reputation at that time, and the Taliban were sensitive in dealing with him. This has changed now. The Taliban gained a lot of experience from the war and their period of governing Afghanistan. They are learning about their successes and mistakes. After the war, I expect the Taliban will make a complete revolution in Afghanistan and in the Islamic world. I expect this but I am not sure of course because nobody can be sure.

12

REFLECTIONS

LF: Although the Arab-Afghan presence in Afghanistan technically ended with their late 2001 withdrawal from the country, the legacy from their stay continues today. It can be seen in a number of Salafi jihadi groups that emerged from the Afghan jihad, and in the conflicts in which they subsequently participated in Asia, North Africa and the Middle East. Indeed, the fate of many of these groups, as well as their behavioural characteristics, is inherently tied to the Arab-Afghan legacy, as the recent conflict and competition between the Jalalabad School and al-Qaeda in Syria clearly shows. Yet, the important role the Arab-Afghan legacy has played since the events following 9/11, and its on-going influence over the jihadist milieu has remained clouded by conventional wisdom, along with a status quo that seems to hold that all that needs to be known about Arab-Afghan history is already known. Our book has shown this is not the case. It reveals that not only is the history of the Arab-Afghans in Afghanistan markedly different to what passes for conventional wisdom; it is also far more complex, and its legacy more influential than what has been commonly assumed.

Unravelling the Arab-Afghan story has also shed new light on the origins of the Taliban. Although important, in and of itself, this new historical detail also has significant bearing on how the development of the Arab-Afghan jihad is contextualised and understood. Nowhere is this more evident than in the similarities between the dynamics that drove the Taliban's genesis—reflected in the reform efforts of Mawlawi Nasrullah Mansur—and in the arguments for the creation of an Arab organisation to oversee the provision of assistance and supplies to the Afghan mujahidin.

Although the reform efforts attempted by Mawlawi Mansur, and those outlined for the proposed Arab organisation (that eventually came into being as Maktab al-Khadamat), differed significantly in their scope and intended implementation, it is striking that both encountered resistance from those for whom reform was not in their interest. For Mansur, anti-reform resistance resulted in sustained efforts to sideline him. For the Arab initiative, efforts were made to influence how the organisation would operate, and to keep Arabs away from the fronts and limit their role to financing and rear supply management. Visits to the front, particularly by influential Arabs, were restricted and managed—leading to a lack of visibility, which in part contributed to Maktab al-Khadamat falling victim to corruption: the very thing it was established to combat.

The same reform dynamic that drove both the Taliban and Maktab al-Khadamat's early development can also be observed in al-Qaeda's genesis. Bin Laden's 1986 separation from Maktab al-Khadamat to begin his own efforts funding and supporting the Afghans was initially for remedial purposes. His unsupervised visit to the front when no Afghan leaders were present was instrumental in his decision to separate from Maktab al-Khadamat. At the front, bin Laden saw that money and supplies were not reaching their destinations as intended but his efforts to remedy the situation also encountered resistance.

While bin Laden's separation from Maktab al-Khadamat has previously been attributed to the mismanagement and corruption that plagued the latter, the significance of his doing so was not fully appreciated. This is because Maktab al-Khadamat's own genesis was not understood as a reform effort for the Afghan jihad. Rather, it was viewed as being established to facilitate Arab-Afghan participation in the jihad. That Maktab al-Khadamat was not solely established for this purpose, but rather as a remedial effort against Afghan corruption, makes its succumbing to mismanagement and corruption all the more significant. It also casts bin Laden's decision to separate from the organisation in a more important light.

Bin Laden was not the only significant figure to leave Maktab al-Khadamat for reasons of ineffectiveness, inefficiency and corruption. Nor was he the only Arab to attempt to initiate reform. As our book has revealed, the proposal for what eventually became Maktab al-Khadamat originated with Mustafa Hamid and a small group of friends. Another of

Hamid's friends, Abu Harith al-Urduni, also attempted reform efforts, which manifested in his split from Maktab al-Khadamat and formation of his own Arab group in Khost.

While Abu Harith and bin Laden's groups subsequently evolved in very different ways, their initial reasons for separating were the same: corruption and inefficiency. What this suggests is that dynamics that have in the past appeared limited to Afghan groups, such as the role corruption played in group formation and the development of splinter groups, are in fact broader; and on closer inspection also present in Arab-Afghan groups.

A fuller picture of organisational evolution in the Afghan and Arab-Afghan jihad has therefore emerged, and with it, the significant role corruption, reform efforts against it, and resistance to such efforts, played in this process. This new insight may be valuable for understanding the dynamics within the Syrian conflict, particularly since what this fuller picture and understanding of the Afghan conflict seems to reveal is that it is not necessarily the nature of the conflict or group that drives the degree of corruption present—or its role in shaping organisational evolution, dynamics and group interaction. The flow of external aid and assistance appears to be a critical factor; something that is common to the Afghan and Syrian conflicts, with many of the same players involved in the provision of aid and assistance. Corruption also seems to have become a problem early on, before group numbers grew significantly, but after external aid and assistance had begun. In the Afghan context, this perhaps might explain why al-Qaeda and Abu Harith did not fall victim to corruption; their role was not one of aid and distribution, and they had separated to work independently and in a limited rather than broad context.

Attempts to manage a broad focus by centralising the administration of aid—as reflected in multiple efforts to create a central Afghan body for receiving and dispersing aid, or an Arab organisation to oversee such activity—did little to prevent corruption. Corruption seems to have instead infiltrated the new groupings. These attempts also appear to have resulted in more splits: each time an initiative was made for unification, or remedial action by the establishment of a new group (Arab-Afghan or Afghan), splits inevitably emerged.

That splits universally emerged as a result of such efforts is perhaps because some of the same dynamics that drove corruption also influenced the exercise of leadership, particularly among the Arab-Afghans. Money, supplies and weapons, along with combat opportunities, 'made' leaders.

While this seems to be a rather obvious statement, in the context of how the Arab-Afghan jihad is commonly understood, it is not. Often the Arab-Afghan jihad is studied in ideological terms and people are perceived to have joined the jihad because of ideology, or more specifically, joined bin Laden or Abdullah Azzam because of their 'ideology', teachings or their ideas. But although religious convictions may have driven people to volunteer for the jihad, many people joined these two leaders not because of ideology but because they wanted to fight, and Azzam and bin Laden were seen as offering the best opportunities to see action. Simply put, on the ground more pragmatic issues often dictated who became leaders, who men followed and how groups formed and disintegrated. Chief among these was a perception of effectiveness, which could quickly change in the Arab-Afghan milieu.

Most often, effectiveness was perceived, particularly by the youth, in terms of victory and participation in combat, and who offered the best opportunities to see combat. This was something bin Laden only came to belatedly understand in the aftermath of Jalalabad, when al-Qaeda's numbers dropped drastically because it was no longer seen as active, and successful and offering such opportunities. The earlier 'defection' of Maktab al-Khadamat followers to al-Qaeda following bin Laden's success in the Battle of Jaji is also testament to this dynamic—as is Abu Harith's successful attraction of volunteers following his military activity in Khost. It is most clear, however, in the change of mood within the youth after the Jalalabad defeat, when not only bin Laden's but also Azzam's historical leadership was rejected because both men were seen by many youth as ineffective and blocking their efforts to fight. This was despite their earlier significant contributions and in bin Laden's case, his significant and famed victory at Jaji.

In the climate following the July 1989 defeat at Jalalabad, these earlier contributions did not matter to the youths. Bin Laden had withdrawn from Jalalabad and he and Azzam did not support further Arab-Afghan involvement in the fighting. Consequently, the youth looked elsewhere and found new 'leaders' who were still fighting or sought to fight. The youth followed them and saw them as not only effective, but also less restrictive. These new leaders established themselves in the surrounds of Jalalabad, setting up their own camps, and essentially followed an 'anything goes' approach to combat. This 'anything goes' school born from the Jalalabad defeat has not only been resurgent in recent years, but is arguably now, as a result of its actions in Syria and elsewhere, a dominant force in the militant Salafist milieu.

MH: In the School of Jalalabad, even the 'leaders' were very young. Most of them were in their twenties; they were not only young in age, but also in experience. Their understanding of politics was poor. Such understanding is rare in the Islamic fields, especially among jihadis, but it was virtually non-existent among the Jalalabad youth. Their military understanding was also poor. They did not know about politics or war, only about fighting, and war is not only about fighting. Many were also tactically inexperienced. Some of them did become very good in this field, but even then they completely ignored strategy. They had no political or strategic understanding and their only focus was on fighting and tactics. For them, it was, as you say, a case of 'anything goes', in the fighting. And it still is in areas where this school is active.

When Abu Abdullah came to realise he had made a big mistake in Jalalabad and that it was in fact a trap for the mujahidin, he withdrew. The youth were angry at his decision to do so. They were also angry with Azzam who had earlier heavily encouraged people to join the battle. The youth thought Abu Abdullah and Azzam had become weak and were incapable of continuing and they thought if they continued in Jalalabad, they could win the war. This is because they did not understand the political and military side or they ignored these aspects.

At the time, they said that according to Shariah, it is the right war. Really, they were looking for a battle and for fighting and they did not recognise Abu Abdullah made the right decision to withdraw from Jalalabad. Instead, the youth considered him weak for leaving the battlefield and argued that the fighting should continue, which was very wrong. Their lack of experience in war and politics made them think this way and made them angry and insistent on continuing in Jalalabad. They would not stop even though it was not successful, and they would accept no leadership on the matter. The same thing continues today, which is why I think in many ways we can call the Jalalabad School the 'School of the Youth' or the 'Teenagers' School of Jihad'.

LF: I wonder if the youths' rejection of bin Laden's decision and his and Azzam's leadership in part happened because of the lack of education in the Arab-Afghan milieu? We have talked a lot about training, and training shortfalls. It seems to me there was a striking lack of education for youths who travelled to join the jihad in Afghanistan during the Soviet conflict and in the time of the Taliban. Throughout the history of the Arab-Afghans in Afghanistan, there were many shiny slogans thrown about but not much in the way of Islamic or political education, or even arguably some aspects of military training.

MH: There was very little education in these areas, and very little research. At the level of training and at the level of Arab military activity, there were no real programmes, no effective strategies and almost nothing in the way of pragmatic, practical thinking. One reason for this was that most Arabs who came to Afghanistan during the jihad against the Soviets did not stay long. Because they were only there for a short time, it was difficult to talk about strategy, planning or organisation, and it was difficult to train the youth under these circumstances, especially when many of them just wanted to go out and fight as soon as possible.

LF: This lack of education seems to have significantly affected the organisation of jihad efforts. Youths came wanting to fight, and went where the fighting and action was. They were quite fickle, and this fickleness had a big impact on the Arab-Afghan jihad. It drove not only a short-term focus but also an individual dynamic in what is meant to be a collective or group activity. In this way, I think it probably contributed to the mind-set where the youth rejected leaders if they were perceived to be hindering their ambitions to fight. They came to fight, expecting to see miracles and hoping to die in combat, which was obviously a short-term agenda. Because it was also an inherently individual motivation, I do not imagine it produced many strategists, planners or even patient fighters. It seems there were plenty of foot soldiers eager for battle and willing to die, but not many skilled leaders emerged.

MH: Exactly. Since the beginning, this fact was known by many Arabs. I remember my friend who had been an officer in the Egyptian army, and was in Afghanistan with us, said, 'We have many soldiers, many surgeons, but no generals have emerged from among the Arabs.' The people who were trained a little and developed were like sergeants. The Arabs had no generals, while the Afghans had quite a few.

This was because many Arabs thought doing basic training and having a gun meant people were prepared to fight a war. There was no focus on the strategic, political and, especially, social elements of the work, which are more important. A communist general highlighted this to me just after the war against the communists had ended. The Afghans were holding him, and I spoke to him and asked him what his conclusions were about the war now that it had finished. He said, 'I realise the social side of the war is more important than the military side.' This is true, but it is a fact that was not clear to the Arabs. It is still is not understood by them, this is clear to see in the conflicts the jihadi groups have been involved in and the damage that has been caused.

A society must be prepared for war. If we are going to go to war, we should be sure that the people are going to accept us doing so; we should be sure it is workable and that the population does not think it is impossible. Fighters, too, need to be educated and prepared for war. They need to be educated in these elements as well as basic training, especially for guerrilla warfare. Otherwise their actions can cause great damage as we have seen.

LF: Do you think because the Arab-Afghans were foreigners in Afghanistan and were removed from their own lands, they did not appreciate these elements and could not grow leaders the way the Afghans could?

MH: Many Arabs thought the mission of jihad was martyrdom and to go to paradise, not to defend the land, or even to win. During the time of the jihad against the Soviets, I said, 'I came to Afghanistan to win and defeat the invaders, not to die.' This shocked those who had come with the goal of martyrdom.

LF: I think they also came because of slogans, which inspired them to think that way. It seems that slogans were very important in the history of the Arab-Afghans—as you have often said—slogans and bright, shiny ideas. This too, seems to have made the youth fickle in terms of whose leadership they followed. Whoever could lead them to the action they had been encouraged by these slogans to seek, was followed. Learning about strategy and building a good programme and foundation were not so popular.

MH: Yes. I remember during the jihad against the Soviets, the youth would come back to Peshawar angrily shouting, 'Where are the miracles?' They had read about miracles in the magazines that were being published about the jihad and then when they got to the fronts they did not see any miracles.

Another reason for the disorganisation was that the Arabs were not stable in who was a leader. The Afghans were very stable in respecting the leadership, but the Arabs were not. It was not only because of the elements you mentioned, which played a role in the making of leaders, but also because Salafism makes everybody able, or theoretically able, to choose for themselves how to follow the religious practice. This means leaders can emerge anywhere. That made the Arab leadership unstable, as we saw with the rejection of the historical leadership of Abu Abdullah and Azzam. We can also see that most of the Arab organisations had divisions or splits. It was a big problem and today too it continues to be a problem with new leaders emerging and divisions and splits like those that are taking place in Syria and everywhere.

LF: Al-Qaeda never had a splinter faction during this period?

MH: Yes, it did. There was never a person who split and took the name of al-Qaeda—because they could not while Abu Abdullah was alive and leading the organisation, but really al-Qaeda had many splits. After Jalalabad, and in the time between then and when it left Sudan, al-Qaeda shrunk from about 10,000 to just fifty. Many of these people split to form other groups—national groups, not by the name of al-Qaeda.

A few takfiris from northern Africa split from al-Qaeda, like Abu Hamid al-Libi. He was from al-Qaeda; in fact, he had worked with me before that on the Khost airport project. There were many examples like him. Another group of Libyans split from al-Qaeda and attacked its guesthouse in Miranshah to take some money. This money was actually for our planned project in Gardez in 1992, which al-Qaeda had agreed to help with. Earlier that day the Libyans had gone to the guesthouse and said to the people there, 'We are still in al-Qaeda.' That night they returned and tried to take the money because they knew the place it was kept. They tried to open the iron case but they could not, so they took the case and ran from the house. When they tried to jump the high wall of the guesthouse with the heavy iron case, they were not able to and were chased and caught.

LF: Would it be correct to say that al-Qaeda did not suffer the same kind of higher profile splits that some other groups did? It is clear from what you have said that splits occurred, but it is striking that outside closed circles these were not widely known. Until the events of February 2014, that is, with what I think is the first ever public split in the form of a disaffiliation by al-Qaeda's leader Ayman Zawahiri of its Iraq franchise, whose operations and violence in Syria have caused a great deal of conflict and discord.

MH: When Abu Abdullah was alive nobody could say 'I am the real al-Qaeda' because he was still there. Who could say that they were al-

Qaeda and Abu Abdullah was not al-Qaeda when he was the founder, and when Abu Hafs al-Masri was still there and Abu Ubaydah al-Banshiri was still there? Nobody could split like this, but they could leave and try to set up another group, like Abu Musab al-Suri did. He split around 1990 with a group of Syrians. In 2000, he formed a group in Kabul and he took some newer al-Qaeda members that he recruited from al-Qaeda's guesthouses. Because of that, al-Qaeda was angry with him.

In the time of the Taliban, Abu Abdullah had more followers than anyone else. Gamaah Islamiyyah and Tanzim al-Jihad were finished in Egypt, and in Afghanistan they only increased their size a little; for Gamaah Islamiyyah, maybe from ten to thirty. Most groups had either collapsed, or were still very small. That meant Abu Abdullah was winning; at that time he was the only horse left in the race. He had fought against the Soviets, he was fighting in Kabul against Masud and Dostum, he was fighting America, he had big training camps and he did media work calling for jihad, calling for joining al-Qaeda. That means he was doing something while everyone else had been stopped or had not really started; so he looked successful. The groups who appeared weak or defeated were the ones who suffered the most splits during this period.

LF: I was thinking about this in the context of al-Qaeda's recent split with its Iraq franchise, which was initially started by Abu Musab al-Zarqawi, who it supported despite him being a part of the Jalalabad School. To borrow bin Laden's term, al-Qaeda went from being the strong horse after 9/11 to being the group appearing weak in the face of a resurgent Jalalabad School and a new front of jihad from which most of its remaining leadership is conspicuously absent.

MH: Back then Abu Abdullah did not look defeated and he did not look corrupted. Because he hit America, he looked like a hero coming on his horse. But in reality, the Arabs in Afghanistan were riding a bus down the mountain, driven by Abu Abdullah. He pressed on the accelerator and he had no brake. All the youth were shouting at him and encouraging him to go faster, and in the end his jihad against America was a disaster: a disaster for Afghanistan, for the Taliban, for the Arab-Afghans and for al-Qaeda. But we should note the disasters that came to the Arab-Afghans in Afghanistan were not only Abu Abdullah's fault. It is also the fault of those around him, who could see the danger. If everybody had stood up earlier, maybe these disasters would not have happened.

LF: I think that's a valid point, and things might have been very different if more people had stood up; although I question who, or when the influence of the Jalalabad School could have been restrained. It's a question I don't have the answer to and I guess depends in part on whether you can restrain the youth and their impetuousness, which are at once the cause of so much damage in the jihadist milieu but also the engine of jihad, so to speak.

Given bin Laden's strong independent streak, and his own background as a young volunteer in the Afghan jihad, it is paradoxical that he fell victim to letting his programme be dictated in part by the whims of these 'shouting youths' encouraging him to go faster down the mountain, as you put it. Bin Laden was popular; he had his own money, or when this was finished, his own donors. You might reasonably assume he should be immune from being influenced by the whims of the youth, especially after his earlier experience during the Afghan jihad. Still, the youths were dominant and had a big impact on his thinking and actions.

MH: At that time al-Qaeda had no real front of its own for fighting, and the youth liked the big projects such as striking America. So too did Abu Abdullah's donors, which also encouraged him towards projects like this. They liked these projects regardless of whether victory was realistically achievable through these methods. Here, I mean strategic victory, not a tactical victory like a successful attack, but whether you can win a war. They are two very different things, but the youths did not think about that. If their leader gives them a big idea and a big project, they will follow and give their blood for the project. In this way, the youth become very important to a project, and their mood is very influential, even though many are not well educated and have no experience. They just want to see action. That was what it was like for al-Qaeda during this time, and I think it is still like this today.

LF: It was also the case during the Afghan jihad; in fact, arguably bin Laden was one of those impatient youths—although a better-connected, better-financed and educated youth. Still, his impetuousness was characteristic of the youths he later found dictating his own programme.

MH: Yes. Abu Abdullah was influenced a lot by his earlier career as the owner of a contracting company. In this work, he had to work quickly and finish as soon as possible. To do that he needed to take risks, he needed money, and equipment and manpower. Abu Abdullah ran al-Qaeda the same way, but war is not like that because war needs the co-operation of all the people, and the people should be content with the decision to go to war and ready to pay its high price—it is not contracting work.

This was one of the big problems that came from privatising jihad, which began with Abu Abdullah and al-Qaeda, and was a major factor in jihad becoming now like the security contracting companies—the 'blackwatering' of the jihad. The roots of this trace back to the privatisation of the jihad by Abu Abdullah and others, and what then happened in Jalalabad with the 'anything goes' school as you say. Its effects can be seen with what has happened in the Arab world after the Arab Spring; Syria is becoming a clear example.

LF: The legacy of the Arab-Afghan jihad might then be characterised as a dictatorship of sorts—of the young and impetuous, and of an 'anything goes' mentality—which continues to manifest in the conflicts that have emerged in the years since the fall of Afghanistan, and particularly since the spate of revolutions that swept the Arab world. The Taliban do not seem to have been as influenced by, or as dependent upon, the youth and their mood, although one could point to the Pakistan Taliban and some of the violence that has taken place in the name of the Taliban and argue otherwise.

MH: In Afghan society, there are very deep beliefs about respecting elders and their advice, and listening to them and obeying and following them. They do not have a mood for shouting and getting excited unless it is a religious matter or women in danger; but normally they sit and think and take the decision and follow their leaders. Also, the Afghan society, even in times of war, was more stable; the people had ties to the land and their families, and to their tribes and societies. The Arabs did not.

The Arabs were foreigners, and they had no elders there in Afghanistan the way the Afghans did. For the Arabs, there was Abu Abdullah or Azzam. What were they? If you have money anyone can be an authority figure, anybody can make a fatwa. We saw the consequences of this after Jalalabad. Today we can see these consequences too, with the blackwatering of the jihad, mostly between the high-level leaders.

LF: Yes, it seems so. Its impact seems to have been intensified by the disconnectedness of many Arab-Afghans, and the groups they formed in, or operated from, Afghanistan. Obviously, these groups were operating at a geographical distance from their constituency, but the problem seems deeper than physical distance. They were removed from events, from the mood of their countries. As a result, they often held beliefs and announced, or attempted to or planned to enforce, solutions that were not accepted in their homelands, or by the Islamic nation more generally.

MH: The Arab groups had lost their connection to their own lands and people, and they had no connection to Afghanistan either. They did not know their own people and they did not think about the Afghan people. They were also very small in size in Afghanistan, and had minimal support in their home countries—although outside the Arab-Afghan yard few people knew this.

LF: It seems to have been a hallmark of groups based in Afghanistan; they appeared stronger than they were. There was also a tendency on the part of some Arab-Afghans to avoid acknowledging and talking about mistakes, and even differences of opinion. This reinforced the appearance of unity among the groups, despite very real differences between them on the ground. A consequence of this seems to be that lessons were not learned, and damaging behaviour was not stopped. If no one would talk about these things, there was nothing to stop the behaviour from being repeated, or to make sure a lesson was learned.

MH: Yes, it was a common problem, to not talk about the bad things. There was some talking taking place, but it was in closed circles, not on the outside. Nobody liked to say something negative, and so everything was shown as good and positive and shiny until some disaster happened.

LF: By not talking about the problems and mistakes and lessons, while saying, 'we want to be a movement for the people', it seems these groups were acting like a movement of the elite, not only in relation to the people of their own countries, but later also to the Taliban and Afghanistan. For example, the Arab-Afghan groups who did not give Mullah Omar an oath, and who disapproved of Afghan religious practices, seemed to be presenting themselves as an elite—as if they were better.

MH: Among the groups, there was a belief that they must show themselves as ideal; they could be nothing less than ideal. They thought because they were calling for the ideal Islam, they must be ideal. This is a noble goal but humans are not ideal, and we must not be afraid to talk about the negatives, even in our own history. But nobody would discuss this. Instead, everything old was treated as gold. This meant that no one learned from the mistakes of the past.

LF: Everything old being gold is a very accurate description of the Arab-Afghan experience in Afghanistan. Success seems to have led to hubris, with the result being the entire history of the Arab-Afghans, particularly against the Soviets, was cloaked in success, and there was no attention focused on mistakes and learning lessons. It is clear to see the impact focusing only on success had on not learning lessons, particularly from events such as Jaji. Al-Qaeda's failures under bin Laden's leadership came in part because of his focus on success at Jaji, which affected his subsequent thinking and calculations.

MH: Abu Abdullah did not recognise the mistakes of Jaji. He and others came to believe that a superpower could be beaten with a small force in the mountains. After the Battle of Jaji and the Soviet withdrawal from Afghanistan, this is what was said and what people came to believe. Abu Abdullah came to believe it. Because of that, he thought he would defeat America from Tora Bora, and from his efforts at Tora Bora America would withdraw from Afghanistan defeated, as the Soviets had done earlier.

LF: I cannot understand how he or others could think like that; I really can't. I know asymmetrical warfare can be very effective but thinking one battle and one tactical victory in a massive and long-term armed resistance in Afghanistan changed the course of the war ignores so many other factors. Claiming so had good propaganda value, but as history shows at Tora Bora, it was a dangerous basis upon which to plan future operations.

MH: It is difficult to understand how people could take these thoughts and plan with them, but they did. I remember the days when I gave lectures to the boys after the Battle of Jaji. I wrote a memo about what needed to be fixed after Jaji; the mistakes of both sides, lessons learned and things like that. I gave a lecture about that, but I can assure you that although they were sitting there, they were not paying attention. No one was listening.

LF: They were not listening, I presume, because they thought they did not need to—because they had won. The hubris that comes from success at a tactical level and somehow seems to make people think a strategic success has been achieved, fascinates me. It is not restricted to the Arab-Afghans, either, but is common to many fighting forces. Taking a tactical success and claiming strategic victory, or ...

MH: ... taking tactical failures and claiming strategic loss.

LF: Yes. Both sides.

MH: If you are going forward, it does not necessarily mean you are winning. You might be trapped. This happened at Jalalabad in 1989. They took the papers I had written and the warnings of others that the forces were falling into a trap—and they threw them to the wind. They said, 'You are wrong, what wrong are we doing? We are winning.' The Taliban going north to finish Masud's forces in late 2001; this was also a trap.

LF: America in Iraq might also qualify, in terms of how the end of combat operations was declared, yet, the conflict raged on for many years. There are a host of examples from both sides; it really does seem to be a widespread problem. A physical trap, or even a trap of thinking and perceiving events differently to what happens on the ground, is a universal problem in conflict.

MH: America's 'big success' in Afghanistan, even if it is a success, might be a big trap. Even if America is controlling the whole world, is it going to be able to control this forever?

LF: Success or perceiving oneself as successful without looking at mistakes really does have massive consequences for operational and strategic decision-making in any organisation. You can see this looking at al-Qaeda and its history. We have discussed at length the notion of al-Qaeda as an organisation of the three big battles: Jaji, Jalalabad and 9/11 and how bin Laden thought it would only take three strikes to force America out, or draw it into conflict and defeat. Only the first of these battles was successful, but it was the one that drove operational and strategic decision-making, even after the other two had failed. You can see this in bin Laden's planning at Tora Bora in late 2001.

MH: Yes, Abu Abdullah thought, 'America will take three hits and the mission will be accomplished.' So he made three battles against America but the third one finished him and his organisation, and it also wiped out nearly three generations of mujahidin—the first, second and third generations were all finished.

The three hits against America resulted in the first generation being finished. Its effect became weak. Since then ideology has changed, the way of thinking has changed and so too has the way of fighting. Now the youths are fighting everywhere in different ways. It truly is a case of anything goes. While this had existed before al-Qaeda was finished, now there is nothing left to challenge it.

The politics too, are completely different. A big gap now exists between the youth and the few left from the Arab-Afghan generations. There is too much difference between them. There is a new flow and a new direction, and the older generations cannot share strongly or effectively in this. Things like the revolutions in the Arab world; it is a new direction that these older generations were not a part of, so there is a gap between them and the new young generation.

The older generation also feels separated; it is harder for them to make a connection with their societies because they were away from them for years, and many things changed. These older generations had different stories and different lives and now things are new. They cannot work in the area of the old ideology, and they do not understand the new ideology, or the new revolutionary politics.

LF: I am not sure I agree that al-Qaeda's last battle finished the organisation, but it certainly transformed it. I agree the third battle finished what little remained of the original al-Qaeda, although I suspect you would argue that even the original al-Qaeda finished much earlier than 2001. Al-Qaeda, as it existed after it left Afghanistan in late 2001, is a very different organisation to the one of the three battles.

From the perspective of achieving goals, I would say bin Laden won tactically if we define winning by achieving his goal. Why? He wanted to draw America into battle in Afghanistan. He achieved that goal, but strategically he lost. His goal of drawing America in was flawed because he could not defeat it on Tora Bora Mountain. Bin Laden got what he wanted. America came to Afghanistan, but what he thought would come next—that he could win with a small force at Tora Bora—did not happen. Strategically, he lost in terms of what he thought would take place and the positive impact he thought it would have for al-Qaeda.

MH: This strategy of drawing America into Afghanistan was an imagined one and it came very late. It did not come before the action. This talk about drawing America into Afghanistan came when it was known that America was already coming to occupy Afghanistan—which became clear after the forming of the World Islamic Front, the embassy operations and the *Cole* attacks.

Al-Qaeda's early slogan was liberating Saudi Arabia from the Americans and it started its actions about this. These actions by al-Qaeda led to the Americans occupying two other countries, which were Iraq and Afghanistan; and what is the genius in that? The problem of occupation then fell on the shoulders of the people of the two countries of Iraq and Afghanistan, and not al-Qaeda who had no deep roots in either of them.

We should also note war was already coming. The Taliban refused to accept the pipelines of oil and gas through Central Asia, and they ordered opium cultivation to be stopped, both of which angered America, and it was clear then that war was coming.

LF: To me the most striking thing about al-Qaeda's history among the Arab-Afghans was how bin Laden thought the 9/11 attack would change everything in his favour. It would not only draw America into what he thought would be a defeat in the mountains of Tora Bora, but also force unity among the Arab-Afghan groups in Afghanistan under al-Qaeda's leadership. This was a long-held but elusive goal. But unity among the groups was short-lived; it did not last after the Taliban's withdrawal order and America was not defeated in the mountains.

What al-Qaeda's attacks did change was America's perception of terrorism and of al-Qaeda's terrorism in particular. Under the Bush Administration, which was in power at 9/11, terrorism became treated as more than a strategic threat. After 9/11, terrorism, and arguably al-Qaeda, was treated as an existential threat, which neither were. This reaction, however, did not change things in bin Laden's favour, as he perhaps imagined it would. There was a failure of perception on the part of both America under the Bush administration and al-Qaeda under bin Laden's leadership. The Bush administration mistook a massive violent attack as being indicative of a power projection and capability that was repeatable. The consequence was that al-Qaeda was treated as an existential threat, when it was not. Was it a threat? Of course. A big threat? Absolutely. 9/11 was a horrific attack that killed thousands and caused billions of dollars of damage. But it did not jeopardise America's existence.

Al-Qaeda, on the other hand, mistook America's over-reaction, and the treatment of the group as posing an existential threat, as evidence of the country's impending defeat. It was not, as America's projection of force, and the continuation of the war in Afghanistan and elsewhere, shows. In fact, neither side has been defeated fully—but in different ways both sides have failed in their objectives of total victory over, or substantive defeat of the other—and both have been weakened by their efforts to achieve this.

MH: This a very interesting point. Both of them failed because they both thought power will solve the problem; war will solve the problem. You cannot solve problems with war only. I advised Abu Abdullah of this; I said, 'We cannot solve the problem with only war. The people need to know about the problem, we have to explain the problem to them.'

When Abu Abdullah was thinking of his three big operations, I said to him. 'This is not suitable; the programme needs to be on the scale of the Ummah, we need to explain the problem to the Ummah. Once they come to understand it we will have a huge power and we can solve this problem even without firing.' But he depended on his three big operations, believing this would finish things.

America, on the other side, made two offensives, and they will try to make another, and then I think they will be finished. Asia will benefit from this. The Western civilisation is not dominating the world, and this is due to thinking that power and force will solve the problems; but it brings more weakness for the user of the power, and more weakness to those who respond to the user of power. Depending on power and power from the gun only means that eventually you lose your position.

LF: You raise a valid point about power not being solely about the gun, so to speak. Yet, despite bin Laden's plans to defeat America at Tora Bora failing, jihad in the purely militarised sense of the gun and the military work, still seems to dominate. I would argue that is in part because of the response of the West. By treating attacks as war and pursuing a military response, it gave political oxygen to al-Qaeda and gave bin Laden a legitimacy he would not have otherwise had, even among those other groups in Afghanistan.

Others who see benefit in provoking such a response have since emulated his actions. While it is true that an armed retaliation by the West essentially plays into the hands of these groups by providing the reaction the attacks were intended to provoke—it is a short-term reaction. This returns us to our earlier discussion about the distinction between tactical and strategic. It may give a tactical victory, but this is no guarantee of a strategic victory. In my view, what both sides have failed to learn or seem determined to ignore is that at some point politics comes into it. For the groups, this includes political interaction with their enemies or with those they seek to recruit for their support base, or those they claim to be representing or defending.

MH: The Arab groups have lost their jihad causes because everywhere they have gone they have depended on explosions and killing people, without giving attention to awakening and raising the nation, to building a solid foundation and to all the other things needed in order to build an Islamic state.

LF: I also noticed that when they go into areas as foreigners, every conflict is treated the same. As foreign fighters, they do not adapt to fit the areas' local customs and, without fail, there is backlash from the local populations, particularly in tribal areas. This was clear during the time of the jihad against the Soviets, and it continues today.

In my view, a lot of this can be traced to the Jalalabad School. Although such actions were present earlier, the emergence of this School really does seem to have contributed to these ways of thinking that have alienated the groups from the populations they claim to be defending. As conflict has spread into a number of countries, it seems the Jalalabad School has come to influence the thinking of the younger generation of fighters. This legacy has not only endured, but in the time since the end of the Arab-Afghan jihad in Afghanistan, has grown; partly it seems because lessons were not learned. There was no speaking up and speaking out early against damaging behaviour, and the consequences of this are writ large across conflicts that have become more and more violent, until it has become almost like bloodlust for its own sake. The legacy of the 'anything goes' Jalalabad School seems to be that people do not fight with the interest of their cause in mind but for fighting's own sake.

MH: The Jalalabad School is a type of thinking now and the majority of the new generation in many groups, and among the fighters more generally, have this type of nature now. This is the way of thinking of the Jalalabad School and they are too near to takfiris. They rely on weapons, and they militarise the jihad. This means it is only about the gun and the reasons of 'kill or be killed' and a desire to be martyred.

They also have the same hostility to local tribal practices that existed in Jalalabad times—and this same Salafi perspective that they cannot accept anything except their way of thinking and behaving and jihad. It is a matter of killing and fighting continuously without any political aim for the work. They do not realise that war and politics are two sides of the same coin. They do not know or care about the history or habits of the area. Then, we can say one major cause of jihad failing is because it is looked at as solely a military action.

LF: To me the militarisation of jihad comes back to education failures, which we spoke of earlier, and training failures, which have been exacerbated by the rise and infiltration of the Jalalabad School.

MH: A big reason for this is the failure to raise good generals and leaders and the poor nature of the training offered for Arab-Afghans. The training camps involved getting recruits, getting money and building a reputation. When it came to preparation for war, the training was very poor—it was the last thing they focused on, and so the trainees did not perform well. Because they were not trained properly, they did not think properly. As a result, many of the trainees graduated from these camps and undertook actions outside Afghanistan that ended up serving their enemies more than their own cause.

The great powers and the world order needs these groups, and needs them to stay thinking and acting in their destructive ways. These groups might cause some harm to the great powers, but the benefits from these groups behaving like that are very good for the great powers. It might kill some people; tactically it might have some consequences, but strategically it brings a lot of benefit to these powers. These groups are performing an essential role in the global strategic programme of America.

LF: We obviously disagree on this point—as I do not see great power involvement the way you do. But I do see problems with the privatisation of armed conflict and jihad, which is something you have commented on at some length. I think it is more widespread than al-Qaeda and the Jalalabad School; the privatisation of armed conflict in the West is also a big problem.

That is one problem, but the other is the private funding of armed conflict. If we look at the issue of leadership in Arab-Afghan groups and in more recently formed groups, we can see how since Jalalabad anyone can become a leader and rise to power quite quickly—and obtain private funding. Of course, the most recent high-profile example of this was Abu Musab al-Zarqawi in Iraq, and I suspect we might see something similar in Syria, in terms of a leader emerging, and possibly from Libya too. The support infrastructure provided by Gulf financiers has been the elephant in the room in the rise of nearly all groups, and I think in the emergence and spread of the Jalalabad School and its way of thinking.

The result of this is a militarisation of jihad, without restraint, without responsibility, because it essentially becomes a private activity—funded and directed by the elite for their own purposes. In relation to your earlier comment about great powers, arguably the same problem exists in terms of the contracted application of armed violence by private organisations on behalf of great powers. Here too, there are actions that are unaccountable and there is a growing view that great powers themselves are increasingly acting as though they are like these contracted armed bands and can act outside international law.

MH: The jihad project has become privatised. Jihad is no longer an activity carried out by the Ummah; it is jihad led by the rich. I said even before Abu Abdullah was killed, 'We are not sure who is coming because it has become a rule that anyone can make his private jihad.' Abu Abdullah was honest; he was not corruptible, he sacrificed everything and so he was trusted. I am sure in the future other leaders will not be honest and good like he was in this way; because jihad brings money now and has become almost akin to being a soldier of fortune.

I remember many years ago my old friend Abdul Aziz Ali warned the youth about taking jihad as a profession. He said, 'Jihad as a profession brings corruption.' Now we have youths who have done exactly this, they have taken jihad as a profession. They are funded by the rich merchants, they lack the proper education for a mujahid and they think they are fighting for a cause—but really, they are fighting for the objectives of others, and they go from conflict to conflict.

Do you know that virtually no one who fought in the Khost battles for their duration took up jihad as a profession, unlike those who fought in Jalalabad, whose mark still appears in the Arab and international arena? At Khost, there was the group of Abu Harith al-Urduani. His group did not contribute to the work outside Afghanistan in the sense that from his group did not emerge a Salafi jihadi current like the Jalalabad School or a 'Salafi jihadi leader' of the weight of Khattab or Azmarai in Jalalabad, or in the camps of Khaldan and Derunta.

The exception was Abu Musab al-Zarqawi who appeared among Abu Harith's group in the early 1990s, but he was never a permanent member or a senior fighter of Abu Harith's group. And also at that time Abu Musab had a good reputation and was loved. His story in Iraq after the US invasion is known and his direction of thought then was extremist in a way that did not exist in the group of Abu Harith, which was away from religious or political debates. Abu Harith's group was instead focused on military effectiveness, alongside Haqqani's forces, and together they managed to capture an essential military town, which was a feat not performed again during the Afghan war.

LF: I think perhaps the key with Abu Harith's group lies in it not being permanent or a profession—it came together for a limited purpose and when that purpose was over, it finished. Do you think the taking of jihad as a profession would have been lessened if people could have returned home after the jihad against the Soviets, or even after the war of 2001?

Many people did not return to their home countries after the jihad finished because, as I understand it, they feared what would happen to them there. If there had been amnesty programmes in place, do you think more people would have gone home, and because of that history might have been a little different? After the Soviet jihad, were the people who remained the ones who had nowhere else to go, who were, or believed themselves to be, wanted?

MH: Not all, but many were like this, and not just from al-Qaeda. Many people felt they could not return home, and so they went elsewhere.

LF: What do you think would have happened if these people could have gone home?

MH: Very few people intended to stay in Afghanistan, or wanted to go to Sudan, they wanted to go home; nearly everyone wanted to go home. Of course, some wanted to go to other fronts too, but many people wanted to go home and could not. I think if countries had behaved normally with us in 1991 and 1992, 9/11 would never have happened.

LF: I have often wondered whether they decided to stay and fight because they felt that they had been put in a corner, where they thought they had no other options, and could not return to their home countries. I do not think that is a justifiable reason for carrying out violence, but I do think it is something that nonetheless must be acknowledged as taking place and accordingly greater attention paid to it because it is not just a legacy of the Arab-Afghans in Afghanistan. Now with what is happening in the aftermath of the Arab Spring, especially in Libya and Syria, there is a chance this could happen again. It seems the narrative of supporting rebel fighters in Syria, even those not associated with the Jalalabad-esque current, could quickly turn to them being considered enemies.

MH: It is a big problem, and it puts the youth in a desperate situation when they cannot return home. I remember this from the jihad against the Soviets, when we all went from being freedom fighters to criminals. Most of those who fought in Afghanistan were youths who went to fight thinking they were fighting for a fair and just cause, and suddenly they found themselves criminals, chased everywhere. It was then they thought the only thing to do was to continue to fight. They were desperate and they thought there was no hope in any place, and so the only solution was to fight. It was the same after the war in 2001.

Of course, there is blame to be put on leaders of the groups—like Abu Abdullah, and those from the Jalalabad School—for their decisions and the consequences they had. But the main fault is with America because they made benefit from the youth and then they turned them into criminals for their own programme.

LF: Well I disagree here as to where the primary fault lies—I think it lies with the leaders of the groups and those who carried out actions that not only killed innocent people but did so on the basis of an authority they did not have. While you raise a valid point about the turn from freedom fighter to criminal, which caught up many young men, in my view this does not excuse the fault of the groups or young men carrying out acts because they felt trapped. Those who carry out and facilitate violence is where, I think, the primary fault must lie. Certainly though, a mistake was made in the past, which sadly seems to be being repeated in Syria. This needs to be recognised, and fixed.

What I think is often overlooked and also needs to be addressed is the vested interests of financiers who pay to send these youths off to fight and see benefit in funding the youth to go from battle to battle. Many of the people who funded the earlier generations of Arab-Afghans remain involved in financing activities, and in my view, they are more responsible for this 'blackwatering of the jihad', as you call it. In fact, it seems to me that they are very active now, with events after the Arab Spring intensifying, in Libya and Syria in particular.

MH: Yes, maybe they will try to make benefit from the youth in Syria who are too badly influenced by the Jalalabad School. This will not end well: not in Syria, or anywhere else. This is because the experience of the Arab-Afghan youth in Afghanistan produced several amazing results, but unfortunately did not have a consistent impact on the ground. Some aspects not only diminished the positive results, but also left a negative legacy that continues to this day.

This negative legacy could have changed if the history of the Arab-Afghans had been studied, but the Arab experience is immune to attempts to review and learn from history. Instead, there is a tendency for history to be read as confirming the beliefs of Salafis or supporting the actions they have already taken. Lessons were not being learned by those who participated in the jihad, or at any time after. Consequently, mistakes continue to be made, as we are now seeing in Syria and elsewhere across the Arab world; not just from the armed movements, but also from among the Salafi groups like Ikhwan Muslimin and others.

Among the dazzling positive results from the Afghan jihad was the Arab youths' discovery of their combat capability. They had not fought wars before like this, and had trained only to a modest level. The youth were courageous, took big risks and made great sacrifices; and they achieved some excellent results in combat in places like Khost and Jaji. Unfortunately, their successes were not consistent and were impacted upon very badly by negatives.

One of the negatives that emerged from the jihad, and which continues to have severe consequences today, was the tendency for the youth to focus not on success and achieving victory and liberating Afghanistan, but on their desire for martyrdom and to enter paradise. They paid little attention to training and strategy, and did not learn how to use their sacrifices in the pursuit of victory over the enemy, and achieving political objectives. This trend continued beyond the Afghan conflict. It produced very negative results because a focus on martyrdom as the goal of participation in combat means that participation became individual, instead of for the benefit of the group or the country where the fight for liberation is taking place. This desire for martyrdom and the rise of a sentiment that nothing matters in war except for retaliation has come to result in suicide operations against civilian targets. It has also resulted in an increase in brutality that has reached the level of bragging in front of the camera while carrying out horrific violent acts.

Concluding reflections

MH: In Afghanistan, the ideological control of the Salafi Wahhabis over armed groups was consolidated, and has since expanded and come to dominate Salafi jihadi yards around the world. This has led to grave consequences for the people of the countries in which these groups operate, not only most recently in Syria, but everywhere they have gone. Chechnya was the first victim at the hands of Khattab, from the Jalalabad School, whose reckless adventure in Dagestan resulted in the Russian re-occupation of Chechnya in 1999. Afghanistan was also a victim at the hands of the Salafi jihadi leader Abu Abdullah, whose actions led to the re-occupation of Afghanistan, an occupation in Iraq, the destruction of these two countries, and tens of thousands of deaths and countless pains for their peoples. Iraq suffered too at the hands of the Salafi jihadi commander, Abu Musab al-Zarqawi, who shifted from fighting against the American occupiers to sectarian fighting between the Sunnis and the Shia that turned Iraq into a failed state and left its people in a miserable condition.

In Libya, the people undertook a revolution, but the Salafi intervention caused infighting within society, destroyed the economy and returned the state to tribal feuding, which made it vulnerable to foreign intervention. In Syria, the Salafi intervention diverted attention away from the revolution and was the cause of the sectarian war that has now led to regional and international intervention, turning Syria into the ruins of a state.

After the revolution in Egypt, Ikhwan Muslimin and their Salafi and jihadi allies assumed the pinnacle of power when their candidate Muhammad Morsi was elected president. They quickly alienated the people because they wanted the state to operate in their Salafi ways. The people rallied against them, and the military returned to power. This was in the interests of America because Egypt returned to its same old strategic directions that the Americans wanted and that the people had revolted against the first time. In reality, what this meant was the Ikhwan–Salafi alliance alienated the people so badly that they not only revolted against them, but they did so knowing they would return to power the regime they had revolted against earlier.

It was in Afghanistan that the elements came together and formed the working mechanisms for the Salafi Wahhabi jihadi current to dominate, as it continues to do today. These elements were: (1) international cover from America; (2) regional cover from Israel; (3) Salafi Wahhabi cover from the scholars of Saudi Arabia and the Gulf; (4) young and ambitious leaders in the Salafi jihadi groups; (5) open fronts for fighting; (6) supplies of money and weapons; and (7) training camps.

Here we must note the availability of Salafi Wahhabi cover means that the first and second elements, regional and international cover, are already plentiful. This is because the Salafi Wahhabi cover provided by the scholars is only possible with international and regional approval, by which I mean the approval of the Saudi regime and the other Gulf petro-states and the Americans and Israelis. The existence of this third element also guarantees the automatic inclusion of the sixth element—the supply of money and arms. The fourth element—young and ambitious youth—cannot also be possible without Salafi Wahhabi scholars; they rally the youth.

These, in fact, were the conditions for the development of the Jalalabad School in the time of the Afghan jihad, which has since spread all over the world. The Jalalabad School was allowed to emerge because it was thought it would weaken al-Qaeda and break the dominance of Abu Abdullah and because of the new phenomenon of forming a multinational Salafi jihadi group, which they called 'global jihad'. I first heard this term in 1988. It made me feel uneasy because not only was it an unusual formulation in the Salafi yard, but it also had very big political implications, which those who supported this new current were unaware of. It was my thought the Arabs were being pushed along a dangerous path that did not benefit them or suit their causes.

All of the jihadi groups that arrived in Afghanistan from the outside were national in character and attached to a specific activity in their homeland. Although their Salafi ideology referred to the *Ummah*, in practice it was nationally focused. There was a lot of talk of the *Ummah* but practically they worked for their own countries, except for Abu Abdullah, who formed his group as a group of the *Ummah*. From the beginning, it was multinational.

Of course, al-Qaeda was not the only international group in the Salafi yard. Ikhwan Muslimin was international too; but it was international in a different way. Ikhwan Muslimin had national branches that came together to form an international union. Abu Abdullah accepted youth from everywhere and so was more international than Ikhwan Muslimin. Salafi thought infiltrated into the ideology of most of the Muslim Brotherhood, as a result of its flight from Egypt, fearing the wrath of Abdul Nasser. It found sanctuary and stability in Saudi Arabia and the Gulf states, which had great wealth, and Ikhwan became close ideologically and politically with the Wahhabis.

This history meant Ikhwan Muslimin's political experience was far more mature than the Salafi jihadi groups, which consisted mostly of youth with little experience but great enthusiasm. But the Salafi jihadis ultimately won the competition for the youth in the Afghan jihad. This was because of their enthusiastic character, and the fact that their groups were filled with enthusiastic and impulsive youth who offered action where Ikhwan Muslimin offered only restrictions.

These Salafi jihadi movements received large numbers of young volunteers who were ready to take risks, happy to move from front to front, and had little time for education and reflection, particularly in the political arena. They were of a fast changing mood and did what they imagined was right in that moment. They did not look forward, or backward to see what could be learned or done.

During the Afghan war, some Salafi jihadi groups managed to succeed in extending their links into the Gulf, and found sources of funding from countries that were beneficiaries of the oil wealth. This brought Salafi and Wahhabis together, which reduced the gap between them and the Ikhwan Muslimin in these areas. But despite growing closer in some areas, the Salafi Ikhwan Muslimin remained in competition with the

Salafi jihadis, who ultimately won. These Salafi jihadi organisations were filled with youth who pushed back against any restrictions, and were characterised by mobility and boldness. Ikhwan Muslimin could not bridge the gap between them because it did not have young cadres who could play a leading role in the Salafi jihadi organisations.

Among these youth, there was a saying that the Ikhwan Muslimin 'was a big refrigerator for the youth'. By that, they meant it was a big power in arresting and freezing their energy. They thought the leadership of Ikhwan Muslimin was too rigid and restrictive. What they said was true. Ikhwan Muslimin not only lacked young leaders, but how could they lead a group that wanted to fight when they were against such fighting—not because they were against fighting in principle, but because it was against their political interests.

The youth knew this and so Ikhwan Muslimin always lost the race with the Salafi jihadis in times of armed crises, as happened in Afghanistan during the jihad against the Soviets, and as is happening now in Syria where we see the Afghan scene repeated. Interestingly now, it seems that al-Qaeda has become in Syria a little like what Ikhwan Muslimin was during the Afghan conflict. By this I mean that some of the youth view it was being too restrictive and instead are drawn towards the Jalalabad School groups. Of course the situation is not identical, but still there is a similarity in the situation al-Qaeda now finds itself in, having won the race against Ikhwan so many years ago. It is now the older, more 'moderate' or 'conservative' group, losing the youth to a younger, more radical and uncontrollable current that has emerged from the conflict.

In Syria too, like in Afghanistan, the Salafi jihadis control the field and the fighting, and Ikhwan Muslimin dominates the money supply and most of the media. During the Afghan jihad, Ikhwan Muslimin was able to control the Afghan aid work and facilitation of those going to fight on the Afghan fronts. Ikhwan Muslimin supported Azzam in Peshawar with money and propaganda of such order that he effectively worked for them. Azzam had been an old member of the Ikhwan Muslimin but he resigned in protest at its passivity towards the question of Palestine and its leaving the Palestinian resistance to be led by secular groups. He continued to show his allegiance to the ideological line of Ikhwan Muslimin, although he did not hide his criticism of them at times.

Azzam further announced himself as a real Salafi when he declared his hatred of the Shia and when he supported the tribes in the North

West Frontier Province in Pakistan in fighting the Shia. He made speeches on this issue, which were mentioned in books made by his followers. In these speeches, Azzam supported Sunnis fighting against Shia, and he allowed the youth from Sadda to join those fighting the Shia in the tribal areas.

It can be said that Azzam had a very big influence on the Salafi jihadi trend, although it did not inherit his focus on Palestine. Azzam was unique in his call for the transfer of the Arab-Afghan experience to Palestine, which he tried to do via his Sadda camp. Salafi jihadi organisations claimed this goal was not possible without first going through the Arab capitals and replacing the systems there with Islamic rule. Azzam's way of thinking was the most dominant among the Arab-Afghans until the rise of Abu Abdullah and al-Qaeda, after which time his influence dropped. It decreased some more after the Soviet withdrawal and the formation of the second interim Afghan government in early 1989, which he supported, but which did not meet Salafi requirements. Azzam supported the government because Sayyaf, the head of Ikhwan Muslimin in Afghanistan was to be prime minister. The Salafi Arabs in Peshawar said that Azzam was responsible for the frustration that hit the hopes of the Arab mujahidin.

Azzam's influence also reduced because of Maktab al-Khadamat's errors in directing aid to the Afghan fronts and overspending in the wrong areas. These reasons were also one of the primary causes of the emergence of Abu Abdullah. He took affairs into his own hands to assist the Afghan mujahidin, and to organise the fighting of the Arabs in Afghanistan, without going through the Ikhwan Muslimin administrators in Peshawar, or the various Afghan parties there. Then he began to build a base on a mountain site in Jaji; and it was after the Battle of Jaji that Abu Abdullah changed from wanting to build a fighting force in Afghanistan to building a fighting force for every place. That force was al-Qaeda.

Looking back on what happened in Peshawar during the emergence of many Salafi jihadi groups, including al-Qaeda, it is clear it was a kind of revolt against Ikhwan Muslimin's distance from combat. Ikhwan Muslimin called for fighting in the way of Allah and attracted young people from all around the world, but would not allow its own to fight. The reason it avoided being involved in any direct action was a fear of what national governments would think of its intentions for armed action within their own countries. This left the arena completely open for a revolt by the youth and for the emergence of the Salafi jihadi groups, including al-Qaeda.

Al-Qaeda later too suffered from a similar revolt. Abu Abdullah's focus on building a group to fight everywhere meant that after Jaji, al-Qaeda turned away from direct participation in hostilities to just training. The Jalalabad battle was the exception. Abu Abdullah engaged in the Jalalabad fight with all of his power, followed by almost all of the Arab-Afghan community. After the failure of that battle, he withdrew to focus the full force of his attention on training and preparation activities for fighting everywhere, although he never specified against whom or where this would take place.

In fact, the ambiguity of Abu Abdullah and al-Qaeda's goals weakened its competitiveness against the national Salafi jihadi organisations who had all declared their areas of focus, and against the other groups who emerged around Jalalabad. Al-Qaeda was very weakened during this period as most of its members left the group and went to these Salafi jihadi organisations.

Al-Qaeda had the largest training camps inside Afghanistan in both the Afghan jihad era and then later during the time of the Taliban. It was open to the field of training—and although this made it popular, it lacked its own front for fighting. During the Afghan jihad, after al-Qaeda withdrew from Jalalabad there was no front, and then during the time of the Taliban there was no fully controlled front, like there was in Jaji or Jalalabad. This weakened al-Qaeda because the organisation that had a training camp and an open front had the largest number of new members or donors.

Al-Qaeda met with strong competition from other jihadist groups who had both a camp and a front, especially the newcomers in Jalalabad, among them many national organisations. It faced severe competition from Khattab who went on to have a front in Tajikistan and after that in Chechnya, while al-Qaeda was busy in Sudan making roads and cultivating land. In Bosnia, al-Qaeda did not participate, while Gamaah Islamiyyah of Egypt shared heavily in events there. Tanzim al-Jihad of Egypt also shared in Chechnya while al-Qaeda did not; except some individuals who went by themselves, exactly like the Ikhwan youth did in Afghanistan in the 1980s.

These fronts and other groups that emerged strongly from Jalalabad became rivals to al-Qaeda. They were characterised by their mobility, the young age of much of their leadership, their often-impetuous decision-making and willingness to fight. In contrast, al-Qaeda at that time had fallen prey to the rigidity of leadership under one man, and had no fighting front in Afghanistan or elsewhere. The new groups in Jalalabad and Khost became more popular because they were involved in the fighting in Afghanistan or, later, elsewhere.

However, it was not only the Jalalabad School that attracted the youth away from al-Qaeda. It was also Abu Harith al-Urduani. His 'School' was the most important in sharing in the direct course of the Afghan war, but the least influential in the Salafi jihadi yard. Abu Harith's School did not have its own training camp, but was dependent on Sadda and Khaldan camps. Untrained volunteers were not accepted, and these two camps were the only ones where the youth could train outside of the influence of any organisation.

What Abu Harith did have was an open front and an excellent reputation among the youth for fighting. His group had no real ideological position of its own, or no political position, except for the liberation of Afghanistan. It was a combat group only, and it was temporary. Its reason for existing was to fight in Afghanistan until the Soviets withdrew and to work in a support role for the Afghans, which Abu Harith did excellently, especially in his work with Haqqani. This is one of the most important reasons why Abu Harith's 'School' ended when the Afghan war finished; there was no purpose beyond fighting the Soviet withdrawal. Abu Harith and his group members did not tie themselves to a future vision or a new role outside of Afghanistan. The Salafi jihadi mujahidin thought this was a shame and a waste and a shortcoming of Abu Harith's approach. In fact, one of Abu Harith's deputies was influenced by this sentiment, and launched a coup against him to continue fighting. He aligned himself with Hekmatyar, and joined the civil war around Kabul, but he was killed and the rest of the group dissolved.

Abu Harith did not like politics and all of the issues around it, and he was only focused on Afghanistan's liberation. He also did not like the Afghan parties, with the exception of Yunis Khalis, and he did not trust Islamic groups like Ikhwan Muslimin, even though his father was one of the Ikhwan leaders in Jordan. Abu Harith's School was active in some of the most important military operations of the Afghan war, which decided the fate of the regime in Kabul. It therefore had great but limited influence. The most famous name associated with Abu Harith's group was Abu Musab al-Zarqawi, although he came late to the war, and was not a permanent member. Later, he ended up being influenced too badly by the Jalalabad School.

We can conclude that the Jalalabad School was the most important of the Arab-Afghan schools in Afghanistan. Its working methods and ideological positions are the most common among the Salafi jihadist groups and movements around the world. Many of the youth who went on to form their own camps in Jalalabad had trained in the camps of Abu Abdullah or Azzam, and then went on to create their own camps and fronts at Jalalabad in co-operation with the Afghan groups, and with financial and religious support from the Gulf.

Among the names in the Jalalabad School was Osama Azmarai who received encouragement from Sayyaf to form an Arab group in that region. Azmarai was a Saudi, and his was among the first groups to have been involved in direct action against America after the end of the war in Afghanistan. Another of the founders of the Jalalabad School and one of its biggest symbols was Khattab, who was also a Saudi. He worked in Tajikistan and then in Chechnya and rose to a great level of fame.

Abdul Hadi al-Iraq was also a part of the Jalalabad School and trained in a camp established by the Iraqi Ikhwan Muslimin after 1990; so too was Ramzi Yousef and Khalid Shaykh Muhammad, who both became famous because of their operations in America against The World Trade Center. The Jalalabad School pioneered attacking America and planted the idea of 9/11 with Abu Abdullah. The bulk of the planning and most of the work originated from this School. Al-Qaeda's role mostly came later with funding and training. In that way, 9/11 can be considered as the infiltration of the Jalalabad School into al-Qaeda and shows the Jalalabad School's impact at the international level has been far greater than al-Qaeda's.

Abu Zubaydah and Ibn Shaykh al-Libi, who took over the Khaldan camp, were also a part of this School. Khaldan came to be popular after the Pakistani authorities made it difficult to get to Jalalabad after the killing of a United Nations staff member at the hands of trainees at one of the camps there. They moved to Khaldan instead, where cadres from Salafi jihadi movements, including those in Algeria, China, Bosnia and Chechnya, were trained. A huge effort was made at this camp to teach the youth the ideas in the writings of Dr Fadl, the former commander of Tanzim al-Jihad of Egypt.

The current at Khaldan was more extreme than al-Qaeda and some other groups. It was close to the Salafi Wahhabi current and operated with Salafi Wahhabi cover and with the blessing of scholars. While the Arab-Afghans had this blessing during the first Afghan jihad, and so too did the Jalalabad School, it is significant that this blessing was not given for the second Afghan jihad against the Americans. The scholars gave their blessing to the Chechen and Bosnian conflicts in the early 1990s, but not the second Afghan jihad against the Americans. These same scholars now bless the Salafi jihadi mujahidin in Syria in their sectarian fighting, and before them, blessed the Salafi jihadi mujahidin in Iraq when they switched from fighting the Americans to sectarian fighting against the Shia.

In general, the Wahhabi and Salafi scholars and the organisations they bless are orientated to fight on a purely religious basis against non-Muslims and then on a purely sectarian basis against the Shia or Sufi. Declaring people *kafir* is an important step for those organisations to get a legitimate blessing to fight, so the first step before the start of the war is to make *takfir* and declare people *kafir*. The Islamic state in their conception is one that must fight the infidel influence and the most important enemies of the Wahhabis, which are the Sufi and the Shia, and to fight them permanently. This state of permanent warfare leads to weakness and external interference and that is to the benefit of America.

The Salafi Wahhabi conception of an Islamic state is removed from any local social or political context. The result has been that the groups who have tried to introduce Islamic states in this manner have not been able to gain the support of the people in their country of origin, or the country in which they are fighting. This is because the people of the land do not care for this focus on just Shariah and on fighting their enemies. They care about having food to eat, having freedom, dignity, social justice and security. They have immediate needs, and so their priorities are different. So too is their understanding of the purpose of jihad and the Islamic concept of a state, and even their understanding of Shariah. The willingness of Salafi jihadis to kill the people of these countries for violations of Shariah or to deny them their perceptions or activities, which they regard as fundamental religious beliefs, turns them against these groups. The Salafi jihadis are rigid on these points; they do not accept nor even try to understand that there might be circumstances that prevent the people from having a better understanding.

Because Salafi jihadi organisations are focused on these things, they easily veer into battles that punish the people of the land and bring down a great disaster upon them. This happened in Afghanistan, Chechnya and Iraq; in fact, in every country these groups have operated in. Even when these groups returned to their home countries, which saw popular revolutions, they could not accept the objectives of the people who brought about these revolutions because they were not in line with Salafi Wahhabi thought. The result has been that not only are these groups losing on the battlefield, they are losing on the Arab street.

The popular uprisings in the countries of the Arab Spring proved an amazing fact: that the people have the ability to bring about a change of regime with minimal losses and minimal violence, and to display their basic demands clearly. This brings into question the claims the underground secret organisations make about their methods, and the need for them to be isolated from the people and the '*jahiliyyat*', as Sayyid Qutb put it. The Arab Spring also brought into question al-Qaeda's methods, and its claim that political change can only be achieved in the Arab world by bombings carried out against America by an organised elite military group.

In Egypt, some Salafi groups did take part in the revolution, like the 'Salafi politicians' Ikhwan, and even some from among the Salafi jihadis. But they took part only after they hesitated for a long time. Then they jumped to the front rows and formed Salafi political parties or allied on a subcontracted basis with Ikhwan Muslimin who received American approval to:

1. come to power; and
2. form an alliance with groups the Americans previously described as terrorists.

Qatar and the Saudis supported this agreement and opened the petrodollar funding pipeline. In return, the leaders of the Ikhwan Muslimin–Salafi alliance gave reassurances to them, to the Americans and Israelis, and to international banks, that they would prevent a true revolution of social justice taking place, meaning the equitable distribution of national wealth. This type of revolutionary goal terrifies the Gulf States more than it terrifies the Americans.

Ikhwan Muslimin and their Salafi and Salafi jihadi allies brought these reassurances to life with a policy of verbal and physical aggression and the use of religious edicts against anyone who tried to bring about these true goals of social justice. They turned any political dispute into a religious one, and they tried to impose their priorities and vision of a state onto the people of the revolution. After Ikhwan Muslimin came to power, the people found there was no significant change in their conditions, which in fact continued to deteriorate. Meanwhile, Ikhwan Muslimin and the groups allied with them contented themselves with shouting Islamic slogans and making threats of violence and intimidation. They relied on the people responding to these religious slogans and forgetting their needs and the misery of their life as their conditions deteriorated. But this did not happen. The people realised what had happened and why their conditions were not improving and turned against them. As infighting grew, more problems emerged. Ikhwan Muslimin and their Salafi and Salafi jihadi allies added new tensions, which were caused by their own religious perceptions. New violence took place against non-Muslims, and secularists were also added to the category of those they considered infidels, and then they turned against the Shia and the Sufi.

What the people in Egypt and in other countries of the Arab Spring have learned is that it is impossible to achieve the political, economic and social goals of the revolution in places where Salafi Wahhabis are present. As long as Salafi Wahhabis, both political and jihadi, are involved and have strong and effective support and political cover from the Gulf oil states, and international and regional cover, they will continue to be an obstacle. The revolutions in the Arab world were to change the lives of the people away from misery and backwardness and repression.

Ultimately, it seems Arab peoples will not be to move forward while Salafi Wahhabism is a key obstacle preventing their access to natural human rights, as described in the first slogans of Egypt's revolution against the American- and Israeli-supported rule of Mubarak: bread, freedom, social justice and human dignity. In this way, the events of the Arab Spring and its aftermath have announced the complete failure of the Islamist project, which in part grew in the soil of Egypt from the hands of Sayyid Qutb, and in Afghanistan from the hands of Azzam, Abu Abdullah and the Jalalabad School. This failure is clearly visible in people's loss of sympathy for the Islamists—and in Egypt, this took only one year.

EPILOGUE

We did not write this book for our peers, but for future generations. When we began we both understood that our co-operation was likely to earn us attacks from all sides. To some, it may seem a moral anathema to cooperate with 'the enemy', even if only on a book. There are some, too, who may not see in this book cooperation towards the shared goal of breaking down myths and building a more accurate historical record, but instead, perhaps made uncomfortable by such cooperation, will question our intent and the accuracy of information we have put forward. It would be a shame if discomfort at such unique cooperation coloured perceptions in such a manner. However, in the event of such charges, our book speaks for itself. Moreover, both of us are already known for our careful attention to detail and for being outspoken in our desire to see myths corrected and accurate information presented.

Most importantly, however, our book shows it is possible for 'enemies' to engage in dialogue, and that if you look, you can find common ground. In fact, by finding some common ground in the process of writing this book, we have somehow managed to wander into no-man's land. We no longer see each other as the enemy, and as such, find ourselves on a journey into uncharted territory. It is our hope others might join us, but if we find ourselves the only ones on this journey, we are comforted with the knowledge we have produced a document for future generations that testifies to the possibility of dialogue, and contributes to the historical record a detailed discussion of this important period and its ongoing legacy. We humbly hope our contribution gives younger generations knowledge, understanding and a desire to reach out and talk; and in doing so, helps to prevent the loss and shattering of more lives.

NOTES

1. INTRODUCING MUSTAFA HAMID

1. Hamid, Mustafa, *Cross Over Kandahar Sky*, 2006, p. 201. http://www.4shared.com/file/15220171/c1e49341/__.html
2. A list of works can be found on Mustafa Hamid's webpage. See http://www.mustafahamed.com/?page_id=558. Some of Hamid's books were obtained by American forces and translated, and can be found on the website of The Combatting Terrorism Centre at West Point. They are catalogued under the name Abu al-Walid al-Misri. See http://www.ctc.usma.edu/programs-resources/harmony-program
3. Muhammad, Basil, *Arab Supporters in Afghanistan*, 2nd edn, Jeddah: House of Learning Printing Press Co., 1991.
4. Al-Suri, Abu Musab, *The Global Islamic Resistance Call*, 2004. http://www.fsboa.com/vw/files/books/2005/mqdoc.zip (site no longer active).
5. See e.g.: al-Zawahiri, Ayman, *Knights under the Prophet's Banner*, 2001. http://rapidshare.de/files/1450673/Knights_Under_the_Proph_11A.pdf.html (site no longer active); and al-Zawahiri, Ayman, *A Treatise on the Exoneration of the Nation of the Pen and Sword on the Denigrating Charge of Being Irresolute and Weak*, 2008, www.fas.org/irp/dni/osc/exoneration.pdf
6. Al-Bahri, Nasser and Georges Malbrunot, *In the Shadow of bin Laden*, Neuilly-sur-Seine: Michel Lafon, 2010.
7. Bin laden, Najwa, Omar bin Laden and Jean Sasson, *Growing up Bin Laden: Osama's Wife and Son Take Us Inside their Secret World*, New York: St. Martin's Press, 2009.
8. Farrall, Leah, 'Detentions Come Back to Bite', *The Australian*, 16 Sep. 2009, http://www.theaustralian.com.au/opinion/detentions-come-back-to-bite/story-e6frg6zo-1225774092712; Hamid, Mustafa, 'The US Soldier in Afghanistan—The First Step for the Release of all Prisoners of the War on Terror', *Sleepwalkers*, 2009, http://www.4shared.com/get/k1roUU_P/__12.html
9. Farrall, Leah, 'Abu Walid al-Masri Renews his Links with Taliban', All Things Counter Terrorism, 9 Oct. 2009, http://www.allthingscounterterrorism.com/2009/10/09/abu-walid-al-masri-renews-his-links-with-the-taliban/

10. Hamid, Mustafa, 'Online Dialogues', *Mafa*, 2010, http://web.archive.org/web/20120319070410/http://mafa.maktoobblog.com/category/%D8%AD%D9%88%D8%A7%D8%B1%D8%A7%D8%AA-%D9%85%D9%81%D8%AA%D9%88%D8%AD%d8%A9/ and Farrall, Leah, 'My Dialogue with Abu Walid al-Masri', All Things Counter Terrorism, http://www.allthingscounterterrorism.com/my-dialogue-with-abu-walid-al-masri/

2. THE ARAB-AFGHAN JIHAD

1. Muhammad, Basil, *Arab Supporters in Afghanistan*, 2nd edn, Jeddah: House of Learning Printing Press Co., 1991, p. 11.
2. Ibid., p. 49. See also al-Suri, Abu Musab, *The Global Islamic Resistance Call*, 2004, p. 714, http://www.fsboa.com/vw/files/books/2005/mqdoc.zip (site no longer active); and Anas cited in Bergen, Peter, *The Osama Bin Laden I Know: A History of Al-Qaeda's Leader*, New York: Simon and Schuster, 2006, p. 41.
3. Yousaf, Mohammad and Mark Adkin, *Afghanistan: The Bear Trap*, Barnsley: Leo Cooper, 1992.
4. Ibid.
5. See e.g., ibid., pp. 55–8, 62, 64.
6. Ibid., p. 20.

3. EARLY TRAINING AND TALIBAN ORIGINS

1. Muhammad, Basil, *Arab Supporters in Afghanistan*, 2nd edn, Jeddah: House of Learning Printing Press Co., 1991, pp. 98–9.
2. 'Formal Request to Integrate Pakistan Officers in Anti-Soviet Jihad (original language)', West Point: The Combating Terrorism Centre, Harmony Database—Document No. AFGP-2002–008588–13, http://www.ctc.usma.edu/posts/formal-request-to-integrate-pakistan-officers-in-anti-soviet-jihad-original-language

4. TWO MEMOS AND AN IDEA THAT SPREAD: THE REAL ORIGINS OF MAKTAB AL-KHADAMAT

1. Muhammad, Basil, *Arab Supporters in Afghanistan*, 2nd edn, Jeddah: House of Learning Printing Press Co., 1991, p. 31. See also Deraz, Essam, *The Lion's Den of Ansar, the Arab Supporters in Afghanistan*, http://www.jehad.net/ansar.zip (site no longer active).
2. Al-Shafey, Mohammed, 'Asharq Al-Awsat Interviews Umm Mohammed: The Wife of Bin Laden's Spiritual Mentor', *Asharq Al-Awsat*, 30 Apr. 2006, http://www.aawsat.net/2006/04/article55266896
3. Muhammad, *Arab Supporters in Afghanistan*, pp. 71–5.
4. Ibid., p. 75.

5. JAJI AND THE ESTABLISHMENT OF AL-MASADAH

1. Muhammad, Basil, *Arab Supporters in Afghanistan*, 2nd edn, Jeddah: House of Learning Printing Press Co., 1991, p. 89.
2. Ibid., pp. 86–100.
3. Ibid., p. 98.
4. Ibid., p. 97.
5. Ibid.
6. Ibid.
7. Ibid., p. 90.
8. Ibid.
9. Ibid., pp. 98–9.
10. Ibid., p. 97.
11. Ibid., pp. 98–9.
12. Hamid, Mustafa, *The Rock Gate Battles*, 2006, pp. 259–60, http://www.mediafire.com/download/yw46eo3qcg3hqo6/Battles-of-The-rocky-Gate-book2.rar
13. Muhammad, *Arab Supporters in Afghanistan*, p. 137.
14. Hamid, *The Rock Gate Battles*, pp. 259–60.

6. CONFUSED ORIGINS: AL-QAEDA'S POST-JAJI EMERGENCE AND THE ARAB ADVISORY COUNCIL

1. Fitzgerald, Patrick, 'Government's Evidentiary Proffer Supporting the Admissibility of Co-Conspirator Statements', United States of America v. Enaam Arnaout, No. 02 CR892, United States District Court, Northern District of Illinois, Eastern Division, 6 Jan. 2003, pp. 21, 34–7, http://news.findlaw.com/wsj/docs/bif/usarnaout10603prof.pdf
2. 'Finding Aid: TareekhOsama 122–123', in Berger, J.M. (ed.), *Beatings and Bureaucracy: The Founding Memos of Al-Qaeda*, Intelwire Press, 2012, Kindle pp. 119–51.
3. 'Finding Aid: TareekhOsama 127–127a', in Berger, *Beatings and Bureaucracy*, Kindle pp. 229–77.
4. 'Finding Aid: TareekhOsama 128–135', in Berger, *Beatings and Bureaucracy*, Kindle pp. 163–218.
5. 'Finding Aid: TareekhOsama 91', in Berger, *Beatings and Bureaucracy*, Kindle pp. 295–343. 'Finding Aid: Tareekh Osama 93', in Berger, *Beatings and Bureaucracy*, Kindle pp. 280–90.
6. '[Al-Qaeda "Founding" Minutes]', Intelwire, p. 1, http://intelfiles.egoplex.com/1988–08–11-founding-of-al-qaeda.pdf
7. '[Al-Qaeda "Founding" Minutes]', Intelwire, p. 3, http://intelfiles.egoplex.com/1988–08–11-al-Qaeda-founding.pdf
8. 'Finding Aid: TareekhOsama 127–127a', in Berger, *Beatings and Bureaucracy*, Kindle pp. 229–77, and 'Finding Aid: TareekhOsama 128–135', in Berger, *Beatings and Bureaucracy*, Kindle pp. 163–218.

9. 'Finding Aid: TareekhOsama 122–123', in Berger, *Beatings and Bureaucracy*, Kindle pp. 119–50.
10. Wright, Lawrence, *The Looming Tower*, New York: Alfred A. Knopf, 2006, p. 131.
11. Ibid., pp. 131–4.
12. 'Finding Aid: TareekhOsama 127–127a', in Berger, *Beatings and Bureaucracy*, Kindle pp. 229–77, and 'Finding Aid: TareekhOsama 128–135', in Berger, *Beatings and Bureaucracy*, Kindle pp. 163–218.
13. Ibid.
14. Ibid.
15. Ibid.
16. 'Finding Aid: TareekhOsama 127–127a', in Berger, *Beatings and Bureaucracy*, Kindle p. 231.
17. 'Finding Aid: TareekhOsama 128–135', in Berger, *Beatings and Bureaucracy*, Kindle pp. 163–218.
18. Ibid., p. 175.
19. Ibid., p. 193.
20. 'Finding Aid: TareekhOsama 127–127a', in Berger, *Beatings and Bureaucracy*, Kindle p. 266.
21. Ibid., pp. 258–69.
22. Ibid., p. 269.
23. '[Al-Qa'eda Members List]', West Point: The Combatting Terrorism Center, Harmony Database—Document No. AFGP-2002–600177, p. 1, http://www.ctc.usma.edu/wp-content/uploads/2012/05/AFGP-2002–600177-Trans.pdf
24. 'Finding Aid: TareekhOsama 127–127a', in Berger, *Beatings and Bureaucracy*, Kindle pp. 229–77.
25. Ibid.
26. 'Direct Testimony of Jamal Ahmed Al-Fadl', United States of America v. Usama Bin Laden, et al., Defendants; S(7)98 Cr.1023, 158: United States District Court, Southern District of New York, 6 Feb. 2001, p. 210, http://fl1.findlaw.com/news.findlaw.com/cnn/docs/binladen/binladen20601tt.pdf
27. Ibid., p. 206.
28. '[Al-Qaeda Employment Contract]', West Point: The Countering Terrorism Center, Harmony Database—Document No. AFGP-2002–6000045, p. 2, https://www.ctc.usma.edu/wp-content/uploads/2010/08/AFGP-2002-600045-Trans.pdf
29. Muhammad, Basil, *Arab Supporters in Afghanistan*, 2nd edn, Jeddah: House of Learning Printing Press Co., 1991, pp. 84–5.
30. 'Finding Aid: TareekhOsama 127–127a', in Berger, *Beatings and Bureaucracy*, Kindle p. 249.
31. Hamid, Mustafa, *Betrayal on the Road*, 2006, pp. 65, 89–90, http://www.4shared.com/file/15213908/ac7f39a4/__.html See also al-Yamani, Mustafa, 'Conflict within the Arab Leaders, Peshawar', *Afghanistan … Memories of the Occupation*, 28 June 2008, http://tokhaleej.jeeran.com/archive/6/597601.html (site no longer active).

32. Hamid, *Betrayal on the Road*, p. 65.
33. Wright, *The Looming Tower*, p. 135.
34. Ibid., pp. 136–7.
35. 'Abdulla Azzam Arbitration 1, Finding Aid: Al Tahdi 88–1 and Abdulla Azzam Arbitration 1 Finding Aid: Al Tahdi 88–5', in Berger, *Beatings and Bureaucracy*, Kindle pp. 783–1045.
36. Ibid.
37. Faraj, Ayman Sabri, *Memoirs of an Afghan Arab: Abu Jafar Al Masri Al-Kandahari*, pp. 25–41. http://www.4shared.com/file/131645895/50da1395/Memories_of_Arab_Afghans.html
38. Harun, Fadil, *The War Against Islam: The Story of Fadil Harun, Part 1. 2009*, p. 64, https://www.ctc.usma.edu/v2/wp-content/uploads/2013/10/The-Story-of-Fazul-Harun-Part-1-O.pdf
39. Hamid, Mustafa, *Big Folly or Goat's War?* 2006, pp. 7–8, http://www.4shared.com/file/36078879/f3bf3b88/4_online.html
40. Ibid., pp. 7–8.
41. Abas, Nasir, *Unveiling Jamaah Islamiyyah*, Jakarta: Grafindo Khazanah Ilmu, 2005, www.swaramuslim.net/ebook/html/015/index.htm (site no longer active).

7. JALALABAD AND THE ARAB-AFGHAN TRAINING STORM

1. Yousaf, Mohammad and Mark Adkin, *Afghanistan: The Bear Trap*, Barnsley: Leo Cooper, 1992, pp. 231–2.
2. Abdul Haq, Mujahidin Commander, 18 May 1988, to Robert D. Kaplan, in Kaplan, Robert D., *Soldiers of God: With Islamic Warriors in Afghanistan and Pakistan*, New York: Vintage Departures, 2001, p. 166.
3. Hamid, Mustafa, *Big Folly or Goat's War?*, 2006, http://www.4shared.com/file/36078879/f3bf3b8/4_online.html
4. Al-Yamani, Mustafa, 'Preparation for the Jalalabad Battle by Osama Bin Laden', *Afghanistan…Memories of the Occupation*, 28 June 2008, http://tokhaleej.jeeran.com/archive/2008/6/597599.html (site no longer active).
5. Hamid, *Big Folly or Goat's War?*, p. 70.
6. 'Direct Testimony of Jamal Ahmed Al-Fadl', United States of America v. Usama Bin Laden, et al., Defendants; S(7)98 Cr.1023, 158: United States District Court, Southern District of New York, 6 Feb. 2001, pp. 190–2, http://fl1.findlaw.com/news.findlaw.com/cnn/docs/binladen/binladen20601tt.pdf
7. Al-Yamani, 'Preparation for the Jalalabad Battle by Osama Bin Laden'.
8. Hamid, *Big Folly or Goat's War?*, p. 63.
9. Mansur, Abdullah, 'The Third Meeting with the Mujahid Brother Abdul Haq (the Emir of the Islamic Party of Turkistan) who Tells the Memories of the Fall of Kabul in 2001', *Voice of Islam*, 4 (26 July 2009), http://ia311004.us.archive.org/1/items/AboYahya_37/MajalahTorkstanAl-Sharqya/Majalah-Torkstan-Al-Sharqya-4-Word.docx (site no longer active). See also Mansur, Abdullah, 'A

Meeting with the Amir of the Islamic Party of Turkistan, the Brother Al-Mujahid Abd-Al-Haq (Part 2)', *Voice of Islam*, 3 (Feb. 2009).

10. Harun, Fadil, *The War Against Islam: The Story of Fadil Harun, Part 1. 2009*, p. 145, http://www.ctc.usma.edu/v2/wp-content/uploads/2013/10/The-Story-of-Fazul-Harun-Part-1-O.pdf
11. Hamid, Mustafa, *Cross in the Kandahar Sky*, 2006. p. 36, http://www.4shared.com/file/15220171/c1e49341/__.html
12. Harun, *The War Against Islam, Part 1*, pp. 64–5.
13. Hamid, Mustafa, *Airport 1990*, 2006, p. 211, http://www.4shared.com/file/15220483/aeb92c49/__90.html

8. THE AFGHAN CIVIL WAR AND ARAB-AFGHAN FLIGHT

1. Harun, Fadil, *The War Against Islam: The Story of Fadil Harun, Part 1. 2009*, p. 94, http://www.ctc.usma.edu/v2/wp-content/uploads/2013/10/The-Story-of-Fazul-Harun-Part-1-O.pdf
2. Such claims were made to Abd al Bari Atwan in his 1996 interview with bin Laden, which originally featured on p. 5 of *Al Quds al Arabi* on 27 Nov. 1996. A copy is available in Foreign Broadcast Information Service (FBIS), 'Compilation of Usama Bin Laden Statements 1994–January 2004', Reston: FBIS, 2004, p. 32, http://www.fas.org/irp/world/para/ubl-fbis.pdf. See also John Miller's interview with bin Laden, available at http://www.pbs.org/wgbh/pages/frontline/shows/binladen/who/interview.html. A letter written by Sayf al-Adl also appears to allude to direct involvement but, on a closer reading, it appears the forces al-Qaeda members were associating with and training, were the ones who in fact carried out these operations. See al-Adl, Sayf, 'A Short Report on the Trip from Nairobi to Cape Kambooni and the Situation in the Southern Region', West Point: The Combating Terrorism Centre, Harmony Database—Document No. AFGP-2002–600113,pp. 4–7,https://www.ctc.usma.edu/posts/a-short-report-on-the-trip-from-nairobi-english-translation-2
3. Al-Suri, Abu Musab, *The Global Islamic Resistance Call*, 2004, p. 709, pp. 771–4, http://www.fsboa.com/vw/files/books/2005/mqdoc.zip (site no longer active).
4. Ibid.
5. Ibid.
6. *Al-Jihad*, No. 60, Feb. 1990, p. 27.
7. Source: As-Sahab Foundation for Media Production, 'The State of the Ummah', Part Two, 2001, https://archive.org/details/stateoftheummah2
8. Al-Suri, *The Global Islamic Resistance Call*, p. 709, pp. 771–4.
9. Ibid.
10. See for example, al-Adl, Sayf, 'A Short Report on the Trip from Nairobi to Cape Kambooni and the Situation in the Southern Region'.
11. Such intimations were made to Abd al Bari Atwan in his 1996 interview with bin Laden. See p. 5 of *Al Quds al Arabi* on 27 Nov. 1996, transcribed in Foreign

Broadcast Information Service (FBIS). 'Compilation of Usama Bin Laden Statements 1994–January 2004', Reston: FBIS, 2004, p. 32, http://www.fas.org/irp/world/para/ubl-fbis.pdf

12. Shama, Muhammad Mustafa Abu, 'The Future of Conflict in Afghanistan (the First Episode): Dr Fadl, Founder of Al-Jihad Writes about the Complete Story of the Birth of al-Qaeda in Afghanistan', *Asharq Al-Awsat*, 25 Jan. 2010, http://www.aawsat.com/details.asp?section=4&article=554311&issueno=11381
13. Hamid, Mustafa, *Cross Over Kandahar Sky*, 2006, pp. 48, 53–4. http://www.4shared.com/file/15220171/c1e493491/__.html
14. Ibid., p. 59.
15. 'Letters from bin Laden: A Collection of Letters from Osama bin Laden to Various Persons in Saudi Arabia Statements 7–21 (Part One)', West Point: The Combating Terrorism Center, Harmony Database—Document No. AFGP-2002–003345 (previously available at http://www.ctc.usma.edu/aq/pdf/-003345_trans1.pdf); 'Letters from bin Laden: A Collection of Letters from Osama bin Laden to Various Persons in Saudi Arabia Statements 7–21 (Part Two)', West Point: The Combating Terrorism Center, Harmony Database—Document No. AFGP-2002–003345 (previously available at http://www.ctc.usma.edu/aq/pdf/AFGP-2002–003345_trans2.pdf); 'Letters from bin Laden: A Collection of Letters from Osama bin Laden to Various Persons in Saudi Arabia Statements 7–21 (Part Three)', West Point: The Combating Terrorism Center, Harmony Database—Document No. AFGP-2002–003345 (previously available at http://www.ctc.usma.edu/aq/pdf/AFGP_trans3.pdf); 'Letters from bin Laden: A Collection of Letters from Osama bin Laden to Various Persons in Saudi Arabia Statements (Part Four)', West Point: The Combating Terrorism Center, Harmony Database—Document No. AFGP-2002–003345 (previously available at http://www.ctc.usma.edu/aq/pdf/AFGP-2002–003345_trans4.pdf); 'Letters from bin Laden: A Collection of Letters from Osama bin Laden to Various Persons in Saudi Arabia Statements (Part Five)', West Point: The Combating Terrorism Center, Harmony Database—Document No. AFGP-2002–003345 (previously available at http://www.ctc.usma.edu/aq/AFGP-2002–003345_trans5.pdf). Collated document, in which the letters have been slightly altered, available at https://www.ctc.usma.edu/wp-content/uploads/2013/10/Letter-from-Bin-Laden-Translation.pdf
16. Many of the assumptions that the group formed in 1999 or just prior come from its release of the following statement that year: 'A Message from the General Command of the Islamic Movement Uzbekistan', 25 Aug. 1999, http://www.e-prism.org/images/balagh01.doc
17. 'Recommendation for Continued Detention Under DoD Control (CD) for Guantanamo Detainee, ISN US9GZ-010016DP', Joint Task Force, Guantanamo, Department of Defense, 2008, p. 2, http://media.mcclatchydc.com/smedia/2011/04/27/19/us9gz-010016dp.source.prod_affiliate.91.pdf
18. Hamid, Mustafa, *Tajikistan Project: Jihad Shifted from the Shamal River*, 2007, pp. 11–12, 15, http://www.4shared.com/file/34339274/dcae60c1/10_online.html

9. THE ARAB-AFGHAN RETURN AND THE RISE OF THE TALIBAN

1. Al-Hamadi, Khalid, 'Al-Qa'ida from the Inside, as Narrated by Abu Jandal (Nasir al-Bahari), bin Ladin's Bodyguard (3); US Embassies in East Africa Targeted because of their Role in Fuelling Ethnic War in Rwanda and Burundi; al-Qa'ida Participated in Warfare in Southern Sudan; Attack on Mubarak's Life was among Training Material in Afghanistan'. *Al-Quds Al-Arabi*, 28 Mar. 2005, http://www.haverford.edu/library/reference/mschaus/jihadimvt/alqaedawithinpt1.pdf
2. Bin Laden, Najwa, Omar bin Laden and Jean Sasson, *Growing up Bin Laden: Osama's Wife and Son take us Inside their Secret World*, New York: St Martin's Press, 2009, pp. 161–3, 184–5.
3. Al-Adl, Sayf, 'Biography of the Leader of the Jihad—Abu Musab Al-Zarqawi', http://203.223.152.151/~/vb/showthread.php?p=6635 (site no longer active).
4. Al-Suri, '[Letter to Bin Laden and Covering Letter for Ayman Al-Zawahiri]', copy provided to Leah Farrall, courtesy of Allan Cullison.
5. Hamid, Mustafa, *Cross over Kandahar Sky*, 2006, pp. 64–79, http://www.4shared.com/file/15220171/c1e49341/_.html
6. Ibid., p. 68.
7. Al-Suri, Abu Musab, *The Global Islamic Resistance Call*, 2004, p. 813, http://www.fsboa.com/vw/files/books/2005/mqdoc.zip (site no longer active).
8. Soufan, Ali H. and Daniel Freedman, *The Black Banners: The Inside Story of 9/11 and the Fight against Al-Qaeda*, New York: W.W. Norton & Company Inc., 2011, pp. 62–3.
9. Al-Hammadi, Khalid, 'Abu-Jandal, Former Personal Bodyguard of Usama Bin Ladin and Leading al-Qai'da Element in Yemen Reveals to Al-Quds Al-Arabi his Intercession in bin Ladin's Marriage to Yemeni Girl', *Al-Quds al-Arabi*, 3 Aug. 2004, p. 4, http://cryptome.org/alqaeda-plans.htm. See also Soufan and Freedman, *The Black Banners*, pp. 62–3; and al-Bahri, Nasser and Georges Malbrunot, *In the Shadow of bin Laden*, Neuilly-sur-Seine: Michel Lafon, 2010.
10. Al-Hammadi, Khalid, 'An Insider's View of Al-Qa'ida as Narrated by Abu-Jandal (Nasir Al-Bahri), bin Ladin's Bodyguard (4); I Tried to Keep Away from Al-Qa'ida After my Experience in Tajikistan; Abu-Abdallah's Quiet Approach Persuaded me to Swear Allegiance; There was Nothing Called Al-Qa'ida; bin-Ladin Worked under Command of Abdallah Azzam at First', *Al-Quds Al-Arabi*, 26 Mar. 2005, http://www.haverford.edu/library/reference/mschaus/jihadimvt/alqaedawithinpt2.pdf
11. Soufan and Freedman, *The Black Banners*, p. 65
12. Hamid, *Cross over Kandahar Sky*, p. 116.
13. 'The Truth about Abu Abdullah Al-Muhajir who Misled Al-Zarqawi and Made him Expand Causing Bloodshed', 2005, http://www.almahdy.net/vb/showthread.php?t=3354 (site no longer active).
14. Al-Suri, '[Letter to Bin Laden and Covering Letter for Ayman Al-Zawahiri]'.
15. Ibid.

16. Ibid.
17. Ibid.
18. Ibid.
19. Hamid, *Tajikistan Project: Jihad Shifted from the Shamal River*, 2007, p. 58, http://www.4shared.com/file/34339274/dcae60c1/10_online.html
20. Soufan and Freedman, *The Black Banners*, pp. 91, 152.
21. The Political Bureau of the Libyan Islamic Fighting Group, 'Statement Number 14: Regarding the US Aggression against Sudan and Afghanistan', 1998, http://web.archive.org/web/20001208170700/www.almuqatila.com/AMEER/bayanat/bayan14.htm
22. Al-Saud, Prince Turki al-Faisal bin Abdulaziz, 'Declaration of His Royal Highness Prince Turki Al-Faisal Bin Abdulaziz Al-Saud', Thomas E. Burnett Sr, et al. v. Al Baraka Investment and Development Corporation et al., Case 1:02-cv-01616-JR, Document 142–2, 5 May 2003, p. 5, http://intelfiles.egoplex.com/affidavit-turki-al-faisal.pdf
23. 'United States of America v. Usama Bin Laden et al., Defendants S(7) 98 Cr. 1023; Day 38, 2 May 2001,' (United States District Court, Southern District of New York, 2001), p. 5482, http://cryptome.org/usa-v-ubl-38.htm

10. STRONG HORSE, WEAK HORSE: ARAB-AFGHAN POLITICS AND AL-QAEDA'S REALPOLITIK

1. Hamid, Mustafa, *Cross Over Kandahar Sky*, 2006, p. 252. http://www.4shared.com/file/15220171/c1e49341/__.html
2. Al-Iraqi, Abd al-Hadi, 'Notes from Abdul Hadi', West Point: The Combating Terrorism Center, 2000. Harmony Database—Document No. AFGP-2002–000091, pp. 1–2, available at https://www.ctc.usma.edu/posts/notes-from-abd-al-hadi-english-translation-2
3. Foreign Broadcast Information Service (FBIS), 'Compilation of Usama Bin Laden Statements 1994–January 2004', Reston: FBIS, 2004, pp. 78, 118, 135, http://www.fas.org/irp/world/para/ubl-fbis.pdf
4. 'A Message from the General Command of the Islamic Movement Uzbekistan', 25 Aug. 1999, http://www.e-prism.org/images/balagh01.doc
5. 'Letters to Abu Khabab', West Point: The Combating Terrorism Center, Harmony Database—Document No. AFGP-2002–001111, pp. 1–4, https://www.ctc.usma.edu/posts/letters-to-abu-khabab-english-translation-2
6. Ibid., pp. 1–4.
7. Al-Adl, Sayf, 'Biography of the Leader of the Jihad—Abu Musab Al-Zarqawi', 2005, http://203.223.152.151/~alfirdaw/vb/showthread.php?p=66 (site no longer active).
8. Ibid.
9. The Turkey way-station provided support to operations in Afghanistan, as well as Chechnya and other locations. From Turkey, Sakka coordinated with Abu

Zubaydah to dispatch trained operatives from Khaldan and Derunta to their final destination. http://media.mcclatchydc.com/smedia/2011/04/27/19/us9gz-0100 16dp.source.prod_affiliate.91.pdf

10. 'The Truth about Abu Abdullah Al-Muhajir who Misled Al-Zarqawi and Made him Expand Causing Bloodshed', 2005, http://www.almahdy.net/vb/showthread.php?t=3354 (site no longer active); and Mansur, Abdullah, 'A Meeting with the Amir of the Islamic Party of Turkistan, the Brother Al-Mujahid Abd-Al-Haq (Part 2)', *Voice of Islam*, 3 (Feb. 2009).
11. United States Department of Defense, 'Abu Zubaydah', The Guantanamo Docket, *The New York Times*, http://projects.nytimes.com/guantanamo/detainees/10016-abu-zubaydah
12. Ibid.
13. Ibid.
14. Two senior al-Qaeda figures indicated the hijackers were diverted from Turkey, according to the National Commission on Terrorist Attacks Against the United States, '9/11 Commission Report', Washington, DC: National Commission on Terrorist Attacks Against the United States, 2004, pp. 233–4, p. 496, fn. 97, p. 525, fn. 107, http://www.9-11commission.gov/report/911Report.pdf. See also Sakka, Lui, 'Interesting Explanations', *Haber Pan*, 3 Apr. 2006, http://www.haberpan.com/lui-sakkanin-ilginc-aciklamalari-haberi/; Yuksel, Gokhan, 'Sakka Trampled the Flag of Israel', *Tum Gazeteler*, 28 Mar. 2008, http://www.tumgazeteler.com/?a=2680686; Stark, Holger, 'Syrian had Inside Knowledge of 9/11 and London Bombings', *Speigel Online International*, 24 Aug. 2005, http://www.spiegel.de/international/0,1518,371201,00.html; Cziesche, Dominik, Juergen Dahlkamp and Holger Stark, 'Aladdin of the Black Forest', *Spiegel Online International*, 15 Sep. 2005, http://www.spiegel.de/international/spiegel/0,1518,371214,00.html; Vick, Karl, 'A Bomb-Builder, "Out of Shadows",' *The Washington Post*, 20 Feb. 2006, http://www.washingtonpost.com/wp-dyn/content/article/2006/02/19/AR2006021901336.html; Gourlay, Chris and John Calvert, 'Al-Qaeda Kingpin: I Trained 9/11 Hijackers', *The Sunday Times*, 25 Nov. 2005, http://www.timesonline.co.uk/tol/news/world/europe/article2936761.ece

11. ARAB-AFGHAN UNITY EFFORTS AND 9/11

1. Al-Mauritani, Abu Hafs, *Islamic Action between the Motives of Unity and Advocates of Conflict*, Pakistan: Center for Islamic Study and Research, 2000, http://www.cybcity.com/antiusa/3amal_islami.zip (site no longer active).
2. Hamid, Mustafa, 'Five Letters to the Africa Corps', West Point: The Combating Terrorism Centre, Harmony Database—Document No. AFGP-2002–600053, https://www.ctc.usma.edu/posts/five-letters-to-the-africa-corps-english-translation-2
3. Hamid, Mustafa, *Cross over Kandahar Sky*, 2006, pp. 146–7, http://www.4shared.com/file/15220171/c1e49341/__.html

4. 'I Was a Neighbour of Al-Zarqawi', 2006, http://www.muslm.net/vb/showthread.php?t=167769; and Mansur, Abdullah, 'A Meeting with the Amir of the Islamic Party of Turkistan, the Brother Al-Mujahid Abd-Al-Haq (Part 2)', *Voice of Islam*, 3 (Feb. 2009).
5. Cullison, Alan, 'Inside Al-Qaeda's Hard Drive', *The Atlantic*, 1 Sep. 2004, http://www.theatlantic.com/magazine/archive/2004/09/inside-al-qaeda-rsquo-s-hard-drive/3428
6. The interview was with Bakr Atyani of MBC and aired on 24 June 2001. For a brief transcript, see http://intelwire.egoplex.com/CIA-911-Binder1.pdf, pp. 176–8.
7. For the list, see Mojdeh, 'Afghanistan under Five Years of Taliban Sovereignty', (unpublished manuscript), p. 36. See also the account of one of the Lackawanna six in Dina Temple-Raston, *The Jihad Next Door: The Lackawanna Six and Rough Justice in the Age of Terror*, New York: PublicAffairs, 2007, p. 111.
8. Hamid, *Cross over Kandahar Sky*, pp. 200–1.
9. Ibid.
10. Ibid.
11. Ibid.
12. Ibid.
13. Ahmad Val Ould Eddin interviews Abu Hafs al Mauritani on 'Special Encounters', Al-Jazeera, 17 Oct. 2012.
14. Al-Adl, Sayf, 'Message to Our People in Iraq and the Gulf Specifically, and to Our Islamic Ummah in General: The Islamic Resistance against the American Invasion of Qandahar and Lessons Learned', 2003, translation available at https://intelcenter.com/Qaeda-Guerrilla-Iraq-v1-0.pdf
15. Ibid.
16. For some accounts of this meeting and events that transpired after see, 'Abu Musab Al-Zarqawi: A Symbol of Courage and Bravery', 2006, http://www.muslm.net/vb/showthread.php?t=164666; 'I Was a Neighbour of Al-Zarqawi'; al-Maqdisi, Abu Ubaydah, *The Leader Abu Zubaydah: This Is How I Knew Him and This Is How He Was Captured*, p. 56; al-Masri, Abu Jihad, '[Episode One through Seven of Al-Masri's Memoirs]', May 2007, http://www.muslm.net/vb/showthread.php?t=234295
17. Ibid.
18. See 'I Was a Neighbour of Al-Zarqawi'; al-Masri, '[Episode One through Seven of Al-Masri's Memoirs]'; al-Adl, 'Message to Our People in Iraq and the Gulf Specifically, and to Our Islamic Ummah in General: the Islamic Resistance against the American Invasion of Qandahar and Lessons Learned'.
19. 'I Was a Neighbour of Al-Zarqawi'; al-Adl, 'Message to Our People in Iraq and the Gulf Specifically, and to Our Islamic Ummah in General: The Islamic Resistance against the American Invasion of Qandahar and Lessons Learned'; al-Masri, '[Episode One through Seven of Al-Masri's Memoirs]'.
20. Al-Masri, '[Episode One through Seven of Al-Masri's Memoirs]'.

21. Al-Adl, Sayf, 'To My Beloved Brother Mukhtar', West Point: The Combating Terrorism Center, 2002, https://www.ctc.usma.edu/wp-content/uploads/2013/10/Al-Adl-Letter-Translation1.pdf

INDEX

Abdul Razak, Mullah: 287
Abu Ubaydah al-Banshiri training camp: 261, 273
Adam, Mawlawi: delegation led by, 34–5
al-Adl, Sayf: 118, 159, 189, 193, 197, 209, 211, 221, 228, 236, 255, 257–8, 268, 277, 279, 281–3; coordination of defence activities, 9, 285–6; family of, 3; Head of Security for al-Qaeda, 3; role in al-Qaeda unity initiatives, 265
al-Adnani, Tamim: 119, 125
Advice and Reform Committee: formation of, 195
Afghan Civil War (1989–92): aerial bombardment campaigns of, 152; Battle of Jalalabad (1989), 24, 62, 96, 105, 107, 114, 118, 121, 123, 125, 136–7, 143, 145–55, 157–8, 160–5, 170–1, 173, 178, 216, 296–7, 305–6; Capture of Khost (1991), 50; Capture of Torghar Mountain (1990), 130; entry of Ikhwan Muslimin into, 162–3; ISI provision of seized weaponry during, 153–4
Afghan Civil War (1992–6): 3, 180–1, 197, 201–3, 227–8, 222; Battle of Kabul, 1, 179, 217–18, 230–3; Capture of Gardez (1992), 191; Capture of Jalalabad (1996), 217–18
Afghan Jihad (Soviet Invasion of Afghanistan)(1979–89): 2, 8, 10–11, 13, 21–2, 27, 30, 32, 34–5, 46, 52, 58, 65, 68, 71, 78, 80–2, 85, 98–9, 102–3, 129, 135, 181, 185, 199, 201, 220, 244, 285, 290, 298–9, 302, 304, 309–10, 312–13, 317; as US-Soviet proxy war, 47; Battle of Jaji (1987), 8, 25, 58, 62, 80–3, 85, 87, 93, 96–101, 103–5, 107–8, 111–14, 117, 122–3, 125–6, 136, 148, 154, 157–60, 216, 247, 269, 281, 283, 286, 296, 305–6, 319; Battle of Lija (1983), 55, 58; Battle of Shahranao, 71; Battle of Urgon (1983–4), 66–7, 142; Battles of Zhawar (1986), 84, 95, 113; financing of, 30, 32, 36–7, 47, 49, 119, 138, 294; ISI influence in, 39–43, 57–8, 71, 73; participation of Syrian fighters in, 24; participation of Yemeni fighters in, 25; signing of Geneva Accords (1988), 145; support from within Pakistan during,

39–43, 45–7, 49–50, 53, 58; training of participants in, 37–40, 42–3, 51–5, 57, 61–2, 65, 69–71; withdrawal of Soviet forces (1989), 32, 103–4, 145–6, 152, 183, 305, 321
Afghanistan: 5, 8, 12, 14, 23, 33–4, 39, 47, 49–50, 53, 56, 59, 66, 69, 77, 86, 89, 99–100, 115, 118–19, 125–6, 132–3, 138, 140, 142–3, 145, 159, 166–7, 175, 179, 184, 190, 192, 195, 204, 211, 228–9, 232–3, 237, 240, 244, 250, 254, 258, 264, 267, 270, 274, 279, 292, 301, 304, 307, 309, 312, 315, 319, 321, 324; Arab-Afghan presence in, 3, 6, 8–11, 23, 33, 220, 298–9; Badakshan Province, 40; Bamian, 270; Garamwak, 258, 261, 273; Gardez, 36, 54–5, 58, 85, 159, 191, 202, 300; Ghazni Province, 58; government of, 97, 210; Herat, 8–9, 35, 257, 273, 285; Jaji, 66, 68, 74, 76–7, 86–7, 89, 91, 94, 96, 102, 112, 139, 314; Jalalabad, 1, 3, 9, 68, 92, 104–5, 146–9, 159, 162–3, 167, 171, 180, 184, 207, 209–12, 217–19, 225, 259–60, 272–3, 275, 283–5, 297, 320–2; Jihadwal, 191; Kabul, 1, 6, 21, 50, 92, 126, 145–7, 173, 177, 183, 197–8, 201, 207, 209–10, 217–18, 222–3, 227–8, 230–2, 241, 248, 254, 256, 261–2, 265–6, 270, 272, 274–6, 285, 301, 321; Kandahar, 1–3, 8–9, 74, 201, 207, 215, 221, 225–7, 234, 236, 248, 261, 266–7, 272, 275, 282, 285, 288; Khost Province, 3, 8, 11, 37, 50, 55, 71, 73, 84–5, 95, 100, 104, 112–13, 121, 129, 137, 157, 165–6, 173, 180, 196, 199, 201–2, 210, 234–5, 238, 240–1, 244, 259, 285, 295–6, 314, 321; Kunar Province, 49, 146, 174; Kunduz Province, 40, 290; Lija, 37, 61; Logar Province, 126, 165, 181, 253, 256, 273; Mazar Sharif, 9, 226, 270; Mes Aynak, 181, 263, 272; Nuristan Province, 75; Paktia Province, 2, 34–6, 58, 67, 71, 77, 89, 93, 125–6, 142, 191; Paktika Province, 35, 58; Pashtun population of, 39–40; return of al-Qaeda to (1996), 3, 113, 194, 196, 204–5, 207–9; Rishikor, 272; Salang Passage, 227–8; Samar Khel Mountain, 146, 155; Shia population of, 19, 270–2; Tajik population of, 40; Takhar Province, 290; Taloqan, 198; Tora Bora Mountains, 8–9, 91–2, 103, 136, 210–12, 214–15, 260, 273, 282–6, 289, 305–8; Torkham, 146, 162, 166–7, 173, 180; Uyghur population of, 247; Uzbek population of, 247, 253; Wardak Province, 201; withdrawal of Arab-Afghans and Taliban from (2001), 247, 287–8, 293, 308; withdrawal of al-Qaeda from (2001), 307; Zhawar, 111–13, 121, 133, 135, 242; Zurmat, 60, 288
Agha, Taheb: 288
Ahmad, Rashid: 59–60; background of, 52–3; departure to Canada (1986), 75; targeted by ISI, 60–1; training provided by, 51–5, 58–9, 65, 70; work in *Al-Surat*, 55–6; working relationship with Jalaluddin Haqqani, 52–6; working relationship with Mawlawi Nasrullah Mansur, 58

Akram, Ali: 70
Algeria: 172, 183, 194, 204, 212, 230, 232, 322; Civil War (1991–2002), 158, 181; Salafi jihadi movement of, 322
Ali, Abdul Aziz: 26, 67, 70, 93, 152, 312; training programme operated by Warsak training camp, 133
Amu Daria: 167
Anas, Abdullah: 33; family of, 123
Arab-Afghans: 12–16, 26, 42–3, 45, 52, 59, 66, 80, 89, 95, 97, 102–4, 108, 121, 126–7, 136, 140, 145, 150–1, 155, 164, 174, 191–2, 200, 210, 231, 247–8, 295, 303–4, 314, 319, 322; backgrounds of, 23; conflicts between, 181; corruption amongst, 295–6; impact of Battle of Jalalabad on (1989), 137, 158–9, 161–2; lack of education amongst, 297; movement of, 165, 180, 183–4; opposition to construction of al-Masadah training base amongst, 90–1, 94, 97–9; organisations founded by, 33, 138, 207; origin of, 21, 23; Saudi, 140; support for jihad in Yemen amongst, 186; Syrian, 24; Taliban support for groups of, 290–1; territory inhabited by, 3, 6, 8–11, 33, 83, 90, 220, 222–3, 298–9; training of, 25–6, 36–7, 39, 52, 84, 133, 141–3, 310; withdrawal from Afghanistan (2001), 247, 287–8; Yemeni, 24–5, 140, 186
Arab Council for Unity: 263, 267; participants in, 265–6; purpose of, 266
Arab Spring: 171, 303, 324; Egyptian Revolution (2011), 316, 325; Libyan Civil War (2011), 313, 315; Syrian Civil War (2011–), 14, 145, 172, 300, 303, 313–16
Arabic (language): 59, 71, 111; media produced in, 69; teaching of, 234
al-Arin base: 111
Arnaout, Enaam: trial of (2003), 108
al-Assad, Hafez: regime of, 24, 84–5
Atta, Abu: 197, 201–2
Australia: Federal Police, 11, 17
Ayoub, Abu: 110
Azmarai, Osama: 169–72, 312, 322; background of, 167, 322; training camps of, 174, 180
Azzam, Abdullah: 65, 69–70, 75, 77, 82, 108–9, 119, 121–2, 125, 151, 161, 172, 213, 303, 319, 325; amir of Maktab al-Khadamat, 79; amir of Sadda training camp, 123; assassination of (1989), 124, 141, 162–3, 166; background of, 26; criticisms of, 157, 161, 172; family of, 123; focus on Palestine, 319; followers of, 296; nominal head of Badr training camp, 81; relationship with Saudi government, 124; training of, 82; participation in Battle of Jaji (1987), 98–9
Azzam School (School of Jihad): 14

Badr training camp: 45–6; establishment of, 81; personnel of, 81; sources of funding for, 45, 81
Bai, Juma: 276–8
Bangladesh: 172
al-Banshiri, Abu Ubaydah: 58, 61, 85, 93, 95, 97, 105, 112, 129, 139, 148, 155, 159–60, 188, 196, 261, 273; background of, 24; co-

founder of al-Qaeda, 24, 58, 142; death of, 207; member of Military Councils of al-Qaeda and Tanzim al-Jidah, 117, 123; participation in Battle of Jaji (1987), 98, 100–1, 160; participation in Battle of Jalalabad (1989), 157
Baradar, Mullah: 287
Barre, Ziad: regime of, 187
Basayev, Shamil: 199
Battle of Kabul (1997): 252, 291
Benevolence International Foundation: Sarajevo office of, 108
al-BM, Abu Abdul Rahman: 122; background of, 24; death of, 98
Bojinka Plot (1995): 169
Bosnia-Herzegovina: 180, 183–4, 230, 232, 322; Salafi jihadi movement of, 322; Sarajevo, 108
Bosnian War (1992–6): participation of foreign fighters in, 180, 189, 193, 212, 230, 320, 323
Brigade of the Humorous: formation of, 84
Burma: 183

Cable News Network (CNN): 249
Canada: 75
Chechnya: 141, 167, 180, 183, 200, 217, 230, 241, 248–9, 252, 258, 260, 322–4; Chechen conflict (early 1990s), 323; mujahidin presence in, 199; presence of Tanzim al-Jihad, 320; al-Qaeda presence in, 184, 193, 315; Russian re-occupation of (1999), 315; Salafi jihadi movement of, 322
China: 19, 172; military hardware from, 54–5; Salafi jihadi movement in, 322
Cold War: 49, 136
communism: 26, 185
Cuba: Guantanamo Bay, 200

Dagestan: 248, 252
Democratic Republic of Afghanistan: 21, 145; fall of (1992), 177; government of, 154; military of, 146–7, 149–52, 155, 191; territory controlled by, 50
Derunta training camp: 255, 259, 312
Dostum, Abdul Rashid: 197, 223, 233, 291, 301; defeated by Jalaluddin Haqqani, 227; followers of, 253; militias of, 150–1, 155, 222

East Turkistan Islamic Movement: 4, 229–30
Egypt: 10, 19, 23, 38, 71, 116–17, 180, 191, 194, 239, 320, 325; government of, 193; military of, 135, 298; Revolution (2011), 316, 325
Egyptian Islamic Jihad: 135

al-Fadl, Jamal: 114, 136, 160; background of, 107–8
al-Faisal, Turki: 243
al-Farsi, Salman: 197
al-Faruq camp: 174, 197, 200–1, 258–9; attacked by US cruise missile (1998), 134, 242; closure of, 203–4; opening of (2000), 248, 261; personnel of, 200; personnel trained at, 198–9, 260–2, 270, 272
Fatah: factions of, 133; fighters trained by, 25–6; training camps, 25–6, 82
fiqh: 113, 140

First World War (1914–18): 92
France: 181
al-Furqan project: 180–1, 192, 197, 209

Gaddafi, Muammar: 205
Gamaah Islamiyyah: 23, 164, 229, 239, 251, 254, 262, 264, 266; establishment of (1987), 116; members of, 237, 241–2, 265, 285, 301; participation in Bosnian War (1992–5), 320; participation in al-Qaeda unity initiatives, 265–6, 268; training camps of, 171, 174, 256, 272
Georgia: 248–9
Goboz (tribe): 134
guerrilla warfare: 38, 55, 58–9, 62, 74, 111, 129, 141; development of, 135–6; opposition to use of, 70; strategies, 92–3, 95–6; training, 52, 135, 143
Gul, Ahmad: 67

al-Hage, Wadih: 52, 57
Hajr, Abu: 109
Hamburg group: role in preparation for 9/11 attacks, 259
Hamid, Mustafa (al-Masri, Abu Walid): 1–2, 5, 10–11, 15–16, 18, 34, 52, 65, 73–4, 135, 294–5; as 'Specially Designated Global Terrorist', 10; background of, 2, 25–6; blacklisted by Ikhwan Muslimin, 56; *Cross in the Sky over Kandahar*, 238; family of, 3; house arrest in Iran, 10, 19; Kandahar Bureau Chief for Al-Jazeera, 10; oath of allegiance to Mullah Omar (1998), 4–5; return to Afghanistan (1996), 207; return to Egypt (2011), 10, 19; visit to Iran (1996), 227–8
Hanafi 37, 75, 143
Haq, Abdul: 152
al-Haq, Amin: 93
ul-Haq, General Zia: 42; direction of ISI activity during Afghan Jihad, 57; intervention against US relations with mujahidin, 40
Haqqani, Ibrahim: confrontation with Taliban, 202; family of, 54, 202; training of, 54
Haqqani, Jalaluddin: 2, 8, 34–6, 52, 56–7, 65–6, 68–9, 74, 85, 129, 171, 191–2, 198, 202, 227, 242; defeat of Dostum and Masud, 228; family of, 54, 202; followers of, 35, 38, 312; hosting of Salafi volunteers, 36–7; ISI provision of weaponry to, 153; role in capture of Khost (1991), 50; working relationship with Abu Harith al-Urdani, 130, 321; working relationship with Rashid Ahmad, 52–6
Haqqani, Khalil: family of, 54; training of, 54
Harakat al-Ansar: members of, 288
Harakat-i-Inqilab i Islami: factional disputes within, 45–7, 49; members of, 45–7
Harun, Fadil: 133, 168, 184
Hekmatyar, Gulbuddin: 83, 98, 100, 138, 197, 201, 321; assassination of Mawlawi Nasrullah Mansur (1993), 60; background of, 40; founder of Lashkar Ethar, 138; ISI support of, 183; role of followers in ISI assassination programme, 42; supporters of, 127, 183; territory controlled by, 113; training camps of, 165

Hizb i Islami-Khalis: 30, 46; members of, 34, 152; offices of, 60
Hussein, Saddam: 153, 175, 188, 244

Ikhwan Muslimin: 23, 56, 76, 78, 123–4, 129, 132–3, 162, 191, 314, 316–21, 324–5; aid distribution activities of, 318; allies of, 316; entry into Afghan Civil War (1989–92), 162–3; failure of, 24; International, 51; Iraqi, 163, 322; members of, 26, 30, 32–3, 84, 100, 124, 187, 193; Syrian, 24, 26, 32, 124; training camps of, 158, 163; training of members of, 38
Imam, Sayyid: 109; alleged member of al-Qaeda Religious Council, 114; amir of Tanzim al-Jihad, 193; *Al-Umdah*, 164
India: 250
Indonesia: 11, 172, 183
Iran: 10–11, 19, 104, 209, 226–8, 288; borders of, 8
Iraq: 18, 23, 38, 92, 153, 183, 258, 300, 312, 323–4; Abu Ghraib Prison, 17; Operation Iraqi Freedom (2003–11), 103, 306, 309; al-Qaeda presence in, 301, 311, 315; Shia population of, 315; Sunni population of, 315
al-Iraqi, Abdul Hadi: 163, 228, 255, 277–8; as member of al-Qaeda, 223; forces led by, 262, 274; letter written to al-Qaeda leadership (1999), 248
al-Iraqi, Abdul Rahman: 52, 57, 59
al-Iraqi, Abu Hajr: 84, 94, 122, 207
Islam: 20, 22–3, 26, 37, 47, 125, 143, 170–1, 191, 212, 239, 244, 304; Hajj, 65–9; Quran, 81–2, 141, 201; Ramadan, 67, 91, 287; Shariah, 46, 51, 58, 234, 238, 323; Shia, 5, 19, 100, 102, 226, 270–2, 315, 318–19, 323, 325; Sufi, 323, 325; Sunnah, 82; Sunni, 203, 315, 319
al-Islambouli, Muhammad: 285
Islamic Movement of Uzbekistan: 4, 229–30; decline of relationship with al-Qaeda, 273, 286; Leadership Council, 251–2; members of, 198–9
Islamist: 159, 325
Israel: 24, 86, 124, 141, 269, 316, 325
Al-Ittihad al-Islamiyyah: 188
Al-Ittihad (newspaper): 2
Ittihad i Islami Tahrir Afghanistan (Islamic Union for the Liberation of Afghanistan): 2; delegation to Abu Dhabi (1980), 27, 30; formation of (1980), 27; members of, 27, 30, 32–3; programme for supporting Afghan Jihad, 32–3; splitting of, 27
al-Ittihad Military Committee: 67, 70

Jafar, Abu: 134
Jalalabad School (School of Youth) (School of Jihad): 14, 166, 170, 173, 257, 259, 293, 297, 301, 321–2, 325; influence of, 165, 169, 212, 257–8, 301–2, 309–11, 313–14; origins of, 145, 165, 316
Jaleel, Mullah: 274
Jamaah Islamiyyah: 138, 166, 194, 204; members of, 137
Jamaah al-Khalifah: ideological development of, 181
Jamal, Dr: former commander of Tanzim al-Jihad, 118, 322

Jamil ul-Rahman: 76; funding of, 49
Jammu and Kashmir: 249
Jandal, Abu: bodyguard of Osama bin Laden, 11
Japan: 7
al-Jazairi, Abdul Majid: background of, 158
al-Jazairi, Abu Usama: 110
al-Jazairi, Dr Ahmad: 116
Al-Jazeera: personnel of, 10
Al-Jihad: 70; articles in, 151
jihad: 17, 66, 186–7, 198, 211, 215, 224, 298, 317; privatisation of, 311
Jihadwal camp: 174, 192, 196–7, 202–3, 235; establishment of, 134; meeting at (1992), 192; personnel of, 200–1, 242
Jordan: 23, 122, 133, 141, 256, 259, 321; Fatah training camps in, 25–6
Julaydan, Wael: 26, 125, 127; as al-Qaeda amir of Peshawar activities, 123
Jundullah: members of, 288

kafir: 228, 271, 323
Kamel, Saleh: funding provided for Badr camp, 45, 81
al-Kanadi, Abu Abdul Rahman: 127, 132, 222–3, 264; background of, 126; 'Challenge Project, The', 126; participation in al-Qaeda unity initiatives, 266
Kenya: 233, 237; US embassy bombing (1998), 5, 107, 136, 232, 238, 242–3, 248, 307
Khaldan training camp: 85, 136, 166–7, 180–1, 230, 255, 291, 312; Beliefs Battalion Institute, 229, 231; closure of, 260; influence of Jalalabad School on, 165; Mujahidin Services Centre, 258–60; operated by Maktab al-Khadamat, 132; personnel of, 259, 322; personnel trained at, 200
Khalid bin Walid camp: 174; establishment of, 135
Khalis, Mawlawi Yunis: 30, 34, 60, 67, 74, 152, 209–10, 321; followers of, 35–6, 38, 46, 55, 60; protection offered to returning al-Qaeda members, 207, 209
Khattab, Ibn: 167, 170–2, 184, 249, 252, 260, 312, 322; death of (2002), 180; expelled from Chechnya and Dagestan, 248–9, 252, 315; followers of, 248; training camps of, 174
Kuchis (ethnic group): 147
Kurds: Syrian, 258
Kuwait: 153, 175; Iraqi Invasion of (1990), 174, 188, 219

bin Laden, Omar: family of, 210
bin Laden, Osama (Abu Abdullah): 1–2, 6, 11, 57, 61–2, 75–8, 81, 85, 92, 94–6, 100–1, 103, 105, 107, 109, 113, 116–18, 121–2, 124–5, 134, 139, 147–9, 154, 168, 174–6, 180, 189–90, 196, 204–5, 211–13, 215–16, 218–21, 225, 232–3, 235–6, 240–3, 245, 252–3, 260, 267, 269, 275, 281, 284, 289–90, 300–3, 306–8, 315, 322, 325; advised against use of Tora Bora Mountains, 9; appointed as amir of the Arabs, 122–3, 127; assassination of (2011), 9–10, 311; attempted assassination of (1997), 225; attempts to start jihad in Yemen, 185; background of, 25, 181; co-founder of al-Qaeda, 25,

301; construction projects of, 89; criticisms of, 155, 157, 161, 163, 172, 175, 231, 269–70; criticisms of Maktab al-Khadamat, 77, 80, 89–90; Declaration of Jihad against USA (1996), 1, 211, 214–18, 223, 231, 237; departure from Pakistan (1992), 196; departure to Saudi Arabia, 160; donors of, 302; escape to Abbottabad, 9–10; establishment of al-Masadah base (1986), 61, 89–93, 294; expansion of networks of, 249; expulsion from Sudan (1996), 3, 195, 204, 208, 230; family of, 11, 196, 210; financing of Afghan Jihad, 30, 86, 91, 93, 96–7, 112, 294; financing of al-Qaeda, 188; focus on Palestine and Saudi Arabia, 269–70; followers of, 103–4, 114, 184, 193–4, 208–10, 269, 296, 317; funding of Tanzim al-Jihad, 194–5, 213; funding provided for Maktab al-Khadamat, 79; influence of Jalalabad School on, 165; media efforts of, 249–50; meetings with Mullah Muhammad Omar, 220–2, 225, 227, 235, 237–8, 250, 280; participation in Battle of Jaji (1987), 93–8, 126, 148, 157–8, 216, 283, 319; participation in Battle of Jalalabad (1989), 137, 150–2, 157–61, 216, 296; return to Pakistan (1991), 177–9; role in al-Qaeda unity initiatives, 265; self-perception of, 77, 86, 122, 148, 151, 280, 305; travel to Sudan, 178–9; use of Arab hospitality customs, 223–4; visit to Afghanistan (1984), 76–7

Lashkar Ethar: establishment of, 138

Lashkar i Taiba: 288

Lebanese Civil War (1975–90): Lebanon War (1982), 22–3, 25; South Lebanon Conflict (1978), 25–6

Lebanon: 23, 25, 213, 256, 258; Beirut, 22–3, 215; US barrack bombings (1983), 215

al-Libi, Ibn Shaykh: 272, 289; amir of Khaldan training camp, 259, 322; head of Sadda training camp, 166; networks of, 230; participation in al-Qaeda unity initiatives, 265

Libya: 172; Civil War (2011), 313, 315

Libyan Islamic Fighting Group: 242–3, 264

al-Mahdi, Qutbi: 195

Mahmud: 207; assassination of, 210

Makkawi, Muhammad: background of, 24; participation in Battle of Jalalabad (1989), 149

Maktab al-Alami al-Islami: members of, 52

Maktab al-Khadamat: 33, 62–3, 75, 85, 87, 89–90, 105, 107, 122, 127, 129–30, 132, 166, 294–5, 319; aid dispersal activity of, 76, 86, 115; corruption in, 80, 86; criticisms of, 77, 80, 172; establishment of (1984), 62, 65, 68, 76, 78–9, 133, 294–5; Finance Committee, 79; funding of, 79, 86, 124, 138; influence of Jalalabad School on, 165; members of, 76, 109–10; Military Council, 81; Shurah Council, 79; supporters of, 78;

training camps established by, 83; training camps operated by, 132
Mansur, Mawlawi Nasrullah: 47, 49, 55, 57, 60, 67, 79, 87, 293; assassination of (1993), 59, 60, 75; followers of, 56; funding provided to *Al-Surat*, 55; leader of Harakat i Inqilab i Islami, 45–7; role in establishment of Qais training camp, 45, 57; Peshawar Special Meeting (1981), 50–1; supporters of, 50; visit to USA (1986), 60; working relationship with Rashid Ahmad, 58
Mansur, Mullah: 287
Mansur, Sayfullah: forces led by, 255
al-Masadah: 91–4, 97, 103, 111, 119, 123, 133; Arab-Afghans based at, 90; as target in Battle of Jaji (1987), 93–8; establishment of (1986), 61, 89–93; opposition to establishment of, 90–1, 94–6
Mashrour, Mustafa: 32–3; guide of Ikhwan Muslimin, 33
al-Masri, Abdul Rahman: 57, 73; death of (1988), 58; training of, 71
al-Masri, Abu Hafs: 2, 45–6, 50, 52, 57, 73, 85, 93, 97, 100, 105, 113, 134, 139, 148, 152, 155, 159–60, 189, 196, 219, 221, 224, 236, 255, 269–70, 277, 283; background of, 24; co-founder of al-Qaeda, 24, 57–8, 142; establishment of Jihadwal, 134; participation in Battle of Jaji (1987), 98, 100–1, 160; participation in Battle of Jalalabad (1989), 157; participation in al-Qaeda unity initiatives, 276; presence in Somalia, 189–90; training of, 71; withdrawal to Peshawar, 149
al-Masri, Abu Islam: travel to Chechnya, 184
al-Masri, Abu Jihad: 129, 219, 265, 285; participation in al-Qaeda unity initiatives, 265–6
al-Masri, Abu Khabab: 254–6, 264, 272; background of, 142
al-Masri, Abu Khalid: 95
al-Masri, Abu Muhammad: 224
al-Masri, Sharif: 285
al-Masri, Shaykh Saeed: 233, 281
Masud, Ahmad Shah: 197, 233, 291, 301; attacks against Taliban forces, 222–3, 227, 305; assassination of (2001), 281; defeated by Jalaluddin Haqqani, 227; leader of Northern Alliance, 5–6, 290, 305
al-Mauritani, Abu Hafs: 207, 234–5, 281; head of al-Qaeda's Shariah Council, 7; *Islamic Action between the Motives of Unity and Advocates of Conflict*, 263, 268
Mes Aynak camp: 248
Middle East Broadcasting Corporation (MBC): 6–7
Morsi, Muhammad: electoral victory of (2012), 316
Mubarak, Hosni: regime of, 117, 325
al-Muhajir, Abu Abdullah: 230; head of Beliefs Battalion Institute of Khaldan training camp, 229, 231
Muhammad, Ali: 135; background of, 84–5, 111; students of, 136; training provided by, 119, 139
Muhammad, Basil: 79, 91, 93–4, 96; *Arab Supporters in Afghanistan, The*, 10
din Muhammad, Hajji: 60–1
Muhammad, Khalid Shaykh:

associates of, 288; capture of (2003), 289; family of, 167; planning of 9/11 attacks, 216–17
Muhammad, Prophet: Companions of, 36
Muhammadi, Ahmed: corrupt practices of, 46–7; family of, 46
Muhammadi, Mawlawi Muhammad Nabi: family of, 46; leader of Harakat i Inqilab i Islami, 46
Mujaddidi, Sigbatullah: 173; president of Mujahidin Interim Government, 145, 154
Mujahid: 207; assassination of, 210
mujahidin: 68, 70, 78–9, 89, 92–4, 147–8, 209, 224, 240, 297, 306, 319; Arab, 163, 174; battalions of, 81; participation in Persian Gulf War (1990–1), 153; proposed creation of support networks for, 293–4; training of, 55
Mujahidin Interim Government: 149, 183; criticisms of, 154; formation of (1989), 140, 145; members of, 145, 154, 173
Muslim-Quraish Wars: Battle of Badr (624), 81
Mutiullah: 36

al-Nahda: 197–8; Shurah Council, 198–9; training of members of, 204
Nasser, Gamal Abdul: 317
North Atlantic Treaty Organization (NATO): personnel of, 168
Northern Alliance: 262, 290; members of, 5–6
Northern Group, The: 228, 232; members of, 224–5, 232, 241, 305; origins of, 223
Nuri, Abdullah: 226
Omar, Mullah Muhammad: 3–6, 104, 234, 236–7, 254–5, 266, 269, 274–8; as 'Amir al-Muminin', 1, 218, 236, 250, 280; leader of Taliban, 46; meetings with Osama bin Laden, 220–2, 225, 227, 235, 237–8, 250, 280; oath of allegiances sworn to, 250–1, 253, 304; order for withdrawal of Arab-Afghans and Taliban, 287, 308; request for al-Qaeda to cease activity, 3–4, 7

Pabbi Military Academy: 137–8
Pakistan: 9, 32, 38, 50, 53, 55, 60, 85, 136, 138, 141, 148–9, 152–4, 166, 168, 176, 183, 196, 207, 209, 226, 244, 250, 288, 290–1, 303; Abbottabad, 9–10; Afghan refugee population of, 32, 47, 49, 79, 289; Arab-Afghan population of, 82, 222–3; Bannu, 289; borders of, 89, 91; Faisalabad, 289; government of, 41, 86, 127, 179; Inter-Services Intelligence (ISI), 38–43, 57, 60–1, 71, 73, 145, 147, 150–1, 153, 183; Islamabad, 40, 79–80, 95, 124, 218, 289; Karachi, 288–9; Lahore, 76, 289; military of, 39, 41, 51–2, 71, 259; Miranshah, 35, 52, 73, 95, 300; North West Frontier Province, 5, 318–19; Peshawar, 21, 27, 32–4, 36, 40, 42, 47, 49–50, 56, 67–70, 76–7, 79–84, 86–7, 90, 102, 109–10, 115, 119, 121–2, 127, 129–30, 132, 138–42, 149, 161–2, 171, 179, 181, 188, 199–200, 210, 288–9, 319; ulama in, 225; Waziristan, 98, 292
Palestine: 124, 141, 163, 256–8,

318–19; Second Intifada (2000–5), 268–9
Palestine War (1948): 22–3, 26, 191
Palestinian Liberation Organisation (PLO): expulsion from Lebanon (1982), 25
Pashtu (language): 55
Pashtuns (ethnic group): 253; members of ISI, 39–40
People's Democratic Republic of Yemen (South Yemen): 187; Soviet influence in, 25–6
Persian (language): 55
Persian Gulf War (1990–1): 168, 188; Iraqi Invasion of Kuwait (1990), 174, 219; participation of mujahidin in, 153; US military presence in Saudi Arabia during, 169; weaponry seized during, 153–4
Philippines: 183
'Preparation of the Ummah' (*Idad al-Ummah*): 143, 164, 170–1

Qadir, Abdul: Governor of Jalalabad, 173, 209
Qadir, Hajji: family of, 225
al-Qaeda: 4–6, 8, 10, 13, 16–17, 61, 84, 87, 93, 100–1, 104–5, 107, 125, 135, 138–9, 142, 148, 150, 162–4, 180, 198, 202, 212, 214–16, 223, 228–9, 232–5, 239–40, 243–4, 247–50, 253, 256–8, 260–1, 263–4, 266, 281–2, 284, 300–1, 303, 313, 320–1, 324; Advisory Councils, 110–11, 119, 121–3, 127, 129; Arab Council, 109; Consultative Council, 122; criticisms of, 203, 238–9, 242, 244; decline of relationship with Islamic Movement of Uzbekistan, 273, 286; departure from Afghanistan (1993), 112–13; departure from Afghanistan (2001), 115; establishment of (1987), 89, 96, 108, 110–11, 115, 125–6, 213; expulsion from Sudan (1996), 196, 204, 208; founding documents of, 108–11; funding of, 179, 188, 217; guesthouses of, 188, 256–7, 262, 271, 273–4, 276, 300–1; impact of Battle of Jalalabad on (1989), 137, 154–5, 157–8, 160–1, 178, 296, 306; influence of Jalalabad School on, 165; Kenya office of, 237; lack of recruitment networks, 249; martyrdom brigades of, 279–80; MBC interview (2001), 6–7; Media Councils, 111, 114, 139–40; members of, 1, 3–4, 7, 9, 11, 16, 24–5, 57–8, 62, 96, 101–2, 110, 112, 115–19, 122, 134, 136–7, 142, 154–5, 157–60, 164, 172–3, 184, 189, 192–3, 196–7, 203, 215, 224, 231, 241, 245, 247, 255, 262, 265, 267–9, 271–3, 275, 277–8, 285–6, 294, 300–1, 320; merger with Tanzim al-Jihad (2001), 278–9; Military Councils, 110, 114, 117; Political Council, 114–15; presence in Chechnya, 184; presence in Somalia, 184–5, 188, 190–1; presence in Syria, 318; presence in Yemen, 187; relationship with Saudi government, 139–40; relationship with Taliban, 239, 241–3; return to Afghanistan (1996), 3, 113, 194, 196, 207–9; Shariah Council, 7, 114; splitting of factions within, 300; 'Tareekh Osama', 108;

Tarnak Farms complex, 261; training camps of, 101–2, 113–14, 118, 121–4, 133–5, 139, 160, 169, 174, 196–7, 200–1, 230, 240, 244, 259, 273; unity initiatives of, 263–7, 276, 278, 286; US embassy bombings (1998), 5, 107, 136, 232, 238, 242–3, 248; use of World Islamic Front, 234–5; withdrawal from Afghanistan (2001), 307; withdrawal from Somalia (1995), 191; withdrawal of Tanzim al-Jihad from, 159
al-Qaeda School (School of Jihad): 14
Qais training camp: 61–2, 70–1; establishment of (1984), 45, 52, 57; influence of, 46, 56, 58; personnel trained at, 58–9, 61–2, 65, 73–5, 95
al-Qaiti, Abu Hamza: 272
Qotada, Abu: alleged member of al-Qaeda Religious Council, 114
Qutb, Sayyid: 324

Rabbani, Burhanuddin: 83, 100, 207, 217; background of, 40
Rahman, General Akhtar Abdul: Pakistani Director of Military Intelligence, 42, 57
Rahman, Omar Abdul: family of, 268; imprisonment of, 241, 268
Rahmani, Arsla: 67
Russian Federation: 248

Sabur, Abdul: 59
Sadat, Anwar: foreign relations with Israel, 25
Sadda training camp: 84, 90, 124, 137, 319; establishment of (1986), 83, 85–6; funding of, 138; operated by Maktab al-Khadamat, 132; personnel of, 84, 123, 135, 166; personnel trained at, 84–5, 94, 121, 126, 141; transfer to Khost, 165–6
al-Saddiq camp: 174; establishment of, 135
Sakka, Luay: 258
Salafism: 36, 61, 75, 78, 102, 104, 143, 164, 170, 228, 231, 235, 239, 273, 300, 314–17, 324; jihadi, 145, 170, 292–3, 312, 317–22, 324–5; militant, 13, 16, 297; Wahhabi, 316, 323
Salahdin: training provided by, 203–4
Salman al-Farsi camp: 174, 203; closure of, 204; opening of, 197
Samha, Abu: participation in al-Qaeda unity initiatives, 265
as-Samia, Abd: 102
al-Sananiry, Kamal: 32
Saudi Arabia: 51, 65, 86, 123–4, 134, 148, 160, 167, 172, 174–9, 188, 211–14, 219, 239, 243, 248, 269, 290; Arab-Afghans from, 140; funding and influence for Afghan Jihad, 47, 49, 126–7, 138; government of, 127, 175–6, 194, 196; Khobar towers bombing (1996), 211–12; National Guard complex attack (1995), 211–¡2; relationship with al-Qaeda, 139–40; Riyadh, 211–12; US military presence in, 169
Sayyaf, Abdul Rasul: 56, 62–3, 65, 67–8, 70–1, 73–7, 79, 86, 91, 132, 322; criticisms of, 99–100; inauguration as leader of Union of Mujahidin Parties, 51, 81; leader of Ittihad i Islami Tahrir

Afghanistan, 27, 32–3; prime minister of Mujahidin Interim Government, 145; territory controlled by, 83; visit to Abu Dhabi (1980), 27
Saznor: 207; assassination of, 210
Second World War (1939–45): 152, 233; Pearl Harbor attack (1941), 7
Shammali: background of, 147
Six-Day War (1967): 23; political impact of, 22, 24
Solidarity Conference (2000): aim of, 268
Somalia: 172, 183–4, 187, 190, 232–3; Battle of Mogadishu (1993), 189, 215; military of, 187; Mogadishu, 189; al-Qaeda presence in, 184–5, 188, 190–1
Soviet Union (USSR): 25, 41, 69, 87, 94, 99, 103–4, 112, 136, 145–6, 152, 168, 181, 183, 185, 283, 291, 304, 321; military hardware of, 39, 54, 187; Special Forces, 89, 97–8
Sudan: 3, 130, 168, 179, 189, 197–8, 243, 260; expulsion of Osama bin Laden and al-Qaeda from (1996), 3, 195–6, 204, 208, 230; government of, 3, 193, 208; movement of Tanzim al-Jihad to, 159–60; al-Qaeda presence in, 193, 196
Sudanese Isra Islamic Relief Agency: 57
Sufism: 37, 75
Sun Tzu: 92–3
Al-Surat: articles in, 55–6; funding of, 55
al-Suri, Abu Burhan: 75–6, 114; 'Afghan Jihad', 85; background of, 84–5; head of Sadda training camp, 84–5, 135, 166; training programme of, 135
al-Suri, Abu Musab: 4, 6, 33, 175, 185–7, 215–16, 229, 238, 251, 254–7, 262, 264, 273–5, 277, 289; criticisms of, 279; *Global Call, The*, 11; oath of allegiance to Mullah Omar (2000), 251
al-Suri, Abu Rida: 109, 183
al-Suri, Abu Rouda: death of, 183
Syria: 23, 25, 84, 124, 256, 258, 292–3, 297; Arab-Afghans from, 24; Civil War (2011–), 14, 145, 172, 300, 303, 313–16; Kurdish population of, 258; presence of al-Qaeda in, 318; Salafi jihadi movement of, 323

Tahir, Mawlawi: 35; family of, 35
Tahir, Muhammad: 253
Tajikistan: 167, 169, 180, 192–3, 198–9, 223, 252, 320, 322
Tajiks (ethnic group): 40, 197–9, 204, 209, 275
takfir: 4, 164, 170, 175, 194, 201, 229, 323; proliferation of, 140–1
Taliban: 4, 8, 10, 16, 62, 168, 201–2, 205, 220–1, 226–7, 229, 232–3, 238–40, 252, 259–60, 270, 289, 291–2, 303–5; Capture of Jalalabad (1996), 217–18; members of, 1–3, 5, 7, 45, 51–2, 56, 58, 201, 218, 223, 227–8, 255, 275, 288; origins of, 45–6, 57, 60, 62, 79, 87; relationship with al-Qaeda, 239, 241–3; rise to power (1996), 11, 21; Shurah, 287; support for Arab-Afghan groups, 290–1; territory controlled by, 5, 9, 202, 217, 222, 227; training of, 51–2; unity initiatives of, 263; withdrawal from Afghanistan (2001), 247, 308

Tanzania: US embassy bombing (1998), 5, 107, 136, 232, 238, 242–3, 248
Tanzim al-Jihad: 23, 84, 99, 116–17, 119, 142, 164, 180, 229, 239, 254, 264–6, 270–1, 276, 278–9; funding of, 194–5, 213; members of, 113, 193, 219, 237, 242, 265, 278, 301, 322; merger with al-Qaeda (2001), 278–9; Military Council, 117; movement to Sudan, 159–60; participation in al-Qaeda unity initiatives, 265–6, 276, 278; presence in Chechnya, 320; splinter factions of, 7; training camps of, 171, 174, 272; withdrawal from al-Qaeda, 159–60
al-Tunisi, Abu Zayd: 153–4
Turkestan: 166
Turkey: 199–200, 258, 260

ulama: 132, 254, 270, 282; funding of, 176; lack of Afghan, 78; Pakistani, 207, 213, 225; Saudi, 239
Union of Mujahidin Parties (Ittihad i Islami Mujahidin Afghanistan): 34, 68; members of, 51, 81
United Arab Emirates (UAE): Abu Dhabi, 2, 27, 30, 34–5, 56
United Kingdom (UK): London, 36–7, 195
United Nations (UN): 173; personnel of, 190, 322
United States of America (USA): 1–2, 40–1, 47, 59, 104, 168, 180–1, 195–6, 215, 217, 223, 237, 240, 243, 260, 279, 301, 306–7, 311, 323; 9/11 attacks, 6, 8, 13, 62, 96, 99, 107, 154, 165, 232, 259–61, 267, 269, 278–9, 281–4, 286, 289, 293, 301, 306–8, 313, 322; Air Force (USAF), 290; Congress, 59–60; military of, 7, 135, 233, 243; Senate, 59; Treasury Department, 10; Washington DC, 60; World Trade Center bombing (1993), 167, 169, 230
al-Urduani, Abu Harith (Khost School of Jihad): 14, 127, 132, 163, 183, 295, 312, 321–2; family of, 129; working relationship with Jalaluddin Haqqani, 130, 321
Uyghur (ethnic group): 166, 238, 251, 260, 275; territory inhabited by, 247
Uzbekistan: 198, 252
Uzbeks: 181, 199, 201, 209, 238, 250–2, 273, 276–7, 286; territory inhabited by, 247, 253

Wahhabism: 170, 220, 292, 315, 317–18; Salafi, 316, 323, 325
Wakil, Abdul: background of, 201
Warsak training camp: personnel of, 133
World Islamic Front: 234, 264; formation of (1998), 4, 169; use by al-Qaeda, 234–5

al-Yamani, Abu Omar: 188
al-Yamani, Mustafa: 155, 161
Yarmuk training camp: 165, 181, 183
Yemen Arab Republic (North Yemen): 25–6, 187
Yemen: 3, 118, 124, 168, 183, 185–6, 188, 203, 259; Aden, 5; Arab-Afghans from, 24–5, 140, 186; Civil War (1994), 195; re-unification of (1990), 187; al-Qaeda

presence in, 187; USS *Cole* bombing (2000), 5, 232, 242, 262, 268–70, 307
Yom Kippur War (1973): 23–4
Yousaf, Muhammad: 145; *Bear Trap, The*, 39–40, 42
Yousef, Ramzi: family of, 167; role in World Trade Center bombing (1993), 230
Yuldashev, Tahir: 251, 253, 273, 277; followers of, 252; founder of Islamic Movement of Uzbekistan, 198–9

Zadran (tribe): 202
al-Zarqawi, Abu Musab: 9, 183, 258, 260, 271, 275, 312, 322; arrival in Afghanistan, 257; influence of Jalalabad School on, 257–8; leader of al-Qaeda presence in Iraq, 301, 311, 315
al-Zawahiri, Ayman: 7, 185, 195, 204, 213, 239, 264–5, 267, 276–7, 280–1; amir of Tanzim al-Jihad, 278; arrival in Afghanistan (1997), 195, 213; as leader of al-Qaeda, 11, 300; departure from Sudan, 204; participation in al-Qaeda unity initiatives, 265
al-Zindani, Abdul Majid: 185
Zubaydah, Abu: 200, 216, 229, 231, 260; arrest and detention of, 181, 200; associates of, 288; head of Mujahidin Services Centre, 258–60; head of Sadda training camp, 166; networks of, 230